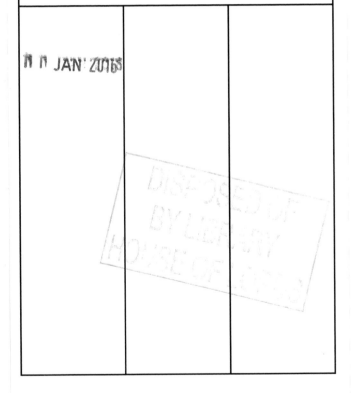

The Law Relating to Children

The Law Relating to Children

Christina M. Lyon LL.B, F.R.S.A.
Solicitor of the Supreme Court, Professor of Law, Keele University

Butterworths
London, Dublin, Edinburgh
1993

United Kingdom	Butterworth & Co (Publishers) Ltd, 88 Kingsway, LONDON WC2B 6AB and 4 Hill Street, EDINBURGH EH2 3JZ
Australia	Butterworths, SYDNEY, MELBOURNE, BRISBANE, ADELAIDE, PERTH, CANBERRA and HOBART
Belgium	Butterworth & Co (Publishers) Ltd, BRUSSELS
Canada	Butterworths Canada Ltd, TORONTO and VANCOUVER
Ireland	Butterworth (Ireland) Ltd, DUBLIN
Malaysia	Malayan Law Journal Sdn Bhd, KUALA LUMPUR
New Zealand	Butterworths of New Zealand Ltd, WELLINGTON and AUCKLAND
Puerto Rico	Equity de Puerto Rico, Inc, HATO REY
Singapore	Butterworths Asia, SINGAPORE
USA	Butterworth Legal Publishers, AUSTIN, Texas; BOSTON, Massachusetts; CLEARWATER, Florida (D & S Publishers); ORFORD, New Hampshire (Equity Publishing); ST PAUL, Minnesota; and SEATTLE, Washington

A CIP Catalogue record for this book is available from the British Library.

ISBN   0 406 01653 4

Printed and bound in Great Britain by William Clowes Limited, Beccles and London

To my children Sasha and David and to all children

Foreword

It is a privilege to be asked to write a foreword to this excellent new work. Professor Lyon, an acknowledged expert in the field, has brought together in one volume a succinct statement of the law relating to children, including a helpful section on the Child Support Act 1991.

The structure of the work is novel but anyone who reads it from cover to cover will find a logical progression throughout. It is a pleasure to find a work which, though not long, gives such a comprehensive and comprehensible treatment to the subject it addresses.

The extensive consideration of the Children Act 1989 is up to date and will be of interest not only to lawyers but to all those who have to deal with children professionally.

I wish this work the success it richly deserves.

David S. Gee
Balderstone
February 1993

Preface

On 14 October 1991 the Children Act 1989 was implemented in full and effected radical changes to the substantive and jurisdictional framework for dealing with children. The principal aim of the Act has been to reform the civil law of England and Wales governing the care and upbringing of children. The new jurisdictional framework and accompanying rules, however, have affected a whole range of civil proceedings as they concern children, and also touched on criminal proceedings through the abolition of the criminal care order. The implementation of the Child Support Act 1991 in April 1993 is also set to have far-reaching effects, not only directly on the law relating to maintenance of children, but indirectly on the whole philosophy underpinning the Children Act 1989. After all, if children become worth "fighting over" in order to avoid high assessments for child support and to increase chances of retaining the matrimonial home, the central message of Parts I and II of the Act: "responsible parenthood in partnership to achieve the paramountcy of children's welfare", may fly out of the window. Practitioners are already being warned that applying for "staying contact orders" on behalf of fathers would be a useful way of reducing liability for child support!

This book is not, however, intended to be another book on the Children Act 1989 although it does aim to be as up to date as possible in its coverage of the treatment by the courts of that Act, as well as all the other Acts encompassed in this work.

The aim of this book is to seek to examine the civil law relating to children in England and Wales, but due principally to limitations on space and cost, it has not been possible to include an analysis of the whole of the law of education.

As far as the construction of the book is concerned, the first chapter attempts to set out the jurisdictional framework in which the civil law relating to children works, including the impact of the Family Law Act 1986 as well as the Children Act 1989. Issues of jurisdiction and all aspects of the law of procedure are further set out in detail in each chapter as it treats particular subjects, together with full cross references to all the statutory forms and current case law. Again, due to limitations of space, but also on the assumption that practitioners will have access to the relevant court rules containing the forms, it was felt inappropriate to reproduce them here. A few forms are set out in the Forms section, either where it is appropriate to highlight them, as in the case of parental responsibility agreements (given their potential importance in practice), or in areas where there are no statutory forms as is the case with child abduction.

Since it was desirable to be clear from the start that children were to be seen as parties to the proceedings which intimately concern them, whether or not the law actually accords them that status, the second chapter deals with this subject. Later chapters go on to consider critically, in what I hope is a logical progression, further matters of vital concern to the child such as: issues of status, parentage and guardianship; the range of provisions dealing with the care and upbringing of children to be found in the Children Act 1989; the mechanisms for sorting out child maintenance; the growing problem of child abduction; the law relating to the adoption of children; the provisions dealing with children's property; and finally, the provisions concerning the exercise of the protective jurisdiction of the High Court over children.

Throughout the work, an attempt has been made to analyse the directions in which the courts are moving in the various areas and to suggest to practitioners who might read this book different ways of approaching possible problems on behalf of their child clients. For the student or academic lawyer, what is offered is an analysis of how the law relating to children is working out in practice, together with extensive references to current case law but, once more due to space and cost limitations, it has been impossible to include many references to the works of other academics and practising lawyers. For other professionals working with children who may have an interest in only one or two of the areas covered by this work, it is hoped that they find the explanation in those areas both interesting and illuminating.

Finally, I should like to express my thanks and appreciation to my husband, Adrian, and to our children, Sasha and David, who endured with unfailing patience the stresses and strains imposed by my writing another book, on top of pre-existing writing commitments.

I have sought to state the law as it stands on 1 January 1993 although it has been possible to incorporate some later amendments and the provisions of the Child Support Act 1991, as described, of course take effect on 5 April 1993.

Christina Lyon
Keele
January 1993

Contents

TABLE OF STATUTES

References in this Table to *Statutes* are to Halsbury's Statutes of England (Fourth Edition) showing the volume and page at which the annotated text of an Act may be found.

Page references in *italic* type are to the Appendices.

TABLE OF STATUTORY INSTRUMENTS

Page references in *italic* type are to the Appendices.

TABLE OF CASES

Page references in *italic* type are to the Appendices

C

D

Q

R

S

V

W

X

CHAPTER 1: DEFINITIONS, JURISDICTION AND PROCEDURE

1: TERMINOLOGY

1. Definitions. Whilst it might have been hoped that, amongst all the reforms consequential upon the enactment of the Children Act, a uniform terminology for referring to children might have been included, such was note the case. In recent years many statutes including the Children Act have used the term "child", where a noun was required[7] to denote a person under the age of 18; where the sense called for an adjective or description the term "infant" has been employed, as in "infant plaintiff"[8], and where a child has been under some sort of legal disability the term "infancy" has gained currency[9]. Yet other recent statutes have employed the term "minor"[10].

In this work where the terminology of statutes has been amended by the Children Act 1989, or that Act itself is under discussion, the term "child" or "children" will be used, and practitioners should note that forms drafted pursuant to that Act demand the use of "child applicant" or "child respondent" or "child as a party"[11]. Where statutes refer to "infants" or "minors" and these statutes are under discussion the terms "infant"[12] or "minor"[13] are employed within the appropriate usage in accordance with the statutory definition. In drafting forms and documents under such statutes for use in the High Court and county court the term "infant plaintiff" should be employed to accord with previous and current practice as well as for aesthetic reasons.

1 Eg Family Proceedings Rules 1991, SI 1991/1247; Family Proceedings Courts (Children Act 1989) Rules 1991, SI 1991/1395; Family Proceedings Courts (Matrimonial Proceedings etc) Rules 1991, SI 1991/1991; Family Proceedings Amendment Rules 1991, SI 1991/2113; The Adoption (Amendment) Rules 1991, SI 1991/1880.
2 Eg applications relating to: guardianship of the person (Paragraphs 79-119 post); residence of the person (Paragraphs 120-140 post); adoption (Paragraphs 228-238 post); holding in secure accommodation (Paragraphs 195-198 post); marriage (Paragraphs 94-97 post); CAre (Paragraphs 173-184 post).
3 This power in the High Court is preserved by Children Act 1989 s 5 (11) but only insofar as provision is made for its exercise by rules of court: Paragraph 119 post. In exercise of the power under ibid s 5 (12) RSC Ord 80 r 13 has been made by RSC (Amendment No 4) 1991, SI 1991/2671 allowing the Court to continue to appoint the Official Solicitor to be a guardian of the child's estate in certain circumstances eg where money is paid into

court on behalf of the child. The power is no longer necessary in most circumstances as "parental responsibility" includes the rights, powers and duties of a guardian of the child's estate: see Children Act 1989 s 3 (2) and (3).

4 Paragraphs 37-59 post.
5 Paragraph 2 post
6 Paragraph 37 post.
7 Children Act 1989 s 105; Adoption Act 1976 s 72.
8 Eg Trustee Act 1925 s 53
9 Ibid s 31 (2).
10 Eg: Mental Health Act 1983 s 33; Minors' Contracts Act 1987; Family Law Reform Act 1969 s 1 (1), (2); the terms "infant", "minor" and "child" are interchangeable in civil law: they mean a person who has not attained the age of 18.
11 Family Proceedings Rules 1991 as amended r 4.7 and App 3 column (iii).
12 Paragraph 65 post.
13 Paragraph 44 post.

2. Infancy, minority, childhood. A child, minor or infant is a person of either sex who has not attained full age. A person attains full age on attaining the age of 18[1], and can only be described as a child whilst under the age of 18. The time at which a person attains a particular age expressed in years is at the beginning of the day on which the relevant anniversary of the birth falls[2].

The onus of proving infancy is on the person alleging it[3]. Infancy is proved by any of the following methods:

1. a certificate under the Births and Deaths Registration Act 1953[4];
2. proof of an entry in the official logbook of a ship of a birth at sea[5];
3. declarations by deceased relatives (in pedigree cases only)[6];
4. evidence of the mother or a person present at the birth;
5. the opinion of witnesses[7];
6. colonial registers (if kept by the law of their own or of this country) and foreign registers (if kept under public authority and recognised by the local tribunals)[8] coupled in each case with the proper identification of the infant with the person referred to.

Infancy is a legal disability which, like mental incapacity, prevents a minor from assuming fully the legal rights and liabilities of an adult. The restrictions which the law therefore imposes upon a minor are in every case such as to enure for the benefit of the minor having regard to his tender years and presumed lack of judgment. Until recently infants were thus only bound by contracts deemed at law to be beneficial to them[9]. The Infants Relief Act 1874 was however repealed by the Minors' Contracts Act 1987[10]. Where the defendant uses his minority at the time of entering into a contract as his defence, which might otherwise render the contract unenforceable, the court may, if it is just and equitable, require him to transfer to the plaintiff any property acquired under the contract or any property representing it[11]. There are other cases in which infancy itself forms part of the cause of action or defence. Special protection is on similar principles afforded to infant litigants.

Proceedings also arise in the courts owing not to the acts of minors but to the fact of their infancy. There is a jurisdiction to protect minors generally and to do on their behalf under the supervision of the court those things which their legal as well as their personal Capacity prevents them from doing for themselves.

1 Family Law Reform Act 1969 s 1.
2 Ibid s 9. This is subject to any relevant enactment, deed, will or other instrument: ibid s 9 (2).

3 There is a presumption that a party to a conveyance is of full age at the date of the conveyance: Law of Property Act 1925 s 15.

4 *Re Wintle* (1870) LR 9 Eq 373, which decided that registration was proof only of the fact of birth before the date of registration, was overruled in *Re Stollery, Weir v Treasury Solicitor* [1926] Ch 284, CA. See also *Jackson v Jackson and Pavan* [1964] P 25, [1960] 3 All ER 621.

5 Merchant Shipping Act 1970 ss 68, 72 (as amended).

6 *Haines v Guthrie* (1884) 13 QBD 818; *Figg v Wedderburne* (1841)11 LJQB 45.

7 *R v Cox* [1898] 1 QB 179.

8 *Sturla v Freccia* (1880) 5 App Cas 623, HL.

9 Eg Where the contract was made for the supply of necessary goods or services, see the Sale of Goods Act 1979 s 3. For goods and for services deemed to be necessary see *Helps v Clayton* (1864) 17 CBNS 553; *De Stacpoole v De Stacpoole* (1887) 37 Ch D 139; *Re Jones (an Infant)* (1883) 48 LT 188. Contracts for necessaries must still however be deemed to be beneficial, see *Flower v London & North Western Ry Co* [1894] 2 QB 65 and also *Buckpitt v Oates* [1968] 1 All ER 1145.

10 For contracts entered into after implementation of the Minors' Contracts Act 1987 on 9 June 1987.

11 Minors' Contracts Act 1987 ss 1, 3

2: JURISDICTION

3. Effects of the Children Act 1989. The principal effect of the Children Act 1989 has not only been to go a long way towards achieving a unified system of the substantive civil law relating to children but also to set this system within a unified courts structure[1]. Pursuant to the establishment of this unified jurisdiction, cases whether of a public law or private law nature can be heard by the magistrates' family proceedings courts at magistrates' court level, by designated trial centre county courts at county court level, and by Family Division Judges at High Court level[2].

1 Children Act 1989 s 92 and Sch 11
2 Children (Allocation of Proceedings) Order 1991, SI 1991/1677.

4. Magistrates' family proceedings courts. Subject to certain limitations all public law and some private law cases concerning children can, pursuant to the Children Act 1989 and consequential rules, be heard in the magistrates' family proceedings courts[1]. By virtue of that Act a family proceedings court may not make any order involving the property of, or held in trust for, a child or any income from such property[2]. Such courts are further restricted in the making of financial provision for children: they are limited to making orders for periodical payments, and lump sums not exceeding £1,000 per child, and cannot make orders for transfers of property to children or secured periodical payments orders in favour of children[3]. Divorce suits can still not be heard in family proceedings courts at magistrates' level, and thus most of the private law applications in respect of children which arise on divorce will continue to be heard at county court level[4]. Many public law applications are required to be commenced at magistrates' courts level[5], but there is then provision to transfer cases either horizontally to another family proceedings court[6] or vertically to the county court[7] or High Court[8] provided certain criteria are satisfied. Public law applications may also be transferred to the higher courts where other proceedings involving the child are pending[9].

1 Children Act 1989 s 92 (1)(3)
2 Ibid s 92 (4).
3 Ibid Sch 1 paras 1 (1)(b) and 5 (2).
4 Children (Allocation of Proceedings) Order 1991, SI 1991/1677,. arts 14 and 15.
5 Ibid art 3.
6 Ibid art 6.
7 Ibid art 7.
8 From the county court by ibid art 12. The magistrates' court cannot transfer direct to the High Court.
9 Ibid art 3 (3).

5. County courts. In respect of both commencement and transfers of family proceedings, county courts have been classified into divorce county courts, family hearing centres and care centres by the Children (Allocation of Proceedings) Order 1991[1]. The judges who can hear proceedings in the designated trial centres, and the types of proceedings to which they are restricted, are provided in the Family Proceedings (Allocation to Judiciary) Directions 1991[2].

Generally private law applications in respect of children arising from divorce suits or adoption will be commenced in the divorce county court[3], but, if opposed[4] or other criteria are met[5], may be transferred to family hearing centres. Opposed applications for Section 8 orders will be heard in the family hearing centres[6], as will cases transferred under the statutory criteria from the High Court to county court level[7].

Public law applications are generally commenced in the magistrates' family proceedings courts[8], but provided the relevant criteria are satisfied may be transferred to a county court care centre[9]. Where an application for a care or supervision order or any associated orders arises from a direction to conduct an investigation made by the High Court or county court under Section 37 of the Children Act 1989, then, provided that court is a county court care centre, the application can be made there[10], or in such care centre as the court which directed the investigation may order[11].

The county courts may make secured periodical payment orders and orders for settlement and transfers of property[12].

1 Children (Allocation of Proceedings) Order 1991, SI 1991/1677 art 2.
2 Issued September 1991 although the Children Act Advisory Committee's First Annual Report (LCD 1992) proposes extending the jurisdiction of the nominated district judges in both private and public law cases to reduce the delays experienced in the first 9 months of implementation..
3 Children (Allocation of Proceedings) Order 1991 art 14.
4 Ibid art 16.
5 Ibid art 10.
6 Ibid art 16 (1).
7 Ibid art 13.
8 Ibid art 3 and note that art 18 (1) does provide for the possibility of applications under Part III, IV or V of the Children Act 1989 being commenced in a care centre.
9 Ibid art 18 (3).
10 Ibid art 3 (2)(a).
11 Ibid art 3 (2)(b).
12 Children Act 1989 Sch 1 para 1 (1)(a).

6. High Court. The High Court has jurisdiction to hear appeals in family proceedings from the magistrates' family proceedings court[1].

Both private law and public law applications under the Children Act 1989 or under the Adoption Act 1976 may be transferred to the High Court, where the county court judge or district judge considers that the proceedings should be determined by the High Court, and that such determination would be in the interests of the child[2].

Proceedings under the inherent jurisdiction of the High Court, including wardship, must be commenced in the High Court[3].

The jurisdiction of each court is considered in more detail under the respective subjects covered in this work.

1 Children Act 1989 s 94 (1)
2 Children (Allocation of Proceedings) Order 1991, SI 1991/1677, art 12.
3 Supreme Court Act 1981 Sch 1 para 3

7. Effect of the Family Law Act 1986. Having briefly outlined the nature of the jurisdiction in family and related proceedings in the three levels of courts, it is important to consider the impact of the Family Law Act 1986[1], as amended by the Children Act 1989[2], on these courts' powers to exercise that jurisdiction.

The Family Law Act 1986 amended the law relating to the jurisdiction of courts in the United Kingdom to make orders relating to the custody or upbringing of children, and to the recognition and enforcement of such orders throughout the United Kingdom. The orders covered by the provisions of the Act as amended include: custody orders made in England and Wales under a range of enactments, repealed in whole or in part by the Children Act 1989[3], before the implementation of that Act[4] or under transitional provisions[5] and which continue in force until they expire or until they are discharged or varied by the making of new orders under the Children Act[6]; custody, care or control, access or education orders or any orders relating to the upbringing of a child other than public law orders, adoption orders or orders made under the Child Abduction and Custody Act 1985, by courts of civil jurisdiction in Scotland[7]; orders relating to the custody, care or control of a child, access to a child or the upbringing of a child made by a court in Northern Ireland[8], including similar orders relating to a child made by the High Court in Northern Ireland in the exercise of its wardship jurisdiction[9]; any orders made by the High Court in England and Wales in the exercise of its wardship jurisdiction relating to the care and control of a child, education of, or access to, a child prior to the implementation of the Children Act 1989[10] or under transitional provisions[11]; any Section 8 orders made by a court in England and Wales under the Children Act 1989, other than orders varying or discharging such orders[12]; and any orders giving care of a child to any person, or providing for contact with, or education of, a child, other than orders varying or revoking such orders, made by a court in England and Wales in the exercise of the inherent jurisdiction of the High Court with respect to children[13].

The jurisdiction of the court under the Family Law Act 1986 depends on whether the child is habitually resident in England and Wales, or alternatively whether he or she is present in England and Wales and not habitually resident in any part of the United Kingdom[14], but in either case is excluded if proceedings for divorce, nullity or separation are continuing in a court in Scotland or Northern Ireland in respect of the marriage of the parents of the child[15]. In addition, the court will have jurisdiction where a ward was resident in England and Wales on the relevant date, and the court considers that the immediate exercise of its powers is necessary for the ward's protection[16].

Recognition and enforcement of the order in other parts of the United Kingdom will be based on its registration with the appropriate court there, in which case it will be regarded as having the same effect as if it had been made by that court[17].

The Family Law Act 1986[18] does not apply generally to public law orders, and the basis for the jurisdiction of the courts in such and other cases will be considered in more detail under the respective subjects covered in the title.

1 Implementation date 4 April 1988 except for those provisions amending the Child Abduction Act 1984 and the Child Abduction and Custody Act 1985 which were implemented on 7 January 1987 and those provisions inserted by the Children Act 1989 which were implemented on 14 October 1991.
2 Implementation date 14 October 1991.
3 Eg custody orders made under the Guardianship of Minors Act 1971 ss 9 (1), 10 (1)(a), 11 (a) and 14A (2); the Guardianship Act 1973 s 2 (4)(b), (5); the Matrimonial Causes Act 1973 ss 42 (1), (2); the Children Act 1975 ss 33 (1) and 34 (5); and the Domestic Proceedings and Magistrates' Courts Act 1978 ss 8 (2) or 19 (1)(ii).
4 On 14 October 1991.
5 See Children Act 1989 Sch 14 and the Children Act 1989 (Commencement and Transitional Provisions) Order 1991, SI 1991/828 and the Children Act 1989 (Commencement No 2 Amendment and Transitional Provisions) Order 1991, SI 1991/1990.
6 Ibid and Family Law Act 1986 s 1 (1)(a)
7 Family Law Act 1986 s 1 (1)(b).
8 Ibid s 1 (1)(c).
9 Ibid s 1 (1)(e) (as substituted by the Children Act 1989 Sch 13 para 63).
10 Ibid s 1 (1)(d) (as substituted by the Children Act 1989 Sch 13 para 63), and see note 5 supra.
11 See note 5 supra.
12 Ibid s 1 (1)(a) (as substituted by the Children Act 1989 Sch 13 para 63).
13 Under the Matrimonial and Family Proceedings Act 1984 s 38 (as substituted by the Children Act 1989 Sch 13 para 51) orders other than those actually making or discharging wardship can be made by county courts.
14 Family Law Act 1986 s 3 (1).
15 Ibid s 3 (2).
16 Ibid s 2 (3) (as substituted by the Children Act 1989 Sch 13 para 64).
17 Ibid ss 25, 27 and 29.
18 Ie under ibid ss 1, 2 and 2A.

3: RULES OF COURT

8. Family proceedings. The Children Act 1989 not only established a unified jurisdiction in children's cases arising out of family proceedings across the three tiers of courts[1], but also provided for the making, where relevant, of common rules of court[2]. It has thus has achieved a close alignment of the provisions governing procedure and evidence in children's cases. The rules which have been issued thus far are: for the High Court and county court, the Family Proceedings Rules 1991[3] as amended by the Family Proceedings (Amendment) Rules 1991[4], the Family Proceedings (Amendment) Rules 1992, the Family Proceedings (Amendment no 2) Rules 1992[5], and, for the magistrates' courts, the Family Proceedings Courts (Children Act 1989) Rules 1991[6], the Family Proceedings Courts (Matrimonial Proceedings) Rules 1991[7] and the Family Proceedings Courts (Miscellaneous Amendments) Rules 1992. Indeed, for public law cases brought under the Children Act 1989, the Rules Committee achieved such a close alignment, that the relevant parts of each set of rules have the same numbering[8]. In addition, both sets of rules have a large number of common forms[9], again particularly in the public law arena, which eases the burden on non-legal professionals working within the system[10] who may have to cope with cases being transferred from one level of court to another[11].

In the case of adoption where rules already provided for the close alignment of the provisions governing procedure and evidence[12], the rules of court have had to be amended to take account of the changes introduced by the Children Act 1989[13].

The relevant rules of court which are peculiar to particular types of proceedings will be considered in detail under the respective subjects, but those procedural and evidential matters governed by the rules which apply commonly to all family proceedings are dealt with here.

1 Pursuant to Children Act 1989 s 92 (6) see Paragraph 3 ante.
2 Ibid s 93.
3 Family Proceedings Rules 1991, SI 1991/1247.
4 Family Proceedings (Amendment) Rules 1991, SI 1991/2113.
5 Family Proceedings (Amendment) Rules 1992, SI 1992/456 and (Amendment No 2) Rules 1992 SI 1992/2067.
6 Family Proceedings Courts (Children Act 1989) Rules 1991, SI 1991/1395 and Family Proceedings Courts (Miscellaneous Amendments) Rules 1992 SI 1992/2068.
7 Family Proceedings Courts (Matrimonial Proceedings etc) Rules 1991, SI 1991/1991.
8 See the Family Proceedings Courts (Children Act 1989) Rules 1991, rr 1-21 and the Family Proceedings Rules 1991 rr 4.1-4.21.
9 See in the Family Proceedings Courts (Children Act 1989) Rules 1991 Sch 1 Forms CHA 1-65, especially Forms CHA 17-55, and the Family Proceedings Rules 1991 App 1 Forms CHA 1-59 (as amended by the Family Proceedings (Amendment) Rules 1991, the Family Proceedings (Amendment) Rules 1992 and the Family Proceedings (Amendment No 2) Rules 1992 SI 1992/2067).
10 See Paragraphs 173-184 post.
11 See Paragraphs 18-28 post.
12 See the Adoption Rules 1984, SI 1984/265 for the High Court and county court and the Magistrates' Courts (Adoption) Rules 1984, SI 1984/611.
13 See the Adoption (Amendment) Rules 1991, SI 1991/1880.

9. Applications. All family proceedings relating to children in all courts and in both private law and public law cases are commenced by way of an application in respect of each child set out in the appropriate form laid down in the rules or, where there is no such form, in writing[1]. The rules provide for the different proceedings in which applications may be made ex parte[2] and for the requisite periods of notice for applications in all other types of proceedings[3].

1 Family Proceedings Rules 1991, SI 1991/1247, r 4.4 (1) and Family Proceedings Courts (Children Act 1989) Rules 1991, SI 1991/1395, r 4 (1).
2 Family Proceedings Rules 1991 r 4.4 (4) and Family Proceedings Courts (Children Act 1989) Rules 1991 r 4 (4) as amended by SI 1992/2067 and SI 1992/2068. Note that the Children Act Advisory Committee's Report (LCD Dec 1992) states at para 4.20 that the Rules Committee has accepted in principle that the requirement for one form per child in private law proceedings should be dispensed with. Practitioners should therefore check for possible 1993 Amendment Rules to effect this change.
3 Family Proceedings Rules 1991 r 4.4 (3) and Family Proceedings Courts (Children Act.1989) Rules 1991 r 4 (3) as amended by SI 1992/2067 and SI 1992/2068.

10. Withdrawal of applications. The leave of the court is required before any application can be withdrawn[1]. The person seeking leave to withdraw an application must file and serve on the parties a written request for leave setting out the reasons for the request[2], unless the request is being made orally in court and the parties and the guardian ad litem or welfare officer are present[3]. Where this is the case, if the parties consent and if the guardian ad litem (if he is involved in the case) has had an opportunity to make written representations, the court can grant the request if it thinks fit[4]. Where the court does so, the justices' clerk or the proper officer, as appropriate, must inform the parties, and the guardian ad litem or welfare officer accordingly[5]. The court may, instead of granting the request, determine that there be a hearing of the request. In the case of the High Court or county court, the court can direct the date to be fixed for the hearing and the proper officer must then give at least seven days' notice of the date fixed to the parties, the guardian ad litem and the welfare officer[6]. Where the request was made to the magistrates' family proceedings court, then the justices' clerk can decide upon and fix a date for a hearing, giving the same notice[7].

1 Family Proceedings Rules 1991, SI 1991/1247, r 4.5 (1) and Family Proceedings Courts (Children Act 1989) Rules 1991, SI 1991/1395, r 5 (1).
2 Family Proceedings Rules 1991 r 4.5 (2) and Family Proceedings Courts (Children Act 1989) Rules 1991 r 5 (2).
3 Family Proceedings Rules 1991 r 4.5 (3) and Family Proceedings Courts (Children Act 1989) Rules 1991 r 5 (3).
4 Family Proceedings Rules 1991 r 4.5 (4) and Family Proceedings Courts (Children Act 1989) Rules 1991 r 5 (4).
5 Ibid.
6 Family Proceedings Rules 1991 r 4.5 (4).
7 Family Proceedings Courts (Children Act 1989) Rules 1991 r 5 (4).

11. Parties. The parties to applications in family proceedings are the applicant, and the respondents prescribed for each type of proceedings in column (iii) of Appendix 3 to the Family Proceedings Rules 1991 in the High Court and county court, and in column (iii) of Schedule 2 to the Family Proceedings Courts (Children Act) Rules 1991 in the magistrates' courts[1]. Other persons may request to be joined as parties to the proceedings[2].

These may include those persons to whom written notice of the proceedings is required to be given as prescribed in column (iv) of Appendix 3 to the Family Proceedings Rules 1991 in the High Court and county court and column (iv) of Schedule 2 to the Family Proceedings Courts (Children Act 1989) Rules 1991 in the magistrates' courts[3]. The intention behind this is to inform those persons who have an interest in the child that legal proceedings are being taken in respect of him, and to provide them with the opportunity to seek leave to be joined as parties to the proceedings. It will be noted from the appendices that that the child is a party in care and associated proceedings, which are described in the Act for purposes to do with representation of the child by a guardian ad litem and solicitir as "specified proceedings"[4].

The lists of respondents and persons to whom notice must be given for each type of family proceedings will be discussed in detail in the relevant parts of this title.

1 Family Proceedings Rules 1991, SI 1991/1247, App 3 column (iii) as amended by Family Proceedings (Amendment No 2) Rules 1992 SI 1992/2067; Family Proceedings Courts (Children Act 1989) Rules 1991, SI 1991/1395, Sch 2 column (iii). The original discrepancy in the two sets of rules has thus been amended by the Rules Committee.
2 Family Proceedings Rules 1991 r 4.7 (2) and Family Proceedings Courts (Children Act 1989) Rules 1991 r 7 (2).

3 Again a discrepancy previously unnoticed by the Rules Committee but now rectified by SI 1992/2067.
4 Children Act 1989 s 41.

12. Service of documents and notices. Any notice or other document required to be served on any person under the Children Act 1989 may be served by personal delivery, registered post or recorded delivery to his proper address[1].

Where, following the refusal of a magistrates' court to order the transfer of a case to the county court, application is made to the county court for such an order, the applicant is required to serve his application and the magistrates' court certificate of refusal personally on all parties to the proceedings[2].

Aside from special rules relating to service on a child, the method of service will depend under the rules on whether the person to be served is known to be acting by a solicitor or not known to be so acting.

Where the person to be served is not known to be acting by a solicitor then service should be effected by personal delivery, registered post or recorded delivery to his proper address[3]. Where the person is known to be acting by a solicitor then there are three means of effecting service: delivery to or sending by first class post to the address which the solicitor has given for service; where that address includes a document exchange box number, by leaving it at that exchange or at a document exchange which transmits documents on every business day to that exchange; or by sending a legible copy of the document to the solicitor's office by facsimile[4].

Service on a party who is a child may be effected by service upon the child's solicitor or, where no solicitor has been instructed, upon the guardian ad litem[5]. Where neither have been appointed then, with the leave of the court, service may be effected on the child himself[6]. If the court does not grant leave it may direct that service be effected in some other way or that the requirement to serve should not apply[7]. Service on behalf of a child who is a party must be effected by the child's solicitor or, if no solicitor, by the guardian ad litem[8]. If the child has neither, then the court must serve the documents on behalf of the child[9].

The rules create a rebuttable presumption that documents are deemed to have been served, in the case of service by first class post, on the second business day after posting and similarly, in the case of documents left at the document exchange, on the second business day after being left[10]. Where one of these two methods of service is employed two additional working days must be added in to the calculation of the particular time limit for service of documents for the proceedings in question[11].

The rules further provide that the applicant is required to file a statement of service before or no later than the time of the first appointment for directions or the hearing. This statement must confirm that the application has been served on each respondent, and that every person to whom notice of the proceedings must be given has been notified[12].

1 Children Act 1989 s 105 (8).
2 Family Proceedings Rules 1991, SI 1991/1247, r 4.6 (1)(b).
3 Family Proceedings Rules 1991 r 4.8 (1)(a) and Family Proceedings Courts (Children Act 1989) Rules 1991, SI 1991/1395, r 8 (1)(a).
4 Family Proceedings Rules 1991 r 4.8 (1)(b) and Family Proceedings Courts (Children Act 1989) Rules 1991 r 8 (1)(b).
5 Family Proceedings Rules 1991 r 4.8 (4)(a), (b) and Family Proceedings Courts (Children Act 1989) Rules 1991 r 8 (4)(a), (b).
6 Family Proceedings Rules 1991 r 4.8 (4)(c) and Family Proceedings Courts (Children Act 1989) Rules 1991 r 8 (4)(c).

7 Family Proceedings Rules 1991 r 4.8 (5), (8) and Family Proceedings Courts (Children Act 1989) Rules 1991 r 8 (5), (8).
8 Family Proceedings Rules 1991 r 4.8 (3)(a), (b) and Family Proceedings Courts (Children Act 1989) Rules 1991, r 8 (3)(a), (b).
9 Family Proceedings Rules 1991 r 4.8 (3)(c) and Family Proceedings Courts (Children Act 1989) Rules 1991, r 8 (3)(c).
10 Family Proceedings Rules 1991 r 4.8 (6) and Family Proceedings Courts (Children Act 1989) Rules 1991, r 8 (6).
11 See time limits for service set out in Family Proceedings Rules 1991 Appendix 3 and Family Proceedings Courts (Children Act 1989) Rules 1991 Sch 2.
12 Family Proceedings Rules 1991 r 4.8 (7) and Family Proceedings Courts (Children Act 1989) Rules 1991 r 8 (7).

13. Directions. The introduction of directions appointments and hearings in all family proceedings cases involving children and across all three tiers of court was thought crucial to ensure the avoidance of the sort of delay which provoked so much criticism under the former law[1]. Early indications however are that directions hearings in care proceedings are having the opposite effect. The Children Act Advisory Committee and many practitioners are reporting that care cases are now taking much longer than they were in the dying days of the former legislation. It would appear that directions are being sought for almost every move each side wishes to make and courts are failing to see through these delaying tactics. In consequence the fate of the children is being adversely affected. Early directions hearings[3] may be necessary in complex cases or in cases where difficulties are likely to arise, though an application for a directions hearing can be made by any party at any stage in the case before the final hearing[2]. Under the provisions of the Act[3] the court is charged with the task of drawing up a timetable for the proceedings and with giving the necessary directions to ensure that the timetable is observed[4]. Certain time limits within which certain steps must be taken in different proceedings are laid down under the Act, and such time limits may be varied by the court[5]. Other matters upon which the court may be asked to give directions include: the attendance of the child at the hearing; the appointment of a guardian ad litem or solicitor for the child; the service of documents; the submission of evidence including experts' reports; the preparation of welfare reports under Section 7 of the Children Act 1989; the transfer of proceedings to another court, and consolidation with other proceedings[6]. The court can also exercise its powers to give, vary or revoke directions in a number of other situations detailed in the rules[7].

1 See Children Act 1989 s 1 (2).
2 Family Proceedings Rules 1991, SI 1991/1247, r 4.14 (3) and Family Proceedings Courts (Children Act 1989) Rules 1991, SI 1991/1395, r 14 (5).
3 Children Act 1989 ss 11 and 32.
4 Family Proceedings Rules 1991 r 4 (14)(2) and Family Proceedings Courts (Children Act 1989) Rules 1991 r 14 (2).
5 Family Proceedings Rules 1991 r 4.14 (2)(b) and Family Proceedings Courts (Children Act 1989) Rules 1991 r 14 (2)(b).
6 Family Proceedings Rules 1991 r 4.14 (2) and Family Proceedings Courts (Children Act 1989) Rules 1991 r 14 (2).
7 Family Proceedings Rules 1991 r 4.14 (3) and Family Proceedings Courts (Children Act 1989) Rules 1991 r 14 (5).

14. Attendance at directions appointments and hearings. All parties must attend directions appointments or hearings of which they have been given notice unless the court otherwise directs[1].

The court may however proceed with the case in the absence of any party, including the child, where this is considered to be in the child's best interests and that party is represented by a solicitor or guardian ad litem[2]. When the court is considering the interests of the child it must give the guardian ad litem, the child's solicitor and, if he is of sufficient understanding, the child himself, an opportunity to make representations[3].

Where an applicant appears at a hearing or directions appointment but one or more of the respondents do not, the court may proceed with the hearing or appointment but should not begin to hear an application in the absence of a respondent unless satisfied that he has received reasonable notice of the hearing date or the circumstances of the case justify proceeding with the hearing[4]. Where one or more respondents appear at the hearing but the applicant does not, the court may refuse the application or, if sufficient evidence has previously been received, proceed in the absence of the applicant[5].

1 Family Proceedings Rules 1991, SI 1991/1247, r 4.16 (1) and Family Proceedings Courts (Children Act 1989) Rules 1991, SI 1991/1395, r 16 (1).
2 Family Proceedings Rules 1991 r 4.16 (2) and Family Proceedings Courts (Children Act 1989) Rules 1991 r 16 (2).
3 Family Proceedings Rules 1991 r 4.16 (2) and Family Proceedings Courts (Children Act 1989) Rules 1991 r 16 (2).
4 Family Proceedings Rules 1991 r 4.16 (3), (4) and Family Proceedings Courts (Children Act 1989) Rules 1991 r 16 (3), (4).
5 Family Proceedings Rules 1991 r 4.16 (5) and Family Proceedings Courts (Children Act 1989) Rules 1991 r 16 (5).

15. Privacy. In the High Court and county court, hearings or directions appointments will take place in chambers unless the court otherwise directs[1]. In the magistrates' family proceedings courts the rules and certain enactments provide for the court, where it considers it expedient in the interests of the child, to hear in private any proceedings brought under the Children Act 1989, under any statutory instrument made under the Act, and under any amendment to the Children Act made by further legislation[2].

1 Family Proceedings Rules 1991, SI 1991/1247, r 4.16 (7).
2 Family Proceedings Courts (Children Act 1989) Rules 1991, SI 1991/1395, r 16 (7) and Children Act 1989 s 97.

16. Evidence. There are a number of new provisions dealing with evidence across the three tiers of courts effected by the rules and the Act. Documentary evidence in the form of affidavits has been replaced in the High Court and county court by written statements of evidence which are also introduced into the magistrates' family proceedings courts for the first time[1]. The rules on documentary evidence are thus common across all three courts and again facilitate the process of transfer where necessary. A party must file and serve on the parties and on any welfare officer or guardian of whose appointment he has had notice, written statements of the substance of the oral evidence which the party intends to adduce at a hearing or directions appointment[2]. Such written statements must be signed and dated by him and contain a declaration that the maker of the statement believes it to be true and understands that it may be placed before the court[3]. He must further file and serve copies of any documents including experts' reports on which he intends to rely[4]. Such statements and copies of documents must be filed and served at or by such time as the court directs or, in the absence of a direction, before the hearing or appointment[5]. Subject to the direction of the court about the timing of statements, a party may also file and serve a supplementary statement[6]. Failure to comply with these rules means that the party cannot adduce evidence or seek to rely upon a document in respect of which he has failed to comply, unless the court grants him leave[7].

There are special rules concerning documentary evidence in relation to applications under Section 8 of the Children Act 1989[8].

The use of expert evidence arising from examination of the child is very strictly controlled. It is provided that no one may, without the leave of the court, cause the child to be medically or psychiatrically examined, or otherwise assessed, for the purpose of the preparation of expert evidence for use in the proceedings[9]. An application for leave must, unless the court otherwise directs, be served on all parties to the proceedings and on the guardian ad litem[10]. Where such leave has not been given, no evidence arising out of an examination or assessment may be adduced without the leave of the court[11].

The court or the justices' clerk or the proper officer is required under the rules to keep a note of the substance of the oral evidence given at a hearing or directions appointment[12].

By Section 96 (2) Children Act 1989 a court in civil proceedings may hear the unsworn evidence of a child if in its opinion the child understands that it is his duty to speak the truth and he has sufficient understanding to justify his evidence being heard, even though the court is of the opinion that he would not understand the nature of an oath[13]. These provisions bring civil proceedings into line with criminal proceedings[14].

The Act further provides the Lord Chancellor with power to make orders for the admissibility of evidence which would otherwise be inadmissible under any rule of law relating to hearsay[15]. The Children Admissibility of Hearsay Evidence Order 1991[16] provides that in civil proceedings before the High Court or a county court and in family proceedings in magistrates' courts, evidence given in connection with the upbringing, maintenance or welfare of a child shall be admissible notwithstanding any rule of law relating to hearsay. The basis for challenging hearsay evidence per se is thus removed. The evidence is admissible but this leaves open the issue of credibility which will have to be determined by the court, which may decide to ignore the hearsay evidence altogether as being too remote. Particularly where the hearsay evidence is that of a child not giving evidence in the proceedings directly, the court will wish to satisfy itself as to the circumstances in which the evidence was given, the age of the child and the nature of the questioning used to elicit the evidence.

The relaxation of the rules governing hearsay represented by the Order is extensive, encompassing: evidence given in any proceedings concerning the upbringing, maintenance or welfare of a child[17] under the Children Act 1989, and the Child Abduction and Custody Act 1985; any property actions which might affect the child's upbringing, maintenance or welfare eg under the Matrimonial Causes Act 1973[18] or the Law of Property Act 1925[19]; and it would seem that the rule might cover proceedings arising out of fatal accidents or personal injury claims or claims under a trust or will where again the child's maintenance or welfare may be substantially affected[20].

Since the Act has two provisions designating proceedings as family proceedings one of which is restrictive[21] and the other all inclusive[22], there was some confusion initially as to whether hearsay evidence would be freely admissible in all proceedings under the Act, most particularly in secure accommodation proceedings and in applications for child assessments orders in the magistrates' courts. In the case of *R(J) v Oxfordshire County Council*[23], Douglas Brown J stated that s 92(2) of the Act took pre-eminence over s 8(3) and since it provided that proceedings under this Act shall be treated as family proceedings in relation to magistrates courts the Children (Admissibility of Hearsay Evidence) Order 1991 would apply.

Finally, the Act provides that the privilege against self-incrimination does not apply to proceedings concerning care or supervision orders under Part IV of the Act or to emergency proceedings under Part V[24]. In such proceedings no person will be excused from giving evidence on any matter or answering any question put to him in the course of his giving evidence on the ground that to do so might incriminate him or his spouse of an offence[25]. This provision is designed to ensure that the court in this child's case has the best evidence before it. Where however a statement or admission is made in these civil proceedings it cannot be used against the witness or his spouse other than in perjury proceedings[26].

1 Family Proceedings Rules 1991, SI 1991/1247, r 4.17 and Family Proceedings Courts (Children Act 1989) Rules 1991, SI 1991/1395, r 17.
2 Family Proceedings Rules 1991 r 4.17 (1)(a) and Family Proceedings Courts (Children Act 1989) Rules 1991 r 17 (1)(a).
3 Ibid.
4 Family Proceedings Rules 1991 r 4.17 (1)(b) and Family Proceedings Courts (Children Act 1989) Rules 1991 r 17 (1)(b).
5 Family Proceedings Rules 1991 r 4.17 (1) and Family Proceedings Courts (Children Act 1989) Rules 1991 r 17 (1).
6 Family Proceedings Rules 1991 r 4.17 (2) and Family Proceedings Courts (Children Act 1989) Rules 1991 r 17 (2).
7 Family Proceedings Rules 1991 r 4.17 (3) and Family Proceedings Courts (Children Act 1989) Rules 1991 r 17 (3).
8 Family Proceedings Rules 1991 r 4.17 (4) and Family Proceedings Courts (Children Act 1989) Rules 1991 r 17 (4).
9 Family Proceedings Rules 1991 r 4 .18 (1) and Family Proceedings Courts (Children Act 1989) Rules 1991 r 18 (1).
10 Family Proceedings Rules 1991 r 4.18 (2) and Family Proceedings Courts (Children Act 1989) Rules 1991 r 18 (2).
11 Family Proceedings Rules 1991 r 4.18 (3) and Family Proceedings Courts (Children Act 1989) Rules 1991 r 18 (3).
12 Family Proceedings Rules 1991 r 4.20 and Family Proceedings Courts (Children Act 1989) Rules 1991 r 20.
13 Children Act 1989 s 96 (1).
14 See Children and Young Persons Act 1938 s 38 (as amended by the Criminal Justice Act 1988 s 34).
15 Children Act 1989 s 96 (3).
16 Children (Admissibility of Hearsay Evidence) Order, SI 1991/1115.
17 Ibid art 2.
18 Matrimonial Causes Act 1973 s 24.
19 Law of Property Act 1925 s 30.
20 See Hershman and McFarlane *Admissibility of Hearsay Evidence* [1990] Fam Law 164.
21 Children Act 1989 s 8(3), (4).
22 Ibid s 92(2).
23 *R(J) v Oxfordshire County Council* [1992] 3 All ER 660.

24 Ibid s 98.
25 Ibid s 98 (1).
26 Ibid s 98 (2).

17. Other proceedings. There is such a multiplicity of other proceedings in which infants may be involved in the county court and High Court, that the rules of court relevant to such proceedings will be considered in detail in the relevant chapter.

4: TRANSFER OF PROCEEDINGS

18. Transfer of family proceedings. Under the Children (Allocation of Proceedings) Order 1991[1] proceedings can be transferred either horizontally or vertically. The provisions in the Order must be read together with supplementary provisions contained in the Family Proceedings Rules 1991[2] as amended and the Family Proceedings Courts (Children Act 1989) Rules 1991[3] as amended.

1 Children (Allocation of Proceedings) Order 1991, SI 1991/1677.
2 Family Proceedings Rules 1991, SI 1991/1247 as amended by SI 1991/2113, SI 1992/456 and SI 1992/2067.
3 Family Proceedings Courts (Children Act 1989) Rules 1991, SI 1991/1395 as amended by SI 1992/2068.

19. Transfer from one magistrates' court to another. A magistrates' court ("the transferring court") must transfer proceedings under the Children Act 1989 or the Adoption Act 1976 to another magistrates' court (the "receiving court") where having regard to the principle that any delay in determining the question is likely to prejudice the welfare of the child, the transferring court considers that the transfer is in the interests of the child[1]. The transferring court may consider this to be the case because it is likely significantly to accelerate the determination of the proceedings[2], or because it would be appropriate for those proceedings to be heard together with other family proceedings which are pending in the receiving court[3], or for some other reason[4]. The receiving court must, through its justices' clerk, also consent to the case being transferred[5].

Where the justices' clerk or a family proceedings court receive a written request from a party to transfer proceedings, he or the court must issue a certificate in Form CHA 64[6] granting, or in Form CHA 65[7] refusing, the request in accordance with the relevant criteria. A copy of the certificate granting the request must be sent to the parties, any guardian ad litem and to the receiving court[8].

1 The Children (Allocation of Proceedings) Order 1991, SI 1991/1677, art 6 (1).
2 Ibid art 6(1)(a)(i).
3 Ibid art 6(1)(a)(ii).
4 Ibid art 6(1)(a)(iii). For an example, see the statement of Sir Stephen Brown P in *Re A D (A Minor)* [1993] Fam Law 43 set out at paragraph 37, post.
5 Ibid art 6(1)(b).
6 See Family Proceedings Courts (Children Act 1989) Rules 1991/1395, Sch 1 Form CHA 64.
7 See ibid Form CHA 65.
8 Ibid r 6 (2).

20. Transfer from magistrates' court to county court. Subject to a considerable number of restrictions[1], a magistrates' court may upon application by a party or of its own motion, transfer to a county court[2] proceedings of any of the kinds mentioned in article 3 (1) of the Children (Allocation of Proceedings) Order 1991[3] where it considers it in the interests of the child to do so having regard to a number of issues. Thus, the court must consider whether: any delay in determining the question raised in the proceedings is likely to prejudice the child's welfare[4]; the proceedings are exceptionally grave, important or complex[5]; it would be appropriate for those proceedings to be heard together with other family proceedings which are pending in another court[6]; whether transfer is likely significantly to accelerate the determination of the proceedings, and no other method of doing so, including transfer to another magistrates' court, is appropriate and delay would seriously prejudice the interests of the child who is the subject of the proceedings[7]. There are restrictions on transfers, however. Thus, applications for the emergency orders[8] for child protection, applications for contribution orders[9], and appeals in child minding and day care registration cases[10] are excluded from the transfer powers, and secure accommodation proceedings[11] and proceedings to give a police constable powers to assist in the removal of children[12] can only be transferred from a magistrates' court to a county court in order to be heard together with other family proceedings, which arise out of the same circumstances as gave rise to the proceedings to be transferred and which are pending in another court[13].

A magistrates' court can also transfer to a county court proceedings under the Children Act 1989 or the Adoption Act 1976 to which the rules set out above do not apply, where it has decided that in the child's interests the proceedings can be dealt with more appropriately in that county court, having regard to the delay principle[14].

As to which county court the case may be transferred, this is governed by special rules concerning the allocation of proceedings to particular levels of county courts[15].

Where the justices' clerk or a family proceedings court has received a written request from a party for a transfer of proceedings to the county court, the procedure to be followed is exactly the same as that following a request to transfer proceedings from one magistrates' court to another[16].

In addition when magistrates are presented with potentially complex or lengthy cases they should consider whether or not to transfer the case to the district judge for his determination as to the appropriate level for the case to be heard. It has already been a matter for concern that a lengthy hearing can cause problems for a bench of magistrates which has to return over a number of separate days[17]. As Thorpe J commented in *Re H (A Minor)*[18] it is vital for the success of the family justice system that has been introduced to accompany the Childrens Act 1989 that the allocation of cases to the appropriate level of court within the three tier system operates effectively. It has also been stressed that cases involving non-accidental injury and assessment of risk should, generally, be transferred to a higher court[19].

1 Set out in the Children (Allocation of Proceedings) Order 1991, SI 1991/1677 arts 7 paras (2), (3) and (4) and arts 15-18.
2 Ibid art 7 (1).
3 Ibid art 3 (1) and the list runs from (a) to (r).
4 Ibid art 7 (1).
5 Ibid art 7 (1)(a): the article suggests proceedings may be so because of complicated or conflicting evidence about the risks involved to the child's physical or moral well-being or about other matters relating to the welfare of the child; because of the number of parties; because of a conflict with the law of another jurisdiction; because of some novel and difficult point of law; or because of some question of general public interest.

6   Ibid art 7 (1)(b).
7   Ibid art 7 (1)(c).
8   Listed in art 3 (1)(g)(j), (l) and (m).
9   Ibid art 3 (1)(p).
10 Ibid art 3 (1)(q).
11 Ibid art 7 (3).
12 Ibid art 7 (3).
13 Ibid art 7 (3).
14 Ibid art 8.
15 Ibid arts 14-20 discussed under Paragraph 5 ante.
16 Family Proceedings Rules 1991, SI 1991/1247 r 4.6 (1).
17 *L v Berkshire County Council* [1992] 1 FCR 481.
18 *Re H (A Minor)* (1992) Times, 5 June, FD, and see also *Sunderland Borough Council v
    A* (1992) Times, 15 May, FD, and *Re J (A Minor) (Change of Name)* [1992] Fam Law 569,
    FD.
19 See per CONNELL J in *S v Oxfordshire CC* [1992] Fam Law 571.

**21. Transfer from magistrates' courts following magistrates' court's refusal to
transfer.** Where a magistrates' court refuses to transfer proceedings to a county
court, any party may apply to the appropriate county court care centre for an order
to transfer the proceedings to that centre[1]. In determining whether or not to transfer
the proceedings to itself, the court must consider the same criteria which the
magistrates' court had to consider when deciding whether or not to grant the request
for a transfer[2]. In so doing the county court may reach the decision that the
proceedings are more appropriate for determination in the High Court and that such
determination would be in the interests of the child[3].

The Family Proceedings Rules 1991 provide for the steps to be taken and the time
within which they should be taken where an application for transfer from a magistrates' court is made to a county court[4]. The applicant is required to file the application
for transfer together with the magistrates' certificate of refusal, and to serve a copy
of the application and of the certificate personally on all parties to the proceedings
which it is sought to transfer within two days after receipt of the certificate by the
applicant[5]. Within two days after receipt of the documents served on him, any party
other than the applicant may file written representations[6].

The court must consider the application not before the fourth day after the filing
of the application unless the parties consent to an earlier consideration, and either
grant the application or direct that a date be fixed for the hearing of the application[7].
If the latter, the proper officer fixes the date and gives not less than one day's notice
of the date to the parties[8]. Strangely, the rules do not provide for a copy of the original
application which it is sought to transfer to be lodged with the county court. It would
clearly assist the district judge so to do.

Where the county court is considering whether to transfer proceedings on to the
High Court, it may, before deciding whether to make or refuse an order for transfer
or whether to fix a date for the hearing or whether such an order should be made, invite
the parties to make written representations within a specified period as to whether
such an order should be made[9]. After consideration of the written representations the
court may make an order for transfer, determine that such an order not be made or set
a date for hearing of the issue[10], as Thorpe J commented however in *Re H* "where it
becomes apparent in family proceedings that a case was more complex that it had
originally appeared, it was essential that action be taken swiftly to transfer it to the
appropriate level of court within the three tier system.[11]"

1 The appropriate centre is the one for the petty sessions area in which the magistrates' court is situated, as listed in the Children (Allocation of Proceedings) Order 1991, SI 1991/1677. The certificate for transfer is made under ibid art 9 (1). See CHA Form 64.
2 Ibid art 9 (2).
3 Ibid art 9 (3). See ante para 21.
4 Family Proceedings Rules 1991, SI 1991/1247, r 4.6 (1).
5 Ibid r 4.6 (1).
6 Ibid r 4.6 (2).
7 Ibid r 4.6 (3).
8 Ibid r 4.6 (3).
9 Ibid r 4.6 (4).
10 Ibid r 4.6 (4).
11 *Re H (A Minor)* (1992) Times, 5 June, FD

22. Transfer from one county court to another. Under the Children (Allocation of Proceedings) Order 1991 the "transferring court'' must transfer proceedings under the Children Act 1989 or Adoption Act 1976 to another county court (the "receiving court'') where having regard to the avoidance of delay principles it considers the transfer to be in the child's interests, and the receiving court is either of the same class or classes as the transferring court or is to be presided over by a judge or district judge who is specified in the Family Proceedings (Allocation to Judiciary) Directions 1991 for the same purposes as the judge or district judge presiding over the transferring court[1].

1 Children (Allocation of Proceedings) Order 1991, SI 1991/1677, art 10 and see the *First Report of the Children Act Advisory Committee* (LCD Dec 1992) Chapter 4.

23. Transfer from county court to magistrates' court. A county court may transfer back to a magistrates' court, before trial, proceedings transferred to it by the magistrates' court, having regard to the avoidance of delay principle and the interests of the child and where the criteria for transfer cited by the magistrates' court as the reason for transfer either did not at the time or no longer apply[1]. Under the Children (Allocation of Proceedings) Appeals Order 1991[2] an appeal from a decision of a district judge lies to a judge of the Family Division of the High Court, or except where the order was made by a district judge or deputy district judge of the Principal Registry of the Family Division, to a circuit judge[3].

1 Children (Allocation of Proceedings) Order 1991, SI 1991/1677, art 11.
2 Children (Allocation of Proceedings) Appeals Order 1991, SI 1991/1801.
3 Children (Allocation of Proceedings) Appeals Order 1991.

24. Transfer from county court to High Court. A county court may transfer proceedings under the Children Act 1989 or the Adoption Act 1976 to the High Court where, having regard to the principle of the avoidance of delay, it considers that the proceedings are appropriate for determination in the High Court, and that such determination would be in the child's interest[1].

1 Children (Allocation of Proceedings) Order 1991, SI 1991/1677, art 12 and see also statement of the President of the Family Division in *Re A D (A Minor)* [1993] Fam Law 43 set out at Paragraph 37.

25. Transfer from High Court to county court. Subject to the provisions governing allocation of proceedings to particular county courts discussed earlier[1], the High Court may transfer to a county court proceedings under the Children Act 1989 or the Adoption Act 1976 where, having regard to the avoidance of delay principle, it considers that the proceedings are appropriate for determination in such a court and that such determination would be in the interests of the child[2].

1   See Paragraph 5 n 7 ante.
2   The Children (Allocation of Proceedings) Order 1991, SI 1991/1677, art 13.

26. Transfers under the Matrimonial and Family Proceedings Act 1984. Under the provisions of this Act the President of the Family Division may with the concurrence of the Lord Chancellor give directions with respect to the distribution and transfer between the High Court and county courts of family business and family proceedings generally[1]. It should be stressed that this power is not exercisable in respect of individual cases, but in respect of whole classes of action or types of business[2], and the President has exercised this power on a number of occasions[3].

The ability of individual parties or of courts to apply for, or make an order for transfer of individual cases from one court to another in family proceedings under the Children Act 1989 or the Adoption Act 1976 has already been discussed[4], but this in effect supplements the existing powers of the High Court and county court to transfer family proceedings under the provisions of the Matrimonial and Family Proceedings Act 1984[5].

1   Matrimonial and Family Proceedings Act 1984 s 37.
2   Ibid s 37 and for definition of "family business" and "family proceedings" see ibid s 32.
3   See eg *Practice Direction* 22 April 1985: Hearing by circuit judges sitting outside the Royal Courts of Justice; and *Practice Direction* [1972] 1 All ER 103.
4   See Paragraph 18 et seq ante.
5   Matrimonial and Family Proceedings Act 1984 ss 38 and 39.

27. Transfers from High Court to county court. Thus, under the 1984 Act, at any stage in family proceedings in the High Court, the High Court may, if the proceedings are transferable, order the transfer of the whole or any part of the proceedings to a county court either of its own motion or on the application of any party to the proceedings[1]. The Act then designates certain family proceedings as being transferable to a county court namely: all family proceedings commenced in the High Court which are within the jurisdiction of a county court or divorce court[2]; wardship proceedings, except applications for an order that a minor be made, or cease to be, a ward of court[3] or any other proceedings which relate to the exercise of the inherent jurisdiction of the High Court with respect to minors[4]; and all family proceedings transferred from a county court to the High Court under Section 39 of the 1984 Act or Section 41 of the County Courts Act 1984[5].

Proceedings transferred under this provision must be transferred to such county court or, in the case of a matrimonial cause or matter within the jurisdiction of a divorce county court only, such divorce county court as the High Court directs[6]. The transfer does not affect any right of appeal from the order directing the transfer, or the right to enforce in the High Court any judgment signed, or order made, in that court before the transfer[7].

Where, pursuant to these provisions in the 1984 Act, proceedings are transferred to a county court, the county court is given jurisdiction to hear and determine those proceedings where it would not otherwise have such jurisdiction[8], and is further granted jurisdiction to award any relief which could have been awarded by the High Court[9].

1   Matrimonial and Family Proceedings Act 1984 s 38 (1).

2   Ibid s 38 (2)(a).
3   Ibid s 38 (2)(b) (as amended by Children Act 1989 s 108 (5), (6) Sch 13 para 51, Sch 14 para 1).
4   Ibid s 38 (2)(b) (as amended by Children Act 1989 s 108 (5), (6) Sch 13 para 51, Sch 14 para 1).
5   Ibid s 38 (2)(c) and County Courts Act 1984 s 41 provides for the transfer of cases to the High Court by order of the High Court.
6   Ibid s 38 (3).
7   Ibid s 38 (4).
8   Ibid s 38 (5)(a).
9   Ibid s 38 (5)(b) for example to grant injunctions based on the inherent jurisdiction of the High Court to protect children from a violent or abusing relative, see *Re T, T v T (Ouster Order)* [1987] 1 FLR 181 or where there is a risk that a child may be removed from the jurisdiction, an order could be obtained from the High Court prohibiting such removal which can if the case is transferred also be granted by the county court in wardship or inherent jurisdiction CAses.

28. Transfer of family proceedings to High Court from county court. The county court may at any stage in family proceedings in the county court, where such proceedings are transferable, order the transfer of the whole or any part of the proceedings to the High Court either of its own motion or on the application of any party to the proceedings[1]. The family proceedings designated as transferable under these provisions are all family proceedings commenced in a county court or divorce county court, and all family proceedings transferred from the High Court to a county court or divorce county court[2].

1   Matrimonial and Family Proceedings Act 1984 s 39 (1).
2   Ibid s 39 (2).

5: APPEALS

29. Appeals in general. Since the procedure to be followed in making appeals against decisions of courts in children's cases varies with each type of proceeding, the relevant appeals process will be examined *in detail in the relevant chapters*. What is offered here is some *general guidance* on the changes to appeals processes effected by the Children Act 1989[1], a consideration of the nature of appeals[2] and the role of the appellate court in children's cases prompted by judicial dicta in recent leading cases[3], and a review of the appellate courts powers.

1   See Children Act 1989 s 94 (1) (as amended by Courts and Legal Services Act 1990, Schedule 16 para 23).
2   For the difficulties faced in such cases see *Re F (A Minor) (Wardship : Appeal)* [1976] 1 All ER 417 at 432 per BROWNE L J and at 439440 per BRIDGE L J ; dicta of SCARMAN LJ in *B v W (Wardship: Appeal)* [1979] 3 All ER 83 at 96; and CUMMING-BRUCE L J in *Clarke-Hunt v Newcombe* (1982) 4 FLR 482 at 488.
3   See principally *G v G* [1985] 2 All ER 225, HL.

30. Appeals from the magistrates' court to the High Court. Under the provisions of the Children Act 1989 an appeal lies to the Family Division of the High Court against the magistrates decision to make or refuse to make any order[1], except in the following situations where there is no right of appeal:

1. against the making or refusal to make an emergency protection order, the granting of an extension of or refusal to extend the effective period of the order, the discharge of or refusal to discharge the order, or the giving or refusal to give any direction in connection with the order[2];
2. where the magistrates' court has exercised its powers to decline jurisdiction because it considers that the case can more conveniently be dealt with by another court[3];
3. against decisions taken by courts on questions arising in respect of the transfer or proposed transfer of proceedings except as provided for by orders made by the Lord Chancellor[4];
4. against the making by the magistrates of an interim order for periodical payments[5].

On hearing the appeal the High Court Family Division can make such orders as may be necessary[6], including such incidental or consequential provision as appears to be just[7], in order to give effect to its determination of the appeal. Any order of the High Court made on appeal, other than one directing a rehearing by the magistrates, shall for the purposes of the enforcement, variation, revival or discharge of the order be treated as if it were an order of the magistrates' court from which the appeal was brought and not an order of the High Court[8].

1 Children Act 1989 s 94 (1).
2 Children Act 1989 s 45 (10) (as substituted by Courts and Legal Services Act 1990 s 116 and Sch 16, para 19) although for the problems this may give rise to in a situation where a child needs protection see *Essex County Council v F* [1992] Fam Law 569, FD and (1992) NLJ 1553.
3 Children Act 1989 s 94 (2).
4 Ibid ss 94 (10) and (11).
5 Under ibid Sch 1. See ibid s 94 (3).
6 Ibid s 94 (4).
7 Ibid s 94 (5).
8 Ibid s 94 (9).

31. Appeals from the county court and High Court to the Court of Appeal. With the exception of providing for appeals to be made against decisions arising out of the transfer or proposed transfer of proceedings from the court making the original order[1], the Children Act 1989 made no further provision in respect of appeals to the higher courts, thus the general rules governing such appeals in family cases are applicable[2].

1 Children Act 1989 ss 94 (10) and (11).
2 Paragraphs 34 and 35 post.

32. Procedure on appeals under the Children Act 1989. Pursuant to the provisions of the Children Act 1989, the Family Proceedings Rules 1991 lay down the procedure to be followed on an appeal to the High Court from the magistrates' court[1], and on an appeal from any decision of a district judge to the judge of the court in which the decision was made[2].

An appeal against a magistrates' court's decision to the High Court will, unless the President otherwise directs, be heard and determined by a single judge[3], although an application to that court to withdraw the appeal, have the appeal dismissed with the consent of all parties, or amend the grounds of appeal may be heard by a district judge[4].

Under the rules the appellant must file and serve on all parties to the proceedings in the lower court, and on any guardian ad litem:

1. notice of the appeal in writing, setting out the grounds upon which he relies[5];
2. a certified copy of the summons or application and of the order appealed against and of any order staying its execution[6];
3. a copy of any notes of the evidence[1] which according to Bracewell J in *Re W & S* should be provided in typescript;
4. a copy of any reasons given for the decision[2] which must have been announced at the time of the decision, and must be set down in the manner prescribed by the Court of Appeal[8].

The notice of appeal must be filed and served within fourteen days after the determination against which the appeal is brought[9], except in the case of an appeal against an interim care or supervision order where the period is within seven days after the making of the order[10], or with the leave of the court to which, or judge to whom, the appeal is to be brought within such other time as that court or judge may direct[11]. Any remaining documents must be filed and served as soon as practicable thereafter subject to any direction of the court to which or judge to whom the appeal is to be brought[12].

Again, except in the case of an appeal against an interim care or supervision order, a respondent who wishes to contend on the appeal that the decision of the court below should be varied either in any event or in the event of the appeal being allowed in whole or in part, or to contend that the decision of the court below should be affirmed on grounds other than those relied upon by that court, or to contend by way of cross-appeal that the decision of the court below was wrong in whole or in part, must, within fourteen days of receipt of the notice of appeal, file and serve on all other parties to the appeal a written notice setting out the grounds upon which he relies[13].

Where the appeal is being brought in the Divisional Court of the Family Division by a party other than the child but the child was a party to the proceedings in the lower court and is affected by the appeal, then the procedure to be followed is laid down in a Practice Direction of 1986[14]. The notice of motion should be served on the guardian ad litem of the child appointed in the court below, and no order is required appointing him guardian ad litem in the Divisional Court proceedings provided his consent to act and his solicitor's certificate, referred to in the rules of court, are filed in the Principal Registry by that solicitor as soon as practicable after service of the notice of motion[15].

It has been emphasised in the case of *Croydon LBC v A*[16] that on an appeal from the magistrates' court under the Children Act 1989 the appeal court has wide ranging powers to consider and deal with the way in which the court below reached its decision, but it is not empowered to hear evidence save in *exceptional* circumstances.

1 Family Proceedings Rules 1991, SI 1991/1247 r 4.22, and see also *Practice Direction (Family Proceedings: Appeals from Magistrates' Courts)* [1992] 1 All ER 864, [1992] 1 WLR 261.
2 Ibid r 4.22.
3 Ibid r 4.22 (8).
4 Ibid r 4.22 (7).
5 Ibid r 4.22 (2)(a).
6 Ibid r 4.22 (2)(b).
7 Ibid r 4.22 (2)(c) and see *Re W & S* [1992] 2 FCR 665, FD.
8 Ibid r 4.22 (2)(d) and see *H v Hillingdon* LBC (1992) 136 Sol Jo LB 191 and *Re B* (1992) Times, 16 July, CA, and *Re O (A Minor) (Care Order: Education)* [1992] 2 FLR 7.

9 Ibid r 4.22 (3)(a).
10 Children Act 1989 s 38 (1) and Family Proceedings Rules 1991 r 4.22 (3)(b).
11 Ibid r 4.22 (3)(c).
12 Ibid r 4.22 (4).
13 Ibid rr 4.22 (5) and (6).
14 *Practice Direction* [1986] 1 All ER 896, [1986] 1 WLR 384.
15 Family Proceedings Rules 1991, SI 1991/1247 r 9.2 (7).
16 [1992] 2 FLR 271.

33. Nature of appeals. The very nature of an appeal in children's cases demands the judgment of Solomon in that the court of first instance is nearly always faced with a choice of two imperfect solutions, but, it has the advantage over an appellate court of seeing the parties in person. Before overturning a decision of the first instance court, the appellate court must therefore be satisfied that the first instance court was plainly wrong and not just that, had it heard the case, it would have come to another conclusion[1]. It is also essential to understand that the making of final orders in proceedings should in the interests of the children be seen to be precisely that, final. The intention behind the reforms in orders in respect of children[2] in divorce and other family proceedings brought about by the Children Act 1989 was partly to impress upon parents the extremely damaging effects on the children of futile warring over who should hold greater powers in respect of the children[3]. By its emphasis on the concept of the joint and enduring nature of parental responsibility and the parent/child relationship[4], it is hoped that the Children Act 1989 will further reduce the potential for damaging and protracted appeals. The Court of Appeal had even gone to the extent in pre-Children Act cases of criticising the legal aid authorities for granting legal aid for an ill-founded appeal[5], though some responsibility clearly lay with the legal advisers, and has intimated that the appellant may incur the risk of an order for costs if the appeal is considered to be unjustifiable[6].

1 See *G v G* [1985] 2 All ER 225.
2 Such as in Children Act 1989 s 1 (5) and in the range of orders available under ibid ss 8, 16.
3 Ibid s 1 (3).
4 Ibid ss 2 (1) and (6).
5 See *Re T (A Minor)* [1986] 16 Fam Law 189, CA.
6 Within the principles laid down by the House of Lords in *G v G* [1985] 2 All ER 225, see also *Re G (A Minor) (Role of the Appellate Courts)* [1987] 1 FLR 164, and *R v R (London Borough of Harrow Intervening)* [1988] Fam Law 171, CA.

34. Role of the appellate courts. In *G v G*[1], the leading case on appeals in cases involving children, the House of Lords laid down clear guidance for the Court of Appeal when reviewing a judge's exercise of discretion in cases involving the welfare of children and this applies also to the exercise of appellate functions by the Divisional Court of the Family Division of the High Court. The House of Lords stated clearly that the principles applicable in such cases were the same as those which applied to the Court of Appeal's general jurisdiction. Thus, having regard to the fact that in such cases there were often no right answers and the court at first instance was faced with choosing the best of two or more imperfect solutions but had the advantage over the appellate court of hearing and seeing the parties in person, the appellate court should only intervene when it considered that the lower court had exceeded the generous ambit within which judicial disagreement was reasonably possible. The appellate court must therefore only intervene where it is satisfied that the lower court was plainly wrong and not where had it itself carried out the balancing exercise of weighing the various issues raised for and against each party, it would have come to a different decision[2].

Lord Fraser further stated that, in cases dealing with the custody of children, the desirability of putting an end to litigation is particularly strong because the longer legal proceedings last, the more are the children, whose welfare is at stake, likely to be disturbed by the uncertainty[3].

Having regard to these principles, one feature which is already emerging, at least on appeals to the Divisional Court, is the importance of demonstrating that full consideration has been given to the welfare check list[4]. One disturbing tendency has been the lower courts' reluctance in private law proceedings[5] seriously to consider children's wishes and feelings if they are below a certain age despite the fact that this is totally contrary to the provisions of the Children Act 1989[6]. Even on appeal, however, some High Court judges are reinforcing this approach by dismissing evidence given as to the children's wishes and feelings as being suspect because the children are too young to know their own wishes and feelings[7]. This approach has been adopted even where court welfare officers have interviewed the children on a number of occasions in neutral environments in order to ascertain their wishes and feelings. If the courts, for the sake of the children's stability, ignore factors provided in the welfare checklist then this, it is submitted, of itself provides grounds of appeal as the court will not have properly carried out the balancing exercise taking into account all relevant factors[8].

1 *G v G* [1985] 2 All ER 225, HL.
2 Leaning heavily on the judgment of BRIDGE LJ in *Re F (A Minor) (Wardship Appeal)* [1976] Fam 238, [1976] 1 All ER 417, CA and see *Re W and S (Minors) (Contact)* [1992] 2 FCR 665.
3 *G v G* [1985] supra at 228.
4 See Children Act 1989 s 1 (3) and see *Re J (A Minor)* (1992) Fam Law 229.
5 Under ibid s 8. See for example *M v M* [1993] 1 FCR 5, CA.
6 Ibid s 1 (3)(a).
7 See for example *Re C (A Minor)* (1992) Fam Law 571 where WAITE J overruled the wishes of a 13 year old girl living in local authority care to return to live with her father.
8 Per *G v G* [1985] 2 All ER 225, HL.

35. Powers of the appellate courts. The power of the appellate courts in children's cases may be exercised in any one of three ways[1]:

1. *Remit the case with directions*—Where the appellate court is satisfied that the order was wrong but is uncertain, on the basis of the evidence before it, as to what order should be made, it may remit the case with such directions for the care of the child in the interim period as are consistent with the paramountcy of the child's welfare[2].

2. *Substitution of orders* — Where the appellate court is satisfied that the lower court's order was plainly wrong in law and it has before it all the relevant evidence then the court may substitute its own order, where it reaches a different conclusion[3].

3. *Hearing the Evidence* — In very exceptional cases the appellate court may hear evidence although where it is the case that either or both of the parties are seeking to put fresh evidence before the court, then great care will be exercised by the court in such circumstances in accordance with the guidance issued by the Court of Appeal[4]. The appellate court may then either allow the appeal and substitute its own orders or dismiss the appeal. In cases where new evidence

suggests the lower court reached its decision without being aware of some crucial factors, the appellate court may remit the case for reconsideration in the wake of such fresh evidence[5].

When drafting a notice of appeal in all these situations, it is crucial that the document reports fully the reasons upon which the lower courts' decision was based[6]. Magistrates as well as judges are required by the court rules to provide written reasons for their decisions which must have been announced at the time of the decision[7], which must be sufficiently detailed for an appellate court to be able to scrutinize them and set down in the manner prescribed by the Court of Appeal[8].

1 Per Lord SCARMAN in *B v W (Wardship : Appeal)* [1979] 3 All ER 83 at 95.
2 See for example in *B v Humberside CC* (1992) Fam Law 569 where BOOTH J discharged an interim care order and remitted the matter back to the justices to consider what order to make.
3 As in *S (B D) v S (D J) (Children : Care and Control)* [1977] Fam 109, [1977] 1 All ER 656, CA and see now *West Glamorgan CC v P (No 2)* [1992] Fam Law 569; and *Nottinghamshire CC v P* [1992] Fam Law 571.
4 In *M v M* [1987] 1 WLR 404, [1987] 2 FLR 146 CA and for a case under the Children Act see *Re A (A Minor) (Care Proceedings)* [1993] 1 FCR 164.
5 *A v A* [1988] 1 FLR 193; and *Re B (Minors) (Custody)* [1991] FCR 428, [1991] 1 FLR 137, CA.
6 Where the sequence of events in the case is very complex it is further helpful to the appellate court to have before it a chronology of events, see *Goodbody (formerly Jupp) v Jupp* (1983) 13 Fam Law 150, and this was constantly emphasised by the High Court judges involved in training on the Children Act.
7 Family Proceedings Courts (Children Act 1989) Rules 1991, SI 1991/1395, r 21 (6) and Family Proceedings Rules 1991, SI 1991/1247, r 4.21 (4), and see *Re W & S* [1992] 2 FCR 665, FD and *H v Hillingdon LBC* (1992) 136 Sol Jo LB 191.
8 Including a chronology where appropriate and see *Re B* (1992) Times, 16 July, CA.

36. Orders pending appeals. Special provision is made in the Children Act 1989 for orders pending appeals in public law cases[1], but in cases under the private law provisions or generally, consideration must be given by the lower court to any orders on the children pending the hearing of the appeal[2]. Appeals should be heard within 28 days[3]. Where it seems appropriate to ask for a stay of execution[4] of an order for example where the child might be removed from the jurisdiction this must be done by the person intending to appeal and should only be for a short period thus enabling the appropriate notice to be filed[5]. The order can be extended by the appellate court[6] up to the hearing date which should be within the 28 day period.

1 Children Act 1989 s 40. It should be noted, however, that it was confirmed in *Croydon London Borough v A and B (No 2)* [1992] 2 FCR 858 that the High Court does not have jurisdiction under s 40(1) to make a care order pending appeal but should instead make an interim care order under s 38 of the 1989 Act.
2 See *Townson v Mahon* [1984] FLR 690 where it was stated that in this case stay of an order should only be allowed for such period as was necessary to file an appeal.
3 *Re W (Minors)* [1984] 3 All ER 58n, sub nom *Practice Note* [1984] 1 WLR 1125, CA.
4 *S v S (Custody Order: Stay of Execution)* [1986] 1 FLR 492.
5 See note 2 supra.
6 See note 3 supra.

CHAPTER 2: MINORS (INFANTS) AND CHILDREN AS PARTIES

1: HIGH COURT

37. Generally. In order to be properly constituted, civil proceedings other than family proceedings in the High Court, where a minor is a party[1], must be conducted on the minor's behalf by an adult[2]. In the case of an infant plaintiff or applicant the adult is known as the "next friend", and in the case of an infant defendant or respondent as the "guardian ad litem"[3]. The next friend or guardian ad litem has the full conduct of the proceedings subject to certain qualifications[4]. If the minor is damnified by the misconduct or negligence of the next friend or guardian ad litem, the matter may be re-opened by original action at any time[5].

Where in any proceedings money is recovered by or on behalf of, or adjudged or ordered or agreed to be paid to or for the benefit of, or money paid into court is accepted by or on behalf of, a minor, the money must be dealt with under the directions of the court[6]. The directions given may provide that the money (or part of it) be paid into court and invested or otherwise dealt with there[7], or such general or special directions may be given as the court thinks fit[8]. Any money paid into court in this way may only be paid out under an order of the court[9].

Under the Children Act 1989 — Amendments to the Family Proceedings Rules have now enabled minors who wish to prosecute or defend any family proceedings (other than specified proceedings under s 41 of the Act[10]) in the High Court to do so without a next friend or guardian ad litem[11]. Where a minor wishes so to do he must either obtain the leave of the court for that purpose or he must convince a solicitor that he is capable of giving instructions in relation to the proceedings or he must already have instructed a solicitor. The rules provide that the minor can apply for leave of the court where he has not already instructed a solicitor by filing a written request for leave setting out the reasons for the application or by making an oral request for leave at any hearing in the proceedings. On considering such a request the court must communicate the decision to the minor and to the other parties, or direct that the request be heard ex parte, when the court must fix a hearing date and give to the minor such notice as the court may direct. Where on the other hand the minor already has a next friend or guardian and wishes to prosecute or defend the remaining stages without one, the minor may apply to the court for leave to have the guardian or next friend removed. It should be noted that following the decision in *Re H (A Minor)*[12] some young people even though emotionally disturbed could have sufficient understanding to instruct solicitors to represent their interests.

The President of the Family Division Sir Stephen Brown has, however, made it plain in *Re A D (A Minor)*[13] that he does not expect applications by children for orders under the Children Act 1989 in private law proceedings to be frequent. Indeed, he emphasised that in his view *any* application by a child to take proceedings under the Children Act ought to be made in the High Court and if commenced elsewhere in either the family proceedings court or the county court it should be transferred to the High Court as soon as possible[14].

1 For minors as plaintiffs, see Paragraph 38 post and Table 1 post; for minors as defendants, see Paragraph 44 post and Table 2 post, and as to the settlement and compromise of actions and approval of arrangements in which minors are involved, see Paragraph 52 post and Table 3 post.
2 RSC Ord 80 r 2, and see Form 2 post.
3 The term "guardian ad litem" has a long legal history but it was also employed in adoption legislation and later adapted in the Children Act 1975 and consequent regulations to describe a non-legal professional, generally a very well qualified social worker who was appointed as a "guardian ad litem" and officer of the court to represent the child's best interests to the court in care and associated proceedings. The function and role of such a "guardian ad litem" differed as between adoption and care proceedings but many social workers and non-legal professionals have come to view the term as as applying only in these situations and have failed to realise that the term has the much wider legal currency described in the text. This has led to considerable confusion when a person is appointed a "guardian ad litem" in cases not connected with care proceedings or adoption and social worker guardians ad litem have not understood why it was not one of their number who was appointed. See Paragraphs 214 and 176 post for details as to those cases where social workers or probation officers may be appointed as guardians ad litem in adoption and in care or associated proceedings. Under the provisions of the Children Act 1989 s 41 the proceedings in which such guardians ad litem may be appointed are described as specified proceedings.
4 Eg the next friend or guardian ad litem cannot validly compromise or settle any proceedings unless the compromise or settlement is in the interest of and for the benefit of the minor; see Paragraph 52 post and Table 3 post. For the qualifications on the making of admissions by a minor see RSC Ord 80 rr 8, 12 (1) and Paragraph 46 post.
5 *Re Hoghton, Hoghton v Fiddey* (1874) LR 18 Eq 573.
6 RSC Ord 80 r 12 (1). The rule applies also where the minor counterclaims: RSC Ord 80 r 12 (5).
7 RSC Ord 80 r 12 (2).
8 RSC Ord 80 r 12 (3).
9 RSC Ord 80 r 12 (4); see also RSC Ord 22 r 4.
10 See Family Proceedings Rules 1991 r 9.2.
11 Family Proceedings (Amendment) Rules 1992 inserting a new Rule 9.2A into the Family Proceedings Rules 1991 SI 1991/1247
12 *Re H (A Minor)* (1992) Times, 5 June 1992, FD.
13 (1993) Fam Law 43.
14 See ante Paragraph 24.

38. Proceedings by minor: the next friend. Any person within the jurisdiction[1] who is not himself incapable of instituting proceedings[2] and is not an accounting party or connected with the defendant[3] or otherwise interested adversely to the minor[4] may be the next friend of an infant plaintiff or applicant[5]. The next friend must act by a solicitor[6]. Preference is given to the father or mother[7] although a guardian of the person, testamentary guardian[8] or even the Official Solicitor[9] may be appointed next friend. The court generally expects him to be a substantial person and thus it is desirable that he be a relation, connection or friend of the family and not a mere volunteer[10].

If a minor is made a plaintiff without a next friend[11] or the next friend is a person incapable of so acting[12], the proceedings may be set aside[13] and the plaintiff's solicitor may be ordered personally to pay the defendant's costs[14]. Before the next friend's name is used he must sign a written consent to act, which must be filed in the Central Office, Chancery Chambers or district registry where the action is proceeding[15]. Where a person is named as next friend without his consent, he can apply to have his name struck out, the solicitor being liable for costs[16].

The next friend is an officer of the court appointed to look after the interests of the minor[17], and although he has the conduct of the proceedings[18] he is not in a sense a party to the proceedings[19] and is not, as next friend, entitled to appear in them in person[20].

All interlocutory applications on behalf of a minor must be made by his next friend[21]. In general anything which in the ordinary conduct of any proceedings is required or authorised by the Rules of the Supreme Court to be done by a party to the proceedings must or may, if the party is a minor, be done by his next friend or guardian ad litem[22].

There is now much greater freedom as to the commencement of family proceedings by a minor[23].

1 A person resident outside the jurisdiction may be appointed next friend, but may be required to provide security for costs: *Didisheim v London and Westminster Bank* [1900] 2 Ch 15, CA; *Jones v Lloyd* (1874) LR 18 Eq 265.
2 *Re Duke of Somerset, Thynne v St Maur* (1887) 34 Ch D 465.
3 The office cannot be filled by the defendant himself (see *Anon* (1847) 11 Jur 258; *Lewis v Nobbs* (1878) 8 Ch D 591 at 593), nor by a friend of the defendant who undertakes the office at his request (*Re Burgess, Burgess v Bottomley* (1883) 25 Ch D 243, CA).
4 *Jacob v Lucas* (1839) 1 Beav 436. See also Paragraph 40 note 2 post.
5 1 Bl Com 464; *Anon* (1739) 1 Atk 570; *Whittaker v Marlar* (1786) 1 Cox Eq Cas 285 at 286; *Harrison v Harrison* (1842) 5 Beav 130; *Jones v Evans* (1886) 31 Sol Jo 11.
6 RSC Ord 80 r 2 (3).
7 *Woolf v Pemberton* (1877) 6 Ch D 19, CA; *Harris v Lightfoot, Harris v Harris* (1861) 10 WR 31.
8 *Harris v Lightfoot, Harris v Harris* (supra).
9 *Re Corsellis, Lawton v Elwes* (1884) 32 WR 965, CA. See also *Re W, W v M* [1907] 2 Ch 557 at 568, CA. The Official Solicitor's costs should be provided for by any order appointing him or by undertaking.
10 *Nalder v Hawkins* (1833) 2 My & K 243; *Foster v Cautley* (1853) 10 Hare App 1.
11 Table 1 Steps 5-11 post; RSC Ord 12 r 1 (1).
12 *Fernée v Gorlitz* [1915] 1 Ch 177, where the next friend was himself a minor.
13 See Table 1 Step 8.
14 *Geilinger v Gibbs* [1897] 1 Ch 479.
15 RSC Ord 80 r 3 (6), (8)(a). See Table 1 Step 12 post and Form 3 post.
16 *Ward v Ward* (1843) 6 Beav 251.
17 *Morgan v Thorne* (1841) 7 M & W 400; *Sinclair v Sinclair* (1845) 13 M & W 640; *Rhodes v Swithenbank* (1889) 22 QBD 577, CA.
18 *Rhodes v Swithenbank* (supra). See also *Re Whittal* [1973] 3 All ER 35, [1973] 1 WLR 1027.

19 *Sinclair v Sinclair* (1845) 13 M & W 640; *Dyke v Stephens* (1885) 30 Ch D 189; but see *Catt v Wood* [1908] 2 KB 458 at 473, CA. In the Chancery Division the next friend's name does not appear in the title to the action but only in the body of the summons or writ: Direction of Chancery Judges, 15 July 1946, *Practice Note (Title of Proceedings)* [1959] 2 All ER 629; in the Queen's Bench Division, the Family Division and the county court the next friend is named in the title as well.

20 *Re Hurst, Addison v Topp (No 2)* (1891) 36 Sol Jo 41, CA; *Murray v Sitwell* [1902] WN 119; *Re Berry, Berry v Berry* [1903] WN 125. See RSC Ord 80 r 2 (3).

21 *Jones v Lewis* (1847) 1 De G & Sm 245. An application adverse to the next friend must be made by a next friend, specially nominated for the purpose: *Cox v Wright* (1863) 32 LJ Ch 770. See *Chaplin v Leslie Frewin (Publishers) Ltd* [1966] Ch 71, [1965] 3 All ER 764, CA.

22 RSC Ord 80 r 2 (2).

23 See Family Proceedings Rules 1991, SI 1991/1247, Part IX, as amended by the Family Proceedings (Amendment) Rules 1992, SI 1992/456 in particular by the insertion of Rule 9.2A which theoretically makes it easier for minors to sue in family proceedings without a next friend. See, however, *Re A D (A Minor)* [1993] Fam Law 43.

39. Inquiry as to proceedings being beneficial to minor. Upon the application of the defendant or of a next friend appointed for the purpose, the court can direct an inquiry whether the proceedings are for the benefit of the minor[1] and, if it appears that they are not, can deal with the proceedings as it thinks fit. Nowadays this power is seldom invoked.

1 *Golds v Kerr* [1884] WN 46; *Re Corsellis, Lawton v Elwes* (1884) 32 WR 965, CA.

40. New next friend. The court can on application[1] remove a next friend if he is an improper person to act as such[2] or if he does not conduct the action properly[3]. A person seeking to remove a parent as next friend and substitute some other person must establish that the relevant person is not acting properly in the interest of the child as his or her next friend, e.g., that the terms of the proposed compromise are so manifestly beneficial to the minor that the refusal of the person concerned to agree or to participate in it must be condemned as prejudicial to the interests of the child[4]. The parent or testamentary guardian is entitled to be substituted for a stranger next friend[5]. It is assumed that a guardian appointed under a duly witnessed and attested document as provided for in the Children Act 1989 would also be entitled to be substituted for a stranger next friend[6].

Where a next friend dies, the nearest paternal relative is entitled to nominate a new next friend[7]. No other person is entitled to act as next friend unless the court makes a substitution order[8], and the original next friend is bound to continue (unless he has died) until an order is made.

A next friend may apply at any stage of the proceedings for his own discharge, although it is unlikely that the application would be granted except in very unusual circumstances, for example, in case of illness or where the minor comes of age and does not within a reasonable time adopt or repudiate the action[9].

The court, where proceedings are commenced under the Inheritance (Provision for Family and Dependants) Act 1975, may consider that a parent or nearest relative is not the appropriate next friend if he has an interest in the estate[10].

1 Table 1 Steps 12-14 post.

2 Eg where he has an interest adverse to that of the minor: *Gee v Gee* (1863) 12 WR 187. If, however, there is no probability of the minor's interests being injuriously affected, the

next friend will not be removed: *Bedwin v Asprey* (1841) 11 Sim 530. See for further examples 24 Halsbury's Laws (4th Edn) para 895:3.

3 *Re Birchall, Wilson v Birchall* (1880) 16 Ch D 41, CA. A next friend will be removed if he improperly refuses to proceed with the action (*Ward v Ward* (1813) 3 Mer 706), or to appeal (*Dupuy v Welsford* (1880) 28 WR 762). In the Chancery Division, the practice now is to issue a summons for such purpose, which should be served on the next friend who is being removed. The order appointing the new next friend may require his consent in writing, and an affidavit of his fitness and that he has no interest adverse to that of the minor. The order may provide that the new next friend shall give security for the defendant's costs up to the time of the order: Direction of Chancery Judges, 21 December 1954.

The order is drawn up by the solicitor (if he so requests at the hearing) under RSC Ord 42 r 6. See also Chancery Masters' Directions No 15A (i)(a): Supreme Court Practice 1991 para 856. In the Queen's Bench Division the practice is to apply by summons under RSC Ord 25. An affidavit is always required.

4 *Re Taylor's Application* [1972] 2 QB 369, [1972] 2 All ER 873, CA (where parents of thalidomide children were not replaced by the Official Solicitor as they had not acted unreasonably in refusing to accept a global settlement).

5 *Woolf v Pemberton* (1877) 6 Ch D 19, CA. See also *Re Taylor's Application* (supra).

6 Children Act 1989 s 6 (2).

7 *Talbot v Talbot* (1874) LR 17 Eq 347.

8 RSC Ord 80 r 3 (4).

9 Table 1 Steps 24-27 post.

10 RSC Ord 99 r 6. The court should consider separate representation as well as conflict of interest with next friend.

41. Infant plaintiff attaining full age. Where a sole infant plaintiff or applicant attains full age while proceedings are pending, he can elect whether the proceedings should continue or not[1]. If he elects to continue[2], the proceedings will be conducted in his name and he will be liable for costs from the commencement[3]. If, however, he elects to discontinue, he may either obtain an order dismissing the proceedings on payment of costs from the commencement[4] or take no steps, in which case the defendant may apply to dismiss the proceedings although he cannot make the minor pay the costs of them[5]. When a minor is co-plaintiff or co-applicant he can, on attaining full age, apply to have his name struck out[6], but if his co-plaintiff or co-applicant so desires he may be added as a defendant or respondent[7].

1 *Brown v Weatherhead* (1844) 4 Hare 122. The next friend should take no further steps in the action other than, if necessary, to apply for his own discharge, but he cannot be interfered with until proof of the minor's majority has been furnished to the court: *Almack v Moore* (1878) 2 LR Ir 90. See also *Carberry (Formerly an Infant but now of Full Age) v Davies* [1968] 2 All ER 817, [1968] 1 WLR 1103, CA (which exemplifies the correct title of such an action in subsequent proceedings). For the procedure on the attainment of full age by a minor see Table 1 Steps 16-27 post.

2 Ibid Step 17.

3 *Bligh v Tredgett* (1815) 5 De G & Sm 74.

4 *Anon* (1819) 4 Madd 461. See Form 14 post.

5 *Turner v Turner* (1726) 2 Stra 708. The repudiation of an action or proceeding by a minor relates back to its commencement so as to override all that has been done in it: *Dunn v Dunn* (1855) 7 De GM & G 25.

6 See Table 1 Step 19.

7 *Bicknell v Bicknell* (1863) 32 Beav 381.

42. Effect of judgment or order on infant plaintiff. An infant plaintiff is as much bound as an adult by a judgment or order[1] even though there may have been irregularities in the conduct of the proceedings[2], unless there has been fraud[3] or gross negligence on the part of the next friend[4]. In special circumstances the minor may be allowed, on coming of age, to amend his claim or bring a fresh action[5]. A minor is not bound by an agreement not to appeal unless the agreement is for his benefit[6].

1 It is the interposition of the court, charged with the duty to watch over the minor's interests, that lends sanctity to a judgment for or against a minor, and binds him: see *Arabian v Tufnal & Taylor Ltd* [1944] KB 685 at 688, [1944] 2 All ER 317 at 319, per WROTTESLEY J.
2 *Morison v Morison* (1838) 4 My & Cr 215.
3 *Colclough v Bolger* (1816) 4 Dow 54, HL.
4 *Re Hoghton, Hoghton v Fiddey* (1874) LR 18 Eq 573 at 576, 577.
5 *Re Hoghton, Hoghton v Fiddey* (supra).
6 *Rhodes v Swithenbank* (1889) 22 QBD 577, CA.

43. Costs: infant plaintiff. An infant plaintiff is not personally liable for the costs of legal proceedings, but the defendant is entitled to recover his costs from the next friend if the proceedings are dismissed[1]. The next friend can recover any proper[2] costs which he has been ordered to pay from any property to which the infant is entitled[3]. Costs in compromise cases are usually ordered to be paid on the standard basis and the infant's solicitor usually waives any claim to any further costs[4]. In any event, unless the court otherwise orders the costs as between the infant plaintiff and his solicitor must be taxed[5].

1 *Catt v Wood* [1908] 2 KB 458, CA. They are recoverable from the next friend even if the proceedings were instituted under the sanction of the court: *Frank v Mainwaring* (1841) 4 Beav 37. As to whether an order for security for costs is to be made against a parent see *Re B (Infants)* [1965] 2 All ER 651n, [1965] 1 WLR 946.
2 Ie if the action was a proper one and brought for the benefit of the minor.
3 *Steeden v Walden* [1910] 2 Ch 393. The next friend can bring an action against the minor to be indemnified against the costs and any damages which he has been ordered to pay, as well as his own costs: *Steeden v Walden* (supra). A solicitor is entitled to a lien on a minor's property recovered by means of his professional services: *Pritchard v Roberts* (1873) LR 17 Eq 222.
4 See the Supreme Court Practice 1991 para 80/12/16 and 80/1011/1.
5 See RSC Ord 62 r 16.

44. Proceedings against minor: the guardian ad litem. A person to fill the office of guardian ad litem of an infant defendant or respondent must be named before any step is taken in the proceedings by either party[1]. The guardian ad litem must have no interest in the matters in question in the proceedings adverse to that of the minor[2]. Preference is given to an adult, competent person who is not already a party to the cause[3], or to a relation, connection or friend of the family[4]. It is a matter of course for the guardian of the minor's person to be his guardian ad litem[5] but, if he desires to act, the Official Solicitor may be appointed[6], subject to his consent, which can properly be withheld if provision for his costs is not made in any order appointing him or by such undertaking as he may consider adequate. Interlocutory applications are dealt with by the guardian ad litem in the same way as by a next friend[7].

Like a next friend[8], a guardian ad litem is not actually a party to the proceedings and cannot appear and be heard in person; he must appear by a solicitor[9].

Except where the rules of court provide otherwise a minor may defend any family proceedings by a guardian ad litem, who need not be appointed by the court[10].

If in any family proceedings it appears to the court that any child ought to be separately represented, the court may appoint the Official Solicitor or some other proper person to be guardian ad litem of the child, with authority to take part in the proceedings on the child's behalf[11]. Such an order may be made by the court of its own motion or on the application of a party to the proceedings or the proposed guardian ad litem, and the court at any stage stay the proceedings for such an application to be made[12].

1 RSC Ord 80 r 2 (1). If an infant acknowledges service, defends or intervenes in any proceedings without a guardian ad litem, the plaintiff should apply, as soon as the fact is known to him, and proceed under RSC Ord 80 r 6, for the appointment of a guardian ad litem by the court.
2 *Smith v Palmer* (1840) 3 Beav 10.
3 *Re Taylor, Taylor v Taylor* [1881] WN 81.
4 For examples of who may act as guardian ad litem see Supreme Court Practice 1991 para 80/3/1.
5 *Sandys v Cooper* (1835) 4 LJ Ch 162.
6 *White v Duvernay* [1891] P 290.
7 RSC Ord 80 r 2 (2); Paragraph 38 ante.
8 Paragraph 38 ante.
9 RSC Ord 80 r 2 (3).
10 Family Proceedings Rules 1991, SI 1991/1247, r 9.2(1)(as amended by the Family Proceedings (Amendment) Rules 1992, SI 1992/456, r 7).
11 Family Proceedings Rules 1991, SI 1991/1247, r 9.2, 9.5 (1).
12 Ibid r 9.5 (3).

45. Default of acknowledgment of service by infant defendant. Where in an action against an infant begun by writ or originating summons no acknowledgment of service is given, the plaintiff may not proceed to enter judgment in default[1] but must apply to the court for the appointment of a guardian ad litem[2]. If the proceedings were begun by petition or motion and the infant does not appear by guardian ad litem at the hearing, the court may appoint a guardian ad litem itself or direct that the petitioner or applicant apply for the appointment[3].

1 RSC Ord 80 r 6 (1).
2 RSC Ord 80 r 6 (3). See further Table 2 Steps 7-13 post. A similar rule applies in third party proceedings: see RSC Ord 80 r 6 (2).
3 RSC Ord 80 r 6 (3).

46. Default of defence by infant defendant. If an infant defendant does not serve a defence or does not traverse the allegations in a statement of claim, they are not taken to be admitted by him[1], and the action cannot be set down on motion for judgment or on a summons for judgment for default, but must be set down for trial as if he had denied the allegations[2]. It is, however, generally necessary for him to serve a defence in order to plead infancy or to allege other matters not put in issue by the plaintiff's allegations[3].

1 RSC Ord 80 r 8.
2 *National Provincial Bank Ltd v Evans* (1881) 30 WR 177. In a simple case, judgment may be obtained on motion for judgment upon an affidavit verifying the statement of claim:

> *Willis v Willis* (1889) 61 LT 610. Evidence has been altogether dispensed with where the inquiries directed by the judgment would sufficiently protect the minor's interests: *Ripley v Sawyer* (1886) 31 Ch D 494.
>
> 3   *Lane v Hardwicke* (1846) 9 Beav 148.

47. New guardian ad litem. If a guardian ad litem acts improperly or against the interests of the minor, or there is good ground for objection to him, he may be removed and another guardian ad litem assigned in his place[1]. If a guardian ad litem dies during the proceedings another will be appointed[2].

1   *Re Duke of Somerset, Thynne v St Maur* (1887) 34 Ch D 465. See Table 2 Steps 15-18 post.
2   *Drant v Vause* (1843) 2 Y & C Ch Cas 524. See Table 2 Steps 15-18 post.

48. Infant defendant attaining full age. When an infant defendant attains full age during the proceedings[1] he may apply for leave to serve a new defence[2] but, if he takes no steps within a reasonable time, he will be bound by what has been done during his infancy[3].

1   Table 2 Steps 19-22 post.
2   *Kelsall v Kelsall* (1834) 2 My & K 409; *Malone v Malone* (1841) 8 Cl & Fin 179, HL.
3   *Monypenny v Dering* (1859) 4 De G & J 175.

49. Effect of judgment or order on infant defendant. A judgment against an infant defendant is as binding as it would be if he were an adult[1] but, if it was obtained on the footing that he was of full age, the court may set it aside[2]. If the plaintiff has signed judgment without applying for the appointment of a guardian ad litem the judgment will be set aside[3].

An injunction may be granted against a minor[4] but not an order for specific performance[5].

1   *Henry v Archibald* (1871) 5 IR Eq 559.
2   *Furnival v Brooke* (1883) 49 LT 134.
3   *Leaver v Torres* (1899) 43 Sol Jo 778; *Stanga v Stanga* [1954] P 10, [1954] 2 All ER 16.
4   *Lempriére v Lange* (1879) 12 Ch D 675. This does not apply where damages could not be sued for: *De Francesco v Barnum* (1889) 43 Ch D 165. See also *Wookey v Wookey; Re S (A Minor)* [1991] Fam 121, [1991] 3 All ER 365, CA, where a non-molestation injunction against an infant was refused on the basis that it would not be enforced by committal.
5   *Lumley v Ravenscroft* [1895] 1 QB 683, CA. Accordingly the court will not generally grant specific performance at a minor's suit: *Flight v Bolland* (1828) 4 Russ 298.

50. Costs: infant defendant. An infant defendant may be ordered to pay costs[1], especially where he has been guilty of fraud[2] or is a respondent[3] or co-respondent[4] on a petition for dissolution of marriage. The costs of a minor's unsuccessful defence may be ordered to be paid out of his property over which the court has jurisdiction[5]. A guardian ad litem is not liable to pay the costs of an unsuccessful defence unless he has been guilty of gross misconduct[6]. In a case where the Official Solicitor was appointed guardian ad litem of a ward of court on a summons by the father to restrain a third party from marrying the ward who went abroad and married, the Official Solicitor's costs were ordered to be paid by the ward's parents as between party and party[7].

1 *Woolf v Woolf* [1899] 1 Ch 343; but see *Elsey v Cox* (1858) 26 Beav 95.
2 *Lempriére v Lange* (1879) 12 Ch D 675 at 679.
3 *Quinn v Quinn* [1920] P 65.
4 *Brockelbank v Brockelbank and Borlase* (1911) 27 TLR 569.
5 *Earl of Orford v Churchill* (1814) 3 Ves & B 59 at 71; *Mandeno v Mandeno* (1853) Kay App ii. The plaintiff may be directed to pay the costs and to recover them out of the minor's property: *Robinson v Aston* (1845) 9 Jur 224.
6 *Morgan v Morgan* (1865) 11 Jur NS 233; *Vivian v Kennelly* (1890) 63 LT 778.
7 *Re P C (An Infant)* [1961] Ch 312, [1961] 2 All ER 308; and see *Re C (An Infant)* [1964] 2 All ER 478, [1964] 1 WLR 857.

51. Service on minor. A document required to be served on a minor in any proceedings must be served on the minor's father or guardian or, if he has no father or guardian, on the person with whom he resides or in whose care he is[1]. If, however, the minor is also a patient, the document must be served on the person, if any, authorised under the Mental Health Act 1983 to conduct the proceedings in the name or on behalf of the minor[2] or, if there is no such person, on the person with whom the minor resides or in whose care he is[3].

Nevertheless the court may order that a document which has been, or is to be, served on a minor or on a person other than one named above be deemed to be duly served on the minor[4].

1 RSC Ord 80 r 16 (2)(a).
2 Mental Health Act 1983 s 96 (1)(i).
3 RSC Ord 80 r 16 (2)(b).
4 RSC Ord 80 r 16 (3).

52. Compromise or settlement. The compromise of an action to which a minor is a party and which affects his interests cannot be effected without the sanction of the court in which the action is pending[1]. The court has full power to sanction a compromise of a money claim made by a minor both before[2] and after[3] proceedings have been begun.

Where an agreement for the compromise or settlement of a money claim made by or on behalf of a minor, whether alone or jointly with any other person, is reached before proceedings are begun, approval of the settlement or compromise may be obtained by originating summons, and no writ need or should be issued[4]. In addition to asking for approval, the originating summons should ask for directions for dealing with the money agreed to be paid[5] and, if the court should decline to approve the settlement or compromise, should also ask for directions as to the further prosecution of the claim[6].

Where a compromise or settlement of a money claim in any proceedings[7] is arrived at, or money is paid into court or money paid in is accepted, after the proceedings have begun, the approval of the court must be obtained to render the settlement valid[8]. Without this approval the compromise or settlement is wholly invalid and unenforceable and is made entirely at the risk of the parties and their solicitors. If the provisional settlement or compromise of such money claim is reached at or during the trial, application for approval should be made to the trial judge; otherwise, application is by summons[9] in the action[10].

In the Chancery Division the judge would normally deal with compromises on behalf of infants but the Chancery master may approve any compromise under the Inheritance (Provision for Family and Dependants) Act 1975 and limited compromises in other actions[11]. The practice is to support the summons[12] with an affidavit by the minor's next friend or guardian ad litem, stating his belief that the proposed compromise or settlement is in the minor's interests, and exhibiting the case to, and opinion of, counsel to this effect[13].

In the Queen's Bench Division, application for approval is by summons before a master. Save in exceptional cases no affidavit is required before the master, although the written consent of the next friend or guardian to the compromise or settlement should be produced. The summons generally seeks directions as to how the money recovered is to be dealt with, and the court's approval and the directions for dealing with the money are generally contained in the same order. Directions may be given that the money is to be paid into court, and may include any general or special directions that the court thinks fit to give as to how the money is to be applied for the maintenance or otherwise for the benefit of the minor or for costs[14]. As soon as the minor attains the age of 18, he is entitled to any fund in court standing to his credit[15] (assuming that he is not also a patient).

In the Family Division, application for approval of a compromise is by summons before a district judge. The practice is to support the summons with an affidavit by the minor's next friend or guardian ad litem, stating that he believes or is advised that the compromise is in the minor's interest, counsel's opinion being exhibited or lodged with the affidavit. Alternatively counsel may attend before the district judge to uphold the compromise or settlement.

In considering whether to approve the compromise or settlement the overriding consideration is the interest of the minor[16], having regard to all the circumstances of the case, such as the risks in the litigation, the chances of recovering any money at all, the adequacy of the amount in question, the desirability of an early end to the litigation, and the amount of costs involved. The court cannot, however, compel a compromise[17] and will not sanction a compromise against the opinion of the minor's next friend or guardian ad litem[18].

Where a compromise or settlement has been sanctioned, it will only be set aside on the same strong grounds of fraud as would justify the setting aside of a compromise between adults[19]. A party to proceedings who agrees to a certain course, knowing that the other parties are minors, cannot afterwards object that his consent does not bind him because the other parties, being minors, could not consent[20].

1 *Hargrave v Hargrave* (1850) 12 Beav 408; *Gray v Paul* (1877) 25 WR 874. For the procedure on a compromise or settlement of claim see Table 3 Post.
2 RSC Ord 80 r 11.
3 RSC Ord 80 r 10.
4 RSC Ord 80 r 11 (1), (5).
5 RSC Ord 80 r 11 (1)(a).
6 RSC Ord 80 r 11 (1)(b).
7 RSC Ord 80 r 10.
8 RSC Ord 80 r 10. Money must promptly be paid into court: *Practice Note (Infants: Settlement of Actions)* [1969] 1 WLR 1284.
9 See Table 3 post.
10 Supreme Court Practice 1985 paras 80/1011/1 et seq.
11 Chancery Master's Practice Direction No 13B: Supreme Court Practice 1991 para 853.
12 See Table 3 post.
13 *Re Birchall, Wilson v Birchall* (1880) 16 Ch D 41, CA.
14 RSC Ord 80 r 12 (3).
15 *Re Embleton* [1947] KB 142, [1946] 2 All ER 542, CA.

16 See *Re Wells, Boyer v Maclean* [1903] 1 Ch 848 at 853 per FARWELL J. The court will not
   sanction a compromise which is in the interest of the next friend but not of the minor:
   Rhodes v Swithenbank (1889) 22 QBD 577 at 578, 579; *Blair v Crawford* [1906] 1 IR 578
   at 587, CA. When the court is asked to sanction a compromise it is the duty of counsel,
   the solicitors and the guardian ad litem or next friend to consider whether the terms of the
   compromise are in the minor's interest: *Re Barbour's Settlement, National Westminster
   Bank Ltd v Barbour* [1974] 1 All ER 1188, [1974] 1 WLR 1198.
17 *Re Birchall, Wilson v Birchall* (supra). See also *Re Whittall* [1973] 3 All ER 35, [1973]
   1 WLR 1027.
18 *Re Birchall, Wilson v Birchall* (supra) at 42, 43. See also *Re Taylor's Application* [1972]
   2 QB 369, [1972] 2 All ER 873, CA.
19 *Brooke v Lord Mostyn* (1864) 2 De GJ & Sm 373; *Fadelle v Bernard* (1871) 19 WR 555.
   See also *Dietz v Lennig Chemicals Ltd* [1969] 1 AC 170, [1967] 2 All ER 282, HL.
20 *Pisani v A-G for Gibraltar* (1874) LR 5 PC 516, PC.

53. Control of money recovered by minor. Where in any proceedings money is
recovered by or on behalf of, or adjudged or ordered or agreed to be paid to or for the
benefit of a minor, or money paid into court is accepted by or on behalf of an infant
plaintiff, the money must be dealt with in accordance with directions given by the
court, and not otherwise[1]. The directions may provide that the money, or part of it,
be paid into the High Court or otherwise dealt with there[2], may include any general
or special directions which the court thinks fit to give and in particular may specify
how the money is to be applied or dealt with, and how, when and to whom any
payments from it are to be made, and may provide for solicitor's costs[3].

Where in pursuance of such directions money is paid into the High Court to be
invested or otherwise dealt with there, the money (including interest on it) may not
be paid out, and securities or dividends on them may not be sold, transferred or paid
out, except in accordance with a court order[4].

Where a plaintiff accepts any sum paid into court in these circumstances it may
not be paid out except in pursuance of a court order, and the order must deal with the
whole costs of the action[5].

1 RSC Ord 80 r 12 (1).
2 RSC Ord 80 r 12 (2).
3 RSC Ord 80 r 12 (3).
4 RSC Ord 80 r 12 (4).
5 RSC Ord 22 r 4 (1)(c).

2: COUNTY COURT

54. Generally. An action by or against a minor may be brought in a county court. A
minor can only sue, or commence proceedings other than family proceedings, or
claim in interpleader proceedings, by his next friend[1], except in one case: he may sue
as if he were of full age where his claim is for a sum of money due to him for wages
or piece work or for work as a servant[2]. A minor may only defend by a guardian ad
litem[3].

Anything which in the ordinary conduct of any proceedings is required or
authorised to be done by a party to the proceedings may, if the party is a minor, be
done by his next friend or guardian ad litem[4].

Special provisions apply to judgments and orders involving minors[5], to
compromise, settlement and payment out of court[6].

In a default action against a minor the plaintiff must, after the expiry of the time provided for service of a defence or admission, apply to the court for the appointment of a guardian ad litem[7].

Under the Children Act 1989 — Amendments to the Family Proceedings Rules have now enabled minors who wish to prosecute or defend any family proceedings (other than specified proceedings under s 41 of the Act[8]) in the county court to do so without a next friend or guardian ad litem[9]. Where a minor wishes so to do he must either obtain the leave of the court for that purpose or he must convince a solicitor that he is capable of giving instructions in relation to the proceedings or he must already have instructed a solicitor. The rules provide that the minor can apply for leave of the court where he has not already instructed a solicitor by filing a written request for leave setting out the reasons for the application or by making an oral request for leave at any hearing in the proceedings. On considering such a request the court must communicate the decision to the minor and to the other parties, or direct that the request be heard ex parte, when the court must fix a hearing date and give to the minor such notice as the court may direct. Where on the other hand the minor already has a next friend or guardian and wishes to prosecute or defend the remaining stages without one, the minor may apply to the court for leave to hear the guardian or next friend removed. It should be noted that following the decision in *Re H (A Minor)*[10] some young people even though emotionally disturbed could have sufficient understanding to instruct solicitors to represent their interests.

As was noted earlier, the President of the Family Division does not anticipate applications by children to be all that frequent, but in *Re A D (A Minor)*[11] he went on to say that in his view any application by a child to take proceedings in the county court should be transferred to the High Court as soon as possible.

1 CCR Ord 10 r 1 (1). See further Paragraph 55 post.
2 County Courts Act 1984 s 47. Whilst this section refers to "the county court limit" it is submitted that, as this would be an action in contract, the court has unlimited jurisdiction under the High Court and County Courts Jurisdiction Order 1991, SI 1991/724.
3 CCR Ord 10 r 1 (2). See further Paragraph 56 post.
4 CCR Ord 10 r 12.
5 See Paragraph 57 post.
6 See Paragraph 58 post.
7 CCR Ord 10 r 6.
8 Family Proceedings Rules 1991 r 9.2 and see Paragraph 37 n 3 ante and Paragraph 176 post.
9 Family Proceedings (Amendment) Rules 1992 inserting a new Rule 9.2A into the Family Proceedings Rules 1991 SI 1991/1247
10 *Re H (A Minor)* (1992) Times, 5 June 1992, FD.
11 [1993] Fam Law 43.

55. Next friend. Before proceedings are commenced or a claim in any proceedings is made by a next friend on behalf of a minor, the next friend must deliver at the court office a written undertaking[1], attested by a solicitor or by an officer of the court authorised to take affidavits, to be responsible for any costs which the minor may be ordered and fail to pay the person against whom the proceedings are brought or the claim is made[2].

Where proceedings are brought or a claim is made by a minor without a next friend, the court may, on application, appoint as next friend any person who gives an undertaking[3] or the court may order that the proceedings be struck out[4].

1 CCR Ord 10 r 2 (b).
2 Ibid.
3 Ie in compliance with CCR Ord 10 r 2 (b).
4 CCR Ord 10 r 3.

56. Guardian ad litem[1]. A person proposing to act as guardian ad litem of a minor need not be appointed by court order if he delivers at the court office on the minor's behalf an admission of or defence to the plaintiff's claim accompanied by a certificate made by the proposed guardian that he is a fit and proper person to act as guardian ad litem of the defendant and has no interest in the matters in question in the proceedings adverse to that of the defendant[2].

Where a minor defendant has no guardian ad litem acting for him, the plaintiff must, after the time for delivering a defence or admission has expired, and before taking any further step in the proceedings, apply to the court for an order that a person named in the application be appointed guardian ad litem of the defendant[3].

The application must be supported by an affidavit showing that the person proposed by the plaintiff for appointment is a fit and proper person to act as guardian ad litem of the defendant, that the proposed person has no interest in the matters in question in the proceedings adverse to that of the defendant and that he consents to act[4].

Notice of the application, together with a copy of the supporting affidavit, must be served on the person on whom the summons in the action was required to be served not less than three days before the hearing of the application[5].

On the hearing of the application the court may appoint the person proposed by the plaintiff or, if not satisfied that the person proposed is a proper person to be appointed, may appoint any other person willing to act or in default of any such person may appoint the district judge[6].

Where a defendant attends the hearing of an action and it appears that he is a minor who has no guardian ad litem, the defendant may name a person as his guardian ad litem who consents to act, and that person must be appointed as guardian ad litem[7]. If the defendant does not name a guardian ad litem, the court may appoint as guardian any person present who is willing to act, or in default of any such person, the court may appoint the district judge to act[8].

1 For an explanation of the different uses of this term see text to Paragraph 37 but principally n 3.
2 CCR Ord 10 r 5.
3 CCR Ord 10 r 6 (1).
4 CCR Ord 10 r 6 (2)(a)(c).
5 CCR Ord 10 r 6 (3).
6 CCR Ord 10 r 6 (4).
7 CCR Ord 10 r 7 (a).
8 CCR Ord 10 r 7 (b). Where a minor is sued for a liquidated sum, the court may, on the application of the plaintiff, direct that CCR Ord 10 rr 6, 7 are not to apply and no appointment of a guardian ad litem will be necessary: CCR Ord 10 r 8. A guardian ad litem will not be personally liable for any costs not occasioned by his personal negligence or misconduct: CCR Ord 10 r 9.

57. Judgments and orders. Where judgment has been obtained or an order made against a defendant who was at the time a minor without a guardian ad litem having been appointed, the judge may set aside the judgment or order and order a new trial, or make such order as he thinks fit[1].

1   Formerly specific provision was made for this in the County Court Rules but the matter is now covered by the general provisions in CCR Ord 37 r 5 which deals with non-compliance with rules.

58. Compromise, settlement and payment out of court. Where in any proceedings money is claimed by or on behalf of a person who is a minor, no settlement, compromise or payment and no acceptance of money paid into court, whenever entered into or made, will so far as it relates to the minor's claim be valid without the approval of the court[1].

Where the sole object of an action in which a claim for money is made by or on behalf of a minor is to obtain the approval of the court to a settlement or compromise of the claim, the particulars of the claim must contain a brief statement of the cause of action together with a request for the approval of the settlement or compromise[2].

Whatever the amount involved, the approval of the court may be given either by the judge or by the district judge and either in chambers or in open court[3].

1   CCR Ord 10 r 10 (1).
2   CCR Ord 10 r 10 (2).
3   CCR Ord 10 r 10 (3).

59.1. Control of money recovered by minor. Where in any proceedings money is recovered by or on behalf of, or adjudged or ordered or agreed to be paid to or for the benefit of a minor, or money paid into court is accepted by or on behalf of a minor then, unless the court otherwise directs, the money will not be paid to the minor, or to his next friend, guardian ad litem or to his solicitor, but will be paid into or remain in court[1] and the money and any interest thereon is to be invested, applied or otherwise dealt with as the court may from time to time direct[2].

An application to the court as to the mode of dealing with the money and any interest thereon may be made by or on behalf of any person interested[3].

Unless the court otherwise directs, the costs payable to his solicitor by any minor plaintiff in the proceedings must be taxed[4] and no costs must be payable to the plaintiff's solicitor except for the amount allowed on taxation[5].

On the taxation of a solicitor's bill to any plaintiff the district judge must also tax any costs payable to that plaintiff in the proceedings and must certify the amount (if any) by which the amount allowed on the taxation of the solicitor's bill exceeds the amount allowed on the taxation of the costs payable to that plaintiff in the proceedings, and where necessary, the proportion of the amount of the excess payable by or out of any money belonging to any party to the proceedings who is a minor[6].

Costs as between the infant plaintiff and the defendant will be dealt with just as in the High Court (subject of course to specific and relevant scale) and will thus normally be taxed on the standard basis[7].

1   CCR Ord 10 r 11 (1).
2   CCR Ord 10 r 11 (2).
3   CCR Ord 10 r 11 (3).
4   Ibid
5   CCR Ord 10 r 11 (4).
6   CCR Ord 10 r 11 (5).
7   See Paragraph 43 notes 4, 5 ante.

3. MAGISTRATES' COURT

59.2. *Under the Children Act 1989* — The only circumstances in which children can be parties in civil proceedings in the magistrates' courts are in family proceedings under the Children Act 1989. In proceedings for any orders under Parts III, IV and V of the Act designated as "specified proceedings"[1], the child is automatically a party[2], and the court must appoint a guardian ad litem for the child unless satisfied that it is not necessary to do so in order to safeguard the child's interests and either the court or the guardian ad litem may go on to appoint a solicitor to represent the child[3]. The child is thus a party to the proceedings whether or not she wishes to make an application for any of the orders under the Act.

By contrast, the child will usually only be made a party to the proceedings under Parts I and II where she has made an application herself[4]. In either case the child must obtain leave of the court to make an application[5], and in the case of an application for a Section 8 order, the court may only grant leave if it is satisfied that she has sufficient understanding to make the proposed application[6]. Where, however, a child does make such an application, the President of the Family Division has already made it clear that he would expect the case to be transferred upwards for hearing ultimately by a High Court judge[7].

1 Children Act 1989 s 41.
2 The Family Proceedings Courts (Children Act 1989) Rules 1991 Sch 2 col (iii).
3 Children Act 1989 s 41.
4 The Family Procedings Courts (Children Act 1989) Rules 1991 Sch 2 col (iii).
5 Children Act 1989 s 4(3)(b); s 6(7)(b); and s 10(8).
6 Ibid s 10(8).
7 In *Re A D (A Minor)* [1993] Fam Law 43.

CHAPTER 3: STATUS AND PARENTAGE

1: STATUS

60. The child's status. It was the intention of the Family Law Reform Act 1987 to end as many differences as possible between the treatment of marital children and non-marital children[1]. Where any differences remain in the law, then it is necessary to proceed rather by reference to the marital status of the child's parents than by labelling the child[2]. To this end since the date of implementation of the Family Law Reform Act 1987[3], any statutory references to any relationship between two persons shall, unless the contrary intention appears, be construed without regard to whether or not the father and mother of either of them, or the father and mother of any person through whom the relationship is deduced, have or had been married to each other at any time.

A child is presumed to be legitimate at common law where his parents were married at the time of his conception or at the time of his birth and that presumption may prove difficult to displace[4]. Legislation has put further glosses on the concept of legitimacy which has thus been expanded by provisions allowing children of void and voidable marriages to be treated as legitimate[5], to allow legitimation by the subsequent marriage of the child's parents[6], to provide in certain circumstances for children conceived by assisted reproduction[7] to be treated as legitimate, and to provide for the legitimation of adopted children in certain circumstances[8].

1 Family Law Reform Act 1987 s 1.
2 Ibid s 1.
3 This governs the enactments of all provisions made after 4 April 1988, the implementation date of the Family Law Reform Act 1987 s 1.
4 See the Law Commission, Second Report on Illegitimacy (Law Com No 157) para 2.1.
5 Legitimacy Act 1976 s 1 (as amended by the Family Law Reform Act 1987 s 28).
6 Legitimacy Act 1976 ss 2, 3.
7 See Human Fertilisation and Embryology Act 1990. See Paragraph 70 post.
8 Legitimacy Act 1976 s 4 (as amended).

61. Children of void marriages. The law provides[1] that a child born of a void marriage shall be treated as the legitimate child of his parents if at the time of the insemination resulting in the birth or, where there was no such insemination, the child's conception (or at the time of the celebration of the marriage if later) both or either of the parents reasonably believed that the marriage was valid[2]. Since this provision settles the question of the status of the child, it is provided that it shall only apply where the child's father was domiciled in England at the time of the child's birth or, if he died before the birth, immediately before his death[3]. No child can be treated as legitimate under these provisions, however, where he or she was born before the parents entered into a void marriage[4].

1 Legitimacy Act 1976 s 1 (as amended by the Family Law Reform Act 1987 s 28).
2 Ibid s 1 (1).
3 Legitimacy Act 1976 s 1 (2).
4 See *Re Spence, Spence v Dennis* [1990] Ch 652, [1990] 2 All ER 827, CA.

62. Children of voidable marriages. The law provides that any children born or conceived between the date of the voidable marriage and the date of the decree of nullity as well as any child legitimated by any such marriage will be treated as legitimate since the marriage itself is treated as having existed up to the date of decree absolute[1].

1 Matrimonial Causes Act 1973 s 16.

63. Legitimacy of children born as a result of assisted reproduction. Any child born in England and Wales, as a result of the artificial insemination of a married woman by the semen of some person other than her husband but with her husband's consent, is treated by law as a child of the parties to the marriage and thus as legitimate[1]. Similarly where a child is born to a married woman as the result of the placing in her of an embryo or of eggs and either before or at the time of the child's birth the woman is married then her husband is deemed to be the father of any child born as a result[2].

1 Family Law Reform Act 1987 s 27; Human Fertilisation and Embryology Act 1990 s 49 (4).
2 Human Fertilisation and Embryology Act 1990 ss 27-29 and see Paragraph 70 post.

64. Legitimation by subsequent marriage. The Legitimacy Act 1976 provides that where the parents of an illegitimate person marry one another, the marriage shall, if the father of the illegitimate person is at the date of the marriage domiciled in England and Wales, render that person, if living, legitimate from the date of the marriage[1]. It will be noted that a person is only legitimated by the operation of this section where his father was domiciled in England and Wales at the time of the marriage[2]. It should further be noted that legitimation does not have retrospective effect, so that a person cannot be legitimated unless he is still alive at the time of his parents' marriage[3]. An adopted child may be legitimated by the subsequent marriage of his parents if either natural parent is the sole adoptive parent[4]. It should be noted that a legitimated person has the same rights and is under the same obligations in respect of the maintenance and support of himself or of any other person as if he had been born legitimate[5]. Any claims that may be made under any statute for damages, allowances, benefits, compensation or otherwise by or in respect of a legitimate child apply equally in the case of a legitimated person[6]. For the purposes of determining whether a person is a British citizen he is to be treated as being born legitimate as from the date of the parents' marriage and is thus able to claim citizenship through his father or his mother[7].

1 Legitimacy Act 1976 s 2.
2 Ibid s 2.

3 Ibid Sch 1 para 1.
4 Legitimacy Act 1976 s 4.
5 Legitimacy Act 1976 s 8.
6 Ibid s 8.
7 British Nationality Act 1981 s 47 (1).

65. Declarations of status and parentage. Under the provisions of the Family Law Act 1986 as amended[1] any person may apply to the High Court or the county court[2] for a declaration:

1. that a person named in the application is or was his parent, or
2. that he is the legitimate child of his parents, or for one of the following declarations,
3. that he has become a legitimated person, or
4. that he has not become a legitimated person[3].

The High Court or county court have jurisdiction to entertain an application only where the applicant is domiciled in England and Wales on the date of the application or has been habitually resident in England or Wales for the period of one year ending with that date[4].

The procedure for making an application is governed by the Family Proceedings Rules 1991 which provide that the application must be laid before the court in the form of a petition supported by an affidavit and the petition must comply with the requirements there set out[5]. Where the court makes a declaration then the form of declaration is set out in the rules[6].

1 Family Law Act 1986 s 56 (as substituted by Family Law Reform Act 1987 s 22).
2 Family Law Act 1986 s 63; See Family Proceedings Rules 1991, SI 1991/1247, rr 3.12-3.16.
3 Family Law Act 1986 ss 56 (1), (2)(as substituted).
4 Ibid s 56 (3) (as amended).
5 Family Proceedings Rules 1991, SI 1991/1247, rr 3.12-3.16 and see also Appendix 2 as well as rr 2.4-2.6.
6 The forms of declaration are set out in Family Proceedings Rules 1991, Appendix 1, Forms M29-M31.

66. Procedure in respect of applications for declarations. An application for a declaration must, as indicated, be in the form of a petition accompanied by an affidavit[1] by the petitioner or where he is under 18 by his next friend[2], confirming the petition and giving particulars of every person whose interest may be affected by the proceedings and that person's relationship to the petitioner[3]. Any petition for a declaration as to marital status must have affixed to it a copy of the certificate of marriage to which the application relates or, as the case may be, a certified copy of any decree of divorce, annulment or order for legal separation to which it relates and, if any such document is not in English, a translation certified by a notary public or authenticated by affidavit[4]. Any petition for a declaration of parentage or of legitimacy or legitimation must have affixed to it a copy of the petitioner's birth certificate[5]. Where the petition is for a declaration of recognition of an overseas adoption it must have affixed to it a copy of the petitioner's birth certificate preferably that which was made after the adoption and, unless otherwise directed, a certified copy of the adoption order effected under the law of any country outside the British Isles, and if not in English such document must be accompanied by a translation certified by a notary public or authenticated by affidavit[6].

Service of the petition on the respondents named is in accordance with the Family Proceedings Rules[7].

The Family Law Act provides for those persons who will be treated as respondents for the purposes of the applications being made[8] and further respondents may be added by the direction of the court after any answers to a petition have been filed[9].

The court is further empowered of its own motion or on the application of any party to the proceedings to direct that all necessary papers in the matter be sent to the Attorney General but whether papers are forwarded or not, the Attorney General may intervene in the proceedings in such manner as he thinks necessary or expedient and argue before the court any question in relation to the application which the court considers it necessary to have fully argued[10]. The rules further make special provision for the procedure in respect of the participation of the Attorney General. One month prior to the filing of the petition a copy of the petition and every document accompanying it must be sent to the Attorney General and this will render further service upon him after the filing of the petition unnecessary[11]. Where the Attorney General wishes to intervene he will notify the court and the court will forward to him a copy of the answer filed in the proceedings[12].

When all answers to the petition have been filed the petitioner must issue and serve on all respondents a request for directions as to whether any other person should be made a respondent or given notice of the proceedings[13].

Where this occurs the Attorney General need not file an answer but must be directed to serve on all parties a summary of his argument[14]. The Attorney General can choose to file an answer however and where he does so may file it within 21 days after directions have been given[15].

Where directions have been given that notice of proceedings should be sent to any person other than named respondents, then such a person shall within 21 days after service of notice upon them be entitled to apply to the district judge to be joined as parties[16]. Directions for trial will not be given until the time limited for the filing of an answer by the Attorney General or for an application by parties to whom notice has been given to be joined as respondents has expired[17]. The rules that direct the proceedings will continue thereafter as though they were a cause[18]. The court hearing an application under this Part may direct that the whole or any part of the proceedings shall be heard in camera[19].

1 Family Law Act 1986 s 63. In the High Court proceedings will be heard in the Family Division: Family Law Act 1986 Sch 1 para 26.
2 Family Law Act 1986 s 60 (2).
3 Family Proceedings Rules 1991, SI 1991/1247, r 3.16 (1).
4 Ibid rr 3.12 (3), (4).
5 Ibid r 3.13 (2), r 3.14 (2).
6 Ibid r 3.15 (2), (3).
7 Ibid r 2.9.
8 In the case of a petition for a declaration as to marital status under Family Law Act 1986 s 55 the parties to the marriage in respect of which a declaration is sought will be the petitioner and respondent respectively, unless the application is made by a third party in which case the parties to the marriage will be respondents. In the case of a petition for a declaration as to parentage under s 56 (1)(a) the respondents will be both parents of the petitioner if they are still alive, and in the case of a petition for legitimacy or legitimation under s 56 (1)(b) and s 56 (2) the petitioner's father and mother or the survivor of them will be respondent. Where the petition is for recognition of an overseas adoption the respondents will be those persons whom the petitioner claims are his adoptive parents for

the purposes of Adoption Act 1976 s 39 or those whom he claims are not his adoptive parents for the purposes of that section. See also Family Proceedings Rules 1991 rr 3.12, 3.13, 3.14, 3.15 and 3.16.

9 Family Proceedings Rules 1991 r 3.16 (6).
10 Family Law Act 1986 s 59.
11 Family Proceedings Rules 1991 r 3.16 (4).
12 Ibid r 3.16 (5).
13 Ibid r 3.16 (6).
14 Ibid rr 3.16 (6), (7).
15 Ibid r 3.16 (9).
16 Ibid r 3.16 (8).
17 Ibid r 3.16 (9).
18 Ibid r 3.16 (12).
19 Family Law Act 1986 s 60 (4) and it should be noted that the application for such a direction will be made in camera unless the court otherwise directs.

67. Evidence. Where legitimacy depends upon the validity of a marriage and matters arise pointing to its invalidity they must specifically be disposed of by the applicant, proof of co-habitation and apparent validity not being sufficient[1]. Where it is proved that one of the parents was previously married to another person the petitioner must at least prove facts from which the cessation of that first marriage can properly be inferred[2]. Where the validity of a foreign marriage or divorce is in issue, expert evidence of the relevant foreign law is necessary[3]. Where the domicile of a deceased parent must be determined before legitimacy can be established, evidence of that parent's statements as to his domiciliary intentions is admissible[4].

The court is further empowered to issue a direction for the use of blood tests to ascertain whether such a party is or is not thereby excluded from being the father of that person, and for the taking, within a period to be specified in the direction of blood samples from that person, the mother of that person and any person alleged to be the father of that person or from any, or any two, of those persons[5]. DNA profiling can be used in respect of such blood samples which have been directed to be taken and where the parties agree DNA profiling of other bodily samples may be taken[6].

1 *Gatty and Gatty v A-G* [1951] P 444.
2 *MacDarmaid v A-G* [1950] P 218, [1950] 1 All ER 497.
3 See also the Civil Evidence Act 1972 s 4.
4 *Scappaticci v A-G* [1955] P 47, [1955] 1 All ER 193. See also *Re Davy* [1935] P 1, *Battle v A-G* [1949] P 358.
5 See Paragraph 73 post and see Blood Tests (Evidence of Paternity) Regulations 1971, SI 1971/1861, Sch, 1 Form 1.
6 See Paragraph 74 post.

68. Making a declaration. Where the truth of the proposition to be declared has been proved to the court's satisfaction, the court must make the declaration unless to do so would be manifestly contrary to public policy[1]. Any declaration binds Her Majesty and all other persons whatsoever[2]. Where a declaration is made, the prescribed officer of the court must notify the Registrar General, in such a manner and within such a period as may be prescribed of the making of that declaration[3]. Where the declaration is refused the court cannot grant a declaration that has not been applied for[4]. Finally it should be pointed out that no declaration can be made by any court that a marriage was at its inception void[5] or that any person is or was illegitimate[6].

Any declaration made under the provisions of the Family Law Act 1986 must be in the form prescribed by Rules of Court[7].

1 Family Law Act 1986 s 58 (1).
2 Ibid s 58 (2).
3 Ibid s 56 (4)(as substituted by the Family Law Reform Act 1987 s 22, Sch 3 para 1).
4 Ibid s 58 (3).
5 Ibid s 58 (5)(a).
6 Ibid s 58 (5)(b).
7 See Family Proceedings Rules 1991, SI 1991/1247, App 1 Forms M30 and M31.

2: REGISTRATION OF THE BIRTH OF A CHILD

69. Entry of names on the Register of Birth. Registration of the birth of a child which includes details of the name of a particular man as father of the child will constitute prima facie proof of his paternity of the child[1]. The birth of every child born in the United Kingdom must be registered by the mother and father of the child at the time of his birth[2] but in the case of a child whose parents were not married to each other at the time of his birth, there is no right and certainly no duty for the father to register himself as such[3]. Under the provisions of the Births and Deaths Registration Act 1953 as amended[4], a father's name in circumstances where the parties are unmarried can be entered on the Register in the following circumstances:

1. where both the mother and father request entry of the father's name and where this is the case both must sign the register;
2. at the request of either the mother or father, where the father has made a statutory declaration of paternity which has been acknowledged by the mother;
3. where the parents have made a parental responsibility agreement in the prescribed form and that is produced together with a declaration also in the prescribed form that the agreement has not been terminated by any court[5];
4. or at the request of either of the parents on the production of a court order which has resulted from a finding of paternity, together with a declaration in the prescribed form that such order has not been terminated by any court[6].

The orders which must be produced include any order under current law giving the father parental responsibility for the child[7] and any order under the old law which gave the father parental rights and duties[8], custody or care and control or legal custody[9], or any orders requiring the father to make financial provision for the child again either under current law[10] or under the former law[11]. In any situation in which the father's name was not entered on the register at the time of his birth and subsequently the parents make agreements with each other or court orders are made, it is provided that the father's name can be added to the Register and re-registration is thus possible[12]. Where any declaration of parentage[13] has been obtained the Register again can be amended to reflect the new situation[14].

1 Births and Deaths Registration Act 1953 s 34 (2)(as amended).
2 Ibid s 2 where the parents are required to register the child's birth within the first 42 days thereafter.
3 Children Act 1989 s 2 (3); Family Law Reform Act 1987 s 1.
4 Under the Births and Deaths Registration Act 1953 s 10 (1)(as substituted by the Family

Law Reform Act 1987 s 24 and further amended by the Children Act 1989 s 108 (4), Sch 12 para 6 (2)); and s 10A (1)(as inserted by the Children Act 1989 s 108 (4), Sch 12 para 6 (3)).

5 See Paragraph 102 for the provisions on parental responsibility agreements and see further Form 1 post.

6 As for those orders which will grant parental responsibility see Paragraph 100 post.

7 Children Act 1989 s 4.

8 Family Law Reform Act 1987 s 4 (repealed by the Children Act 1989 s 108 (7), Sch 15).

9 Guardianship of Minors Act 1971 s 9 (repealed by the Children Act 1989 s 108 (6), Sch 14, paras 5-11).

10 Children Act 1989 s 15 and Sch 1.

11 Guardianship of Minors Act 1971 ss 9, 11B (repealed by the Children Act 1989 s 108 (7), Sch 15) and Affiliation Proceedings Act 1957 s 4 (repealed by the Family Law Reform Act 1987 ss 17, 33 (4), Sch 4).

12 Births and Deaths Registration Act 1953 s 10A (1)(as amended by Family Law Reform Act 1987 s 25 and further amended by Children Act 1989 s 108 (4), Sch 12 para 6 (2)); and s 10A (1A)(as inserted by Children Act 1989, Sch 12 para 6 (3)).

13 See Paragraph 65 ante.

14 See Births and Deaths Registration Act 1953 s 14A (as inserted by Family Law Reform Act 1987 s 26).

3: PARENTAGE

70. Who are the child's legal parents? *Definition of mother* — Prior to the recent progress made by medical science in human fertilisation and embryology processes, it always used to be the case that a woman who gave birth to a child was legally deemed to be the mother. As a result of the scientific advances made, however, a woman is now able to give birth to a child who is not genetically related to her[1]. It has therefore been necessary to provide in statutory form for the legal definition of a child's mother and this is provided under the Human Fertilisation and Embryology Act 1990[2]. This Act provides that "a woman who is carrying or has carried a child as a result of the placing in her of an embryo or of sperm and eggs, and no other woman, is to be treated as the mother of the child"[3]. For these purposes, therefore, it is the woman who has given birth to the child and no other woman who will be treated as the child's mother, unless an order is made under s 30 of the Human Fertilisation and Embryology Act 1990[4] or the child is later adopted[5]. The Act does not appear to be retrospective but it would appear that the Act's definition applies in all situations where the placing of the embryo, sperm or eggs took place on or after the implementation date of the Act[6].

Definition of a child's legal father — As with the legal definition of motherhood, fatherhood is now complicated by issues arising from gamete donation and placement, and artificial insemination. Under the provisions of the Family Law Reform Act 1987 where a child was born to a married woman as the result of having been artificially inseminated with the sperm of some person other than her husband, then the husband is to be treated as the father of the child unless it is proved to the satisfaction of any court that the husband did not consent to the insemination[7]. The provisions of the Human Fertilisation and Embryology Act 1990 further extend the definition of fatherhood to cover the situation where the birth of a child is the result of placement of embryo or sperm and eggs in the married woman and the donor of the sperm was not in fact the husband[8]. The husband in such a situation will nevertheless be treated in law as the father for all purposes[9] but it should be noted that the parties must be married at the time of placement or insemination and should not be judicially separated, although the rule does extend to confer fatherhood in the situation of a void marriage if either or both of the parties to the marriage reasonably believed at the time of placement or insemination that the marriage was valid[10].

Therefore, where the husband has consented to his wife being artificially inseminated there will not be a problem about fatherhood, but where the husband has not so consented, the child will effectively be fatherless for all purposes since the sperm donor has provided sperm for the purposes of treatment of others and is not to be regarded as the child's father[11].

Where the couple undergoing treatment are not married but are living together then again the male cohabiting partner is treated as the child's father at law[12].

Where a child is born as a result of the artificial insemination of the mother using a deceased man's sperm, that man is not to be treated as the child's father[13].

1 For example where an embryo or eggs and semen have been placed in the mother's body so that she is effectively acting as a house mother. See for a detailed treatment of the legislation on this difficult subject *Blackstone's Guide to the Human Fertilisation and Embryology Act 1990* by D Morgan and R G Lee (Blackstones 1991).

2 See the Human Fertilisation and Embryology Act 1990 s 27 but see also the position at common law where the respective status of a woman giving birth and of the genetically related women was left undecided in *Re W (Minors)(Surrogacy)* [1991] FCR 419, [1991] 1 FLR 385.

3 Human Fertilisation and Embryology Act 1990 s 27 (1).

4 Ibid s 30, not yet in force at the time of writing.

5 Ibid s 27 (2).

6 Ibid s 49 (3) implementation date 1 August 1991. It should be noted that the provisions of s 27 apply irrespective of whether the woman was in the United Kingdom or elsewhere at the time of placement.

7 Family Law Reform Act 1987 s 27 which effectively governs the period between 4 April 1988 and 1 August 1991 which is the implementation date of the Human Fertilisation and Embryology Act 1990 ss 27, 28.

8 Ibid s 28 which then governs the situation from 1 August 1991 implementation date of Human Fertilisation and Embryology Act 1990 ss 27-29. After August 1991 only s 30 of the Act and s 48(1) insofar as it relates to s 30 remain unimplemented.

9 Ibid s 29 (1).

10 Ibid s 28 (7).

11 Ibid Sch 3 para 5.

12 Ibid s 28 (6) though in order to obtain parental responsibility he must seek a court order or make an agreement with the child's mother under Children Act 1989 s 4 or seek a residence order under s 8 which has the effect of conferring parental responsibility: s 12 (2).

13 Human Fertilisation and Embryology Act 1990 ss 28 (3), 28 (6), 29 (1) and see further s 29 (2)-(4).

71. Parental orders for gamete donors. Once the provisions of s 30 of the Human Fertilisation and Embryology Act 1990[1] are actually brought into force (and this had still not happened by the end of 1992), the High Court, county court or a magistrates' court[2] is empowered to make an order providing for a child to be treated in law as the child of the parties to a marriage where the child was carried by a woman other than the wife as the result of the placing in her of an embryo or sperm and eggs or her artificial insemination[3] and the gametes of the husband or the wife or both were used to bring about the creation of the embryo.

A number of conditions have to be fulfilled before the court will make an order and these are:

1. An application for an order can only be made by a husband and wife, both of whom must be over the age of 18 and at least one of whom must be domiciled in part of the United Kingdom or the Channel Islands or the Isle of Man[4].
2. The application must be made within six months of the child's birth or in the case of a child born before the Act came into force, within six months of its commencement[5].
3. At the time of the application the child's home must be with the husband and wife[6].
4. The carrying woman and the father including someone who is treated as the father[7], have freely and with full understanding of what is involved, agreed unconditionally to the making of an order[8].
5. Unless authorised by the court, no money or other benefit[9] has been given, paid or received by the spouses in connection with the making of the parental order, the giving of agreement, handing over of the child or the making of any arrangements with a view to the making of the order[10].

1   Human Fertilisation and Embryology Act 1990 s 30 from a day still to be appointed even at the end of 1992.
2   Ibid s 30 (8). It should be noted that proceedings under ibid s 30 relating to applications for a parental order are classified as Family Proceedings; see further ibid s 30 (8)(a).
3   Ibid s 30 (1)(a). Under ibid s 30 (11) an application can be made whether or not the woman was in the United Kingdom at the time of the placement or the insemination.
4   Ibid s 30 (2), (3)(a), (4).
5   Ibid s 30 (2). Note in the case of children born before the Act came into force an action would therefore have to have been commenced before the end of the six month period immediately following implementation.
6   Ibid s 30 (3)(a).
7   Ibid s 28 (2).
8   Ibid s 30 (5). Note that the unconditionality of the agreement relates to the making of an order and not to the making of an application.
9   With the exception of expenses reasonably incurred.
10 Ibid s 30 (7).

72. Presumption of paternity. Where a child is born to a married woman, the common law presumption that a child born of a married woman during the subsistence of her marriage is presumed to be the child of her husband operates and therefore if that presumption is not challenged by the husband or by another man claiming to be the father, the law provides that the husband will be treated as the child's father[1]. The burden of rebutting the common law presumption falls upon the husband or any other man claiming to be the father of the child, and where there is such a challenge, the standard of proof required is high[2], since the consequences of rebuttal will be very serious indeed for the child[3]. There are, however, now a range of scientific tests available to enable someone seeking to rebut the presumption of legitimacy successfully to do so[4]. These tests include blood testing and DNA fingerprinting[5].

1   See for example Glanvil, 7 chapter 12; Bracton, fol 6; Co litt 373; Blackstone's Commentaries i 457; *Gardner v Gardner* (1877) 2 App Cas 723, HL; *R v Luffe* (1807) 8 East 193 and *Re Heath* [1945] Ch 417 at 422, per Cohen J.
2   See for example *Serio v Serio* (1983) 4 FLR 756; *W v K (Proof of Paternity)* [1988] 1 FLR 86.

3 See Paragraphs 75 post and see also *Re F (Minor: Paternity Tests)* (1992) 2 FCR 725, FD.
4 See Paragraphs 73, 74 post.
5 See Paragraphs 73, 74 post.

73. Blood testing to establish paternity. Under the provisions of the Family Law Reform Act 1969 in any civil proceedings in which the paternity of any person falls to be determined by the court, the court may, on an application by any party to the proceedings, give a direction for the use of blood tests to ascertain whether such tests show that a party to the proceedings is, or is not, thereby excluded from being the father of that person[1]. Blood tests as such cannot be used to demonstrate conclusively that any particular man is the father of a child, but they can show positively that a given man could or could not be the father of the child[2]. The chance of excluding a non-father using blood tests on the father, child and mother is in the region of 97-99%. Where the test does not exclude a person alleged to be the father of the child, then the particular blood group characteristics are determined and the frequency of these occurring is expressed as a percentage of the general population. Where the presence of such men in the population is not high and the alleged father is one of this group, then the court is likely to decide that he is the father[3].

As the result of an amendment to regulations effected in 1989 it is now possible to extend the examination of blood specimens to include DNA profiling on the specimens[4]. Amendments effected to the Family Law Reform Act 1969 by the Family Law Reform Act 1987 which confer power on the court to direct the use of scientific tests and taking of other bodily samples have not yet been implemented but it is open to the parties to the application to agree to such a profiling of other samples[5].

The circumstances in which blood tests may be sought to establish paternity are:

1. where an application is being sought or financial proceedings in relation to a child of unmarried parents[6];
2. where a husband is seeking to establish that his wife's child is not his and that she has therefore committed adultery[7];
3. where one of the parties to the marriage is alleging that a child is not a child of the family for the purposes of any applications which may have been made in respect of the child[8];
4. where an unmarried father is seeking to establish paternity in order to succeed in an application for an order granting him parental responsibility[9];
5. where a husband is alleging that a marriage is voidable because of his wife's pregnancy by another person at the time of their marriage[10];
6. where entitlement under the terms of a trust is dependent upon a child being a child of married parents[11];

and in all cases a court has a discretion on an application being made, to give a direction for the use of blood tests[12] and for the taking of blood samples[13] from that person, the mother of that person and any party[14] alleged to be the father of that person, or from any one or two of those persons[15].

The courts empowered to direct blood tests are the High Court, county court and the magistrates' court[16] and when application[17] is made to the court it should specify who is to carry out the tests[18] but it should be noted that the court may either confirm the tester referred to in the application or, where it deems that person inappropriate[19], the court may decline to give the direction[20].

Where a direction is made the court will specify the period within which the samples must be taken and the court may revoke or vary a direction which it has previously given[21]. Where a direction has been given, the court must send a copy to every party to the proceedings and to every other person from whom the direction involves the taking of a blood sample. The proceedings will be adjourned[22] to a date when the court has received the report, at which time the court will send a copy to every party to the proceedings and to every other person from whom the direction involves the taking of blood samples[23].

The report should resolve the issue but where it does not the proceedings may be restored for further directions, for example for the court to consider the appointment of a guardian ad litem for the child (usually the Official Solicitor) if no such appointment has been made earlier in the proceedings[24].

The cost of taking and testing the blood samples including any expenses reasonably incurred and of making a report, is the responsibility of the party who made the application[25].

Where all parties agree to the blood tests being taken, then it is unnecessary to obtain any further direction from the court unless a guardian ad litem lodges an objection that the test would be against the child's interests[26]. Where one of the parties is refusing consent, the court is only empowered to direct that a blood sample be taken and cannot compel the taking of a blood sample. In the case of a minor under the age of 16, the consent of the person having care and control of him is required[27]. In such circumstances where the child wishes to refuse to give consent, it would appear that the parental consent would override this[28]. Under the provisions of the Family Law Reform Act 1969 the consent of a minor aged 16 or over is effective for the purposes of consent to medical treatment and it is therefore unnecessary to obtain the consent of anyone else[29].

1 Family Law Reform Act 1969 s 20 (1)(as amended) and see Blood Tests (Evidence of Paternity) Regulations 1971/1861, Sch 1 Form 1.
2 See *S v S, W v Official Solicitor* [1970] 3 All ER 107 at 109, HL, per LORD REID and see *Dodd and Lincoln* [1987] Law Society Gazette 2163.
3 *Dodd and Lincoln* (supra) at 2164.
4 Blood Tests (Evidence of Paternity) Regulations 1971, SI 1971/1861, Sch 1 Form 2 (as amended by the Blood Tests (Evidence of Paternity) (Amendment) Regulations 1989, SI 1989/776, reg 4), which amends the form in order to reflect the fact that the range of blood tests is not limited to blood group investigation.
5 Family Law Reform Act 1969 s 20 (as amended by Family Law Reform Act 1987 s 23). Where parties agree to DNA profiling, however, the testing is available from Cellmark Diagnostics and University Diagnostics Limited: see (1990) 140 NLJ 580.
6 See Children Act 1989 s 15 (1), Sch 1 and further see Paragraph 142.
7 See for example *F v F* (1968) P 506, [1968] 1 All ER 242.
8 See Matrimonial Causes Act 1973 s 52 (1) (as amended by Children Act 1989 s 108 (4), Sch 12 para 33); Domestic Proceedings and Magistrates' Courts Act 1978 s 88 (1)(as amended by Children Act 1989 s 108 (5), Sch 13 para 43 (b)) and also see *Dixon v Dixon* (1983) 4 FLR 99, CA.
9 See Children Act 1989 s 4.
10 See Matrimonial Causes Act 1973 s 12 (f) and *W v W (No 4)* [1964] P 67, 2 All ER 841, CA.
11 See for example *B v A-G (NEB Intervening)* [1965] P 278, [1963] 1 All ER 62; and *B v A-G (B Intervening)* [1966] 2 All ER 145n.
12 See Family Law Reform Act 1969 s 25 (to be repealed by the Family Law Reform Act 1987 s 23, Sch 3 para 1 as from a day to be appointed).
13 Blood samples refers to blood taken for the purpose of the blood tests.
14 This includes any party to the proceedings.

15 Family Law Reform Act 1969 s 20 (1)(as amended).

16 Ibid s 20 (1A)(as inserted by Children Act 1989 s 89 and amended by the Courts and Legal Services Act 1990, Sch 16 para 3).

17 Family Law Reform Act 1969 s 20 (1)(as amended). Note that unopposed applications in the county court may be heard by a district judge, but where the application is opposed, it is desirable that the application should be transferred to a judge, if possible to a High Court judge. See *R v R (Blood Test: Jurisdiction)* [1973] 3 All ER 933n.

18 An application may be made by any party to the proceedings but it should be noted that the blood tests are to be used to determine whether such tests show that a party to the proceedings is not excluded from being the father of the person whose paternity is in issue, and thus they are not available in respect of a person who is not a party to the proceedings. It is therefore necessary to join as a party anyone who is alleged to be the child's father. Both the High Court and the county court have power to direct that a person from whom it is desired to take a blood sample should be joined as a party but there is no corresponding power available in the magistrates courts: see RSC Ord 112 r 4; CCR Ord 47 r 5 (3).

19 Family Law Reform Act 1969 s 22.

20 Family Law Reform Act 1969 s 20 (1B)(as inserted by Children Act 1989 s 89 and amended by the Courts and Legal Services Act 1990 s 116, Sch 16 para 3) and see *Re F (Minor: Paternity Tests)* (1992) Times July 31, FD.

21 Family Law Reform Act 1969 s 20 (1)(as amended).

22 RSC Ord 112 r 5; CCR Ord 47 r 5 (5).

23 RSC Ord 117 r 6; CCR Ord 47 r 5 (6); and see Magistrates Courts (Blood Tests) Rules 1971, SI 1971/1991, r 14.

24 There are various circumstances which the court should take into account in deciding whether or not to appoint the Official Solicitor: see *Practice Direction* [1975] 1 All ER 319.

25 Family Law Reform Act 1969 s 20 (6).

26 See *Re L (An Infant)* [1968] P 119, [1968] 1 All ER 20, CA.

27 Family Law Reform Act 1969 s 21 (3).

28 See for example LORD REID in *S v S* [1973] 3 All ER 107 at 111.

29 Family Law Reform Act 1969 s 21 (2).

74. DNA testing. When the provisions come into force allowing for the courts to make directions for scientific testing on bodily samples other than blood under the Family Law Reform Act 1987, it will be possible to perform tasks on such bodily samples as semen, saliva, hair roots as well as on samples of blood[1]. The disadvantage of such DNA tests is that they are more expensive than the blood tests which routinely used to be done and it is now possible following the increase in the level of fees to be charged to obtain a test result from one of two organisations approved by the Home Office for the performance of such tests[2]. Until such time as the provisions of the Family Law Reform Act 1987 are implemented, it is, however, open as previously noted to the parties to agree to such profiling[3].

1 Family Law Reform Act 1987 s 23 (from a day to be so appointed).

2 The approved testing agencies are Cellmark Diagnostics and University Diagnostics Limited: see (1990) 140 NLJ 580.

3 See Paragraph 73 ante.

75. Circumstances under which blood testing will be directed. It is possible for the parties to an application to agree to submit to blood testing without requiring a direction from the court[1]. In any situation however where the parties do not agree, the legislation provides that the court has a discretion whether or not to direct the taking of blood samples[2]. The courts have however indicated that this discretion is not unfettered and must be exercised judicially.

Since such proceedings are not family proceedings for the purposes of the Children Act 1989, the issue of whether or not to direct blood tests would not appear to have to be determined solely by reference to the principle of the paramountcy of the child's welfare, but also on the common law principles of justice and the availability of the best evidence before the court[3]. The House of Lords has stated that the proper test to be applied is that the court should direct a blood test unless it is satisfied that to do so would be against the child's interests, which it is submitted would only be in rare cases[4]. It has therefore been suggested that in divorce proceedings it is better to have all the relevant evidence available before the court than to rely on the presumption of legitimacy and thus a direction for a blood test will usually be given as requested[5]. This would appear to reflect the view that there is really little significance attached to the status of illegitimacy under current law[6]. Thus, just because a blood test can prove that a child is a child of unmarried parents, this is not a sufficient reason to refuse to make a direction[7], and indeed a refusal to direct a blood test may increase rather than allay doubts as to paternity which may in turn prejudice the child's interests[8]. However, where the sole purpose of the application is "of a fishing nature, designed for some ulterior motive to call in question the legitimacy, otherwise unimpeached, of a child who had enjoyed legitimate status"[9], then the court is likely to exercise its discretion to refuse to direct a blood test in the circumstances[10].

1 In the situation where the court issues a direction under Family Law Reform Act 1969 s 20 then it has the advantage that it appoints the testers.
2 See *S v S, W v Official Solicitor* [1972] AC 24, [1970] 3 All ER 107, HL.
3 See *S v S, W v Official Solicitor* (supra) and see *Re T (A Minor) (Blood Tests)* [1992] 2 FCR 663, CA.
4 See *S v S, W v Official Solicitor* (supra) but see *Re F (Minor: Paternity Tests)* [1992] 2 FCR 725, FD.
5 See *Practice Direction* [1975] 1 All ER 223, but see also *R v R (Blood Test: Jurisdiction)* [1973] 3 All ER 933n. It should be noted that in divorce proceedings where no point is taken by either petitioner or respondent as to the paternity of children who are accepted as children of the family, the court does not then have jurisdiction to direct a blood test to be carried out on the children; see *Hodgkiss v Hodgkiss* [1984] FLR 563.
6 See Family Law Reform Act 1987 s 1.
7 See for example *W v Official Solicitor* (supra); *P v P* (1969) 113 Sol Jo 343, CA.
8 See ORMROD J in *H v H (H by his Guardian Intervening)* [1966] 1 All ER 356 at 357.
9 *S v S; W v Official Solicitor* [1973] 3 All ER 107 at 115 per LORD McDERMOTT.
10 See further *M(D) v M(S) and G(M)(D A Intervening)* [1969] 2 All ER 243.

76. Refusal to comply with directions. Failure to comply with the court's direction for the taking of blood samples[1], or to supply information as to the persons having care and control of a child under 16 or a patient, or by failing to supply a photograph or medical certificate before taking such a blood sample[2] allows the court to draw such inferences, if any, as appear proper in the circumstances[3]. Such inferences will usually, but not necessarily[4], be adverse to the refusing party. A refusal by the alleged father to comply with the direction to submit to a blood test is generally taken to be evidence capable of corroborating the mother's evidence that he is the father of the child[5].

Where in any proceedings in which the parentage of any person falls to be determined by the court and there is a presumption of law that that person is legitimate, then if a direction for blood testing is given under Section 20 in the proceedings and any party who is claiming relief in the proceedings, is entitled to rely on the presumption and fails to take any step required of him in relation to the blood testing, then the court may adjourn the hearing for such period as it thinks fit to enable that party to take any such step. If after the period of the adjournment that party has still failed without reasonable cause to take the relevant step, then the court may dismiss his claim for relief notwithstanding the absence of evidence to rebut the presumption[6]. It is a criminal offence for any person to impersonate another for purposes of providing a blood sample or to proffer a child knowing that he is not the child named in the direction for blood testing[7].

1 Family Law Reform Act 1969 s 23 (3).
2 The Blood Tests (Evidence of Paternity) Regulations 1971, SI 1971/1861, reg 6 (2).
3 Family Law Reform Act 1969 s 23 (1)(to be amended by the Family Law Reform Act 1987 s 33 (1), Sch 2, para 24 from a day to be so appointed).
4 See *B v B and E (B Intervening)* [1969] 3 All ER 1106.
5 *McVeigh v Beattie* [1988] Fam 69, [1988] 2 All ER 500.
6 Family Law Reform Act 1969 s 23 (2).
7 Ibid s 24 (to be amended by the Family Law Reform Act 1987 s 33 (1), Sch 2 para 25 from a day to be so appointed).

77. Procedure in the High Court and county court. An application for a direction for the use of blood tests must be made, except where the court grants leave, on notice to every party to the proceedings and to any other person from whom the direction involves the taking of a blood sample[1]. In the High Court if the application is made otherwise than at the hearing of the proceedings, it is made by summons[2]. Service of any notice of application or summons on a person who is not a party to the proceedings must be on him personally[3] and he should be joined as a party to the proceedings[4]. Where a direction is sought in respect of a person under the age of 16, or suffering from mental disorder within the meaning of the Mental Health Act 1983[5], who is such that he is incapable of understanding the nature and purpose of the blood testing, a notice of application or summons must state the name and address of the person having the care and control of that person and shall be served on the person having care and control[6].

Where a direction for blood testing has been made by the Family Division of the High Court or the county court, then the solicitor acting for the applicant[7] must arrange for the taking and testing of the blood samples[8]. The solicitor should, on receipt of the direction, apply to the court for the necessary number of copies of the prescribed direction form[9]. A separate form is required in respect of each person to be tested and the solicitor should agree with the solicitors for the other parties as to who is to be the tester[10] and should inform the tester that a direction for blood tests has been made and in which proceedings, stating the number of persons covered by the direction and the area in which they live[11].

Wherever practicable, all samples should be tested by the same tester, the tester should be asked when it will be convenient for him to receive the samples and he should also suggest the name of any sampler who could appropriately take the samples[12]. Where the parties are unable to agree the arrangements, then the applicant's solicitor should refer the matter back to court for further directions. Where at any stage it appears to the tester that he is unable to make tests in accordance with the direction, he must inform the court, giving his reasons and must return the direction forms in his possession to the court[13]. It is further provided that a tester shall not make tests on any samples unless he will, in his opinion, be able to show from the results of those tests that a person is or is not excluded from being the father of a person whose paternity is in dispute[14].

As soon as the solicitor has made arrangements for blood testing, he should complete the relevant parts of the direction form in respect of each person to be tested and attend with the forms before the district judge by whom the direction was given, or, if it was not given by a district judge, before the district judge[15]. If the district judge is satisfied with the arrangements, he must sign each form and return them to the solicitor[16]. The solicitor must then include a photograph of the applicant unless he or she has not attained the age of twelve months or is suffering from mental disorder[17]. If necessary, applications should be made to the solicitors for the other parties for photographs of the subjects they represent.

The solicitor should forward the direction forms with the notes of guidance to the nominated sampler and make arrangements with him as to the attendance of the various parties. A person who is under the age of 16 or who is a patient, must be accompanied by a person of full age who will then be able to identify him to the sampler[18]. In a situation where no photograph can be obtained of a patient, then a direction form should be accompanied by a medical certificate stating that the party is suffering from a mental disorder and that a photograph cannot, or should not, be taken[19]. No samples should be taken unless the relevant parts of the direction form have been completed[20], and the direction form has been signed by the proper officer of the court or some other person on his behalf[21].

The sampler can make whatever arrangements are appropriate for the taking of samples and is free to change any arrangements or make alternative arrangements[22]. In certain circumstances the sampler can decide not to take a sample from a person where he has reason to believe that that person has had a blood transfusion within the last three months, or tests taken from that person at that time could not effectively be carried out for the purposes of the direction, or if in his opinion the taking of a sample might have an adverse effect on the health of that person[23].

Wherever there is reason to suppose that any person may refuse to give a sample, the sampler should be advised as soon as possible of this situation so that samples are not taken from other parties to no avail. It is particularly important that a sample should not be taken from a child unnecessarily and that a child's sample should, wherever possible, be taken last. Where it proves impossible to take a sample from a party and no arrangements have been made, the sampler should return the direction form, stating on it the reason for not taking the sample and any reasons given by a party, or the person having care and control of the party for their non-attendance[24]. Under the provisions of the regulations, a solicitor representing any party may accompany him or her for the purposes of the sample being taken[25].

Where the tests have been completed, the person responsible for carrying them out must make a report to the court in the appropriate form[26], stating the result of the tests, whether the party to whom the report relates is excluded from being the father of the child, and if not, the value, if any, of the results in determining paternity[27]. The court must send a copy of the report to every party to the proceedings and to every other person from whom samples were taken pursuant to the court's directions[28]. Upon receipt of the tester's report via the court, any party may, with the court's leave, obtain from the person who made the report a written statement explaining or expanding upon any statement made in the report, and that statement shall be deemed to form part of the report[29].

A party to the proceedings is not entitled to call the tester or any person by whom any aspect of the test was performed, as a witness, unless within 14 days of receipt of the report he serves notice of his intention to call that person on the other parties to the proceedings, or on such of the parties as the court directs. Where the tester or such other person is called, the party who called him is entitled to cross examine[30].

1 RSC Ord 112 r 2 (1); CCR Ord 47 r 5 (2).
2 RSC Ord 112 r 2 (2) and see also RSC Ord.32.
3 RSC Ord 112 r 2 (3); CCR Ord 47 r 5 (3).
4 RSC Ord 112 r 4; CCR Ord 47 r 5 (3).
5 Mental Health Act 1983 s 1.
6 RSC Ord 112 r 3; CCR Ord.47 r 5 (4).
7 *Practice Direction* [1972] 1 All ER 640.
8 As to the meaning of "sample" see Blood Tests (Evidence of Paternity) Regulations 1971, SI 1971/1861, reg 2 (1).
9 See ibid Sch 1 Form 1.
10 "Tester" means a person appointed by the Secretary of State to carry out blood tests under the regulations: reg 2 (1). A list of authorised testers can be supplied, see Home Office Circular No 2481971 para 5.
11 See Blood Tests (Evidence of Paternity) Regulations 1971, reg 9 (1).
12 "Sampler" means a registered medical practitioner or tester nominated in a direction form to take blood samples for the purposes of the direction: ibid reg 2 (1).
13 Ibid reg 11.
14 Ibid reg 9 (2).
15 Ibid reg 3.
16 The forms should be returned to the solicitors together with a copy of the notes for guidance of samplers.
17 Ibid reg 6 (2), 2 (1).
18 Ibid reg 4.
19 Ibid reg 6 (2).
20 Ibid Sch 1 Form 1.
21 Ibid reg 3.
22 Ibid reg 5 (1).
23 Ibid reg 5 (3).
24 Ibid reg 5 (5).
25 Ibid reg 5 (6).
26 Ibid Sch 1 Form 2 (as amended by Blood Tests (Evidence of Paternity) (Amendment) Regulations 1989, SI 1989/776, reg 4).
27 Family Law Reform Act 1969 s 20 (2)(as substituted by Family Law Reform Act 1987 s 23 (1) as from a day to be appointed). See further *Turner v Blunden* [1986] Fam 120, [1986] 2 All ER 75.
28 RSC Ord 112 r 6; County Rules 1981 Ord 47 r 5 (6).
29 Family Law Reform Act 1969 s 30.
30 Family Law Reform Act 1969 s 2 (5).

78. Procedure in the magistrates' courts. Under the relevant court rules where any person makes a complaint to the magistrates' court and the justices' clerk determines that in the hearing of such a complaint the paternity of any person will fall to be determined, then the rules require that a form explaining the procedure about blood tests[1] be served upon the complainant and upon any person who is served with a summons to answer such a complaint[2]. The form can be delivered personally or by sending it by first class post to him at his last known or usual place of abode, or to his solicitor at his office[3]. A party to any proceedings may apply in writing to the court for a direction at any time after the making of the complaint, and upon receipt of the application the justices' clerk must inform the other party to the proceedings that the application has been made and that he may consent to the court giving a direction before the commencement of the hearing of the complaint[4].

A court may give a direction for blood tests in the absence of the applicant and the other party to the proceedings if it appears that that other party, or, where he is under a disability, the person having the care and control of him has consented to the giving of the direction for blood tests[5]. The court, when giving a direction, shall name the person appearing to the court to have the care and control of any subject who is under a disability[6], and the direction shall be set out in the appropriate form with a copy being served on every subject or, where the subject is under a disability, on the person named in the direction as having the care and control of him[7]. Where any person has not consented to the court giving a direction for blood tests in advance of the hearing or an application has not been made until the hearing itself, then the applicant may seek a direction at the hearing and the court will have to decide whether or not to exercise its powers to direct a test. Where the court decides to exercise its discretion and direct a blood test, it should issue a direction even though the party is unlikely to comply, so that the court may draw such inferences as may be appropriate[8].

Within 14 days[9] of the giving of any direction, the applicant[10] shall pay to the justices' clerk such sum as appears to the clerk to be the probable cost of paying the fees of the sampler and tester[11]. The clerk must pay the fee due and repay the balance if any due to the applicant[12]. The applicant is also responsible for the subject's expenses, but the court has powers to deal with these expenses when it makes an order for costs[13]. Within 14 days of service of a copy of the direction for blood tests, each subject who is not under a disability and the person having care and control of the subject who is under a disability but has attained the age of 12 months by the date of the direction, shall furnish to the clerk a photograph of the subject[14]. Again, as in the High Court, this provision does not apply if the subject is suffering from a mental disorder and the medical practitioner in whose care he is certifies that a photograph cannot or should not be taken of the subject in the circumstances[15].

Unlike the situation in the High Court[16], the arrangements for taking and testing blood can be made either by the clerk or the justices' clerk can arrange for the party's solicitor to make the arrangements on his behalf[17]. Whoever is responsible for making arrangements follows the same procedure as laid down in respect of the High Court and county court, with the tester indicating when it would be convenient for him to receive the samples and suggesting the names of the persons who could appropriately take the samples[18]. As soon as the arrangements have been made, the justices' clerk should notify the subject[19], or where a subject is under disability the person having care and control of the subject. The justices' clerk should then complete the relevant parts of the direction form[20] in respect of each subject and forward it to the sampler. The procedure for the taking of the samples is identical to that in the High Court and county court[21]. As soon as the tests have been completed, the tester will forward a copy of his report to the court upon receipt of which the justices' clerk must send out a copy of the report to each of the parties to the proceedings[22]. The procedure to be followed upon receipt of a direction form not accompanied by a report is again exactly the same as for the High Court and county court[23].

1 Under the Magistrates' Court (Blood Tests) Rules 1971, SI 1971/1991, Sch 1 Form 1.
2 Ibid r 3 (as amended by SI 1989/384 r 3).
3 Ibid r 16.
4 Ibid r 4.
5 Ibid rr 2, 3, 5.
6 Ibid r 6.
7 Ibid r 7 and see Sch 1, Form 2.

8   See Paragraph 76 ante (dealing with court's exercise of its discretion in these cases).
9   Or such longer period as the court may order: Magistrates' Court (Blood Tests) Rules 1971, r 9.
10 Where the applicant has not been granted legal aid.
11 Magistrates' Court (Blood Tests) Rules 1971, r 8.
12 Ibid r 15.
13 Note that the sampler's and tester's fees are to be treated as costs incurred by the applicant in the proceedings.
14 Magistrates' Court (Blood Tests) Rules 1971 r 9.
15 Ibid r 9.
16 See Paragraph 77 ante.
17 Ibid r 11 and see Home Office Circular 248/1971 as amended.
18 Ibid r 2 (1).
19 Ibid in Sch 1 Form 3 and see r 12.
20 Blood Tests (Evidence of Paternity) Regulations 1971 (as amended), Sch 1 Form 1.
21 See Paragraph 77 ante.
22 Magistrates' Courts (Blood Tests) Rules 1971, r 14.
23 Ibid r 14 and see Paragraph 77 ante.

CHAPTER 4: PARENTAL RESPONSIBILITY AND GUARDIANSHIP

1: PARENTAL RESPONSIBILITY

79. Definition of parental responsibility. Parental responsibility is defined in the Children Act 1989 as meaning "all the rights, duties, powers, responsibilities and authority which by law a parent of a child has in relation to the child and his property"[1]. It is noteworthy that within the space of two years from the enactment of the Family Law Reform Act 1987 to that of the Children Act 1989 the emphasis has shifted from parental rights to parental responsibilities[2]. It has also come to be recognised that even the rights referred to under the Children Act 1989 are subject to the decision in *Gillick v West Norfolk and Wisbech Area Health Authority*[3]. Thus in certain situations the parents' rights yield to the child's right to make his own decisions when he reaches sufficient understanding and intelligence to be capable of making up his own mind on the matter requiring decision[4]. It must be stressed that the child's competance to make such decisions must however be a continuing state unaffected by psychosis, mental illness or an imbalance arising from physical deterioration and may be overridden by the exercise by the High Court of its inherent jurisdiction over minors to act in the minor's best interests.[5]

The problem with the provision in the Children Act defining parental responsibility is that it does not give a precise list of what those rights, powers, duties and responsibilities include[6]. Whilst this follows the recommendation of the Law Commission[7] it is nevertheless important to know what these rights, duties, powers, and responsibilities are, for they are the ones which are likely to come up for consideration when applications are made to the court for orders under Section 8 of the Children Act 1989[8]. What follows is an attempt to draw up a list of the more important rights, powers, duties and responsibilities which might be affected by the making of Section 8 orders[9].

1   Children Act 1989 s 3 (1).
2   Contrast the Family Law Reform Act 1987 s 4 (6 Halsbury's Statutes (4th Edn) CHILDREN) with the Children Act 1989 s 4.
3   *Gillick v West Norfolk and Wisbech Area Health Authority* [1986] AC 112, [1985] 3 All ER 402, HL.
4   *Gillick v West Norfolk and Wisbech Area Health Authority* (supra).

5 See now the Court of Appeal's decisions in *Re R (A Minor) (Wardship: Medical Treatment)* [1992] 1 FLR 190, CA and *Re J (a Minor) (Inherent Jurisdiction : Consent to Treatment)* [1993] 1 FLR 1, CA.
6 *Gillick v West Norfolk and Wisbech Area Health Authority* (supra).
7 Law Commission No 172: Family Law Review of Child Law Guardianship and Custody, HC 594 at paras 2.6 et seq.
8 See Paragraphs 123-126 post.
9 The Law Commission list (See note 6 supra) was described as not being exhaustive.

80. Physical care of the child. Probably the most important facet of parental responsibility will be that of physical care and control of the child. It would appear that those with parental responsibility have a duty to provide a home for the child and the power to determine where a child should live. Whether that power extends to being able to tell the child what to do depends on the child's age and understanding[1]. Where a child is removed by force or fraud without his consent[2] then the parents may be guilty of the common law offence of kidnapping the child and removal of a child under the age of 16 outside the United Kingdom without either the consent of any parent[3], guardian, or person in whose favour a residence order had been made in respect of the child[4] or without the leave of the court. A parent has no right of action or a remedy in damages against a stranger who interferes with the parent's rights in respect of his relationship with his children[5].

1 See *Gillick v West Norfolk and Wisbech Area Health Authority* [1986] AC 112, [1985] 3 All ER 402, HL as circumscribed by the decisions in *Re R (A Minor) (Wardship : Medical Treatment)*[1992] 1 FLR 190, CA and *Re W (A Minor) (Inherent Jurisdiction : Consent to Treatment)* (1992) Times, 15 July, CA, *Hewer v Bryant* [1969] 3 All ER 578 at 582.
2 See *R v D* [1984] AC 778, [1984] 2 All ER 449, HL.
3 Child Abduction Act 1984 s 1 (as amended by Children Act 1989 s.108 (4) and Sch 12, para 37 as from a day to be appointed) (12 Halsbury's Statutes (4th Edn) CRIMINAL LAW).
4 For an account of residence orders see Paragraph 123 post.
5 See *F v Wirral Metropolitan Borough Council* [1991] Fam 69, [1991] 2 All ER 648, CA.

81. Discipline. The law with regard to the right of a parent to exercise discipline over a child is somewhat grey. However it is assumed by implication from the provisions of the Children and Young Persons Act 1933[1] that a parent has a right to exercise discipline over the child, though this right is restricted by the corresponding rights of local authorities to intervene in children's cases, where they believe that a child might be at risk of suffering significant harm[2].

1 Children and Young Persons Act 1933 s 1 (as amended by the Children Act 1989 s 108(5), Sch 13, para 2).
2 Children Act 1989 s 31.

82. Protection. Arising out of the same statute there is also a duty upon those who have the care and control of a child to protect the child from unnecessary suffering or injury as a result of criminal behaviour[1]. It should however be noted that whilst local authorities who look after children are placed under a statutory duty to safeguard and promote the child's welfare a parent is not under a corresponding duty to promote the welfare of his or her own child[2]. It has however been held in relation to adoption law that parents have a natural and moral duty to show affection, care and interest towards their children[3].

1   Children and Young Persons Act 1933 Pt I.
2   Children Act 1989 s 22 (3).
3   Per PENNYCUICK J in *Re P (Infants)* [1962] 3 All ER 789.

83. Maintenance. Under various statutory provisions a parent has a duty to maintain his or her child[1], and under the provisions of the Children Act 1989 and the Child Support Act 1991 the fact that a person has or does not have parental responsibility for a child does not affect any obligation which he may have in relation to the child[2]. This means that an unmarried father who has not been granted parental responsibility under the relevant provisions of the Children Act 1989[3] may nevertheless be held liable to maintain his child as the child's liable relative under the provisions of the Social Security Legislation[4] or as the parent of a qualifying child under the provisions of the Child Support Act 1991. Where, however, the absent parent denies that he is one of the child's parents, then the Child Support Agency will not be able to make a maintenance assessment on the assumption that the alleged parent is one of the child's parents[6], unless the case falls within one of a number of specified pre-conditions laid down in the statute[7], or the Child Support Agency refer the case to court and obtain a declaration of parentage against the alleged parent[8]. Furthermore a step-parent who has treated the step-child as a child of the family may, in matrimonial proceedings, be ordered to maintain the child, even where the step-parent has not been granted a residence order[9].

1   See Social Security Act 1986 s 26.
2   Children Act 1989 s 3 (4)(a).
3   Children Act 1989 ss 4, 8, 12 (2).
4   See Social Security Act 1986 ss 24, 24A (inserted by the Social Security Act 1990 s 8 (1)) and the Maintenance Enforcement Act 1991 ss 9 (the latter coming into force from a day to be appointed), 26.
5   Child Support Act 1991, ss1, 4.
6   Child Support Act 1991 s 26(1).
7   Ibid s 26(2) (A-F).
8   Ibid s 27.
9   See Matrimonial Causes Act 1973 s 25 (as substituted).

84. Contact. Whilst parental responsibility necessarily includes seeing and having contact with the child it has nevertheless been stated that is a basic right of the child rather than of the parent[1]. Given the provisions of the Children Act 1989 it may be said that parental responsibility towards a child includes the duty to allow the child to have contact with other persons having parental responsibility[2]. Where problems about contact with another person having parental responsibility or indeed with any other person seeking to have contact with the child arise, then the situation may be resolved with the making of a contact order under the Children Act where contact is to be permitted or a prohibited steps order where contact is to be prevented[3].

1   See the comments of WRANGHAM J and LATEY J in *M v M (Child: Access)* [1973] 2 All ER 81 at 88 and 85 respectively.
2   Children Act 1989 s 3 (1).
3   Under the provisions of ibid s 8 (1).

85. Education. Every person who has parental responsibility for a child or full-time care of a child is under a duty to ensure that where the child is of compulsory school age he or she receives an efficient full-time education[1]. Such a person also has the right to choose a school[2] and the local Education Authority must have regard to parental wishes[3] and preferences[4] and must make sufficient schools available[5]. It must consult parents before deciding whether or not to close or amalgamate any of its schools[6]. Where the parent wishes to do so he or she may choose to educate the child privately, but in the event of any dispute between parents arising either before or after divorce then an application could be made to the court to determine the matter by the issuing of a specific issue or prohibited steps order under the Children Act 1989[7].

1   Education Act 1944 s 36.
2   Education Act 1944 ss 114 (1D)-(1F) (as inserted by Children Act 1989 s108 (5), Sch 13 para 10).
3   Education Act 1944 s 76.
4   Education Act 1980 s 6.
5   Education Act 1944 s 8.
6   Education Act 1980 ss 12, 14, 16 and see *R v Brent London Borough Council ex p Gunning* (1985) 84 LGR 168.
7   See Children Act 1989 s 8 (1).

86. Religious upbringing. A parent or person exercising parental responsibility has the right to determine the religion in which the child should be brought up. This right to determine the child's religion will continue to vest in the parent or other person exercising parental responsibility even where a care order vests other parental responsibilities in a local authority[1]. Where the child is old enough to form his own views then it must be expected that this will be considered to be of greater validity than those of the parents[2]. It has, however, been stressed in the case of *Re R*[3] by the Court of Appeal that there is no rule or legal principle that it could never be right to force a child to abandon his religious beliefs. There is a right in the parent or other person with parental responsibility for the child to require that the child not be included in religious study lessons in school or in school assembly[4].

Where a religion in which the child is being caused to be brought up by the parents involves a risk of serious harm to the child then an order could be granted prohibiting the child being brought up in such a religion[5], or if a risk arises as a result of a particular belief of the parents' religion which the child is following, then a specific issue order dealing with the consequences of that particular belief may also be issued[6].

1   Children Act 1989 s 33(6)(a).
2   See *Gillick v West Norfolk and Wisbech Area Health Authority* [1986] AC 112, [1985] 3 All ER 402, HL.
3   *Re R (A Minor)* (1992) Times, 3 November, CA
4   Education Reform Act 1988 s 9.
5   For example as in *Re B and G (Minors)(Custody)* [1985] FLR 493 and see also the post Children Act case of *Re R (A Minor)* (1992) Times, 3 November, CA.
6   As for example in *Re T (Minors)(Custody : Religious Upbringing)* (1975) 2 FLR 239, CA.

87. Medical treatment. Any person over the age of sixteen who has the care of a child under the age of sixteen is under a duty to obtain or to take steps to obtain essential medical treatment for the child[1]. Once a child has attained the age of sixteen, the child may give a valid consent to medical treatment without the need of the consent of the parents but where his mental capacity is impaired to such a degree that he cannot give an effective consent then the parent may do so on his behalf[2]. Where the child is under the age of sixteen then the parent is normally in the position of being able to give a valid consent but this gives way to the principle established in the *Gillick* case that, if the child is of sufficient understanding and intelligence to enable him to understand fully what is involved, then he may give consent on his own behalf[3]. Since the decisions in *Re R*[4] and *Re W*[5] however, it must be stressed that the child's ability to give such a consent must be a continuing one and not affected by any psychoses, mental illness or imbalances arising from physical deterioration. It would further appear as a result of the decisions in *Re R* and *Re W* that the Court of Appeal is of the view (and in subsequent cases this view would be persuasive but not binding) that where a competent child refuses treatment, a valid consent may be obtained from someone with parental responsibility, or where this is not possible from the High Court in the exercise of its inherent jurisdiction. Where however the child is under the age of sixteen and the parents are refusing to give consent to treatment, then previous case law has suggested the best course of action is to seek the court's views on the performance of medical treatment[6]. Previously, such authority would have to have been given in wardship proceedings[7]; it is now the case that authority to perform or withhold treatment will be sought by means of a specific issue order or a prohibited steps order[8] or by invoking the inherent jurisdiction of the High Court in very difficult cases.

1 Children and Young Persons Act 1933 s 1 (1)(as amended by the Children Act 1989 s 108(5), Sch 13, para 2), (2)(a)(as amended by the Children Act 1989 s 108(4), Sch 12, para 2).
2 Family Law Reform Act 1969 s 8(1).
3 See *Gillick v West Norfolk and Wisbech Area Health Authority* [1986] AC 112, [1985] 3 All ER 402, HL.
4 *Re R (A Minor) (Wardship Medical Treatment)* [1992] 1 FLR 190, CA.
5 In *Re W (A Minor) (Inherent Jurisdiction : Consent to Treatment)* [1993] 1 FLR 1, CA.
6 See LORD TEMPLEMAN in *Re B (A Minor) (Wardship : Sterilisation)* [1988] 1 AC 199, [1987] 2 All ER 206, HL at pp 205206 and 214215 and see further *Practice Note (Official Solicitor: Sterilization)* [1989] 2 FLR 447, although see further *Re E (A Minor) (Medical Treatment)* [1991] 2 FLR 585, [1992] Fam Law 15.
7 As for example in *Re B (A Minor) (Wardship : Medical Treatment)* [1990] 3 All ER 927, [1981] 1 WLR 1421, *Re C (A Minor) (Wardship : Medical Treatment) (No 2)* (1990) Fam 39, [1989] 2 All ER 791.
8 Under the provisions of the Children Act 1989 s 8 (1).

88. Agreement to adoption. Before an adoption order can be made or an order freeing a child for adoption, the agreement of every parent who has parental responsibility for the child is necessary unless the court dispenses with that agreement on specified grounds[1]. The right to agree or refuse to agree to the making of an adoption or a freeing order does not pass to the local authority on the making of a care order[2].

1 See Adoption Act 1976 ss 16, 72 (as amended by Children Act 1989 s 88 (1), Sch 10, paras 5, 30).
2 Children Act 1989 s 33(6)(b).

89. Appointment of a guardian. Any parent who has parental responsibility for a child may appoint one or more individuals to be the child's guardian on his death[1] though whether such an appointment will take effect may be determined by whether the deceased parent had a sole residence or custody care and control order in their favour at the time of their death. Where no such order was in force then the appointment by the deceased parent of a guardian will only take effect where there is no parent with parental responsibility surviving. Thus where the child's father has parental responsibility and he survives, the mother's appointment of a guardian does not take effect[2]. The right to appoint a guardian for the child does not pass to the local authority on the making of a care order[3].

1　Children Act 1989 s 5 (3).
2　Children Act 1989 s 5 (8). See further Paragraph 98 et seq post.
3　Children Act 1989 s 33 (6)(b)(iii).

90. Child's surname. A child, whose parents were married to each other at the time of his birth, generally takes the surname of his father[1], but there is nothing in the relevant regulations which requires the father's name to take precedence over the mother's and thus it seems that the mother is equally entitled to register the child in her name[2]. A child whose parents are not married will usually take the surname of his mother but he may equally be known by the father's surname. The provisions of the Children Act 1989 make it clear that where a residence order is in existence the holder of the residence order is not thereby entitled to change the child's surname without either the written consent of every person who has parental responsibility for the child or the leave of the court[3]. Application for leave to change the child's name should be made in the appropriate form[4] and in deciding whether to grant leave the court must be guided by the principles set out in Section 1 of the Children Act 1989[5].

Where no residence order is in force then the position would seem to be that whilst one parent may seek to change the child's name the other parent can apply for a prohibited steps order to prevent the change[6].

Finally, it should be noted that whilst a care order is in force with respect to the child the local authority does not have the right nor does any other person have the right to cause the child to be known by a new surname without either the written consent of every person who has parental responsibility for the child or the leave of the court[7].

1　*Du Boulay v Du Boulay* (1869) LR 2 PC 430 at 442 and see the Registration of Births, Deaths and Marriages Regulations 1968, SI 1968/2049 .
2　*D v B* [1979] Fam 38, [1979] 1 All ER 92, CA.
3　Children Act 1989 s 13 (1).
4　See Form CHA 11 in Family Proceedings Rules 1991 SI 1991/1247 Appendix 1.
5　See Children Act 1989 s 1 (1) and also see *W v A (Child : Surname)* [1981] Fam 14, [1981] 1 All ER 100, CA.
6　See Children Act 1989 s 8 (1).
7　Children Act 1989 s 33 (7) and see now *Re J (A Minor) (Change of Name)* [1992] Fam Law 569, [1993] FCR 74, FD.

91. Removal of the child out of the jurisdiction. Under normal circumstances a parent has the ability to give or refuse consent to his child being taken out of the jurisdiction as a result of his power to exercise parental rights[1]. Application can be made to the Passport Office for the children's names to be entered on the passport of either one of married parents, or in the case of unmarried parents, on that of the unmarried mother[2].

If a residence order is in force with respect to a child no person may cause the child to be removed from the United Kingdom without either the written consent of every person who has parental responsibility for the child or the leave of the court, application having been made in the prescribed form[3]. Where such an order has been made, however, it does not prevent the removal of a child for a period of less than one month for example for a holiday by the person in whose favour the residence order has been made[4]. In making a residence order with respect to a child the court may grant the leave required either generally or for specified purposes where there is a known reason for regular absences[5]. Where the parent who does not hold the residence order is concerned about the number of trips abroad or as to the possibility of the risk of abduction, a variation of the residence order could be sought attaching conditions restricting removal of the child from the United Kingdom, or alternatively steps could be taken to apply for a prohibited steps order[6]. Where a care order has been made no person may remove the child from the United Kingdom without either the written consent of every person who has parental responsibility for the child or the leave of the court unless such removal is to be for a period of less than one month by the local authority[7]. Local authorities can however make arrangements with the approval of the court and the consent of every person who has parental responsibility for the child to live outside England and Wales[8].

Where either parent seeks leave to emigrate with the child this will be decided in accordance with the paramountcy of the child's welfare[9].

Finally, where there is in force any court order prohibiting or restricting removal of a child from the United Kingdom, the court which made the order may require the surrender of the child's passport or of any adult's passport containing particulars of the child[10].

1 Children Act 1989 s 3 (1).
2 The Passport Department's information on passport facilities for minors is reproduced at [1986] Fam Law 50.
3 Children Act 1989 s 13 (1)(b), and see CHA Form 11A, which is the same form for use in the High Court, county court and magistrates' courts. As to the consequences of not returning a child in respect of whom leave for removal had been granted, see *Re D (A Minor) (Child Removal from Jurisdiction)* [1992] 1 FLR 637, CA.
4 Ibid s 13 (2) and see CHA Form 12 post for the order which is the same form for use in the High Court, county court and magistrates' court.
5 Ibid s 13 (3).
6 Such conditions or restrictions can be included in any order under the provisions of the Children Act 1989 s 11 (7).
7 Children Act 1989 s 33 (8)(a).
8 Children Act 1989 s 33 (8)(b) and such arrangements are governed by Children Act 1989 Sch 2 para 19.
9 See for example in *P (LM) (Otherwise E) v P (GE)* [1970] 3 All ER 659; *Barnes v Tyrrell* (1981) 3 FLR 240, CA; *Lonslow v Hennig (Formerly Lonslow)* [1986] 2 FLR 378; and for a case where leave was refused see *Tyler v Tyler* [1990] FCR 22, [1989] 2 FLR 158, CA.
10 Family Law Act 1986 s 37.

92. Legal representation. A parent has the right to act on behalf of a child in legal proceedings as the child's next friend or guardian ad litem[1]. Another person will only be substituted if it is established that the parent has acted improperly and against the child's interests[2]. Some other person may be substituted as the child's next friend where it appears that a parent's decision to discontinue an action or not to appeal against a decision is not in the child's best interest[3].

Under the provisions of the Children Act 1989 children are able to seek leave to make an application for a Section 8 order either through a next friend or by acting in their own right[4]. It should also be pointed out that a parent is not deemed to be representing the child in care proceedings as the child is deemed to be a party in his own right to the proceedings[5].

1 *Woolf v Pemberton* (1877) 6 Ch D 19 and for definition of this term see Paragraph 37 n 3.
2 *Re Birchall, Wilson v Birchall* (1880) 16 Ch D 41, CA; and *Re Taylor's Application* [1972] 2 QB 369, [1972] 2 All ER 873, CA.
3 *Kinnear v DHSS* [1989] Fam Law 146.
4 Children Act 1989 s 10 (8) and see Family Proceedings Rules 1991, SI 1991/1247, r 9.2A (as inserted by the Family Proceedings (Amendment) Rules 1992, SI 1992/456, r 6).
5 Family Proceedings Rules 1991, App 3, Col iv and Family Proceedings Courts (Children Act 1989) Rules 1991, SI 1991/1395, Sch 2 Col iii.

93. Burial of child. The parent of a child has both a right and a duty to bury his deceased child[1]. This duty, like so many other important parental rights and duties, remains unaffected by the making of a care order[2].

1 See *R v Vann* (1851) 2 Den 325, 15 JP 802 approved in *Clarke v London General Omnibus Co Ltd* [1906] 2 KB 648, CA.
2 See *R v Gwynedd County Council, ex p B* [1991] 2 FLR 365, [1991] Fam Law 377, CA.

94. Consent to marriage. Where a child is to marry between the ages of sixteen and eighteen then under the terms of the Marriage Act 1949 he must have the requisite consent[1]. Where a party to an intended marriage, not being a widower or widow, is a minor and the marriage is intended to be solemnised on the authority of a Superintendent Registrar's certificate, whether by licence or without licence (or on the issue of a common licence by an ecclesiastical authority having power to issue it[2]) the consent of the following persons is required[3]:

1. each parent (if any) of the child who has parental responsibility for him; and each guardian (if any) of the child;
2. where a residence order is in force with respect to the child, the person or persons with whom he lives, or is to live, as a result of the order (instead of the consents of those persons mentioned in paragraph 1);
3. where a care order is in force with respect to the child, the local authority designated in the care order (in addition to the persons whose consent is necessary under paragraph 1); and
4. where at the time of consent being required neither a residence order nor care order is still in force but a residence order was in force with respect to the child immediately before he reached the age of sixteen, the person or persons with whom he lived or was to live as a result of the order instead of the persons referred to in paragraph 1[4].

It should be noted that where the minor is a ward of court the court's consent will be required[5]. Indeed wardship proceedings are sometimes instituted with a view to preventing undesirable associations and runaway marriages[6]. Where the Superintendent Registrar (or ecclesiastical authority)[7] is satisfied that the consent of any necessary person cannot be obtained by reason of his absence, inaccessibility or disability, the necessity for the consent will be dispensed with if there is any other person whose consent is also required[8]; and if there is no such other person the Registrar General (or master of the faculties[9]) may dispense with the necessity of obtaining any consent or the court[10] may give the necessary consent[11]. If any person whose consent is required refuses his consent the court may give the necessary consent[12].

A marriage solemnized without any necessary consent is nevertheless valid unless void for some other reason[13].

Consent is not required for the marriage of a minor, not being a widower or widow, after the publication of banns, but any person whose consent would have been required had the marriage been on a Superintendent Registrar's certificate, or a common licence, may openly and publicly declare his dissent in the church or chapel in which the banns are published at the time of the publication, whereupon the publication of the banns is void[14].

Similarly, any person whose consent is required to the issue of a Registrar's certificate may forbid the issue of such a certificate by writing "forbidden" opposite the entry in the marriage notice book and his name, address and the capacity in which he forbids the issue of the certificate, whereupon (unless the consent of the court is obtained) the notice of marriage and all proceedings thereon shall be void[15].

1 See the Marriage Act 1949 s 3 (as amended by Family Law Reform Act 1987, s 33 (1), Sch 2 para 9 and by Children Act 1989 s 108 (4), (7), Sch 12, para 5, Sch 15).
2 Marriage Act 1949 s 3 (2).
3 Ibid s 3 (1) (as amended).
4 Ibid s 3 (1A) (as inserted by Children Act 1989).
5 Ibid s 3 (6).
6 See Paragraph 228 post, and see also Table 7.
7 Marriage Act 1949 s 3 (1)(as amended).
8 In the case of a common licence: ibid s 3 (2). Ibid s 3 (1)(a).
9 The master of the faculties is the Dean of the Arches Court of Canterbury and Auditor of the Chancery Court of York; see the Ecclesiastical Jurisdiction Measure 1963 s 13 (1). Marriage Act 1949 s 3 (1) (as amended).
10 Court means the High Court, the county court for the district in which any applicant or respondent resides or a magistrates' court; ibid s 3 (5)(as amended).
11 Ibid s 3 (1)(b).
12 Ibid s 3 (1)(b).
13 See *R v Birmingham Inhabitants* (1828) 8 B & C 29.
14 Marriage Act 1949 s 3 (3).
15 Ibid s 30.

95. Application for consent to marry: High Court. Application for the court's consent to a minor's marriage where a necessary consent[1] is unobtainable[2] or has been refused[3], may be made to the High Court[4] although such applications are rare. Unless wardship proceedings are pending[5] application is by an originating summons[6] intituled in the matter of the minor and in the matter of the Marriage Act 1949. Usually the minor, by his next friend, will be the plaintiff and the parents or other persons whose consent is necessary will be the defendants. The summons must be served on each person whose necessary consent has been refused. Application should be made to the Family Division and the procedure is governed by the Family Proceedings Rules[7]. The application may be heard and determined by a district judge[8].

1 See Paragraph 94 ante.
2 See Paragraph 94 text to note 12 ante.
3 See Paragraph 94 text to note 13 ante.
4 Marriage Act 1949 s 3 (5)(as amended).
5 For applications to marry in the case of wards see Paragraph 236.
6 Family Proceedings Rules 1991, SI 1991/1247, r 3.20 which does not specify how the application is to be made. It is submitted that the correct procedure is as stated, using RSC App A Form No 10.

7 Family Proceedings Rules 1991, SI 1991/1247.
8 Ibid r 3.20 (2).

96. Application for consent to marry: county court. Application for the court's consent to a minor's marriage where a necessary consent is unobtainable or has been refused[1] may be made to the county court of the district in which the applicant or respondent resides[2]. The respondents are the persons whose consent is necessary and who have refused consent[3]. Application is by originating application a copy of which together with a notice of the hearing[4] must be served on each respondent not less than seven clear days before the date fixed for hearing[5]. It is not necessary for the application to be made by the applicant's next friend unless the court so directs[6]. The application may be heard and determined by a district judge[7] from whom an appeal lies to a judge.

1 See Paragraph 94 ante.
2 Marriage Act 1949 s 3 (5)(as amended).
3 Family Proceedings Rules 1991, SI 1991/1247, r 3.20 (4).
4 See County Court Form N8.
5 See Family Proceedings Rules 1991, r 3.20 (5).
6 Ibid r 3.20 (3).
7 Ibid r 3.20 (2).

97. Application for consent to marry: magistrates' court. Where a necessary consent[1] to a minor's marriage is unobtainable[2] or has been refused[3], personal application may be made for the court's consent, either orally or in writing[4], to a justice of the peace or to a magistrates' court having jurisdiction in the place in which any applicant or respondent resides[5]. Where the application is made in consequence of a refusal to give consent, the justice or the court may issue a notice of the application and of the time and place appointed for the hearing, directed to the person refusing consent[6]. Any such notice must be served on the person to whom it is directed in the same manner as if it were a summons[7]. The application is heard in the same way as if it were a complaint for an order[8], proceedings for obtaining the court's consent to marry are family proceedings[9] and special rules apply as to the composition of the court and the persons who may be present at the hearing[10]. The court's consent if given, should be in writing signed by one of the justices.

1 See Paragraph 94 ante.
2 See Paragraph 94 text to note 12 ante.
3 See ante Paragraph 94 text to note 13 ante.
4 See Magistrates' Courts (Guardianship of Minors) Rules 1974, SI 1974/706, r 5.(1)(as amended by SI 1979//953, SI 1980/1585 and SI 1989/384 and further amended and saved by the Family Proceedings Courts (Matrimonial Proceedings etc) Rules 1991, SI 1991/1991, Schs 2, 3).
5 Marriage Act 1949 s 3 (5)(as amended) and see Magistrates' Courts (Guardianship of Minors) Rules 1974 and note 4 supra.
6 See Magistrates' Courts (Guardianship of Minors) Rules 1974, r 5 (2)(as amended).
7 Ibid r 5 (3)(as amended).
8 See Magistrates' Courts (Guardianship of Minors) Rules 1974, r 5 (4)(as amended).
9 See Magistrates' Courts Act 1980 s 65 (1)(e)(as amended by the Children Act 1989 s 92 (1)).
10 Ibid s 69 (2)(as substituted by the Courts and Legal Services Act 1990 s 125 (3), Sch 18, para 25 and amended by the Children Act 1989 s 92 (1)).

2: ACQUISITION OF PARENTAL
RESPONSIBILITY

98. Married parents. Under the provisions of the Children Act 1989 where a child's father and mother are married to each other at the time of his birth they are each to have parental responsibility for the child[1]. Where a child is treated as legitimate under a range of different provisions[2] or is an adopted child[3] then his parents are treated as having parental responsibility[4].

1   Children Act 1989 s 2 (1).
2   See ibid s 2 (3) and the Legitimacy Act 1976 ss 1 (as amended by Family Law Reform Act 1987 s 28 (1)), 10.
3   Adoption Act 1976 Pt IV.
4   Children Act 1989 s 2 (3).

99. Unmarried parents. The Children Act provides[1] that where a child's father and mother were not married to each other at the time of his birth then the mother shall have parental responsibility for the child and the father shall not have parental responsibility for the child unless he acquires it as a result of a court order giving him parental responsibility[2] or he makes an agreement with the mother in the prescribed form[3] .The unmarried father may also obtain parental responsibility by being appointed a guardian of the child[4] or by marrying the mother[5] or by having a residence order made in his favour[6].

1   Children Act 1989 s 2 (2).
2   Children Act 1989 s 4 (1)(a).
3   Ibid s 4 (1)(b).
4   By the mother or by the court under ibid s 5.
5   See Paragraph 60 ante.
6   Children Act 1989 s 12 (1).

100. Parental responsibility orders. Under the provisions of the Children Act 1989 the court may upon the application by the child's father where the father and mother were not married to each other at the time of the child's birth and have not married since, order that the father have parental responsibility for the child[1]. Where there is any dispute as to the child's paternity this will have to be established before the court can proceed to make a parental responsibility order[2]. In deciding whether or not to make an order for parental responsibility the court must have regard to the principles laid down in Section 1 of the Act. Although the court is not specifically directed for the purposes of such an application to consider the welfare check list set out in the Act[3] nevertheless these factors are likely to be considered relevant and certainly the intention behind the legislation was to promote relationships between parents and children even where the parents were unmarried. Such orders under the old law were made even where there was likely to be extreme opposition from the other parent, where the child was in local authority care or was about to be freed for adoption[4].

1   Children Act 1989 s 4 (1)(a) and see *Re H (A Minor) (Contact and Parental Responsibility)* [1993] 1 FCR 85.
2   See Paragraphs 70-78 ante on establishing parentage.
3   See Children Act 1989 s 1 (3).
4   See *Re C (Minors) (Parental Rights)* [1992] 2 All ER 86, CA, [1992] 1 FLR 1. See *D v Hereford and Worcester County Council* [1991] Fam 14, [1991] 2 All ER 177; *Re H*

(Minors) (Local Authority: Parental Rights (No 3)) [1991] Fam 151, [1991] 2 All ER 185 and see now *Re H* sup cit n 1. See also *Children First? Reports in Unmarried Parent Cases* [1991] JSWFL 442.

101. Procedure governing applications for parental responsibility orders. The procedure governing applications for parental responsibility orders under Section 4 is laid down in the relevant rules of court[1] and is exactly the same in all points as for any application made under the Children Act 1989[2]. As far as an application for a parental responsibility order is concerned the applicant must file the application in respect of each child in the appropriate form set out in the rules[3]. Where the court decides to make a parental responsibility order it must be set out in the appropriate form of an order as set out in the rules and again served in the normal way[4].

1 Family Proceedings Rules 1991, SI 1991/1247 and Family Proceedings Courts (Children Act 1989) Rules 1991, SI 1991/1395.
2 See Paragraphs 9-27 ante.
3 See Form CHA 2.
4 See Form CHA 1.

102. Parental responsibility agreements. Under the provisions of the Children Act 1989 where a child's father and mother were not married to each other at the time of his birth, then the father and mother may by an agreement termed a "parental responsibility agreement" provide for the father also to have parental responsibility for the child[1]. Such an agreement has to be made in the prescribed form[2] and recorded in the prescribed manner. The form is expressed in clear and comprehensible language and warns the parents that the agreement seriously affects their legal position, and advises them to seek legal advice before completing it[3]. The form goes on to explain the circumstances in which the agreement can come to an end[4]. The relevant regulations provide that the agreement is to be recorded by filing it together with two copies at the Principal Registry of the Family Division of the High Court[5]. There is no fee charged. The Registry will then forward a sealed copy to the mother[6]. The record of any agreement is open to inspection by any person upon written request and payment of a fee[7].

1 Children Act 1989 s 4 (1)(b).
2 Parental Responsibility Agreement Regulations 1991, SI 1991/1478, Reg 2, Schedule and see Form 1 post.
3 Children Act 1989 s 4 (2)(a), (b).
4 See the Form as set out in the Schedule to the Parental Responsibility Agreement Regulations 1991: Form 1 post.
5 Ibid reg 3 (1).
6 Ibid reg 3 (2).
7 Ibid reg 3 (3).

103. Consequences of the making of parental responsibility orders and agreements. Wherever a parental responsibility order has been made by the court or a properly recorded parental responsibility agreement has been made and filed at the Principal Registry of the Family Division then parental responsibility will be conferred upon the unmarried father[1]. Such parental responsibility will be shared with the mother[2] or where the mother has died with the mother's formerly appointed guardian[3]. The unmarried father may also be sharing parental responsibility with some other third person in whose favour a residence order has been made[4]. Once the unmarried father has parental responsibility by virtue of a court order or an agreement, then these responsibilities are the same as those possessed by any other parent[5]. Whilst, however, the making of an order or an agreement gives parental responsibility to the unmarried father it does not affect the child's status. Thus, the child will not be able to take British citizenship through his unmarried father nor will he be able to succeed to a title of honour through his parents[6]. As with the former law relating to parental rights orders, it is likely that an order granting a father parental responsibility would still be made not withstanding that a number of the rights associated with such an order would be unenforceable under prevailing conditions in any particular case. Thus, in *Re C*[7] where the first instance judge had declined to make a parental rights order on the ground of unenforceability due to the mother's implacable opposition, the Court of Appeal ruled that the father's conduct had shown sufficient commitment to justify giving him the legal status of a legitimate father, and that an inability to exercise the full range of parental rights was no reason to refuse an order.

1 Children Act 1989 s 4.
2 Ibid s 2 (2).
3 Ibid s 5.
4 Ibid ss 8, 12 (2), and s 2 (5), (6).
5 See Paragraphs 7994 ante.
6 See British Nationality Act 1981 s 50 (1).
7 *Re C (Minors) (Parental Rights)* [1992] 2 All ER 86, CA and see also *Re H* sup cit Paragraph 100 n 1 where the opposition came from the stepfather and prevented a contact order being made to a father, who had been granted a parental responsibility order.

104. Duration of parental responsibility orders or agreements. A parental responsibility order or agreement will automatically come to an end when the child reaches the age of eighteen[1]. It is submitted that where the child's father subsequently marries the mother, the child is legitimated by the marriage and, therefore, falls within the extended definition of a child whose parents were married to each other at the time of his birth[2]. In such circumstances the fact of marriage gives parental responsibility to the father and this cannot subsequently be ended by anything other than the child's adoption[3].

A parental responsibility order or agreement may only be brought to an end by application being made to the court for a court order to that effect. An application may be made by anyone who had parental responsibility for the child including the father himself[4] and an application may also be made by the child himself provided the court is convinced that he has sufficient understanding[5]. In determining whether or not to terminate a parental responsibility order or agreement, the court is bound by the welfare principle[6] and also by the consideration that discharging an order must be deemed to be better than making no order at all[7]. It should be noted that the procedural provisions relating to applications for a parental responsibility order will also apply to applications to terminate an order or a parental responsibility agreement but no special forms of application or forms of order for termination are laid down in the relevant provisions in the rules[8].

1 Children Act 1989 s 91 (7), (8).
2 Ibid s 2 (3) and Family Law Reform Act 1987 s 1.
3 Children Act 1989 s 2 (1).
4 Ibid s 4 (3)(a).
5 Ibid s 4 (3)(b).
6 Ibid s 1 (1).
7 Ibid s 1 (5).

8   See Family Proceedings Rules 1991, SI 1991/1247, r. 4.3 (1) or Family Proceedings
    Courts (Children Act 1989) Rules 1991, SI 1991/1395, r 3 (1).

105. Appointment of unmarried father as the child's guardian. A further way in
which an unmarried father may acquire parental responsibility will be where the
mother has appointed him guardian upon her death[1] or where an unmarried father
applies after the mother's death to be appointed as guardian[2] instead of applying for
parental responsibility under the provisions of Section 4 of the Children Act 1989.
In practice, however, it should be pointed out that there would seem to be no reason
why an unmarried father should seek to apply to court for appointment as guardian
where in reality he would be better off with an order for parental responsibility under
the provisions of Section 4 of the Children Act 1989[3].

1   Children Act 1989 s 5 (3).
2   Ibid s 5 (1).
3   Compare ibid s 4 (3), (4) with ibid s 6 (7). See *Re H (A Minor) (Contact and Parental
    Responsibility)* [1993] 1 FCR 85.

106. Acquisition of parental responsibility by other persons. In addition to
unmarried fathers seeking to acquire parental responsibility by means of court
orders, other persons who obtain a residence order may acquire parental
responsibility as a result of the making of such an order[1]. Special provision has been
made to enable a person in whose favour a residence order has been made to have
parental responsibility whilst the order remains in force[2]. It should, however, be
pointed out that such persons do not have the same extensive rights as married
parents or unmarried fathers who have obtained a parental responsibility order or
made a parental responsibility agreement[3]. Thus those persons who acquire parental
responsibility as the result of a residence order do not acquire the right to consent to,
or to refuse to consent to, the making of an application to free a child for adoption,
nor to agree or refuse to agree to the making of an adoption order nor the right to
appoint a guardian[4]. Where a local authority acquires parental responsibilities under
the provisions of a care order[5], it, too, is subject to a number of restrictions which are,
however, more extensive than those which apply to ordinary individuals. Thus the
local authority cannot agree to the making of a freeing order nor to the making of an
adoption order and nor can it appoint a guardian for the child[6], nor is the authority
able to cause the child to be brought up in any religious persuasion other than that in
which he would have been brought up if the order had not been made[7] nor are they
permitted to change the child's surname[8].

1   Children Act 1989 s 12 (2). See also Paragraph 123 post.
2   See the Children Act 1989 ss 5 (6) and 12(2).
3   Ibid s 12.
4   Ibid s 12 (3) and see Paragraph 123 post.
5   Children Act 1989 s 33 (3)(a).
6   Ibid s 33 (6)(b).
7   Ibid s 33 (6)(a).
8   Ibid s 33 (7). See Paragraph 177 post and also Paragraph 90 ante.

107. Sharing parental responsibility for the child. The provisions of the Children
Act 1989 lay down clearly that more than one person may have parental
responsibility for the same child at the same time[1]. It is also emphasised that a parent
does not cease to have parental responsibilities solely because some other person
acquires such responsibility[2], and indeed it should be pointed out that the holder of

a residence order will not lose parental responsibility solely because an unmarried father obtains it[3]. However, where it is a non-parent who holds parental responsibility by virtue of a residence order, then when the residence order is discharged the non-parent will lose parental responsibility[4]. Where those sharing parental responsibility do not agree as to its exercise then any problem may have to be sorted out using either a prohibited steps order or a specific issue order[5].

1 Children Act 1989 s 2 (5).
2 Ibid s 2 (6).
3 Ibid s 4.
4 Ibid s 12 (2).
5 Ibid s 8 (1).

108. Independent exercise of parental responsibility. The Children Act 1989 expressly provides that each person who holds parental responsibility may act alone and without the other or others in meeting that responsibility[1]. Clearly there is every expectation that those with parental responsibility will consult together and reach an agreement on any steps to be taken, but there is also recognition of the fact that one cannot have a legally enforceable duty to consult[2]. Where one parent or any other person with parental responsibility proposes to take a step which any other persons with parental responsibility object to then they have the right to take action to prevent the independent exercise of parental responsibility by applying to the court for a prohibited steps order or in certain circumstances for a specific issue order[3].

This ability to take independent action is subject to two restrictions. The Children Act provides that no steps shall be taken to affect the operation of any enactment which requires the consent of more than one person in a matter affecting the child and thus agreement to adoption, consent to marriage, and consent to removal of the child from the United Kingdom under the provisions of the Child Abduction Act 1984 cannot be exercised without all those persons with parental responsibility giving their consent[4]. The second restriction is that any step which a person with parental responsibility takes must be one which is compatible with any orders which have been made with respect to the child under the provisions of the Children Act[5].

1 Children Act 1989 s 2 (7).
2 See the recommendations of the Law Commission Review of Family Law, Child Law, Guardianship and Custody, Law Commission Paper no. 172, para 2.10.
3 Under the provisions of the Children Act 1989 s 8.
4 Children Act 1989 s 2 (7) and see Adoption Act 1976, Marriage Act 1949 Statutes and Child Abduction Act 1984 s 1 (as amended by Children Act 1989 s 108 (4), Sch 12 para 37).
5 Children Act 1989 s 2 (8).

109. Surrender, transfer or delegation of parental responsibility. The Children Act 1989 further provides that a person who has parental responsibility for a child may not surrender or transfer any part of that responsibility to another person but may, however, arrange for some or all of it to be met by one or more persons acting on his behalf[1]. This, therefore, allows the delegation of parental responsibility and that can be made to someone who already has parental responsibility or to those persons who do not, for example nannies, child-minders, schools or other persons looking after the child[2]. Where persons to whom parental responsibility is delegated under these provisions do not have parental responsibility themselves then they may have to rely on the provision in the Children Act which allows them to take whatever steps are necessary where they have physical possession of the child provided such steps can be shown to be for the purposes of safeguarding or promoting the child's welfare[3]. Such steps would encompass giving consent to emergency medical treatment or to a tetanus injection following a road accident, but would not encompass giving consent to prophylactic vaccinations. In such circumstances, the parent or other person holding parental responsibility must have been given the necessary information in order to be able to decide whether to give consent or not. Health personnel would be ill-advised to proceed with such vaccinations of a child accompanied by the parent's delegate without having obtained a signed consent form from a person holding parental responsibility. Any consent form should further provide for an acknowledgment of receipt of all the relevant information necessary to enable a proper evaluation of risks attendant upon such vaccinations. Wherever a parent has delegated parental responsibility this does not, however, discharge him from any liability for failure on his part to meet his parental responsibilities for the child[4].

1 Children Act 1989 s 2 (9).
2 Ibid s 2 (10).
3 Ibid s 3 (5).
4 Ibid s 2 (11).

3: GUARDIANSHIP

110. Introduction. The Children Act 1989 effected fundamental reforms of the law of guardianship. The Children Act 1989 repealed the provisions of the Guardianship of Minors Act 1971 and of the Guardianship Act 1973[1] and thus the rule that a father was the natural guardian of his legitimate child and that on the death of one of the married parents of a child the other became the child's guardian[2] have both been repealed. As has already been seen the new emphasis in the Children Act is on the concept of joint equal parental responsibility for a child possessed by both the child's parents provided that they were at the time of the child's birth married or later married to each other[3]. The effect of the Children Act 1989 therefore is to draw a very clear distinction between parents who are able to exercise the full range of parental responsibilities and guardians who are subject to some limitations in the exercise of their powers[4]. It is for this reason that it would be generally accepted that an unmarried father should apply for parental responsibility under the Act rather than apply to be appointed a guardian of his child in the event of the mother's death[5]. Nevertheless an unmarried father may acquire the limited range of guardian's parental responsibilities by having been appointed the child's guardian by the child's mother[6].

1 Children Act 1989, s 108 (7), Sch 15.
2 Ibid s 2 (4) and by the operation of the repeal of Guardianship of Minors Act 1971 s 3.
3 Children Act 1989 s 2 (1).
4 Ibid ss 5, 6.
5 Ibid s 5 but note a court appointment can be brought to an end by order of the court: ibid s 6 (7).
6 See Paragraph 105 ante.

111. Court's power to appoint guardians. Under the provisions of the Children Act 1989 a High Court, county court or magistrates' court[1] may appoint an individual to be a child's guardian, where the child has no parent with parental responsibility for him, or a residence order has been made with respect to the child in favour of a parent or guardian of his who has died whilst the order was in force[2], although this may be extended to include more than one person[3]. It should be noted for these purposes therefore that the court could make an order appointing someone to be the child's guardian even where the child's unmarried father was alive provided he has not obtained an order for parental responsibility or made an agreement with the mother[4]. The court's powers to appoint a guardian may be exercised in any family proceedings either upon an application being made in the prescribed form[5] or where the court considers that the order should be made even though no application has actually been made[6]. The order should be made in the prescribed form laid down in the rules[7].

1 Children Act 1989 s 92 (7).
2 Ibid s 5 (1).
3 Ibid and see also Interpretation Act 1978 s 6 (c).
4 See Paragraph 104 ante.
5 See Form CHA 3.
6 Children Act 1989 s 5 (2).
7 See Form CHA 4.

112. Making an application. Any person may apply to the court to be appointed as a guardian of a child and there is no provision requiring for leave of the court to be sought before an application is made[1]. There appears to be a grey area around the issue of whether an appointment would be made in respect of a married child[2]. Exactly the same procedural rules relating to applications for parental responsibility orders apply to applications to appoint a child's guardian[3]. Application must be made in the appropriate form laid down in the rules and it is provided that the applicant must state his reasons for making the application and his plans for the child therein[4]. Where the court determines on making an order appointing a guardian then, again, this must be done in the form laid down in the rules[5].

1 Children Act 1989 s 5 (1).
2 See ibid s 105 (1) which defines "child" as "a person under the age of 18".
3 See Paragraph 100 ante.
4 See Family Proceedings Rules 1991, SI 1991/1247, App 1 Form CHA 3.
5 Ibid Form CHA 4.

113. Exercise of the courts' powers. In determining whether or not to make an appointment of a guardian for the child the court is, of course, bound by the welfare paramountcy principle[1]. Where the court is only being requested to make an order relating to the appointment of a guardian, it will not be required to have regard to the statutory check list, although in practice this will be done. Where, however, an application is also being made by the guardian for a Section 8 residence order and that application is being opposed by for example an unmarried father, then the check list must be applied[2]. In trying to determine what order if any the court should make there are now new powers to allow the court to order a welfare report which were not formerly available to courts under the previous legislation[3].

1 Children Act 1989 s 1 (1), (5).
2 Ibid s 1 (4) applying s 1 (3).
3 Ibid s 7.

114. Appointments of guardians by parents and guardians. Any parent with parental responsibility and any guardian may appoint another individual to be the child's guardian in the event of their death[1]. As noted earlier a parent or guardian may appoint more than one person as a guardian[2] although an additional guardian can be appointed at a later date[3]. The Children Act further expressly provides there is nothing to prevent an appointment being made by two or more persons jointly[4]. The previously strict controls requiring the appointment of a guardian to be made in a will or by deed have now been relaxed by virtue of the provisions in the Children Act[5], and such an appointment may therefore be made by means of either a deed or will since these would satisfy the requirements of the Children Act but an appointment may also be made by means of some document provided it is signed at the direction of the person making the appointment, in his presence and in the presence of two witnesses who each attest the signature[6]. It should be stressed that no special document is therefore needed and indeed it should be pointed out that a minor who is a parent and wishes to appoint a guardian of the child[7] would have to do so by document since they are not capable of making a valid will[8].

1 Children Act 1989 s 5 (3), (4).
2 See Paragraph 89 ante.
3 Children Act 1989 s 6 (1).
4 Ibid s 5 (10).
5 Ibid s 5 (5)(a).
6 Ibid s 5 (5)(b).
7 It should be clear from the document that there is an obvious intention to appoint a guardian.
8 Wills Act 1837 s 7.

115. Revocation and disclaimer of appointment. The Children Act provides[1] that a later appointment revokes an earlier appointment of a guardian including one which is made in an unrevoked will or codicil unless it is clear expressly or by implication that the purpose of the later appointment is in fact to appoint an additional guardian[2]. The Children Act goes on to provide that an appointment can be expressly revoked by a written and dated document which is signed by the parent or guardian or at his direction in his presence and in the presence of two witnesses who each attest his signature[3]. An appointment may also be revoked (other than one made in a will or codicil) if, intending to revoke it, the appointor destroys the document by which it was made or has someone else destroy it in his presence[4]. Where an appointment was made in a will or codicil, it is automatically revoked if the will or codicil is revoked[5], whether intentionally or by operation of law[6].

The Children Act provides, further, for an appointee to disclaim his appointment as guardian[7]. The disclaimer must be in the form of a written instrument signed by the appointee[8] and must be recorded in accordance with any regulations made by the Lord Chancellor[9]. The decision to disclaim must be made within a reasonable time of the appointee's knowing that the appointment has taken effect. In exceptional situations where the appointee will be sharing parental responsibility with the surviving parent[10], it is likely that the parent will wish to press for a decision as to whether or not the guardian has accepted his appointment. There seems to be no provision to cater for the situation where the guardian seeks to disclaim too late and thus it would appear that the guardian's appointment would take effect. It is clear therefore that parents should seek to obtain a clear indication from a person to be appointed as a guardian that they will accept the appointment.

1   Children Act 1989 s 6.
2   Ibid s 6 (1).
3   Ibid s 6 (2).
4   Ibid s 6 (3).
5   Ibid s 6 (4).
6   For example by a subsequent marriage.
7   Children Act 1989 s 6 (5) and (6). Under the old law the guardian had the right to refuse the appointment, see the Guardianship of Minors Act 1971 s 3.
8   There are no express provisions for the appointee to be able to direct someone else to sign on his behalf unlike the provisions relating to the appointments of a guardian, nor is there express provision requiring that the instrument be dated although this clearly ought to be done.
9   No such regulations have yet been made.
10 See Paragraph 107 ante.

116. Date when appointment takes effect. A major change effected by the Children Act 1989, and one little appreciated by most of the population, is that the appointment of a guardian for the child no longer automatically takes effect upon the death of the appointing parent[1]. The Children Act provides that an appointment only takes effect immediately upon the death of the appointing person where immediately following that person's death the child has no parent with parental responsibility[2] or where there was a residence order (or existing custody order) in favour of the person making the appointment immediately before his death, unless that a residence order (or existing custody order) was also made in favour of the surviving parent[3]. Where the child therefore does have a surviving parent who holds parental responsibility the new law provides that the appointment of the guardian by the deceased parent will only take effect upon the death of the surviving parent with parental responsibility[4]. It should be noted that the Children Act provides under the transitional provisions that those who were guardians at the date of the commencement of the Act should continue to be treated as guardians provided that such appointment had taken effect before the implementation of the Act[5].

1   Children Act 1989 s 5 (7).
2   Ibid s 5 (7). See also ibid Sch 14 para 8 (2).
3   Ibid s 5 (8) ie where a joint residence or custody order had been made the surviving joint order holder automatically steps into the deceased's parents shoes and has sole parental responsibility.
4   Ibid s 5. See also ibid Sch 14 paras 12-14.
5   Ibid Sch 14 para 12 (1).

117. Effects of guardianship under the provisions of the Children Act. A guardian is deemed to have parental responsibility for the child and thus stands in the same position as a parent with regard to the exercise of rights, duties, powers, responsibilities and authority which a parent has[1]. However, the responsibility of the guardian does not include liability to maintain a child out of his own income, unlike parents[2], nor is he liable for social security purposes[3] nor for the purposes of contribution orders to local authorities[4] where the child is being looked after by the local authority[5].

A guardian appointed under the provisions of the Children Act can himself appoint a guardian to take his place in the event of his death[6]. However, guardians have no rights of succession upon the child's death, nor can a child derive a right to

British citizenship from his guardian. Guardians do, however, gain certain rights which others holding a residence order do not obtain which include the right to consent or withhold consent to adoption or freeing for adoption or indeed the right to appoint a guardian[7].

1 Children Act 1989 ss 5 (6) applying ibid s 3 (1).
2 Child Support Act 1991 s 1
3 Social Security Act 1986 s 26.
4 Children Act 1989 s 29 (4).
5 See also Sch 2 Part III para 21 (3).
6 Ibid s 5 (4).
7 See Paragraph 114 ante.

118. Termination of guardianship. The duties of a guardian will come to an end when a child reaches the age of eighteen[1]. They will also come to an end when a child dies[2]. The death of the sole guardian will also bring guardianship to an end unless he has taken the step of appointing a successor[3]. Guardianship may also be brought to an end upon an application being made to the High Court, a county court or magistrates' court on the application of anyone with parental responsibility for the child, on the application of the child where he is given leave to apply[4] and by the court of its own motion in any family proceedings[5]. An application must be made in the appropriate form[6] and as with an application to appoint a guardian the applicant must state on the form his reasons for applying to terminate the guardianship and any plans for the child[7]. Where the court orders termination of the appointment[8] it may take the step of appointing another person to be the guardian of the child where it considers that this is in the paramount interests of the child[9]. In trying to reach its decision the court may call for a welfare officer's report and may also though it is not required to do so take into account the welfare check list laid down in the Act[10]. As noted before, the effect of the child's marriage on guardianship is still a grey area and it is unfortunate that the opportunity was not taken in the Children Act to clarify this matter. Guardianship will of course come to an end on the child reaching the age of majority but it seems likely that even if the guardianship is presumed to continue it is unlikely that the guardian would seek to exercise his powers under the Act[11].

1 Children Act 1989 s 91 (7), (8).
2 See also Paragraph 93 ante.
3 Children Act 1989 s 5 (4).
4 Ibid s 6 (7).
5 Ibid s 6 (7)(c).
6 The application must be made in Form CHA 5.
7 Ibid s 6 (7)(c).
8 The court order must be in Form CHA 6.
9 Children Act 1989 ss 1 (1), 5 (2).
10 Ibid ss 1 (3), 7.
11 See Children Act 1989 ss 5, 6.

119. Guardian to receive foreign legacy. The High Court has always had an inherent jurisdiction to appoint a guardian of a minor's estate. This has commonly been done where a minor has been a beneficiary under a foreign will, or where he has been awarded damages abroad, and someone has been needed who can give a valid discharge on his behalf. Another example has been where shares have been vested in a minor and upon amalgamation or reconstruction it has been necessary to seek the court's appointment of a guardian to sign the necessary share transfers, subject, of course, to being satisfied that the transaction is in the minor's interest. However, this jurisdiction has now been removed, except in so far as rules of court provide for its exercise[1]. The jurisdiction is not now likely to be invoked as the Children Act gives anyone with parental responsibility "the rights, powers and duties which a guardian of the child's estate (appointed, before the commencement of Section 5, to act generally) would have had in relation to the child and his property"[2]. Rules of court have made provision for the appointment of the Official Solicitor to be a guardian of the estate of a child in certain circumstances[3].

1 Children Act 1989 s 5 (11), (12).
2 Ibid s 3 (2).
3 RSC Ord 80 r 13 (as inserted by RSC (Amendment No 4) 1991, SI 1991/2671). For an example see RSC Appendix A Form No 11.

CHAPTER 5: RESIDENCE, CONTACT AND ASSOCIATED ORDERS

120. Introduction. Residence, contact, specific issue, prohibited steps[1] and family assistance[2] orders are all orders which can be made by the courts in "family proceedings" as defined by the Children Act 1989[3]. The definition of family proceedings is very wide and embraces: proceedings under the inherent jurisdiction of the High Court in relation to children; proceedings under Parts I (e.g. applications for parental responsibility by unmarried fathers), II (e.g. applications for orders in matrimonial or adoption proceedings) and IV (e.g. applications for care, supervision or education supervision orders) of the Children Act 1989; and to proceedings under the Matrimonial Causes Act 1973, the Domestic Violence and Matrimonial Proceedings Act 1976, the Adoption Act 1976, the Domestic Proceedings and Magistrates' Courts Act 1978, proceedings under Sections 1 and 9 of the Matrimonial Homes Act 1983, and finally to proceedings under Part III of the Matrimonial and Family Proceedings Act 1984[4].

It should be noted that for the purpose of making Section 8 orders the definition of family proceedings does not include proceedings for emergency protection, child assessment or recovery orders under Part V of the Act, but it does encompass care and supervision order proceedings under Part IV of the Children Act 1989. Thus the closer alignment of public law and private law proceedings is underlined by allowing the making of Section 8 and Section 16 orders in care and associated proceedings wherever this would be in the paramount interests of the child[5].

It is not, however, any longer possible for courts hearing matrimonial and other private law proceedings involving children to make committal to care or supervision orders. Where the court is concerned in private law proceedings about a child and the possibility of harm, it can now under Section 37 of the Children Act 1989 only direct the local authority to investigate the circumstances and determine whether or not to apply for a care or supervision order[6]. Where the court is concerned about more short term problems or the effects of adjustments in family relationships or of orders following proceedings in circumstances where it might previously have made a supervision order, it can now make a family assistance order under Section 16 of the Children Act 1989[7]. Domestic violence and adoption proceedings are also included within the wide definition of "family proceedings", again to emphasise the increased range of options available to the courts when trying to meet the needs of children. The basic intention of the Children Act 1989 is to fit the orders to the child and not the child to the orders. It must be pointed out, however, that in domestic violence proceedings, unlike divorce proceedings in the county court or applications for financial provision in the magistrates' courts, there is no requirement that the court should first consider the needs of the child when granting orders[8] and in a lot of cases the need to obtain an emergency order may well be the primary concern.

The fact that wardship proceedings under the inherent jurisdiction of the High Court are included in the definition of "family proceedings" further emphasises the fact that there is little point in invoking that jurisdiction if the outcome, the making of Section 8 orders, is likely to be exactly the same as making an application in proceedings proceedings under Parts I and II[9] or making a free standing[10] application for such orders.

Applications for orders for financial provision in respect of children can be made under the provisions in Section 15 and Schedule 1 of the Children Act 1989[11]. The scheme of provision in Schedule 1 replaces provision for financial orders formerly found in the Family Law Reform Act 1969[12], Guardianship of Minors Act 1971 and Guardianship Act 1973[13], Children Act 1975[14] and the Family Law Reform Act 1987[15] as all these financial provisions and most of the statutes are now repealed by the Children Act 1989[16]. Thus, where proceedings relate to the child alone and are not linked to matrimonial proceedings, applicants must use the provisions of Schedule 1[17]. Where the issue of financial provision for children arises in matrimonial proceedings, then the court may still make orders pursuant to the provisions in the Matrimonial Causes Act 1973[18] or the Domestic Proceedings and Magistrates' Courts Act 1978[19].

It should be noted that the Child Support Act 1991 comes into force fully in April 1993[20] and thus the system just described will thenceforward only apply in respect of children who are not "*qualifying children*"[21] within the provisions of that Act, for example stepchildren or children who are living abroad, or for payments which are other than for maintenance for example, school fees, or capital payments, or to cover special situations for example children with disabilities. For all other children, the scheme introduced by the 1991 Act applies. Thus a "*person with care*"[22] of a "*qualifying child*"[23] (and it has been suggested that this could include a local authority with care of the child[24]) may apply to a "*child support officer*"[25] for a "*maintenance assessment*"[26] in order for the quantum of child support maintenance to be fixed by reference to formulae set out in a Schedule to the Act[27] as expanded upon by Regulations.[28] The process is a bureaucratic and not a judicial one, and any appeals against the amount of an assessment will go in the first instance to Child Support Appeal Tribunal[29], thence to a hearing before the Child Support Commissioner[30], and only on a point of law could a matter go further to the Court of Appeal[31].

1   Children Act 1989 s 8 (1).
2   Ibid s 16.
3   Ibid s 8 (3), (4).
4   Children Act 1989; Matrimonial Causes Act 1973; Domestic Violence and Matrimonial Proceedings Act 1976 ; Adoption Act 1976; Domestic Proceedings and Magistrates' Court Act 1978; Matrimonial Homes Act 1983 ss 1, 9; Matrimonial and Family Proceedings Act 1984.
5   Ibid s 1 (3)(g), (4), (5).
6   Children Act 1989 s 37 (1).
7   Children Act 1989 s 15 and Paragraph 140 post.
8   As there is under Domestic Proceedings and Magistrates Courts Act 1978 s 3 (1) and Matrimonial Causes Act 1973 s 25 (1).

9   Children Act 1989 ss 8, 16.
10 An application for orders under ibid s 8 can be made by anyone who is entitled to do so
    under the provisions of s 10 (2)(5) and by anyone else who obtains the leave of the court
    to make an application by satisfying the criteria laid down in s 10 (9).
11 Children Act 1989 s 15 and see s 16.
12 Family Law Reform Act 1969 s 6.
13 Guardianship of Minors Act 1971 ss 913, Guardianship Act 1973 s 2 (4).
14 Children Act 1975 ss 34-35.
15 Family Law Reform Act 1987 s 4.
16 Children Act 1989 s 108 (7) and Sch 15.
17 Children Act 1989 s 15. Orders for financial provision for children are treated separately,
    see Paragraphs 142-158.
18 Matrimonial Causes Act 1973 s 23.
19 Domestic Proceedings and Magistrates' Courts Act 1978 ss 2, 6, 7.
20 5th April 1993. For further detail see post Paragraph 141.
21 As defined by Child Support Act 1991 s 3(1)
22 Ibid as defined in s 3(3)
23 Ibid s 1 and s 3(1)
24 See post Paragraph 141 and see "Child Maintenance : The New Law" R Bird (Jordans)
    (1991) at p42.
25 Child Support Act 1991 s 13
26 Ibid s 54
27 Ibid Sch 1
28 See The Child Support (Maintenance Assessment Procedure) Regulations 1992 SI 1992/
    1813; The Child Support (Maintenance Assessments and Special Cases) Regulations
    1992 SI 1992/1815
29 Child Support Act 1991 s 18
30 Ibid s 24
31 Ibid s 25

121. Jurisdiction. *General* — As was noted earlier[1] orders made under Section 8 of
the Children Act 1989[2], other than variations or discharges, are Part I orders within
the meaning of the Family Law Act 1986[3]. Orders made pursuant to the exercise of
the High Court's inherent jurisdiction where these deal with the residence of, contact
with or education of, the child are also Part I orders[4]. Provided, therefore,
jurisdiction is not excluded under the terms of the Family Law Act 1986, the court
has power to make any of the orders in Part II of the Children Act 1989. In
proceedings for divorce, nullity or judicial separation in the county court and High
Court and in proceedings for financial provision in the magistrates' courts, the court
concerned must decide whether there are any children of the family in relation to
whom it should exercise any of its powers under the Children Act 1989[5].

  Children of the Family — A child of the family is defined in both the
Matrimonial Causes Act 1973[6] and the Domestic Proceedings and Magistrates'
Courts Act 1978[7] as a child of both parties to a marriage, and any other child who is
not a foster child and who has been "treated" by both of those parties as a child of their
family. "Child" in relation to one or both parties to a marriage includes an illegitimate
or adopted child of that party, or as the case may be, of both parties. A child will be
held to be a child of the family even where one party treated the child as such in the
erroneous belief that the child was his[8]. A child being cared for by relatives does not
qualify as a child of the relative's family for the purposes of these pieces of
legislation. The courts will thus have jurisdiction where the child is a "child of the

family", and in the magistrates' courts may exercise their powers to make orders in respect of children up to the age of eighteen[9], whereas in proceedings in the county court and High Court the court can exercise its powers in divorce, nullity and judicial separation proceedings in relation to children of the family under the age of sixteen or in respect of a child who has reached that age and the court specifically directs that the powers shall be applied[10].

Protection of Children's Welfare — In proceedings for divorce, nullity or judicial separation the decision whether or not to exercise any powers to make orders under the Children Act 1989 is made initially by a District Judge on considering the parties' written statements of the arrangements for the children[11]. Where having scrutinised the available documentary evidence, the District Judge is satisfied that the court need not exercise such powers he must certify accordingly and there will be no court hearing[12]. Where he is not so satisfied, the District Judge may give one of a number of directions: that either of the parties shall file further evidence relating to the arrangements for the children (and the direction shall specify the matters to be dealt with in the further evidence); that a welfare report on the children or any of them be prepared; that the parties or any of them shall attend a hearing before him at a specified time and place; and the parties must be notified accordingly[13]. Where the court gives such a direction, notice must be given to all the parties. Where after receipt of further evidence or a welfare report the District Judge determines that the court must exercise its powers under the Act, or upon one of the parties filing an application for an order which is opposed the case must be listed for hearing before an appropriate judge designated as a divorce county court or family hearing centre judge[14]. In such circumstances the District Judge may direct that the decree of divorce or nullity is not to be made absolute, or the decree of judicial separation is not to be granted until the court orders otherwise but only where there are exceptional circumstances which make this desirable in the interest of the child[15].

As far as the magistrates' court is concerned, when an application for financial provision is made under the Domestic Proceedings and Magistrates' Courts Act 1978, the court must not dismiss the application or make a final order until it has decided whether or not to exercise any of its powers under the Children Act 1989[16].

Applications involving children not linked to divorce or financial provision — Applications for Section 8 orders not linked to divorce or applications for financial provision can be made in any family proceedings[17] pursuant to s 10 of the Children Act 1989 and the application itself may be the start of such proceedings or in proceedings invoking the inherent jurisdiction of the High Court. Applications under Section 10 of the Children Act 1989 may be instituted in any one of the three courts but the jurisdictional rules applicable under the Family Law Act 1986 as amended by the Children Act apply, thus the child must be habitually resident in England and Wales or present in England and Wales and not habitually resident in Scotland or Northern Ireland[18], and at the time of application there must be no pending matrimonial proceedings in Scotland or Northern Ireland[19].

1 See Paragraph 3 ante.
2 Children Act 1989 s 8.
3 Family Law Act 1986 s 1 (1)(a)(as substituted by the Children Act 1989 s 108 (5) Sch 13 para 63).
4 Ibid s 1 (1)(d)(as substituted) but does not include variations or revocations of such orders.
5 Under Matrimonial Causes Act 1973 s 41 (1)(as substituted by the Children Act 1989 s 108 (4) Sch 12 para 31) and Domestic Proceedings and Magistrates' Courts Act 1978 s 8 (1)(as substituted by the Children Act 1989 s 108 (5) Sch 13 para 36).

6 Matrimonial Causes Act 1973 s 52 (1)(as amended by the Children Act 1989 s 108 (4) Sch 12 para 33).
7 Domestic Proceedings and Magistrates' Courts Act 1978 s 88 (1).
8 *W (R J) v W (S J)* [1972] Fam 152, [1971] 3 All ER 303.
9 Domestic Proceedings and Magistrates' Courts Act 1978 s 3 (1). Although in the case of Section 8 orders the court is constrained by Children Act 1989 s 9 (6).
10 Matrimonial Causes Act 1973 s 41 (3)(as substituted by the Children Act 1989 s 108 (4) Sch 12 para 31) and Children Act 1989 s 9 (6).
11 Family Proceedings Rules 1991, SI 1991/1247, r 2.39 (1).
12 Ibid r 2.39 (2).
13 Ibid r 2.39 (3).
14 See Family Proceedings (Allocation to Judiciary) Directions 1991 Schedule 1 and The Children (Allocation of Proceedings) Order 1991, SI 1991/1677, art 15. Where an application is opposed it must be transferred to a family hearing centre, ibid art 16 (1).
15 Matrimonial Causes Act 1973 s 41 (2)(as substituted by the Children Act 1989 s 108 (4) Sch 12 para 31).
16 Domestic Proceedings and Magistrates' Courts Act 1978 s 8 (1).
17 Children Act 1989 s 8 (4).
18 Family Law Act 1986 ss 2 (2), 3 (as substituted by the Children Act 1989 s 108 (5) Sch 13 para 36).
19 Ibid s 3 (2)(as substituted by the Children Act 1989 s 108 (5) Sch 13 para 64).

122. The court's powers to make orders. The court has power in any family proceedings to make orders under Section 8 of the Children Act 1989[1], and to make an order under Section 16 of the Act[2]. The court can make any Section 8 orders in response to an application by any person qualified under the terms of the Children Act to apply[3], but it is also empowered to make such orders as it thinks fit under Section 8 even though no application has been made[4]. Thus, where, for example, a grandparent is reluctant to go to court to ask for a contact order, but a divorce court welfare officer's report refers to such contact as being valuable and in the child's best interests, then the court could go ahead and make an order in favour of the grandmother[5], though it will probably wish to be satisfied that she does actually want the order[6].

In exercising its powers to make any of the Section 8 orders the court also has power to direct how the order should be carried into effect[7], impose conditions[8], provide for its duration[9] and to make such incidental, supplemental or consequential provision as the court thinks fit[10]. This seemingly limitless power of the court to attach any condition it thinks fit has already been construed as being subject to some limitations. Thus Booth J in *Leeds City Council v C*[11] overturned a stipendary magistrate's decision to the extent that he had ordered supervision of a contact order in favour of three children's mother and grandmother by the local authority at two weekly intervals. The judge found that the proper course of action would have been to have made a family assistance order under Section 16. In contrast however imaginative use of a residence order with conditions attached was made in *Re C*[12]. In this case there had been an application for a care order but the magistrates had made a supervision order. In Ward J's view both were wrong. He directed that a better approach, given the absence of a final assessment, would be to make a residence order in favour of the parents subject to the conditions that the parents undertook a programme of assessment and contact with the child, and further to make an interim supervision order subject to the condition that the child be medically assessed on a periodic basis.

The principles contained in section 1 of the Children Act 1989 — The first part of section 1 provides that when any court is determining any question with respect to the upbringing of a child or the administration of a child's property or the application of any income arising from it, the child's welfare shall be the court's paramount consideration. This provision confirms the position previously applied under the Guardianship of Minors Act 1971 although it should be noted that whilst the former legislation provided that the welfare of the child was to be the court's "first and paramount consideration", the words "first and" have now been ommitted. The reason for this is that these words were felt to be superfluous and as adding nothing to the sense of the provision. As to what the phrase "paramount consideration" actually means one can do no better than to look at the judgment of Lord MacDermott in *J v C*. He stated that the principle of the court placing the child's welfare as its paramount consideration involved "a process whereby, when all the relevant facts, relationships, claims and wishes of parents, risks, traces and other circumstances are taken into account and weighed, the course to be followed will be that which is most in the interests of the child's welfare as that term is now to be understood. That is the first consideration because it is of first importance and the paramount consideration because it rules upon or determines the course to be followed". Whilst the Act has provided that the child's welfare is its paramount consideration it does not necessarily mean that other factors cannot be considered such as the wishes of a child's parent, other relatives or anyone else who is deemed to be relevant for the purposes of determining the child's welfare or indeed that the court should not consider other circumstances which may be relevant in helping it to determine what is in the best interests of the child.

The second provision within section 1 states that "in any proceedings in which any question with respect to the upbringing of a child arises, the court shall have regard to the general principle that any delay in determining the question is likely to prejudice the welfare of the child". This provision links in with the powers of the courts to determine their own timetables but judges in a large number of cases have since implementation of the act emphasised that delays should be kept to a minimum.[13] In certain cases however delay may well be beneficial to the child. In the case of *Re C*[14] the court acknowledged that delay would ordinarily be inimical to the welfare of the child, but the court acknowledged in that case that "a planned and purposeful delay might well be justified". In the circumstances of the case delaying a final decision for the purpose of an assessment was "proper delay" and was to be encouraged; it was wholly consistent with the welfare of the child to allow a matter of months to elapse for a proper programme of assessment to be undertaken.

Section 1(3) provides the all important welfare checklist to which the court is under a duty to have regard to in the circumstances laid down in the next subsection. These circumstances are that the court is considering whether to make, vary or discharge a section 8 order, and the making, variation or discharge of the order is opposed by any party to the proceedings, or the court is considering whether to make, vary or discharge an order under part 4 of the act.[15] Thus the court must in those circumstances have regard in particular to —

a. the ascertainable wishes and feelings of the child concerned (considered in the light of his age and understanding) —In the case of *Re P*[16] it was stressed that whilst the court must have regard to the ascertainable wishes of the child, at the end of the day it was for the court to make the decision and not the child. In two other cases also known as *Re P* and *M v M*[17] the court stated that it was important for the court to listen and pay respect to the views of older children, who were of an age and maturity to make up their minds as to what they thought was best for them. The case of *Re W*[18] also examined the issue of the relevance of the wishes of children in determining where they should reside. The judge in that case had found that both the mother and the father could properly meet the needs of the children, who were aged 12 and 10. The children wished to live with their father and the judge had made a residence order in favour of the father, with contact to the mother. The Court of Appeal held that there was no ground for saying that the judge had plainly been wrong in finding that the children's wishes should be the main factor in these circumstances. The judge had indeed recognised that the wishes of the children are not automatically to be followed as they are only one item on the welfare check list but that nevertheless where other factors are evenly balanced the wishes of the children may tip the scales in one or the other party's favour.

b. *His physical, emotional and educational needs* — It has been stressed in two recent cases that there is no presumption that one parent is to be preferred to another parent for the purpose of looking after a child at a particular age. Both in the case of *Re S*[19] and the case *Re A*[20] it was stated however that it was likely that a young child, particularly a little girl, would be expected to be with her mother, but that that was subject to the overriding factor that the child's welfare was the paramount consideration. The court stated that it was natural for young children to be with mothers, but that where there was a dispute, it was a consideration rather than a presumption. In the latter case of *Re A* it was further stated that where very young children had remained throughout with the mother, the unbroken relationship of mother and child would be difficult to displace unless the mother was unsuitable to care for the child. Where however as in the circumstances of this case the mother and child had been separated and the mother then sought the child's return, other considerations would apply. There was no presumption which required the mother, as mother, to be considered as the primary caretaker in preference to the father. The court again reiterated the principle that the welfare of the child was paramount and that each parent should be assessed carefully before one could be chosen as the parent to look after the child. As to the presumption that babies should reside with their mothers this came up for consideration in the case of *Re W*.[21]. In *Re W* the mother had formed a relationship with the father, become pregnant and then the relationship had broken down. The mother had a three year old child from a previous marriage and reached an agreement with the father that when the child was born it would be cared for by the father and he employed a nanny for that purpose. The day after the birth the mother left hospital in order to care for her three year old child and two days later the child was collected by the father from the hospital and looked after by the nanny and himself. Three days after the birth, the mother signed a parental responsibility agreement giving parental rights to the father which she later asserted was done under pressure. A short while later the mother wrote to the father stating that she wished the child to live with her and made an application for an interim ex-parte residence order which was heard ten days later. At the hearing the mother indicated that she wished to commence breast feeding although she had not done so prior to the hearing. The judge ordered that the status quo should be maintained and that the child should remain with the father pending the outcome of the court welfare officer's report which was ordered. The mother appealed and the Court of Appeal allowed the appeal stating that although there was no presumption of law that a child of any given age was better off with one parent or the other, and that although the only legal principle involved was that the welfare of the child was the paramount consideration, no court could be ignorant of what would be the natural position if other things were equal. There was a rebutable presumption of fact that a baby's best interests were served by being with its mother, although the situation might be different with older children.

c. *The likely effect on him of any change in his circumstances* — This was also considered in the case of *Re W* which involved the dispute between the unmarried parents of a three week old baby.[21] In the case the Court of Appeal ruled that the decision as to the child's placement which had been the subject of an interim application should not have been left until the final hearing. The pressure on the courts and welfare services might not have enabled the case to have been heard for a further three months and this would have meant that the party which had had the child in the meantime had an inbuilt advantage because when the case returned before the court the status quo assumed an even greater importance than originally. In those circumstances, the judge at first instance should have considered which was likely to be better for the child's welfare. The child in question was less than four weeks old and her welfare required that for the time being she should have been with her mother. The Court of Appeal went on further to state that although there was a well established principle that when enquiries were being made in order to decide what were the best arrangements for a child the status quo should not be disturbed, it was not really possible to establish a status quo within a period of three weeks at the beginning of a child's life. By contrast however the case of *Re G*[22] emphasised the fact that when the court is dealing with small children, there is a "working rule" that the status quo should not be disturbed unless there is good reason to do so. In the case of *Re R*[32] it should be noted that the Court of Appeal refused a residence order in favour of the mother of a member of a strict religious sect, thus disturbing the status quo. The Court of Appeal confirmed that the judge at first instance is under no duty to interview a child in private when deciding whether to make a residence order, but more importantly that there was no rule or legal principle that it could never be right to force a child to abandon its religious beliefs.

d. His age, sex, background and any characteristics of his which the court considers relevant — It should be pointed out for those familiar with looking at parts III and IV of the Act that the duty upon the court is couched in slightly different language from that cast upon local authorities. Thus local authorities when reaching any decision with regard to a child are required to take into account not only the child's wishes and feelings but also they are required to look to the child's religious persuasion, racial origin and cultural and linguistic background. It is submitted that of course courts would be expected under the provision in section 1(3)(d) to look at these other factors, which local authorities are required to look at, in any way in which the court considers relevant.[23]

e. Any harm which he has suffered or is at risk of suffering — This inevitably will involve the court in a risk balancing exercise, and the court may be forced into a choice which it may believe is not wholly and necessarily the right one. This was illustrated most graphically in the case of *Re P*[24] where the Court of Appeal in the particular case upheld the decision of a judge to return a child home to a family in which it was understood there had been abuse of the child of a sexual nature by the child's stepfather. The Court of Appeal stated that the judge had considered all relevant matters and recognised that his decision carried risks but there was no better solution. This was said the Court of Appeal a case where there was no right solution only two alternative wrong solutions. In such circumstances the judge had to decide which of two bad solutions was the least dangerous having regard to the long term interests of the child. It could not be said that the judge was plainly wrong on the principles set out in the case of *G v G*. The risk balancing approach was further followed by the Court of Appeal in the case of *Re H*[26]. In that case in the Court of Appeal Balcombe LJ stated that "no one would deny that the sexual abuse of a child is an evil which can cause lasting damage to the child. Society is rightly astute to protect children from that evil. The danger is that in seeking to protect children from sexual abuse, society may cause other, and possibly greater, harm to the children it seeks to protect. To take children away from the only home they may have known, from parents (however inadequate) to whom they are attached, and to put them into the care of foster parents (however loving and skilled), or into a residential home, clearly carries a risk of causing harm to those children. It is the balancing of those risks in a particular case which is the object of the exercise of the judicial discretion".

f. How capable each of his parents, and any other person in relation to whom the court considers the question to be relevant, is of meeting his needs — In the case of *Re W*[27] the court had found that both the mother and father could properly meet the needs of the children and where this was the case some other factor in this particular case children's wishes and feelings, would have to be looked to in order to achieve some determination in the case. It seems clear though that whenever the court is considering any application from any adult or from any other person seeking an order under the act, that it will carefully consider the capability of such persons in terms of meeting the child's needs. It is therefore particularly important when the issue of residence or contact with another party is being considered that all aspects of a situation have been thoroughly investigated. For example, where a welfare officer is recommending that a child should be looked after by the mother together with a new stepfather or by father together with a new stepmother then both parties should be interviewed and the welfare officer make some assessment of the new partner's relationship with the children and also of any new siblings which the children may be expected to have as a result of new living arrangements. To do otherwise would lay the decision open to the allegation that the court could not possibly have proceeded in a particular way because it did not have all the relevant information before it.

g. The range of powers available to the court under this act in the proceedings in question — It has to be remembered that the court is not only able to make not just orders under Section 8 or Section 16 of the Act but may also direct an investigation under Section 37 where it believes that a child is suffering or is likely to suffer significant harm and that it might require the taking of care or supervision order proceedings. It should also be noted that of course the court may in care or supervision order proceedings make any of the Section 8 or Section 16 orders as it thinks fit. The courts further have the power to make orders other than those for which an application has been made.[28]. A Section 8 order can further be granted to anyone without application[29]. Finally it should be noted that the court also has the power to prevent further applications being made[30.]

The fourth provision which is a key principle contained in section 1 is the so-called principle of "judicial non-intervention" or as the writer prefers "the positive advantage principle". Thus Section 1(5) provides that *"where a court is considering whether or not to make one or more orders under this Act with respect to a child, it shall not make the order or any of the orders unless it considers that doing so would be better for the child than making no order at all"*— In practice in every case it will now be up to those seeking to have an order made to establish that a particular order will be beneficial to the child's interests. Whilst this provision may have a very considerable impact in public law proceedings where local authorities will have to establish that, in each particular case, care is better for the child than not making a care order and this might be difficult given recent controversies, nevertheless the first case on this point has been in the private law area involving a Section 8 application. This was the case of *B v B* in which magistrates originally refused to make a residence order in favour of the child's grandmother on the basis that there was no likelihood of the child's residence with the grandmother being disturbed and that for this reason making an order would not be better for the child than making no order at all[31.] On the grandmother's appeal however the family division judge pointed out that the magistrates had not fully considered all the circumstances of the case and in particular had not given due weight to issues concerning the child's health and welfare which might need the consent of a person with parental responsibility as a matter of urgency. In the circumstances the grandmother's appeal was allowed and a residence order was made in her favour. This case further illustrates the point that practitioners involved in private law applications should be expected to put forward every piece of evidence which would go towards showing that an order would be better for the child in all the circumstances of the case than making no order at all.

1　Children Act 1989 s 8 (4) although not it is thought in proceedings under s 25. See The Children Act 1989 Guidance and Regulations Vol I Court Orders para 2.36.
2　Ibid s 16 (1).
3　Ibid s 10 (1)(a).
4　Ibid s 10 (1)(b).
5　Ibid s 10 (1)(b).
6　Ibid s 1 (1).
7　Ibid s 11 (7)(a).
8　Ibid s 11 (7)(b).
9　Ibid s 11 (7)(c).
10 Ibid s 11 (7)(d).
11 *Leeds City Council v C* (1992) Times, 15 July, FD.
12 *Re C* [1991] 2 FCR 341, FD.
13 Children Act 1989 section 1(2) and see *Re P* (1992) Times, 11 May, and *Re W (A Minor) (Residence Order)* [1992] 2 FLR 332.
14 [1992] 2 FCR p 341 at p 357.
15 Children Act 1989 s 1(4).
16 *Re P (a Minor)* (1992) Times 11 May and see also *Re C (A Minor)* [1992] Fam Law 571.
17 *Re P (A Minor) (Education; Child's Wishes)* [1992] 1 FCR 145 and see also *M v M (Children: Removal from Jurisdiction)* [1993] 1 FCR 5.
18 *Re W* (1992) 156 JPN 476, CA.
19 [1991] 2 FLR 388.
20 [1991] 2 FLR 394.
21 [1992] 2 FLR 332.
22 *Re G (A Minor) (Custody)* 1992 2 FCR 279.
23 See Children Act 1989 s 22 (4) and s 22 (5) and see *R v R* [1992] Fam Law 571 and *Re P (A Minor) (Transracial Placement)* [1990] FCR 260.
24 *Re P* [1991] FCR 283.
25 *G v G* [1985] 2 All ER 225, [1985] 1 WLR 647.
26 *Re H (Minors) (Wardship: Sexual Abuse)* [1991] 2 FOR 424.
27 156 JPN 476, CA.
28 Children Act 1989 s 10(1).
29 Ibid s 10 (1)(b).
30 Ibid s 91 (14) although *F v Kent County Council* (1992) 136 Sol Jo LB 258 which states that such powers should be used sparingly.
31 [1992] 2 FLR 327. See also *S v R* [1993] Fam Law 42.
32 (1992) Times, 3 November,(1992) Fam Law 571, CA.

123. Residence order. Although the Section 8 orders are listed in the Children Act 1989[1] in alphabetical order with the residence orders appearing third, it is here considered first because it will be deemed by most to have the greatest significance. The Children Act 1989 defines a residence order as an order settling the arrangements as to the person with whom a child is to live. Where a residence order is made in favour of some person other than a parent then it will have the effect of further conferring parental responsibility on the holder so long as the order remains in force[2]. Whilst Section 8 orders were perceived as merely intended to determine practical issues regarding child care, whoever holds a residence order, will clearly be in a stronger position to influence the child's upbringing, and the rights of the holder of a residence order are further recognised in the Children Act to be superior[3] to others merely holding parental responsibility. This has further been acknowledged to be the case in the court's decision in *B v B*[4]. In this case magistrates had originally refused to make a residence order in favour of the child's grandmother with whom she had lived for all but the first six weeks of her eleven year life. The magistrates had found that there was no risk of the child being removed by the mother since the grandmother's application had been made with the support of the mother and therefore held that they could not make the order, because it could not be shown that the child would be better off were a residence order made. The grandmother appealed, and, on appeal, the Family Division judge pointed out that this application for a residence order had been made by a grandparent, and not by one of two parents each having parental responsibility. The grandmother's appeal would be allowed and a residence order granted on the basis that this would confer parental responsibility upon her, and she would be able to deal on a day to day basis with such bodies as health and education authorities.

Before making a residence order the court must consider the items on the welfare checklist in Section 1(3), and certainly where children are older, or have expressed very fixed views of their attitudes to residence with one or the other of their parents, more weight will have to be attached to their views. This was emphasised clearly by the court in *Re P*[5], whilst at the same time acknowledging that, at the end of the day, it must be recognised that it is the court which makes the decision and not the child. In this case, the children were aged thirteen and eleven. In *Re W*[6] the judge at first instance had found that both the mother and the father could probably meet the needs of the children who were aged 12 and 10. The children wished to live with their father and so the court had made a residence order in favour of the father, with contact to the mother. The Court of Appeal held that there was no ground for saying that the judge had been plainly wrong in finding that the children's wishes should be the main factor in these circumstances. All the other factors in this case were evenly balanced and the wishes of the children being an aspect of their welfare tipped the scales in their father's favour. In the case of *M v M*[7] the Court of Appeal found that the first instance judge had erred in failing to do more than pay lip service to the wishes of intelligent and articulate children aged 10 and 11, and in failing to take account of the welfare officer's recommendation that the children should stay in England with their father rather than go to Israel to live with their mother. The Court of Appeal allowed the father's appeal and made a residence order in his favour.

Residence orders may be made in favour of more than one person[8], for example in favour of a parent and step-parent, grandparents, other relatives or foster parents. Residence orders can also be made in favour of two or more persons who do not live together. Thus under the provisions of the Act it is possible to make a joint residence order in favour of each parent and their new partners. Where such an order in favour of two or more persons is made, the order may specify the periods during which the child is to live in the different household[9].

Department of Health Guidance on court orders under the Children Act 1989 suggests that orders could be expressed to provide for weekdays with one parent and weekends with the other or to provide for the child to spend alternate weeks with each parent or to provide further for the division of the child's time in school holidays between both parents[10]. As the Guidance points out a joint residence order also has the psychological advantage that it removes any impression that one parent is good and responsible whereas the other is not. Against any notion that joint residence orders will become the norm, however, the Guidance properly cautioned that, "it is not expected that it will become a common form of order because most children will still need the stability of a single home, and partly because in the cases where shared care is appropriate there is less likely to be a need for the court to make an order at all. However, a shared care order has the advantage of being more realistic in those cases where the child is to spend considerable amounts of time with both parents, and brings with it certain other benefits (including the right to remove the child from accommodation provided by a local authority under Section 20)"[11].

A joint residence order may further come in useful where both parents, who have prior to divorce shared a council tenancy, are seeking to convince the housing authority of the necessity of providing two sufficiently spacious units of accommodation to house the children for different parts of the week with both parents.

The need to convince housing authorities of the requirement for accommodation may equally be a reason for one of the parties to press for the making of a sole residence order in his or her favour upon divorce[12]. Another reason for pressing for a sole residence order may be related to guardianship since, if either parent dies after October 14th 1991, then the other parent is deemed to step into the deceased parent's shoes[13] and unless the deceased held a sole residence order[14], the appointment of their guardian does not take effect and the surviving parent can act untrammelled by any restrictions which a guardian may have sought to make.

Where, as the result of the making of a residence order, the child lives or is to live with one of two parents and each has parental responsibility for him, the order ceases to have effect if the parents live together for a continuous period of more than six months[15]. It should be noted that this provision applies whether or not the parents are married or unmarried provided each has parental responsibility for the child. It does not of course apply where a residence order had been made in favour of a grandmother and then the mother of the child went to live with the grandmother also.

The Family Proceedings Rules have now been amended[16] to provide that applications for any orders under Sction 8 can be made ex parte. This reflects the Court of Appeal'sdecision in the case of *Re B*[17] where the court emphasised that such ex parte orders should only be made in exceptional circumstances, a point repeated in *Re G*[18] and *M v C*[19].

1   Children Act 1989 s 8 (1).
2   Ibid s 12 (2).
3   Ibid ss 20 (9), 5 (1)(b).
4   *B v B* [1992] 2 FLR 327
5   (1992) Times, 11 May, CA
6   (1992) 156 JPJO 476, CA.
7   (1992) Times, 12 August, CA.
8   Ibid s 11 (4).
9   Ibid s 11 (4).
10 As in the terms of the agreed order in *J v J (A Minor) (Joint Case and Control)* [1991] 2 FLR 385, CA and see *The Children Act 1989 Guidance and Regulations,* Vol 1 Court Orders (Department of Health, HMSO 1991) para 2.28.
11 Ibid para 2.28 and see *J v J* [1991] 2 FLR 385, CA.
12 See the *Children Act Advisory Committee's First Annual Report.*
13 Children Act 1989 s 5 (8).
14 Ibid s 5 (7)(b).
15 Ibid s 11 (5).

16 Family Proceedings Rules 1991 r 4.4.(4) as amended and Family Proceedings Courts
   (Children Act 1989) Rules 1991 r 4 (4).
17 [1992] 3 All ER 867, CA.
18 (1992) Times, 9 October, CA.
19 (1993) Fam Law 41.

124. Contact order. A contact order under Section 8 of the Children Act 1989 is
according to the First Report of the Children Act Advisory Committee the most
popular type of order in private law proceedings a prediction borne out by the initial
statistics published in the Children Act Advisory Committee's First Annual
Report. A contact order is defined as an order requiring the person with whom a child
lives, or is to live, to allow the child to visit or stay with the person named in the
order, or for that person and the child otherwise to have contact with each other[1].
Contact under Section 8 is thus very broadly defined, and it is submitted, is much
wider than the old access provisions which it replaces[2]. The order also emphasises
the idea that it is in favour of the child, rather than a parent or any other person who
has actually sought and obtained the order[3]. That this is indeed to be the approach
under the new provisions was confirmed by the Court of Appeal in *Re C*[3] reaffirming
the guidance set out in the 1973 case of *M v M*[3]. The Court stated that contact between
children and non-resident parents should not be refused unless there are cogent
reasons to deny it. The Court of Appeal held that there was no material difference
between cases involving assertions that existing contact should be terminated and
those where the claim was that contact be resumed.

Under the terms of a contact order it may be required that a child should be
allowed to have physical visiting or staying contact with another person, or that he
should be allowed other contact such as by letter, telephone[4], networking on a
computer, audio-tape, video tape or the receipt of birthday and Christmas cards. As
with residence orders, contact orders can be made ex parte and subject to such
directions, conditions, duration or incidental supplemental or consequential direction as the court thinks fit[5]. It should be noted however that where it is felt desirable
to have contact supervised this cannot be done by inserting a condition to be attached
to the contact order, but must instead be achieved by the making of a s 16 family
assistance order[6].

Again, as with residence orders it should be noted that it is not just parents who
can apply for orders but anyone (other than a local authority) who is either entitled
to apply under special provisions in the Act[7], or who applies for, and is granted, leave
of the court to make an application[8]. This could cover a wide variety of people in a
child's life including siblings, grandparents and other relatives, friends, godparents
and anyone else whom the court agrees should be granted leave. It should be noted
however, that such other people should not be given leave where their interests are
identical to those of another party to the proceedings. This was the decision of the
Court of Appeal in *Re M*[9], where Butler Sloss LJ stated that where the grandparents'
interests were identical to the mother's she could not see the purpose of their being
separately represented, their intervention had lengthened the proceedings, and had
thereby increased the costs of all the parties. Grandparents, she stated, like others,
should only intervene where they had a separate view to put forward[10].

In the case of *Re CB*[11], a mother had appealed against the first instance judge's
decision to allow the child's grandfather, who had a conviction of indecent assault
against the mother while she was a child, staying in contact with the child. The
welfare officer had also recommended against contact arguing that where a person
with a history of abuse was involved, protection for the child was the court's
paramount concern. Since the grandfather in this case was denying the justice of his

conviction, the risk of further abuse could not be controlled since he refused to work towards changing his behaviour. The judge however found there was no risk to the child and ordered contact. The Court of Appeal allowed the mother's appeal, and held that the judge had erred in questioning the conviction, in failing to investigate the mother's allegations of subsequent abuse, and in departing from the welfare officer's recommendations without taking further assistance from that officer in the form of oral evidence. The Court of Appeal transferred the case for rehearing by a Family Division judge.

Where the applicant for a contact order is a non blood relative, then the absence of a blood tie will be taken into account in deciding whether future contact will be ordered. This factor was of relevance in the case of *Re C*[12] where a step-father was seeking contact with his step-daughter. The child had at one time believed him to be her father but the mother had now formed a relationship with another man, and the judge at first instance had refused to allow a contact order holding that in the long term it would be disruptive and contrary to her welfare. This decision was upheld by the Court of Appeal, despite the applicant's claim that, because he had lived with the child for some time as her father, there must be some compelling reason to justify denying him access. The Court of Appeal rejected this argument, pointing out that the judge at first instance had considered the impact of contact very carefully and there was no basis upon which his assessment that it would not benefit the child could be displaced. In those cases where fathers may be seeking to resume contact with children after a long break it is evident that in the period running up to implementation of the Children Act 1989, the Court of Appeal reached conflicting decisions. In the first case of *Re H*[13] it was held that *the test is not whether there is a positive advantage* to resuming contact, but whether there are cogent reasons why the children should be denied the opportunity of seeing their father. By contrast in the slightly later case of *Re GF*[14] the Court of Appeal stated that the crucial questions in such cases is whether starting contact after the long lapse of time will be of any *positive benefit* to the child. Where the reintroduction could only cause disruption to the child and to the mother, because of the father's attitudes to them both, then, said the Court of Appeal, contact should be refused. In a later case also known as *Re H*[24] an unmarried father sought both a parental responsibility order and a contact order in relation to his child with whom he had had regular contact ever since the mother had married the step-father some six months later but contact continued for another six months until it became clear that contact was causing a rift in the marriage of the mother and step-father and the step-father had threatened to leave if contact continued. The first instance judge ruled that whilst there would be considerable benefit to the child in seeing the father and building up a relationship with him this would be far outweighed by the risk of bringing to an end the family, home and security which the child had. The judge thus refused the contact order and for much the same reasons the parental responsibility order. The Court of Appeal confirmed the refusal to make a contact order but made a parental responsibility order. Whilst this may have seemed a good compromise to the Court of Appeal one can only lament the refusal of the contact order in such circumstances given the signals such a decision may give to step-parents and wonder at the naivety of the belief that granting a parental responsibility order would not cause just as much trouble and present a greater threat to the stepfather as the making of a contact order.

Where a child is being "accommodated" by a local authority, and a relative or friend feels they have been excluded by the terms of agreement reached between the local authority and the parents from being allowed contact, then they too will be able to seek leave to make an application for a contact order[15] under Section 8. In addition, of course, it should be remembered that where a child is of sufficient understanding he may apply for an order[16].

It should also be noted that a court will not generally make a contact order to have effect for a period, which will end after the child reaches the age of sixteen unless it is satisfied that the circumstances of the case are exceptional[17].

Contact orders may be made in favour of more than one person[18] but a contact order which requires the parent with whom the child lives to be allowed contact with his other parent shall cease to have effect if the parents live together for a continuous period of more than six months[19].

There is no limitation as to where contact may take place. Thus the courts may make orders providing for contact to take place abroad[20].

It should also be noted as is pointed out in the Guidance on Court Orders that "a Section 8 contact order is a positive order in the sense that it requires contact to be allowed between an individual and a child and cannot be used to deny contact"[21]. Thus if any person is seeking to stop contact with the child, he would have to apply for a prohibited steps order[22].

Finally, it should be pointed out that under no circumstances should solicitors ever advise their clients to obstruct contact in breach of a court order. In *Re K*[23] the Family Division considered what action should be taken against solicitors who, prima facie, appeared to have incited their client to obstruct contact between a father and his children in breach of a court order. This had happened on only one occasion and contact had been resumed satisfactorily. Hollis J found that there were mitigating circumstances and in the light of this the condign punishment which would usually be required for so grave an offence was inappropriate. It would be wrong in this particular case to order the solicitors to bear the costs of the action because no more than a prima facie case had been proved against them, but more severe action would be taken in more serious cases.

1 Children Act 1989 s 8 (1). See CHA Form 7. More than 20,000 contact orders were made in the first 9 months' operation of the Act — CAAC First Annual Report 1991/92.
2 See for example *Allette v Allette* [1986] 2 FLR 427, [1986] Fam Law 333, CA and *Wickes v Benfield* [1991] FCR 499, (1991) Times, 26 March.
3 [1992] 1 FLR 148, CA and see Children Act 1989 s 8 (1). This accords with the emphasis given by WRANGHAM J in the pre-Children Act case of *M v M (Child Access)* [1973] 2 All ER 81 at 85.
4 Such contact is suggested in *Guidance under the Children Act 1989 and Regulations,* Vol 1 Court Orders (Department of Health, HMSO 1991) at para 2.29.
5 Children Act 1989 s 11 (7).
6 *Leeds City Council v C* (1992) Times, 15 July, FD.
7 Ibid s 10 (1)-(5).
8 Ibid s 10 (9).
9 *In re M (Minors)(Representation)*(1992) Times, 19 November.
10 Ibid.
11 (1992) 156 JPN 234, [1992] 1 FLR 309.
12 [1992] 1 FLR 148.
13 [1992] 1 FCR 237.
15 Again as suggested in *Guidance under the Children Act 1989 and Regulations,* Vol 1 Court Orders (Department of Health, HMSO 1991) at para 2.29.
16 Children Act 1989 s 10 (8).
17 Ibid s 9 (6).
18 Ibid s 8 (1).

19 Ibid s 11(6).
20 Since this could be done under the old law on access there seems no reason why similar provision should not be made under the new law, see *Re F (A Minor) (Access Out of Jurisdiction)* [1973] Fam 198, [1973] 3 All ER 493.
21 See note 4 supra at para 2.30.
22 Ibid.
23 [1992] 2 FLR 108, FD.
24 [1993] 1 FCR 85.

125. Prohibited steps order. A prohibited steps order is defined in the Act as an order that no step which could be taken by a parent in meeting his parental responsibility for a child, and which is of a kind specified in the order shall be taken by any person without the consent of the court[1].

As was indicated earlier, the order may be used to prevent contact between the child and some other person[2] but may be employed far more widely to prevent any step which is akin to the exercise of any parental responsibility in respect of the child[3] being taken by any person and not just a parent. It was pointed out however in *Croydon LBC v A*[4] that a prohibited steps order cannot be made to prohibit a mother and father from having any contact with each other. This cannot be dealt with by the court making a prohibited steps order because this is not a step which could be taken by a parent in meeting his parental responsibility for the child. The Family Division judge further held that the justices had been wrong to make a prohibited steps order without informing the parties, which here included the local authority who had sought interim care orders, of their intention to do so and without giving them the opportunity to make representations to the court. The first order made by the justices prohibiting the father from contacting the children was possible, unlike the second, but the order would not fully protect the children, and so in the circumstances the local authority's appeal was allowed in full.

The real intention behind giving all courts hearing family proceedings the power to make both prohibited steps and a specific issue order is to enable all courts to have the power to deal with problems which would previously have resulted in a resort to the wardship court[5].

A prohibited steps order may, like a specific issue order, deal with a single issue such as ordering no contact with a particular person[6], prohibiting removal of the child from the United Kingdom where no residence order has been made[7], or preventing the removal of the child from his home. In the case of *Re D*[8] a child had been retained by the mother in Turkey in breach of an undertaking to return her. The father applied ex parte for a specific issue order that the child be returned to the jurisdiction and for a prohibited steps order preventing mother from removing the child once she was returned. The orders were made ex parte because the mother was in Turkey and the orders were apparently of value to the father in the proceedings in the Turkish courts. A prohibited steps order could not, however, be used, for example to restrict publicity about a child[9] since this is not within the scope of parental responsibility and it is only those issues which can be affected by the making of such an order[10]. As with a residence or contact order, a prohibited steps order can be applied for ex parte[11]. It should be noted that a local authority may apply for a prohibited steps order but not relating to a child subject to a care order[12].

In *Nottinghamshire CC v P*[13] Ward J emphasised that a local authority should also not try to circumvent the prohibition on local authorities applying for residence and contact orders[14] by seeking a prohibited steps order with conditions which would have the same effect. The case concerned the local authority's concern over two girls aged 16 and 13 whom the local authority believed to be at serious risk of sexual abuse from the father. They had in consequence applied for a prohibited steps order that the father vacate the household and that the children have no contact with him except under supervision. Ward J ruled that under the Act the court must enquire on a local authority's application for a prohibited steps order whether the purpose was to achieve the result of a residence order or a contact order by the back door.[15] In this case, it clearly was and local authorities should be advised to use care or supervision order proceedings in such circumstances. In those circumstances however the case was before the court and the father had sought a residence order. The court held that it would make a residence order that the children reside at the family home with the mother and that the father be excluded and that the younger sisters had no contact with the father unless that contact was supervised. It is unclear from the report whether this last order issued in the form of a prohibited steps order with conditions attached.

1 Children Act 1989 s 8 (1). See Form CHA Form 10 and see *Re M* [1992] 1 FR 415.
2 See Paragraphs 84 and 124 ante.
3 Children Act 1989 s 8 (1). See *Re M (Prohibited Steps Order: Application for Leave)* (1993) Fam Law 76 for an attempt by a guardian ad litem to obtain such an order.
4 [1992] 3 All ER 788, FD
5 *The Children Act 1989 Guidance and Regulations,* Vol 1 Court Orders (Department of Health, HMSO 1991) at paras 2.31 and 2.33.
6 See ibid para. 2.30. Note there should be very good reasons to deny contact to a non-residential parent.
7 See Children Act 1989 s 13 (1)(b).
8 [1991] 1 All ER 892
9 See note 4 supra.
10 Children Act 1989 s 8 (1).
11 Family Proceedings Rules 1991, SI 1991/1247, r 4.4(4) and Family Proceedings Courts (Children Act 1989) Rules 1991, SI 1991/1395, r 4(4), though this should only be done in exceptional circumstances, see *Re M (Prohibited Steps Order: Application for Leave)* [1993] 1 FCR 78.
12 Children Act 1989 s 9 (2).
13 [1993] 1 FCR 78, FD.
14 Children Act 1989, s9(5).
15 Ibid.

126. Specific issue order. A specific issue order is defined as meaning an order giving directions for the purpose of determining a specific question which has arisen or which may arise, in connection with any aspect of parental responsibility for a child[1]. A specific issue order may thus be used to settle such matters as which school a child should attend[2]; in which religious denomination or faith he should be brought up; where a child lives with a Jehovah's Witness parent, that the other's consent to blood transfusions or operative treatment be good against the Jehovah's Witness parent's opposition[3]; and a dispute about the performance of surgical treatment upon a child[4].

As with prohibited steps orders, a specific issue order can be made on its own or together with a residence or contact order and it must be made in the prescribed form[5]. Where an order is made together with a residence or contact order it might be advisable to request that the court include a condition that any decision concerning an issue which is the subject of a specific issue order is not to be taken without informing the parent so that he would be able to object[6].

Again, as with prohibited steps orders, a specific issue order may be the subject of an application by a local authority[7], provided it obtains leave[8]. The availability of a specific issue order means that local authorities will now be able to resolve speedily and cheaply certain issues such as whether an accommodated child whose parents cannot be contacted should have an operation[9], without having to resort to the wardship jurisdiction[10]. A local authority may also seek to apply for a specific issue order where it wishes for example to compel a parent to take up services being offered for the child pursuant to Sections 17 and 27 of the Children Act 1989[11].

An application for a specific issue order may also be made ex parte under the relevant court rules[12]. An example of where this was done in a child abduction case can be seen in *Re D*[13]. In this case the mother had failed to return the child to England after a holiday in Turkey in breach of an undertaking to the court. The father sought a specific issue order ex parte that the mother return the child within twenty-eight days, a residence order in his favour and a prohibited steps order restraining the mother from removing the child from the jurisdiction again. The judge refused to make the orders saying that the would be unenforceable because the mother was outside the jurisdiction. The father appealed and the Court of Appeal held that there was jurisdiction under the Children Act 1989 since despite possible difficulties of enforcement the orders would have some value. The father had apparently been advised that the specific issue order would assist him in his efforts to secure the return of the child through the Turkish courts. It was therefore wholly appropriate to make the specific issue and prohibited steps orders, and the father did not press ahead with his application for a residence order.

1   Children Act 1989 s 8 (1).
2   See *The Children Act 1989 Guidance and Regulations,* Vol 1 Court Orders (Department of Health, HMSO 1991) at para 2.32.
3   See under the old law for example *Jane v Jane* (1983) 4 FLR 712, 13 Fam Law 209, CA.
4   For an apparent reluctance to use the new order see *Devon County Council v S* (1993) Fam Law 40..
5   Children Act 1989 s 8 (1). The order will be made in CHA Form 10.
6   Ibid s 11 (7).
7   Ibid s 9 (2). Application should be made on CHA Form 10.
8   Ibid s 10 (9).
9   Note 2 supra at para 2.33.
10 Ibid at para 2.33.
11 Children Act 1989 s 27. See *The Children Act 1989 Guidance and Regulations,* Vol 2 Family Support Day Care and Educational Provision for Young Children (Department of Health, HMSO 1991) Ch. 2.
12 Family Proceedings Rules 1991, SI 1991/1247, r 4.4 (4) and Family Proceedings Courts (Children Act 1989) Rules 1991, SI 1991/1395, r 4 (4) and using CHA Form 10.
13 [1992] 1 All ER 892.

127. Court's powers to make additional directions, conditions etc. It has already been noted in relation to all the orders under Section 8 of the Children Act 1989[1] that the court is given very wide powers to make such directions, conditions and incidental, supplemental or consequential provision as it thinks fit[2]. By virtue of Section 11(7) the persons upon whom such conditions may be imposed are very restricted[11] and the court cannot attach conditions requiring supervision by a local authority of a contact order. Where such supervision is required, then the court in *Leeds City Council v C*[12] stated that the proper course of action would have been to have applied for a family assistance order. The wide scope of Section 11 is to enable the new orders to be as flexible as possible and so reduce or remove the need to resort to wardship[3]. It has also been suggested that it is under this provision that the court could make an interim order pending appeal[4], where interim orders are not otherwise provided for under the Act, and certainly an order could be made for a limited period containing a further direction that the case be brought back to court by a specified date[5].

Where the court seeks to impose conditions the Act provides that these can be made to apply to four categories of person[6]:

1. Any person in whose favour the order was made[7], for example a residence order may impose a condition as to where the child and the person in whose favour the order is made is to live;
2. Any person who is a parent of the child[8], which will include an unmarried father who has not obtained a parental responsibility order or a residence order which has the effect of granting him parental responsibility;
3. Any person who is not a parent of the child but who has parental responsibility for him[9], for example where a relative has been granted a residence order and the court in making a contact order in favour of the parent wishes to impose on the relative conditions under which contact with the child is to be permitted;
4. Any person with whom the child is living[10], thus for example where the child is living with someone who is not of the same religious persuasion as the child a contact order may contain a direction that that contact is to take place so as to enable the person in whose favour it is made to take steps to allow the child to pursue his religious upbringing.

1 Children Act 1989 s 8. See Paragraphs 3 ante.
2 Children Act 1989 s 11 (7) and see CHA Forms 7-9.
3 *The Children Act 1989 Guidance and Regulations,* Vol 1 Court Orders (Department of Health, HMSO 1991) at para. 2.22.
4 See *Clarke Hall & Morrison on Children* (10th Edition) at 1 [223].
5 Children Act 1989 s 11 (7)(c).
6 Ibid s 11 (7)(b).
7 Ibid s 11 (7)(b)(i).
8 Ibid s 11 (7)(b)(ii).
9 Ibid s 11 (7)(b)(iii).
10 Ibid s 11 (7)(b)(iv).
11 See infra Conditions 1-4.
12 (1992) Times, 15th July, FD.

128. Duration of orders made under Section 8. There are a number of provisions which limit the duration of orders made under Section 8, and these are listed:

1. No court can make an order which is to have effect for a period which will end after the child has reached the age of sixteen unless it is satisfied that there are exceptional circumstances[1];
2. No court can make any Section 8 order other than one varying or discharging such an order with respect to a child who has reached the age of sixteen unless it is satisfied that the circumstances of the case are exceptional[2];
3. Where orders have been made or extended in such exceptional circumstances, they automatically terminate upon the child reaching the age of eighteen[3];
4. An order may be brought to an end by a court making a new order before the expiry of the old order[4]. Note that the making of a care order brings to an end any Section 8 order[5];
5. A residence order is also terminated by the making of an order for the child's return under Part I of the Child Abduction and Custody Act 1985, or where a decision has been registered under Section 17 of that Act[6].

6. Under the provisions of the Family Law Act 1986[7], if a court in Scotland or Northern Ireland makes or varies a Part I order in respect of a child who is the subject of a Part I order made by a court in England and Wales, then the Scottish or Northern Ireland order has precedence over the English order to the extent that they overlap. The English court then loses the power to vary its own order so as to take account of matters covered by the later Scottish or Northern Ireland order[8].

7. Where matrimonial proceedings[9] are pending in Scotland or Northern Ireland in respect of the marriage of the child's parents[10], and an application is made[11] to the English court to vary any Section 8 orders previously made, the English court cannot do so unless, either the court in Scotland or Northern Ireland waives jurisdiction to make an order or stays proceedings before it in favour of the English court[12], or the Section 8 order was made in matrimonial proceedings in the English court and those proceedings are continuing[13].

1 Children Act 1989 s 9 (6).
2 Ibid s 9 (7).
3 Ibid s 91 (11).
4 By the bringing of proceedings set out in ibid s 8 (4).
5 Ibid s 91 (2).
6 Child Abduction and Custody Act 1985 ss 25 (1), 27 (1) and Sch 3, para 1 (1)(as amended by the Children Act 1989 s 108 (5) and Sch 13 para 57).
7 Family Law Act 1986 s 6 (1).
8 Ibid s 6 (2).
9 Ibid s 7 (b)(as substituted by the Children Act 1989 s 108 (5) Sch 13 para 67).
10 Ibid s 6 (3)(as substituted by the Children Act 1989 s 108 (5) Sch 13 para 66).
11 Ie this is the relevant date, see ibid s 7 (c)(as substituted by the Children Act 1989 s 108 (5) Sch 13 para 67).
12 Ibid s 6 (4).
13 Ibid s 6 (3A), (3B)(as substituted by the Children Act 1989 s 108 (5) Sch 13 para 66).

129. Restrictions on making Section 8 orders. The Children Act 1989 imposes a number of restrictions on the making of Section 8 orders chiefly in respect of local authorities[1].

Where a child is in the care of a local authority then the court cannot make any Section 8 order other than a residence order[2], and the making of the residence order has the effect of terminating the care order[3]. The ability of the court to make a residence order in response to an application where the child is already the subject of a care order represents an important limitation on the local authority's virtually unfettered discretion to make decisions in respect of a child subject to a care order without fear of successful challenge by a relative or anyone else with an interest in the child[4]. Thus, where relatives do wish to provide a home for the child[5], or the child was made the subject of a care order following care proceedings arising out of divorce proceedings[6] and one of the parents can provide a home, then an application could be made under Section 8[7]. It is also important to note that under the Review of Children's Cases Regulations 1991 children must be advised as appropriate of their right to apply for any of the Section 8 orders[8]. Furthermore, unmarried fathers, who without parental responsibility cannot apply for the discharge of a care order, may nevertheless apply for a Section 8 residence order[9].

Local authorities may not themselves apply for a residence order on behalf for example of foster parents, nor are they allowed under any circumstances to apply for a contact order[10] nor is the court allowed to make such an order of its own motion.

These restrictions apply whether the child is being accommodated or is the subject of a care order.[10]

Where, however, a child is being accommodated, or is the subject of a supervision order, a local authority may apply for a prohibited steps order or a specific issues order[11], but as has been noted earlier[12] these must relate to an aspect of parental responsibility, so for example a prohibited steps order might be used to stop contact with a particular relative[13], or a specific issue order to deal with medical treatment in a situation of possible absence of the parent[14].

It should be noted however, that a further general restriction applies to the making of prohibited steps and specific issue orders and that is that neither order can be made by the court with a view to achieving a result which could be achieved by making a residence order or contact order[15], or in any way which is denied to the High Court in the exercise of its inherent jurisdiction with respect to children[16]. The first restriction is to protect against the risk especially in uncontested cases, that these orders might be used to achieve the same practical results as residence or contact orders but without the same legal effects[17]. The second restriction stops local authorities from using the orders as a means of obtaining the care accommodation or supervision of children, or the ability to exercise any aspect of parental responsibility over such children[18]. Thus, a prohibited steps order could not be made to prevent a parent exercising his right to remove his child from local authority accommodation[19].

1 Children Act 1989 s 9.
2 Ibid s 9 (1).
3 Ibid s 91 (1).
4 See for example under the former law *A v Liverpool City Council* [1982] AC 363, [1981] 2 All ER 385, HL, and *Re W (A Minor) (Wardship: Jurisdiction)* [1985] AC 791, [1985] 2 All ER 301, HL.
5 As in *Re W* (supra).
6 Via a direction made under Children Act 1989 s 37.
7 Ibid s 8 (1), (4).
8 Review of Childrens' Cases Regulations 1991, SI 1991/895, Sch 1 para 5.
9 Children Act 1989 s 10 (4)(a).
10 Ibid s 9 (2) and see *Nottinghamshire County Council v P* [1993] 1 FCR 180.
11 Ibid s 9 (1), (2).
12 See Paragraphs 124126 ante.
13 Necessary because a contact order is framed in the positive sense only, see Paragraph 124 ante.
14 See Paragraph 126 ante.
15 Children Act 1989 s 9 (5)(a) and see *Nottinghamshire County Council v P* sup cit n 10..
16 Ibid s 9 (5)(b).
17 See *The Children Act 1989 Guidance and Regulations*, Vol 1 Court Orders (Department of Health, HMSO 1991) at para 2.34.
18 Ibid at para 2.33.
19 Given to the parent or person with parental responsibility by virtue of Children Act 1989 s 20 (7), (8).

130. Who may apply for Section 8 orders. The Act provides for certain categories of people to be able to apply for any[1] or some[2] of the Section 8 orders as of right and without having to seek leave[3], whilst others will have to satisfy the criteria laid down before the court can consider whether or not to grant them leave to apply for a particular Section 8 order[4]. The court can, of course, make any Section 8 order of its own motion in favour of someone who has not sought leave to make an application[5], but would doubtless consider the criteria laid down in the Act when taking such a step[6].

Persons entitled to apply for any of the Section 8 orders — Presumably because of their close relationship to the child, the following persons are entitled as of right to make an application for any of the Section 8 orders: any parent (which includes an unmarried father without parental responsibility)[7]; or guardian of the child[8]; any person in whose favour a residence order is in force[9]; and under the transitional provisions anyone who holds a custody, care or control order under the former law applicable to the making of orders on children in divorce, matrimonial and other proceedings[10].

Persons entitled to apply for residence or contact orders — It seems strange to have provided for a group of persons who can automatically apply for residence or contact orders, but who must seek leave to apply for a prohibited steps or a specific issue order. The basis for this group being automatically entitled to apply for a residence order or contact order would again seem to relate to their having a sufficiently close connection to the child[11]. In this group the following persons are entitled to apply: any party to a marriage whether or not subsisting in relation to whom the child is a child of the family though it should be empasised that as a result of *Re C*, the absence of any blood tie between the child and the step parent may weaken the case of step parent applicants.[12]; any person with whom the child has lived for a period of at least three years[13]; any person who has, in any case where a residence order is in force with respect to the child, the consent of each of the persons in whose favour the order was made[14]; any person who in any case where the child is the subject of a local authority care order, has the consent of that authority[15]; any person who, in any other case, has the consent of each of those (if any) who have parental responsibility for the child[16]; any person who is not entitled under these previous provisions to apply for variation or discharge of a Section 8 order shall be entitled to do so if the order was made on his application or in the case of a contact order he is named in the order[17]; any person who has access to a child by virtue of an order under the former law applicable is entitled to apply for a contact order[18]; and finally it is provided that rules of court may be made entitling further persons to apply without leave but so far no rules have been made[19].

Persons who must seek leave to apply for Section 8 orders — Anyone else may apply to the court for leave to make an application, and this might include relatives, older siblings, godparents or other friends of the child[20].

Local authority foster parents, unless they are relatives of the child[21], or the child has lived with them for at least three years preceding the application[22], may not apply to the court for leave without the specific consent of the local authority[23]. The Guidance makes it clear that the rationale for these restrictions is to prevent applications by foster parents at a stage when the local authority is still trying to assess what is best for the child in the long term, and also so that parents will not be deterred from making for or agreeing to their child to be accommodated with a local authority foster parent if the need arises[24].

Criteria to be considered by the court in deciding whether or not to grant leave — These criteria are laid down in the Act and thus in making its decision the court must have particular regard to:

1. the nature of the proposed application for the Section 8 order;
2. the applicant's connection with the child;
3. any risk there might be of that proposed application disrupting the child's life to such an extent that he would be harmed by it; and

4. where the child is being looked after by a local authority:
    4.1. the authority's plans for the child's future; and
    4.2. the wishes and feelings of the child's parents[25].

It should be noted that the courts decision under these provisions to grant leave is not a decision as to the care and upbrining of a child and thus the court is not obliged to regard the child's welfare as its paramount consideration. This was confirmed in the case of *Re A and W*[26]. Where a foster mother had sought, and been granted, leave to apply for residence orders in respect of four children in local authority care. They had also refused to direct that the children's mother be informed of the proceedings. The local authority had appealed and the Court of Appeal held that the judge was wrong to regard the children's welfare as the paramount consideration because this conflicted with the relevant provisions of the Act[27], which directed the court to have regard to a number of matters that would be irrelevant if the welfare principle was to determine the outcome of the proceedings. The failure to inform the mother prevented the judge considering one of the specified factors[28], the wishes and feelings of the parents, and he was thus unable to exercise his discretion properly. The Court of Appeal rejected the argument that the court should have been bound by the principle laid down in *A v Liverpool City Council*[29], and should have accepted a local authority's plans for the children's future save in exceptional circumstances. The court accepted that this principle of judicial non-intervention when Parliament has entrusted decisions to local authorities was generally observed by the provisions of the Children Act 1989, but it was expressly excluded as far as the court's power to make a residence order in respect of a child in care is concerned[30]. This did not mean that the local authority's views were irrelevant because the court was directed to pay special attention to their plans[31.] The court should acknowledge that those plans would have been formulated expressly to promote the child's welfare and to depart from them might well harm the child[32.] The Court of Appeal considered the merits of the case with the assistance of the Official Solicitor's report and the mother's statement, and exercised its discretion to refuse the foster mother's application for leave to apply for a residence order.

Application by a child — Different criteria apply when the court is considering an application for leave to apply for a Section 8 order by a child. The court in such circumstances may only grant leave if it is satisfied that he has sufficient understanding to make the proposed application for the order[33]. It is suggested that this does not mean that the child should understand the legal technicalities of making an application, but that he is taken to be old enough to press through the courts for his desire to live with or see or not see particular persons. The ability of the child to proceed with an application may be particularly important where those with whom he is living or those whom he wishes to see would not themselves qualify for legal aid or might for some other reason be reluctant to press ahead with an application.

1 Children Act 1989 s 10 (4).
2 Ibid s 10 (5).
3 Ibid under s 10 (1)(a)(i).
4 Ibid s 10 (1)(a)(ii).
5 Ibid s 10 (1)(b).
6 Ibid s 10 (9).
7 Ibid s 10 (4)(a) and see *M v C and Calderdale MBC* [1992] Fam Law 571, CA.
8 Ibid s 10 (4)(a).
9 Ibid s 10 (4)(b).

10 Children Act 1989 Sch 14 para 8(3).
11 Ibid, see s 10 (5).
12 [1992] 1 FLR 309 and see Children Act 1989 s 10 (5)(a).
13 Ibid s 10 (5)(b).
14 Ibid s 10 (5)(c)(i).
15 Ibid s 10 (5)(c)(ii).
16 Ibid s 10 (5)(c)(iii).
17 Ibid s 10 (6).
18 Ibid Sch 14 para 5 (1)(c)(iii).
19 Ibid s 10 (7).
20 Pursuing the "open door" policy of the Children Act 1989.
21 Ibid s 9 (3)(b).
22 Ibid s 9 (3)(c).
23 Ibid s 9 (3)(a).
24 *The Children Act 1989 Guidance and Regulations*, Vol 1 Court Orders (Department of Health, HMSO 1991) at para 2.45 (d).
25 Children Act 1989 s 10 (9).
26 *Re A and W (Minors)(Residence Order : Leave to Apply)*[1992] 2 FLR 154; also reported as *J R v Merton London Borough* [1992] 2 FCR 176.
27 Children Act 1989, s 10(9).
28 Ibid s 10(9)(c).
29 [1981] 2 All ER 385, HL.
30 Children Act 1989, s 9(1).
31 Ibid s 10(9)(d).
32 Ibid s 22(3).
33 See *Re A D (A MInor)* [1993] Fam Law 43, FD.

131. Procedure for seeking leave to make an application. Any person seeking leave must file a written request for leave setting out the reasons for the application and a draft of the application for the making of which leave is sought[1]. The draft should be in writing[2] and there should be sufficient copies for one to be served on each respondent. Under the court rules, the court can either grant the request for leave whereupon the proper officer or the justices clerk must inform the applicant, or it can direct that a date be fixed for hearing the request, in which case the proper officer or justices' clerk fixes the date and gives such notice of it as the court directs to the applicant and such other persons as the court requires to be notified[3]. These are likely to be those persons who will be respondents if the application for a Section 8 order goes ahead[4].

1 Family Proceedings Rules 1991, SI 1991/1247, r 4.3 (1), Family Proceedings Courts (Children Act 1989) Rules 1991, SI 1991/1395, r 3 (1).
2 The Rules allow for the existence of a prescribed form, but one is not included.
3 Family Proceedings Rules 1991 r 4.3 (2) and Family Proceedings Courts (Children Act 1989) Rules 1991, r 3 (2).
4 See Family Proceedings Rules 1991 App 3 col (iii) as amended or Family Proceedings Courts (Children Act 1989) Rules 1991 Sch 2 col (iii).

132. Procedure for applying for Section 8 orders. Applications are commenced by filing an application in the prescribed form[1] in respect of each child, together with sufficient copies for one to be served on each respondent[2]. Except in the case of divorce, nullity or judicial separation proceedings (where one application includes all "children of the family"), an application has to be filed in respect of each child and a case number will be allotted to each application although as aresult of the recommendations of theChildren Act Advisory Committee, the Rules Committee is considering amending this to one per family.

Upon receipt of the filed documents, the court must fix the date, time and place for a hearing or directions appointment, indorse the date fixed on the filed copies and return them to the applicant[3]. The applicant must then serve a duly indorsed copy of the application on each respondent a minimum of 14 days prior to the hearing or directions appointment[4]. The respondents listed in the rules include: every person whom the applicant believes to have parental responsibility for the child; where the child is the subject of a care order, every person whom the applicant believes to have had parental responsibility immediately prior to the making of the care order and in the case of an application to extend, vary or discharge an order, the parties to the proceedings leading to the order which it is sought to have extended, varied or discharged[5].

The applicant must at the same time as effecting service, give written notice of the proceedings and of the date, time and place of hearing to: a local authority providing accommodation for the child; persons who are caring for the child at the time the proceedings are commenced; in the case of proceedings brought on a child who is staying in a refuge, the person who is providing the refuge; every person whom the applicant believes to be named in a current court order on the child, to be a party to pending proceedings in respect of the same child, or to be a person with whom the child has lived for at least three years, unless in respect of the former two, the applicant believes that the court order or pending proceedings are not relevant to the application[6].

It is further open to any person to file a written request that he or some other person be joined as a party to the proceedings, or that he should cease to be a party[7]. The court also has power to direct that a person who would not otherwise be a respondent be joined as a party to the proceedings or that a party to the proceedings should cease to be so[8].

When an application has been made it can only be withdrawn with the leave of the court[9].

Within 14 days of service of an application for a Section 8 order, every respondent must file and serve on all the parties an answer to the application in the prescribed form[10].

1 See CHA Form 10A-D.
2 Family Proceedings Rules 1991, SI 1991/1247, r 4.4 (1)(a), App 3 col (iii) as amended by Family Proceedings (Amendment No 2) Rules 1992, Family Proceedings Courts (Children Act 1989) Rules 1991, SI 1991/1395, r 4 (1)(a), Sch 2 col (iii).
3 See Family Proceedings Rules 1991 r 4.4 (2), Family Proceedings Courts (Children Act 1989) Rules 1991 r 4 (2).
4 Family Proceedings Rules 1991 r 4.4 (1)(b) as amended by The Family Proceedings (Amendment No 2) Rules 1992 SI 1992/2067 and Family Proceedings Courts (Children Act 1989) Rules 1991 r 4 (1)(b) and for rules as to service see respectively r 4.8 and r 8.
5 Family Proceedings Rules 1991 Appendix 3 col (iii), and Family Proceedings Courts (Children Act 1989) Rules 1991 Sch 2 col (iii).
6 Family Proceedings Rules 1991 App 3 col (iv), and Family Proceedings Courts (Children Act 1989) Rules 1991 Sch 2 col (iv).
7 Family Proceedings Rules 1991 r 4.7 (2) and Family Proceedings Courts (Children Act 1989) Rules 1991 r 7 (2).
8 Family Proceedings Rules 1991 r 4.7 (5) and Family Proceedings Courts (Children Act 1989) Rules 1991 r 7 (5).

9 Family Proceedings Rules 1991 r 4.5 and Family Proceedings Courts (Children Act 1989)
   Rules 1991 r 5 and see Paragraph 10 ante.
10 See CHA Form 10A.

133. Ex parte applications. Ex parte applications may now be made in respect of residence, contact prohibited steps and specific issue orders[1], and in the magistrates' court only with the leave of the justices' clerk[2]. Applications in respect of each child[3] and in the prescribed form[4] must be filed either at once or, where the application is made by telephone, within 24 hours after the making of the application[5]. The applicant must then serve a copy of the application on each respondent within 48 hours after the making of the order[6]. Ex parte applications would generally take place within usual court hours with applications out of hours being kept for quite exceptional cases.

Where the court refuses an order on an ex parte application, it may direct that the application be made inter partes[7].

1 Family Proceedings Rules 1991, SI 1991/1247, r 4.4 (4) as amended by The Family Proceedings (Amendment No 2) Rules 1992. The Rules were amended as a direct result of the decision in *Re B (A Minor) (Residence Order: Ex Parte)* [1992] 2 FLR 1. Such orders should however only be granted occasionally and in exceptional circumstances. See also *M v C (Minors) (Residence Order: Ex Parte)* [1993] Fam Law 53.
2 Family Proceedings Courts (Children Act 1989) Rules 1991, SI 1991/1395, r 4 (4) as amended by Family Proceedings Courts (Miscellaneous Amendments) Rules 1992.
3 Family Proceedings Rules 1991 r 4.4 (4)(i) and Family Proceedings Courts (Children Act 1989) Rules 1991 r 4 (4)(i).
4 Ibid Form CHA 10.
5 Family Proceedings Rules 1991 r 4.4 (4)(i)(a).
6 Family Proceedings Rules 1991 r 4.4 (4)(ii) and Family Proceedings Courts (Children Act 1989) Rules 1991 r 4 (4)(ii).
7 Family Proceedings Rules 1991 r 4.4 (5) and Family Proceedings Courts (Children Act 1989) Rules 1991 r 4 (5).

134. Transfer of proceedings. Any application for a Section 8 order is deemed to be relevant proceedings for the purposes of the rules relating to the transfer of proceedings[1].

1 See Paragraph 121 ante.

135. Directions hearings. The general rules governing the giving, variation or revocation of directions for the conduct of proceedings and attendance at directions appointments have already been discussed[1] but particular issues in relation to Section 8 orders applications may be dealt with in directions hearings or pursuant to them.

Directions will be sought to obtain the court's leave before a child may be medically or psychiatrically examined or otherwise assessed for the purpose of the preparation of expert evidence for use in the proceedings[2].

1 See Paragraph 123 ante.
2 See Family Proceedings Rules 1991, SI 1991/1247, r 4.18(1) and Family Proceedings Courts (Children Act 1989) Rules 1991, SI 1991/1395, r 18(1).

136. Other evidence admissible at a hearing.
Hearsay Evidence — Pursuant to the Children (Admissibility of Hearsay Evidence) Order 1991 in civil proceedings before the High Court, county court and in family proceedings in the magistrates' court, evidence given in connection with the upbringing, maintenance or welfare of a child is admissible notwithstanding any rule of law relating to hearsay[1].

Welfare Reports — The court considering any question with respect to a child has the power under the Children Act 1989 to ask either a probation officer or a local authority to report to the court on such matters relating to the welfare of that child as are required to be dealt with in the report[2]. Whilst it should be noted that this power exists in relation to any issue to be decided under the Act, and could thus include a power to order such reports in care proceedings, in most care or supervision order proceedings a guardian ad litem will have been appointed[3]. The functions of welfare officers are fundamentally different from those of guardians ad litem. The former report to the court about the child's background[4] whereas the latter are concerned with representing the child's best interests[5] although both will rely heavily on the welfare checklist in Section 1 (3)[6]. It should be noted that the court in *Re S*[28] stated that where there is a report in the proceedings from a guardian ad litem, it is then inappropriate to order a welfare report.

Under the provisions of the Act, courts are given the power to choose whether they wish welfare reports to be provided by local authorities or by probation officers[7] dependent upon the circumstances. Generally, it has turned out to be the case that for the vast majority of cases, probation officers have been appointed, but where social services already have a connection with the child or his family it may be more appropriate to ask the local authority to provide for the report to be done either by one of their officers or such other person (other than a probation officer) as the authority consider appropriate[8]. The court now has much greater control over what it wants covered in such welfare reports[9], and this, together with the requirement to consider all the elements contained in the welfare checklist should mean that welfare officers' reports be much more clearly focused in future.

In deciding whether or not to call for a welfare report to be provided the court may have regard to all the principles set out in Section 1 of the Act. Thus, the advantage of having a report[10] may be outweighed by the delay its preparation might entail[11]. To save delay, however, the court would require the report to be made orally[12] or alternatively might set a time limit within which the report must be prepared[13]. The welfare officer must file his report either pursuant to such a direction or in the absence of a direction at least fourteen days before the hearing at which it will be considered[14] and a copy must be served on the parties as soon as practicable by the proper officer or the justices' clerk[15]. The report is confidential and should not be disclosed to anyone other than the parties, their legal representatives and the Legal Aid Board without the leave of the courts[16]. Despite the fact that the Act allows the court to take account of any statement contained in, or evidence given in respect of matters referred to in the report[17], it is important that where second-hand evidence is relied upon this is made explicit in the report as should the source of the information and the welfare officer's reasons if he has any for agreeing with reported opinions[18].

The welfare officer must attend the hearing at which his report will be given or considered, unless the court or the justices' clerk excuses his attendance[19]. Any party may question the welfare officer about his report at such a hearing[20], but the judge or justices should not discuss the case privately with the welfare officer in the absence of the parties[21]. It was stated in the case of *Re CB*[29] that it is wrong for a judge to proceed to form conclusions that are directly contrary to the welfare officer's recommendations without first receiving oral evidence from the officer.

Courts are not bound by the recommendations made in welfare reports but since all levels of court must now record in writing the reasons for their decisions[22], the courts should indicate their reasons for deviating from the course of action recommended by a welfare officer[23].

A divorce county court had jurisdiction under the old law to grant leave for information contained in a welfare report in an earlier case to be reused in the case before it, and there seems to be no reason why this should not continue to be good law[24].

Interviewing the child — Provided the welfare officer has done his job properly there should really be no need for the court to interview children in private[25] unless the child is insisting on making his views known to the judge. The relevant court rules do not, however, deal with the issue and thus it must be assumed that the practice which applied before 14th October 1991 continues to be applicable. Thus the judges in the High Court and county court will continue to have a power to interview children in the course of the proceedings in a private room, but they must not promise the child that the exchange of views will be kept private[26]. Previous law had also established that magistrates have no powers to interview children in private[27].

1 Children (Admissibility of Hearsay Evidence) Order 1991, SI 1991/1115.
2 Children Act 1989 s 7 (1).
3 Ibid under s 41.
4 Ibid s 7 (1).
5 Family Proceedings Rules 1991, SI 1991/1247, r 4.11; Family Proceedings Courts (Children Act 1989) Rules 1991, SI 1991/1395, r 11.
6 Children Act 1989 s 1 (3).
7 Ibid 1989 s 7 (1)(a), (b).
8 Ibid s 7 (1)(b)(i), (ii).
9 Ibid see for example s 7 (1), (2), (3), (4).
10 In that it may assist with a determination pursuant to ibid s 1 (1).
11 See Children Act 1989 s 1 (2).
12 Ibid s 7 (3).
13 Family Proceedings Rules 1991 r 4.14(2)(g) or Family Proceedings Courts (Children Act 1989) Rules 1991 r 14 (2)(9).
14 Family Proceedings Rules 1991 r 4.13 (2) as amended by Family Proceedings (Amendment No 2) Rules SI 1992/2067 or Family Proceedings Courts (Children Act 1989) Rules 1991 r 13 (2) as amended by Family Proceedings Courts (Miscellaneous Amendments) Rules 1992.
15 Family Proceedings Rules 1991 r 4.13 (2) or Family Proceedings Courts (Children Act 1989) Rules 1991 r 13 (2).
16 Family Proceedings Rules 1991 r 4.23 (1) and Family Proceedings Courts (Children Act 1989) Rules 1991 r 23 (1).
17 Children Act 1989 s 7 (4).
18 See *Thompson v Thompson* [1986] 1 FLR 212n and further also *Edwards v Edwards* [1986] 1 FLR 205, [1986] Fam Law 99, CA, and *H v H (A Minor), K v K* [1990] Fam 86, [1989] 3 All ER 740, CA.
19 Family Proceedings Rules 1991 r 4.13 and Family Proceedings Courts (Children Act 1989) Rules 1991 r 13 (1).
20 Family Proceedings Rules 1991 r 4.13 and Family Proceedings Courts (Children Act 1989) Rules 1991 r 13 (1).
21 See *Re C (A Minor)* [1991] 2 FLR 438, [1991] FCR 308.
22 Family Proceedings Rules 1991 r 4.21 (4) and Family Proceedings Courts (Children Act 1989) Rules 1991 r 21 (5)(b).
23 See *Re T (A Minor) (Welfare Report Recommendation)* (1977) 1 FLR 59, and *Stephenson v Stephenson* [1985] FLR 1140, [1985] Fam Law 253, CA and *W v W (Custody of Child)* [1988] 2 FLR 505, CA.
24 See *Brown v Matthews* [1990] Ch. 662, [1990] 2 All ER 155 CA.
25 See for example the welfare checklist in the Children Act 1989 s 1 (3) which provides for the court to have regard to the child's ascertainable wishes and feelings.
26 See *Elder v Elder* [1986] 1 FLR 610, [1986] Fam Law 190, CA.

27 See *Re W (Minors)* (1980) 10 Fam Law 120 and *Re T (A Minor) (Welfare Report Recommendations)* [1977] 1 FLR 59.
28 See *Re S (A Minor)* [1992] Fam Law 320, CA.
29 [1992] 1 FCR 320.

137. Hearing of applications for Section 8 orders. The date for the final hearing of any applications for Section 8 orders will be fixed by the justices' clerk, the court or a proper officer[1]. The justices' clerk at a directions appointment, or the court at a hearing or directions appointment may give directions as to the order of speeches and evidence at a hearing[2]. Subject to any such directions being given, the parties must adduce their evidence in the following order:

1. the applicant;
2. any party with parental responsibility for the child;
3. other respondents;
4. the guardian ad litem;
5. the child, if he is a party to the proceedings[3].

In deciding whether or not to make a Section 8 order the court is bound by the requirement to regard the child's welfare as its paramount consideration[4]. Where the application for the Section 8 order is opposed, the court must further have regard to the welfare checklist[5] set out to assist the court in reaching the right decision. Finally, the court when considering all the options must not make an order or any of the orders unless it considers that doing so would be better for the child than making no order at all[6]. This last provision has been termed the principle of judicial non-intervention, and it is clear that it is up to the applicant to persuade the court that an order should be made. The Guidance indicates that the court may be inclined to consider making a residence order where it is shown that the child's need for security and stability may be better served by the making of an order, where it is necessary to protect the child from the risk of abduction, or where it is shown to be desirable to obtain a sole residence order in order that the applicant's appointment of a guardian for the child will take effect in the event of the applicant's death[7].

After the final hearing of the proceeding the court is required to deliver its judgment or reach its decision as soon as is practicable[8].

The court is required to state any findings of fact and the reasons for the court's decision when making any order or when refusing an application[9]. Where a Section 8 order is made, it must be recorded in the appropriate form[10], and a copy must be served as soon as practicable by the justices' clerk or the proper officer on the parties, and any person with whom the child is living[11]. In the case of ex parte prohibited steps or specific issue orders, a copy must be served within 48 hours on each party and on any person who has actual care of the child or who had such care immediately prior to the making of the order[12].

1 Family Proceedings Rules 1991, SI 1991/1247, r 4.15; Family Proceedings Courts (Children Act 1989) Rules 1991, SI 1991/1395, r 15.
2 Family Proceedings Rules 1991, r 4.21 (1) and Family Proceedings Courts (Children Act 1989) Rules 1991, r 21 (1).
3 Family Proceedings Rules 1991, r 4.21.(2) and Family Proceedings Courts (Children Act 1989) Rules 1991, r 21 (2).
4 Children Act 1989 s 1 (1).
5 Ibid s 1 (3), (4).
6 Ibid s 1 (5).
7 The Children Act 1989 Guidance and Regulations Volume 1 Court Orders at para 2.56.

8 Family Proceedings Rules 1991, r 4.21 (3) and Family Proceedings Courts (Children Act 1989) Rules 1991, r 21 (4).

10 Ibid Form CHA 7 for a residence or contact order, Form CHA 8 a prohibited steps order or Form CHA 9 for a specific issue order.

11 Family Proceedings Rules 1991, r 4.21 (6) and Family Proceedings Courts (Children Act 1989) Rules 1991, r 21 (7)(b).

12 Family Proceedings Rules 1991, r 4.21 (7) and Family Proceedings Courts (Children Act 1989) Rules 1991, r 21 (8).

138. Enforcement of orders. Any order made in the magistrates' court, other than for payment of money can be enforced under the general rules pertaining to the enforcement of magistrates' court orders. The orders can be enforced under the provisions of Section 63 of the Magistrates' Courts Act 1980[1] by either the payment of a sum not exceeding £5,000 or up to £50 for every day in default but not exceeding a maximum of £5,000, or committal to custody until compliance with the order or for a period of two months, whichever is the shorter. Whilst Section 63 is specifically stated in the Children Act 1989 to apply to residence orders[2], the terms of the Section would seem to indicate that it is actually more applicable to the other Section 8 orders[3] and the reason for the specific extension for residence orders is that these might otherwise have been thought to be declaratory only and not capable of enforcement[4].

The failure by any person to obey the terms of a Section 8 order made by the High Court or a county court, is punishable in the usual ways by committal to prison or sequestration until the child is produced to any person named in the order[5]. Given the restrictions on the magistrates' courts enforcement powers, where it is anticipated that enforcement may be a problem, this may constitute a good reason for allocating the case to the county court.

Where a child is not produced following the making of a residence order, then alternative action such as proceedings for an emergency protection[6], interim care or interim supervision order with directions must be considered[7], although only local authorities or the NSPCC are able to apply for the interim care or supervision order. Where very real immediate fears exist for the child's safety it may be appropriate to ask the police to exercise their powers of protection[8].

Where there are alleged breaches of any of the other orders, the court before it would make any committal order would have to be satisfied that a court order has been breached and that the relevant penal notice has been served[9]. Even in those cases where the court has been satisfied that an order has been deliberately breached by the defendant it has tended to view its enforcement powers both under the 1980 Act and in the higher courts for contempt to imprison or fine the defendant as very much a remedy of last resort[10]. This has most particularly been the case where contact has been denied by one parent to the other since enforcement is likely further to aggravate hostility and possibly turn the child against the parent seeking to enforce the order. In recent cases however it has been stated that where an order has been consistently and deliberately flouted then imprisonment for contempt may be deemed appropriate[11].

Finally, where a person is required by a Part I order under the Family Law Act 1986, or an order for the enforcement of a Part I order, to surrender the child to another person and the court which made the order is satisfied that the child has not been given up, it may make an order authorising an officer of the court or a constable to take charge of the child and deliver the child to that other person[12]. The Act further provides that the authorisation includes authority to enter and search the premises and to use such force as may be necessary[13]. Where no such order has been made however the police are not under a duty to intervene, unless there is a threat of danger or a breach of the peace[14], although they are under a duty to help a parent to enforce the law by preventing the child being wrongfully removed or kept from the parent even where there is no such threat.

1 Magistrates' Courts Act 1980 s 63.
2 Children Act 1989 s 14 (1).
3 Ibid see s 8 (1).
4 Following *Webster v Southwark London Borough Council* [1983] QB 698, [1983] 2 WLR 217.
5 RSC Ord 45 rr 1, 5; CCR Ord 29 r 1.
6 Children Act 1989 s 44 (1)(a).
7 Ibid s 38.
9 See *D v D (Access: Contempt: Committal)* [1991] FCR 323, [1991] 2 FLR 34, [1991] Fam Law 365, CA and *Re P (Minors) (Custody Order: Penal Notice)* [1990] 1 WLR 613, [1990] FCR 223 and note that the Family Proceedings (Amendment No 2) Rules 1992 have amended CCR Order 29 r 1 so that in the case of a Section 8 order enforceability by a committed order the judge may on the application of a person entitled to enforce the order, direct that a proper officer issues the order indorsed with a penal notice.
10 See eg ORMROD LJ in *Ansah v Ansah* [1977] Fam 138, [1977] 2 All ER 638, CA.
11 By BUTLER-SLOSS LJ in *C v C (Access Order: Enforcement)* [1990] 1 FLR 462, [1990] FCR 682, CA.
12 Family Law Act 1986 s 34 (1).
13 Ibid s 34 (2).
14 So held in *R v Chief Constable of Cheshire, ex p K* [1990] FCR 201, [1990] 1 FLR 70.

139. Appeals and the appellate courts powers. The position on appeals in respect of applications under the Children Act 1989 has been considered earlier[1] together with the appropriate court rules[2]. The powers of the appellate courts in cases concerning children have also been subjected to detailed consideration[3].

1 See Paragraphs 29-36 ante.
2 Family Proceedings Rules 1991, SI 1991/1247, r 4.22.
3 See Paragraph 35 ante and particularly dicta in *G v G* [1985] 2 All ER 225, [1985] 1 WLR 647, HL and *Re G (A Minor)(Role of the Appellate Court)* [1987] 1 FLR 164, [1987] Fam Law 52, CA.

140. Family assistance orders. The Children Act empowers courts in family proceedings, whether or not any Section 8 orders have been made, to make what is termed a family assistance order[1]. The order requires a probation officer to be made available or a local authority to make an officer of the authority available to advise, assist and where appropriate befriend any person named in the order[2]. The persons who may be named in the order are any parent or guardian of the child, any person with whom the child is living or in whose favour a contact order is in force with respect to the child, or the child himself[3]. The order is time-limited up to a maximum of six months[4] but there is nothing in the Act which would prevent the court making a further order if it thought this would be in the interests of the child.

The court's power to make a family assistance order under Section 16 has been described as replacing the former power in a range of proceedings[5] to make a supervision order and indeed this was said to be the correct approach in the case of *Leeds City Council v C.*[6] Supervision orders are now only available after proceedings have been issued under Section 31[7], but it was felt appropriate that the court should be empowered to make an order to assist families in trying to adjust in the often traumatic and stressful period after family breakdown. It was felt that such an order might be particularly useful in situations where there are problems over contact between the child and one of his parents or another relative[8].

It should be noted, however, that the order should only be made if the court deems the circumstances of the cases are exceptional[9], and, very importantly, provided the court has obtained the consent of every person to be named in the order other than the child[10]. The fact that the child's consent is not necessary emphasises the fact that the order is primarily focused on the adults who may be having difficulties coping with the situation rather than the child.

A family assistance order may include directions that the person named in the order or such one of them as may be specified in the order, should take such steps as may be specified with a view to enabling the probation officer or social worker designated in the order, to be kept informed of the address of any person named in the order and to be allowed to visit any such person[11].

The powers held by such an officer where a family assistance order is in force alongside a Section 8 order are really quite considerable. Thus, where a family assistance order has been made to ease a difficult contact situation governed by a Section 8 contact order, the officer concerned can of his own motion refer to the court the question as to whether the Section 8 order should be varied or discharged[12]. If there is a residence order in force as well as the contact order and the difficulties with contact are being caused by the parent holding the residence order, then he or she must realise that the officer could refer the question of the variation or discharge of the residence order to the court[13].

Whilst the courts powers to make family assistance orders may chiefly be linked to Section 8 orders, they may exercise such powers in any family proceedings in which the court has power to make an order under Part II of the Children Act 1989. Thus, the power extends to proceedings involving orders for financial provision[14]. In situations where it is possible that problems may be experienced over implementing orders for financial provision, the court may deem it appropriate to make a family assistance order to assist in dealing with them.

1   Children Act 1989 s 16 and see CHA Form 16.
2   Ibid s 16 (1).
3   Ibid s 16 (2).
4   Ibid s 16 (5).
5   For example under Matrimonial Causes Act 1973 s 44 (1); Guardianship Act 1973 s 2 (2)(a); Domestic Proceedings and Magistrates' Courts Act 1978 s 9; Adoption Act 1976 s 26 all of which are repealed by Children Act 1989 s 108 (7) Sch 15; and in wardship proceedings pursuant to Family Law Reform Act 1969, s 7 (4) which is repealed by Children Act 1989, s 100 (1).
6   (1992) Times 15th July FD and see *The Children Act 1989 Guidance and Regulations*, Vol 1 Court Orders (Department of Health, HMSO 1991) at para 2.50.
7   Children Act 1989 s 31 although the effect and terms of the new supervision order are laid down in s 35 and Sch 3 Pt I and II.
8   See note 6 supra at paras 2.502.53.
9   Children Act 1989 s 16 (3)(a).
10 Ibid s 16 (3)(b).
11 Ibid s 16 (4).
12 Ibid s 16 (6).
13 Ibid s 16 (6).
14 Ibid s 15 and Sch 1.

CHAPTER 6: ORDERS FOR FINANCIAL PROVISION FOR CHILDREN

1:UNDER THE CHILD SUPPORT ACT 1991

141 Child support Even as early as the 1970s defects in the system of private law maintenance had been in turn been pointed up and investigated. The Finer[1] Committee Report on one parent families published in 1974 made a number of proposals under which many problems relating to the assessment and enforcement of maintenance support obligations could be dealt with by an administrative agency rather than by the courts. The report also put forward the idea of the Guaranteed Maintenance Allowance which was intended to provide a guaranteed level of income for single parent families set at a much higher rate than the basic subsistence level supplementary benefit rates. The proposals of the Finer Committee were never implemented but by the late 1980s the huge increase in the number of single parent families dependent on income support and the dwindling proportion of those absent parents who were actually paying maintenance for their own children became a matter of considerable concern to the government. At that stage the Conservative government decided to undertake a review of the current system of maintenance support for children.[2] Both evidence released around the time of the review[3] and that made available to the review itself[4] revealed some remarkable statistics all of which had the effect of spurring the government on to action. The most significant of the statistics revealed, as far as the government was concerned, was that approximately 770,000 lone parents or around two-thirds of the total number of lone parent families were dependent upon income support in 1989. This contrasted with a figure of some 330,000 families in 1980. Of the 770,000 fewer than 25% of these families were receiving any maintenance at all whilst the cost to the Treasury of paying benefits out to these families amounted to some 3.2 billion pounds in 1988/89[5]. Other evidence available merely confirmed earlier findings that maintenance awards were generally of an extremely low level with wide variations in practice[6] but high proportions of maintenance orders made were in fact in arrears[7]. The correlation between the low levels of maintenance awarded and the issue of arrears is obvious when one notes that this is little incentive to seek the enforcement of low awards especially where the recipient of maintenance would in any event be in receipt of social security benefits. The review also found however[8] that even where the Department of Social Security had the power to seek enforcement against liable relatives, in only 23% of the cases was the full amount of arrears of maintenance actually recovered. The results of the review prompted the government to push forward with the outline proposals contained in *Children Come First* and legislation followed in the form the Child Support Act 1991. The legislation was intended to ensure that parents met their responsibilities to their children whenever they could and thus to reduce the dependence on state benefits. It was also intended that a much fairer system of income maintenance be provided by the scheme contained in the act so that: children would receive fairer levels of maintenance whilst at the same time ensuring that the paying parent had sufficient income left to meet their needs and any new responsibilities; that the system should be seen to be fair and producing consistent results across the country; and that parents incentives to work should be maintained.

The Act introduces a formula which is to be applied to calculate the amount of maintenance needed by the child and to be met by the absent parent. The actual assessment, collection and enforcement of the maintenance payments are to be performed by the Child Support Agency which is responsible to the Department of Social Security and thus the jurisdiction of the courts in respect of children qualifying to be dealt with under the act is ousted. The courts will now only deal with certain aspects of maintenance which will include top-up maintenance for disabled children, maintenance for step-children and maintenance for additional items like school fees. In addition the Child Support Agency will not deal with anything other than income maintenance support and thus any applications for lump sum provisions in respect of a child will still fall to be dealt with by the courts.

The Child Support Agency is staffed by child support officers under the direction of the Chief Child Support Officer whose duty is to advise officers on their functions, to keep under review the operation of the act, and to make annual reports to the Secretary of State[9]. Transition arrangements have been made to enable the Child Support Agency to take on the work of making some 3 million assessments annually in separate phases. The effectiveness of the agency would be impaired if its final full operational capacity was attempted from the very beginning so it has been provided that the scheme will not be fully operational until 1997, although the majority of cases will have been taken on by 1996. The phased timetable provides that from April 1993, any new case whether or not the parent is on income support, family credit or disability working allowance, will be taken on by the agency. This means that if any parent with care of a qualifying child feels that their maintenance being paid on a voluntary basis is insufficient they, or their solicitor on their behalf, will be able to take their case to the Child Support Agency for the maintenance assessment to be worked out by the agency. From April 1993 to April 1996 those claimants who are currently receiving income support, family credit and disability working allowance will be taken on and maintenance assessments made although priority will be given to those cases where a change of circumstances has occurred which affects maintenance. For those existing cases with court orders where none of the benefits referred to above are in payment, parties may retain the court order if they wish to and where they feel the maintenance assessed was sufficient. The courts will no longer however have the power to vary the orders. These cases therefore will have phased access to the child support agency assessments between April 1996 to January 1997 according to the surname of the person with care of the children[10]. Enforcement of the maintenance assessments made will be possible either through collection from an absent parent's bank account[11], or from his earnings[12], or by application to the magistrate's court for a liability order[13] which then enables enforcement of payment by distress[14] or an action may be taken in the County Court for example by way of a garnishee or charging order[15]. Enforcement may also take place by committal to prison[16]. From April 1994 onwards awards made by the courts may under the provisions of Section 8 of the Child Support Act 1991 be collected and enforced by the agency. These will include such items of maintenance as school fees, maintenance in respect of disability, and any extra maintenance payable because of the absent parent's high income. From April 1996 spousal maintenance, and other maintenance outside the agency's scope may be collected and enforced by the agency and this will include such items as step child maintenance where the agency is already collecting and enforcing child support maintenance. It should be noted however that whilst the agency will be able to take on responsibility for collection and enforcement it will not be responsible for the determination of awards of other forms of maintenance such as spousal maintenance. The courts will retain their functions in these areas for the time being.

1 Report of the Finer Committee on One Parent Families (1974).
2 *Children Come First* Cm 1264.
3 Edwards, Gould and Halpern *The Continuing Saga of Maintaining the Family After Divorce* [1990] Fam Law 31.
4 See the White Paper *Children Come First* Vol 2, para 5.1.2 and see also Gibson *The future for maintenance* [1991] CJQ 330.
5 See *Children Come First* vol 2, p i.
6 Ibid para 1.5.
7 See Edwards, Gould and Halpern Sub set note 4.
8 See *Children Come First* vol 2 para 5.1.2.
9 Child Support Act 1991 s 13.
10 See Child Support - A New Approach Department of Social Security 1992, para 84.
11 Child Support Act 1991 s 29 (3)(e).
12 Ibid s 31.
13 Ibid s 33.
14 Ibid s 35.
15 Ibid s 36.
16 Ibid s 40.

141A Conditions for Liability. Under the provisions of the Child Support Act 1991 each parent of a qualifying child is responsible for maintaining him and the absent parent discharges that responsibility by paying maintenance under the act calculated in accordance with any maintenance assessment made by the Child Support Agency[1]. A qualifying child in respect of whom child support will be assessed, is a child whose parent or parents is absent from him,[2] and who is under the age of 16 or 19 and receiving full time education[3]. Liability to make payments of child support falls on the absent parent who is the parent not living in the same household as the child who has his home with the person with care. Child support will generally be payable to the person with care who is the person or persons with whom the child has his home or usually provides day to day care for the child. Liability to make payments of child support under the act can only fall on a parent. The act provides that a parent is any person who is in law the mother or father of the child subject to the provisions of the Human Fertilisation And Embryology Act 1990 and it will include adoptive parents but not step parents[4]. Under the provisions of the act an absent parent is taken to have met his responsibility to maintain any qualifying child of his by making periodical payments of maintenance with respect to the child in accordance with the formula set out in the act[5].

1 Child Support Act 1991 s 1(3).
2 Ibid s 3(1).
3 Ibid s 55(1).
4 Ibid s 2.
5 Ibid Sch 1.

141B Applications for assessments. Either the person with care of the child or the absent parent may apply to the Child Support Agency for a maintenance assessment to be made by a Child Support Officer with respect to the qualifying child[1]. Application may also be made to the agency to arrange for the collection and enforcement of the child support maintenance once it has been assessed[2]. Where the person with care is the child's parent and is dependent on income support, family credit or other benefits, then she is required by the act to authorise the agency to take action to recover child support from the absent parent by completing a "maintenance application form"[3].

1   Child Support Act 1991 s 4.
2   Ibid s 29(1) (b).
3   Ibid s 6(1).

141C Provision of information to make the assessment. Any person applying for a maintenance assessment or who is under a duty to authorise the agency to enforce maintenance must as far as is reasonably possible supply information to the agency to enable the absent parent to be traced if necessary and for the agency to make the maintenance assessment[1]. Where there are concerns that a parent dependant upon benefits may not wish to reveal the identity of an absent parent to the agency because she fears violence from him or the circumstances surrounding conception of the child were particularly unhappy or unfortunate then the agency is able to waive the requirement to give authorisation or to provide information where it considers that there are reasonable grounds for believing that abiding by the provisions would lead to the claimant or any child living with her suffering harm or undue distress as a result[2]. This is an area calling for the exercise of discretion and is therefore one in which the Child Support Officer can have regard to the welfare of any child likely to be affected by his decision[3]. This duty can scarcely be compared with that to be found in legislation binding the courts[4] but it does relate to considering the welfare of any child who might be affected by the decision and not just the child in respect of whom maintenance is being assessed. The act however gives no guidance on how welfare is to be taken into account nor on how the benefit officers should strike a balance between the different children who might be affected by his decision[5]. Where however the Child Support Officer considers that there are no reasonable grounds for the failure to give information then he may give a "reduced benefit direction"[6] under which the amount of benefit payable would be reduced by an amount equivalent to 20% of the income support adult rate for the first six months and for the next twelve months an amount equivalent to 10% of the income support full adult rate. Under the provisions of the Child Support Act and the relevant regulations[7] the absent parent is required to furnish information or any such other evidence as will enable the Child Support Officers to make the necessary assessments for child support purposes. Under provisions of the act the Child Support Agency can also obtain information from the Inland Revenue, and from local authorities administering housing benefit as to the income or housing costs of an absent parent or person with care. In addition, Section 15 of the act provides the agency with some quite draconian powers to enable them to obtain information under the act. Thus it is provided that inspectors may be appointed to exercise powers of entry and enquiry and they can at all reasonable times enter any premises other than those used solely as a dwelling house in order to question any person aged 18 or over on the premises. It is further laid down under this provision that any occupier of the premises, and any employer or employee working there, any person carrying on a trade, profession, vocation or business or who is an employee or agent of these is required to furnish to the inspectors all such information and documents as he may reasonable require[8]. As has been pointed out elsewhere[9] the main aim is doubtless to obtain information from an absent parent's employer, but there appears to be nothing to prevent an inspector going to other premises such as the parent's bank or solicitor. The act does provide that where a child support officer has insufficient information upon which to base a final assessment then he can make an interim maintenance assessment[9]. Such interim assessments may well be higher than final ones but this could be argued to be useful as a means of encouraging the parties to part with information so that a reduction may be made in the final assessment.

1 Child Support Act 1991 s4 and s 6.
2 Ibid s 6(2) and s 46(3).
3 Ibid s 2.
4 See for example Matrimonial Causes Act 1973 s 25(1) and Children Act 1989 s 1
5 Child Support Act 1991.
6 See regulation 36 Child Support (Maintenance Assessment Procedure) Regulations 1992 SI1992/1813.
7 Child Support (Maintenance Assessments and Special Cases) Regulations 1992 SI 1992/1815.
8 Child Support Act 1991 s 15 (4) and (6).
9 Child Support Act 1991 s 12.

141D Issues of Parentage. Liability under the provisions of the Child Support Act 1991 depends upon a determination that one is the legal parent of the child. It is provided under the act that where a person who is alleged to be a parent of the child denies that he or she is one of the child's parents, then the Child Support Officer concerned shall not make a maintenance assessment on the assumption that that person is one of the child's parents, unless there has been a court order which resolves the question of parentage[1]. Any court orders which might have been made so that the child benefit officer can proceed with an assessment include an adoption order; a parental order under Section 30 of the Human Fertilisation and Embryology Act 1990; a declaration under Section 56 of the Family Law Act 1986 that the alleged parent is the parent of the child; a declaration under Section 27 of the Child Support Act; and a court finding that the alleged parent is or is adjudged to be the father of the child[2]. When an alleged parent is denying parentage and none of the above orders have been made then the Child Support Officer is entitled under the provisions of the act[2] to apply to the court[3] for a declaration that he is, or is not, a parent of the child, but such a declaration will only have effect for the purposes of the act itself[4].

1 Child Support Act 1991 s 26.
2 Child Support Act 1991 s 27.
3 Under Child Support Act 1991 s 27 (4) "court" means, subject to any provision made under Schedule 11 to the Children Act 1989, the High Court, County Court or Magistrate's Court.
4 See Child Support Act s 27 (3).

141E The Formula. The basis upon which the calculation of the maintenance payable by way of child support is made is contained in the formula set out in Schedule 1 of the Act. The provisions in Schedule 1 to the Act are amplified by the provisions in regulations which give the precise amounts and percentages of income which the letters used in the schedule were taken to represent[1.]

a. The maintenance requirement —The Act provides that the first step is to calculate the child's maintenance requirement which is defined as the minimum amount necessary for the maintenance of the qualifying child, or where there is more than one qualifying child all of them[2]. The formula used to assess the maintenance requirement is MR=AG-CB. In this formula MR is taken to indicate the maintenance requirement, AG means the aggregate of the amounts to be taken into account under the act to arrive at the basic day to day costs of supporting the children and this is calculated by adding the child allowance set at current income support levels, the amount of any income support family premium, the amount of income support lone parent premium, and the adult over 25 income support personal allowance. From this aggregate is then deducted CB which is the child benefit payable for the child. The amount of child benefit to be deducted includes the eldest child allowance but does not include one parent benefit so in a family with one child £9.65 would be deducted for that one child and in a family with a second or subsequent children £7.80 in respect of each other child would be deducted[3].

b. Assessable income — The next step is to calculate assessable income and set against it exempt income. Thus the calculation at this stage is represented in the act by the formula A=N-E. A means the absent parent's assessable income which is the income available to each parent after making allowance for day to day expenditure. In order to arrive at net income, income tax, national insurance contributions and half the parent's pension contributions are deducted. This will then produce a figure for net income. E means the absent parent's exempt income which comprises the parent's own essential expenses which must be met before maintenance is paid. This is set as the income support personal allowance payable for him but does not include an allowance for any new partner, the income support allowances for any of the absent parent's own children living with him, half the income support allowance for any child of the parent and the new partner (in recognition of the fact that the new partner will bear half of the liability for the child); any premiums payable for such children and the absent parent's housing costs but only a half of these will be allowed where the absent parent is living with another partner. Thus the absent parent's assessable income will consist of his net income after the deduction of the exempt income to cover his basic needs. An almost identical calculation is then done for the person with care using the formula set out in the schedule of C=M-F. In this formula C is equal to the assessable income of the person with care, M is equal to the person's net income and F is their exempt income. The regulations provide that the amounts used to calculate assessable income net income and exempt income are exactly the same as those used for the absent parent[5].

c. The assessment of maintenance — Once the child's maintenance requirement and the parents' assessable incomes have been calculated the Child Support Officer must then calculate the maintenance payable. This is calculated with reference to the formula (A+C)xP. The calculation is thus achieved by adding the two assessable incomes and multiplying them by 0.5 or 50%[6]. Where the result of this calculation is a sum equal to, or less than the child's maintenance requirement, then under the act[7] the absent parent must pay an amount equal to half his assessable income. It should be noted however that where total assessable income exceeds the maintenance requirement then an additional levy of child support is made at 25% of the balance of the assessable income after deducting the amount for the maintenance requirement. Provided the additional element payment does not exceed the maximum amount then this would be the amount of additional maintenance by way of child support which the absent parent should pay. There is however a ceiling on the amount of additional maintenance which can be paid and this is calculated by adding the amount of the income support personal allowance for the child as included in the maintenance requirement to the amount of the income support family premium and then multiplying the total of these by three. The multiplier and the use of the income support rates were chosen as a straightforward way of arriving at a reasonable level of maximum maintenance which would be regularly uprated[8].

d. Minimum payments — Where no payment is assessed as being payable due to the low income of the absent parent or where the absent parent is on income support or other benefits the absent parent is taken as having no assessable income. It was nevertheless felt desirable to include in the act some recognition of parental obligations towards the maintenance of their children and thus it was provided that 5% of the absent parent's income support should be deducted in order to emphasise the importance of this responsibility to his children[9]. Where however the absent parent is receiving benefits for children living with him then no deductions will be made[10].

e. Protected Income — In order to ensure that the absent parent would be left with an amount sufficient to cover his own needs, those of any children living with him and any new dependants as well as his housing costs the act provides[11] that the amount of any assessment shall be adjusted "with a view to securing so far as is reasonably practicable that payments by the absent parent of the amount so assessed will not reduce his disposable income below his protected income level." The protected level of income reflects the day to day expenses of the absent parent and his or her family that is including any partner and step children and other dependant children but not foster children living with them. In the same way as exempt income allowances made for children who live with the absent parent for part of the week. The protected income calculation does not include non-dependant people living in the same house or any person who has reached 16 and has left school. The protected income calculation includes the amount of the income support adult personal allowance for someone aged 25 or over or where the absent parent has a partner the amount of income support personal allowance for a couple where both are aged over 18 and in addition for each child the amount of income support personal allowance that would be appropriate for a child of the same age and in addition the amount of any income support premiums which would be applicable if income support were claimed and in addition reasonable housing costs for the whole family; plus any council tax liability for the members of the family after deducting any council tax benefit plus a standard margin of £8 in all cases together with a further margin of 10% of income above the basic protected income level. The extra margins of £8 and 10% are intended to ensure that the absent parent is left with an income in excess of the appropriate income support level in order to encourage that parent to work.

1 Child Support (Maintenance Assessment and Special Cases) Regulations 1992 SI 1992/1815.
2 Child Support Act 1991 Sch 1 para 1.
3 Child Support (Maintenance Assessments and Special Cases) Regulations 1992.
4 See *Children Come First* vol 1 para 3.8.
5 Child Support (Maintenance Assessments and Special Cases) Regulations 1992 SI 1992/1815 reg 3.
6 Ibid.
7 Child Support Act 1991 Sch 1 para 2 (2).
8 Child Support (Maintenance Assessments and Special Cases) Regulations 1992 SI 1992/1815 reg 4.
9 Child Support Act 1991 s 43.
10 Child Support (Maintenance Assessments and Special Cases) Regulations 1992 SI 1992/1815 reg 4.
11 Child Support Act 1991 Sch 1 para 6.

141F Review of assessments. The act provides that in order to keep pace with inflation or to meet changed circumstances the regulations will provide for the maintenance assessment to be reviewed by a Child Support Officer as soon as is reasonably practicable after the end of the prescribed period[1]. Alternatively the absent parent or the person with care can also seek a review themselves of a maintenance assessment on the grounds of a reasonable change of circumstances since the original assessment the amount of child support payable would be significantly different if it was to be reassessed[2]. Under either provision once a review is completed the Child Support Officer must make a fresh maintenance assessment. In order to allow any mistakes in an assessment to be corrected and to remove the necessity for a person with care or an absent parent themselves to seek a review, the act further provides that the Child Support Officer himself can make a fresh maintenance assessment where he is satisfied that the one currently in force is defective by reason of having been made in ignorance of material facts, or based on mistakes as to material facts, or being wrong in law, or that it would be appropriate to make a fresh assessment[3].

1 See Child Support Act 1991 s 16.
2 Ibid s 17.
3 Ibid s 19.

141G Reviewing the Child Support Officer's Decision. Under the provisions of the act[1] a person who is aggrieved by a Child Support Officers decision is able to seek a review by another officer who was not involved in the original decisions. A review can be requested against a refusal to grant an application for a maintenance assessment under Section 4, or to carry out a review under Section 17, or to challenge a current maintenance assessment or a cancellation or refusal of cancellation of such an assessment. The other officer need not carry out the review where he is satisfied that there are no reasonable grounds for supposing that the decision was made in ignorance of the material fact, was based on a mistake as to a material fact or was wrong in law. Where however as a result of the review the Officer is satisfied that a maintenance assessment or fresh assessment should be made then he should proceed to do so[2].

An appeal against a Child Support Officer's review or his refusal to carry out such a review lies to a child support appeal tribunal[3]. Such a tribunal is similar in composition and function to social security appeal tribunals[4]. The appeal must be brought within 28 days of the application unless leave is obtained from the chairman of the tribunal.[5] Where the appeal succeeds the tribunal must remit the case to be dealt with by a Child Support Officer and may give such directions as it considers appropriate. Further appeals on questions of law may be made to a Child Support Commissioner[6] and there is a further right of appeal to the Court of Appeal[7].

1 Child Support Act 1991 s 18.
2 Ibid ss 18, 19.
3 Ibid s 20.
4 Ibid s 21.
5 Ibid s 20(2).
6 Ibid s 22.
7 Ibid s 24 and 25.

141H Termination of assessments. Under the provisions of the act an assessment ceases to have effect on the death of the absent parent or the person with care or where there is no longer a qualifying child to benefit from the assessment. The assessment will also cease where the absent parent ceases to be the child's parent or where the absent parent or person with care have been living together for a continuous period of six months. In addition where a new maintenance assessment has been made by the Child Support Officer the original one ceases to take effect once the new assessment is notified[1]. There are further provisions under the act which allow for those persons who applied for assessments under Section 4 to request cancellation in which case the Child Support Officer must comply[2] and cancellation can also be achieved where an assessment was originally made when the parent with care was dependant on benefit and that parent is now no longer dependant upon benefits[3]. Finally under the provisions of the act a Child Support Officer may cancel an assessment where the person with care is on benefits provided he is satisfied that the person with care and the absent parent are now living together[4].

1 Child Support Act 1991 Sch 1 para 16.
2 Ibid para 2.
3 Ibid para 3.
4 Ibid para 6.

2: UNDER THE CHILDREN ACT 1989

142. Introduction. The general power of the courts to make orders for financial provision for children who are not covered by the provisions of the Child Support Act is to be found in Section 15 and Schedule 1 of the Children Act 1989. Schedule 1 seeks to provide a single statutory scheme for financial provision for children to replace the multiplicity of provisions under different pieces of legislation[1] now repealed by the Children Act 1989[2]. The Act does not however implement new provisions but re-enacts with consequential amendments and modifications the previous range of orders available for financial relief for children[3]. The ability of the courts to grant financial relief under Schedule 1 in a variety of different situations is, however, without prejudice to the court's powers to make orders in matrimonial proceedings under the Matrimonial Causes Act 1973[4] or the Domestic Proceedings and Magistrates' Courts Act 1978[5].

Where, therefore, the proceedings are exclusively concerned with the children, then parents, spouses or others seeking orders for financial provision from either or both parents must do so using the statutory scheme laid down in Schedule 1[6]. Where, however, the question of financial provision comes up in matrimonial proceedings, the courts may make orders under the relevant matrimonial legislation[7], which may be more appropriate where an adult is seeking relief for herself and the children at the same time.

For the purposes of the Children Act 1989 a "child" is defined as a person under the age of eighteen[8], but the powers to make or vary orders are extended in favour of persons over the age of eighteen where certain conditions are fulfilled[9].

A "parent" is defined for the purposes of the Act so as to include any party to a marriage (whether or not subsisting) in relation to whom the child concerned is a child of the family, and any reference to either or both parents of a child must be construed as references to any and all of his parents[10]. The only circumstances in which this definition of a parent does not apply is when the court is considering liability to pay maintenance beyond the age of eighteen or where the local authority is considering making payment of a residence order allowance[11].

Orders for financial relief will generally only be made upon an application by a specified person or persons, but in two situations, the court may make orders even though no application has been made. In the first, the court can make a financial order where it is making, varying or discharging a residence order[12], and in the second where the child concerned is a ward of court[13].

The courts which are able to make orders under Schedule 1 and the matrimonial legislation are the magistrates' courts, county courts and High Court[14] although the magistrates' powers are more limited than those of the higher courts[15].

1 Ie under the Family Law Reform Act 1969 s 6 (repealed), the Guardianship of Minors Act 1971 (repealed), Guardianship Act 1973 (repealed), the Children Act 1975 (repealed), and Family Law Reform Act 1987 ss 15, 16 (repealed).
2 Children Act 1989 Sch 15.
3 Ibid s 15 (1).
4 Matrimonial Causes Act 1973 ss 22, 23, 24, 24A, 25, 27, 29.
5 Domestic Proceedings and Magistrates Courts Act 1978 ss 17 (27 Halsbury's Statutes (4th Edn) MATRIMONIAL LAW).
6 Children Act 1989. Note there is no power to seek an order against a guardian.
7 For relevant provisions in the Matrimonial Causes Act 1973 and the Domestic Proceedings and Magistrates' Courts Act 1978 see respectively notes 4 and 5 supra.
8 Children Act 1989 s 105.
9 Ibid Sch 1 para 2 (1), (2).
10 Ibid Sch 1 para 16 (2).
11 Ibid. In which case the definition includes a natural parent.
12 Ibid Sch 1 para 1 (6).
13 Ibid Sch 1 para 1 (7)(as amended by the Courts and Legal Services Act 1990 s 116, Sch 16 para 10 (2)).
14 Ibid Sch 1 para 1.
15 Ibid Sch 1 para 1 (1)(b).

143. Making an application. Application can be made for orders for financial provision in respect of children who are not qualifying children under the Child Support Act or for such provision as lump sums, against a parent by the other parent, a guardian or anyone holding a residence order[1] filing the appropriate form[2] in respect of each child with the court. The application form together with sufficient numbers of copies for service[3] must be accompanied by a statement of means[4] also with copies for service, in the appropriate form on which the applicant should set out the financial details relevant to the application. The respondents to the application are: every person whom the applicant believes to have parental responsibility for the child and those persons whom the applicant believes to be interested in or affected by the proceedings[5]. The rules further require that the applicant must give notice of the proceedings to certain other persons which are: a local authority providing accommodation for the child; any person looking after the child at the time the proceedings are commenced; and if the child is staying in a refuge certificated under the Children Act, the person providing the refuge[6]. The proper officer or the justices' clerk will fix a date and time for the directions hearing, which will be indorsed on the notice of hearing[7] and then the applicant must serve a copy of the application, a notice of hearing and a statement of means on each respondent not less than 14 days prior to the date fixed for the hearing[8]. The applicant must further send a copy of the notice of hearing to every person to whom notice of the proceedings is required to be given[9].

An answer to an application for financial relief should be made in the appropriate form[10] and filed with the court together with a copy for each of the other parties to an application within 14 days of service of the original documents[11].

Apart from any financial statements which must be in the appropriate form[12], any other statement which is to be adduced at the hearing must be set out in the required form and served on the other parties prior to the hearing[13]. The normal rules relating to documentary evidence in family proceedings apply, and thus such evidence may not be relied upon unless it has been served or the court grants leave[14]. Documents already filed and served may not be amended without the leave of the court, which should be requested in writing[15]. Once an application has been made it can only be withdrawn with the leave of the court[16].

1 Children Act 1989 Sch 1 para 1 (1).
2 See CHA Form 13.
3 Family Proceedings Rules 1991, SI 1991/1247, r 4.4 (1)(a) and Family Proceedings Courts (Children Act 1989) Rules 1991, SI 1991/1395, r 4 (1)(a).
4 See CHA Form 14.
5 Family Proceedings Rules 1991 App 3 col (iv) and Family Proceedings Courts (Children Act 1989) Rules 1991 Sch 2 col (iii).
6 Family Proceedings Rules 1991 App 3 col (iii) and Family Proceedings Courts (Children Act 1989) Rules 1991 Sch 2 col (iv).
7 Family Proceedings Rules 1991 r 4.4 (2) and Family Proceedings Courts (Children Act 1989) Rules 1991 r 4 (2).
8 Family Proceedings Rules 1991 Appendix 3 col (ii) and Family Proceedings Courts (Children Act 1989) Rules 1991 Sch 2 col (ii).
9 Family Proceedings Rules 1991 r 4.4 (3) and Family Proceedings Courts (Children Act 1989) Rules 1991 r 4 (3.).
10 See CHA Form 13A.
11 Family Proceedings Rules 1991 r 4.9 (1) and Family Proceedings Courts (Children Act 1989) Rules 1991 r 9 (1).
12 Family Proceedings Rules 1991 r 4.4 (6) and Family Proceedings Courts (Children Act 1989) Rules 1991 r 4 (6).
13 Family Proceedings Rules 1991 r 4.17 (1) and Family Proceedings Courts (Children Act 1989) Rules 1991 r 17 (1).
14 Family Proceedings Rules 1991 r 4.17 (3) and Family Proceedings Courts (Children Act 1989) Rules 1991 r 17 (3).
15 Family Proceedings Rules 1991 r 4.19 (1) and Family Proceedings Courts (Children Act 1989) Rules 1991 r 19 (1).
16 Family Proceedings Rules 1991 r 4.5 (1) and Family Proceedings Courts (Children Act 1989) Rules 1991 r 5 (1).

144. The powers of the court. The High Court, county court and magistrates' courts may order the making of unsecured periodical payments either to the applicant for the benefit of the non-qualifying child[1] or to the child himself for such term as may be specified in the order[2]. The same courts may order lump sum payments[3], although in the magistrates' courts orders are limited to up to a prescribed maximum of £1,000[4]. A lump sum order may be made to defray expenses or liabilities incurred in connection with the birth of the child, or in maintaining the child[5], which were reasonably incurred before the order was made[6], although in the light of the ability of the parent with care to approach the child support agency for a maintenance assessment, some caution should now be exercised when acting for those against whom a lump sum order has been requested. The court may provide for any lump sum order to be paid by instalments[7], although where the court does so provide, the order may be varied on the application of the payer or recipient in terms of the number of instalments, the amount of each instalment and the date on which any instalment becomes payable[8].

The High Court and county court possess further powers to order the making of secured periodical payments[9], settlements of property[10] and transfers of property[11]. Unlike the other orders which can be made to the applicant for the benefit of the child or to the child himself, a settlement of property to which a parent is entitled, either in possession or reversion, must be made for the benefit of the child and to the satisfaction of the court[12]. Only one order for a settlement or for a transfer of property may be made against a parent for the same child[13], but there is no restriction on the number of periodical payments or lump sum orders which can be made in respect of a child before he reaches the age of eighteen[14].

All courts have the power to make interim orders for periodical payments pending the final disposal of the application[15]. An interim order can require either or both parents to make such periodical payments at such times and for such term as the court thinks fit[16] and the court may also give any directions it deems appropriate[17]. The court cannot make an order backdating payments to a date before which the substantive application was made[18], although payments may be ordered to begin at a later date[19]. Interim orders will end either when the application is finally disposed of, or on such date as is specified in the interim order[20] although this can be varied by substituting a later date[21].

It must be noted again that applications for financial provision are treated as family proceedings under the Children Act 1989[22]. Thus the court has power to make Section 8 or 16 orders even though no application for such orders has been made[23], and to direct an investigation of the child's circumstances under the provisions of Section 37[24].

1 Children Act 1989 Sch 1 para 1 (2)(a)(i).
2 Ibid para 1 (2)(a)(ii). Since the Finance Act 1988 there are no financial advantages to be gained in making payments direct to a child, although there may be in making payments to the ex-spouse in favour of the child, provided that she does not remarry.
3 Children Act 1989 Sch 1 para 1 (2)(c).
4 Ibid para 5 (2).
5 Ibid para 5(1)(a).
6 Ibid para 5 (1)(b).
7 Ibid para 5 (5).
8 Ibid para 5 (6)(a)-(c).
9 Ibid paras 1 (1)(a), 1 (2)(b).
10 Ibid paras 1 (1)(a), 1 (2)(d).
11 Ibid paras 1 (1)(a), 1 (2)(e).
12 Ibid para 1 (2)(d). See *K v K (Property Transfer)* [1992] 2 All ER 727.
13 Ibid para 1 (5)(b).
14 Ibid para 1 (5)(a).
15 Ibid para 9.
16 Ibid para 9 (1)(a).
17 Ibid para 9 (1)(b).
18 Ibid para 9 (2).
19 Ibid para 9 (2).
20 Ibid para 9 (3).
21 Ibid para 9 (4).

22 Children Act 1989 s 8 (4) covers proceedings under Part II, applications are made under s 15 and the Court has the powers given to it in Sch 1.

23 Ibid s 10 (1)(b).

24 Ibid s 37 (1).

145. Criteria to be applied when making orders. In deciding whether to exercise its powers in respect of non-qualifying children or to make orders for which no provision is made in the Child Support Act 1991, and if so in what manner, the court is directed to have regard to all the circumstances of the case including:

1. the income, earning capacity, property and other financial resources which each relevant person has or is likely to have in the foreseeable future;
2. the financial needs, obligations and responsibilities which each relevant person has or is likely to have in the foreseeable future;
3. the financial needs of the child;
4. the income, earning capacity (if any) and other financial resources of the child;
5. any physical or mental disability of the child, and
6. the manner in which the child was being, or was expected to be, educated or trained[1].

The relevant persons whose circumstances must be considered apart from the child are any parent[2], the applicant for the order[3] and any other person in whose favour the court proposes to make an order[4].

In deciding whether and how to exercise its powers to make an order against a step-parent of a child, the court is further directed to have regard to whether that person had assumed responsibility for the maintenance of the child and if so, the extent to which and the basis on which he assumed that responsibility and the length of period during which he assumed that responsibility; whether he did so knowing the child was not his; and the liability of any other person to maintain the child[5].

This provision mirrors similar ones in the relevant divorce[6] and matrimonial[7] legislation and although it means that orders against step-parents could be made outside the matrimonial legislation, it is just as likely that it will be step-parents who will be making applications for orders.

It is further provided that where the court makes an order for financial provision against a person who is not the father of the child, it must record in the order that it has been made on the basis that the person concerned is not the child's father[8].

1 Children Act 1989 Sch 1 para 4 (1).
2 Ibid para 4 (4)(a).
3 Ibid para 4 (4)(c).
4 Ibid para 4 (4)(d).
5 Ibid para 4 (2).
6 See Matrimonial Causes Act 1973 s 25 (4).
7 Domestic Proceedings and Magistrates' Courts Act 1978 s 3 (4).
8 Children Act 1989 Sch 1 para 4 (3).

146. Duration of orders. An order for unsecured or secured periodical payments may begin with the date of the application, or any later date but cannot in the first instance extend beyond the child's seventeenth birthday unless the court thinks it right in the circumstances of the case to specify a later date[1]. An order shall not in any event extend beyond the child's eighteenth birthday unless it appears to the court that the child is or will be or if an order were made would be receiving instruction at an educational establishment or undergoing training for a trade, profession or vocation whether or not whilst in gainful employment or there are special circumstances which justify the making of the order[2].

Where an order for the making of, or securing of, periodical payments ceases to have effect on the child reaching sixteen, or at any time thereafter but before he reaches eighteen, then the child may apply to the court which made the order for its revival[3]. The court can provide for the order to be revived where the child is receiving educational instruction or training for a trade profession or vocation or again where there are special circumstances[4]. The court's powers to revive the order can only be backdated to the making of the application[5].

Any order for periodical payments made against a parent while the child is under eighteen ceases to have effect where the parent making or securing the payments and the parent receiving them live together for more than six months[6].

Further, any unsecured periodical payments order ceases to have effect on the death of the payer[7].

1   Children Act 1989 Sch 1 para 3 (1)(a).
2   Ibid Sch 1 para 3 (1)(b), (2).
3   Ibid Sch 1 para 6 (5).
4   Ibid Sch 1 para 6 (6).
5   Ibid Sch 1 para 6 (6).
6   Ibid Sch 1 para 3 (4).
7   Ibid Sch 1 para 3 (3).

147. Orders for financial provision for persons over eighteen. The Act provides (following on from the provision made in the Family Law Reform Act 1987) that a person who has reached the age of eighteen may apply to the court for periodical payments or lump sum order against either or both parents[1]. The court may make the order or orders if it is satisfied that the person is, or would be if an order was made, receiving instruction at an education institution or undergoing training for a trade profession or vocation[2], or that there are special circumstances justifying an order[3].

An application may not be made for an order by the person, if immediately before he reached the age of sixteen there was a periodical payments order in force in respect of him[4], and no order can be made when the parents of the applicant are living together in the same household[5].

In determining what orders should be made, the court is bound by the same considerations to which it has regard in the case of other applications for financial provision for children under the Act[6].

The orders may be varied or discharged on the application of the person in whose favour the order was made, or on the application of any person by whom the order was to be paid[7]. There is no power to vary a lump sum order except where the sum has been ordered to be paid in instalments when it is possible to vary the number or amount or date of the instalments payable[8].

1   Children Act 1989 Sch 1 para 2 (1), (2).
2   Ibid Sch 1 para 2 (1)(a).
3   Ibid Sch 1 para 2 (1)(b).
4   Ibid Sch 1 para 2 (3).
5   Ibid Sch 1 para 2 (4).
6   Ibid Sch 1 para 4 (1).
7   Ibid Sch 1 para 2 (5).
8   Ibid Sch 1 para 5 (6).

148. Variation of orders and Appeals. The Act provides that any order for secured or unsecured periodical payments may subsequently be varied or discharged upon the application of any person by or to whom payments were required to be made[1], or by the child himself, if he has reached the age of sixteen[2]. An order for the making or securing of periodical payments may be varied or discharged after the death of either parent on the application of a guardian of the child concerned[3]. In addition secured periodical payment orders may be varied or discharged on application being made by the personal representatives of the deceased parent's estate[4]. It should be noted however that the court's permission will be required if the application is made more than six months after the date on which representation in respect of the estate of the deceased parent was first taken out[5]. Where a lump sum order is payable by instalments, application may be made to vary the number, amount or date of the instalments[6].

An application for variation should be made in the prescribed form[7] together with the relevant number of copies for service and the normal provisions with regard to the requirements for service and for giving notice under the provisions of the Act should be adhered to[8].

Where the court is considering an application to vary an order the court may consider temporarily suspending periodical payments orders and may subsequently revive them[9]. The court is further able, provided the child has not yet reached the age of eighteen, to make further orders for periodical payments and lump sums[10].

When considering an application to vary an order the court is bound to have regard to the matters laid down for the court's consideration when it made the original order[11].

It should be noted that under the Maintenance Enforcement Act 1991 magistrates further have the power where satisfied that payments have not been made in accordance with the terms of the order to provide that payments be made directly to a creditor or to a clerk of the court; or that they should be made payable by standing order or that they should be made the subject of an Attachment of Earnings order under the provisions of the Attachment of Earnings Act 1971[12].

Appeals — Reference should be made to the detailed discussion earlier with regard to appeals and the powers of the appellate courts, but in the context of financial provision it should be noted that an appeal lies against the making, variation or revocation of an order, against the terms of an order and against the refusal to make, vary or revoke an order and that such appeals lie from the magistrates' court to the High Court, and from a district judge to a circuit judge[13]. An appeal from a circuit judge lies to the Court of Appeal[14]. It should be noted in particular that no appeal lies against the making or refusal to make an interim periodical payments order[15]. Where the appeal relates to the making of a periodical payments order, the High Court may order that its determination of the appeal shall have effect from such date, consistent with the Rules of Court, as it thinks fit to specify[16]. Where the High Court reduces the payments or discharges the order it may order the payee to return the sums paid as it thinks fit, and may order the remittance of any arrears in whole or in part[17].

1 Children Act 1989 Sch 1 para 1 (4).
2 Ibid Sch 1 para 6 (4).
3 Ibid Sch 1 para 6 (8).
4 Ibid Sch 1 para 7 (1).
5 Ibid Sch 1 para 7 (2).
6 Ibid Sch 1 para 5 (6).
7 See Form 116 post.

8 See Family Proceedings Rules 1991, SI 1991/1247, r 4.4 generally and see rr 4.4 (6), 4.8 and Appendix 3 col ii, iii and iv; and also see Family Proceedings Courts (Children Act 1989) Rules 1991, SI 1991/1395, rr 4 (1), 4 (8) and Sch 2 col (ii), (iii) and (iv).
9 Children Act 1989 Sch 1 para 6 (2).
10 Ibid Sch 1 para 1 (5)(a).
11 Ibid Sch 1 para 1 (5)(b).
12 Children Act 1989 Sch 1 para 6A (as inserted by the Maintenance Enforcement Act 1991 s 6). See Paragraph 6 ante.
13 See Paragraph 6 ante.
14 See Paragraph 6 ante.
15 Children Act 1989 s 94 (3).
16 Ibid s 94 (6), (7).
17 Ibid s 94 (8).

149. Financial provision for children living abroad. The Act further provides[1] that courts can make orders for secured and unsecured periodical payments[2] against a parent living in England and Wales where the child is living outside England and Wales with the other parent, a guardian, or a person in whose favour a residence order is in force with respect to the child[3]. It should be noted that the child cannot make an application himself but he may apply for a variation of an order when he has attained the age of sixteen[4]. It would seem that an order for the maintenance of a person over the age of eighteen cannot be made if that person lives outside England and Wales[5].

1 Children Act 1989 Sch 1 para 14.
2 Ibid Sch 1 para 14 (1).
3 Ibid Sch 1 para 14 (1)(a), (b), (c).
4 Ibid Sch 1 para 6 (4).
5 Ibid Sch 1 para 14 (1).

3: UNDER THE MATRIMONIAL CAUSES ACT 1973

150. Court's powers to make orders. In any proceedings for divorce, nullity of marriage or judicial separation, the court, before granting a decree or on granting a decree or at any time thereafter[1] or, where any such proceedings are dismissed, either forthwith or within a reasonable period after dismissal[2] may make orders for periodical payments, secured periodical payments and a lump sum to be paid by a party to the marriage in favour of such person as may be specified for the benefit of a child or to a child of the family[3]. It should be noted that in all new cases arising after April 1993 the court's jurisdiction to make orders for the maintenance of qualifying children is ousted by the provisions of the Child Support Act. The court's powers to make orders for lump sums or in respect of certain children such as step children is not however affected and so the provisions set out below will continue to apply in these circumstances.[4] An order may be made for the payment of a lump sum to or for the benefit of a child of the family for the specific purpose of enabling any liabilities or expenses reasonably incurred by or for the benefit of that child to be met[5]. It should be noted that the court may order that periodical payments be made to such person as may be specified in the order for the benefit of the child or to the child himself[6].

The court is further empowered to order the transfer of property to or for the benefit of a child of the family or that it should be settled for his benefit and the court may further vary, for the benefit of such a child any antenuptial or post-nuptial settlement[7] and may make an order for the sale of property[8].

1   Matrimonial Causes Act 1973 s 23 (1).
2   Ibid s 23 (2).
3   Ibid see s 23 (1)(c)-(f).
4   See ante para 141.
5   Ibid s 23 (3).
6   Ibid s 23 (1)(d).
7   Ibid s 24 (1)(a), (b), (c).
8   Ibid s 24A.

151. Criteria for the making of, and duration of orders under the Matrimonial Causes Act 1973. In deciding whether or not to exercise its powers to order financial provision to or for the benefit of a child of a family not dealt with by child support, the court is required to give first consideration to the welfare while a minor, of any child of the family who has not attained the age of eighteen[1]. When determining whether to exercise its powers to make orders for financial provision by way of periodical payments, lump sum provision or by a variation of property arrangements against a party to a marriage, the court is required to consider[2]:

1. the income, earning capacity, property and other financial resources which each of the parties to the marriage has or is likely to have in the foreseeable future, including in the case of earning capacity any increase in that capacity which it would in the opinion of the court be reasonable to expect a party to the marriage to take steps to acquire;
2. the financial needs, obligations and responsibilities which each of the parties to the marriage has or is likely to have in the foreseeable future;
3. the standard of living enjoyed by the family before the breakdown of marriage;
4. the age of each party to the marriage and the duration of the marriage;
5. any physical or mental disability of either of the parties to the marriage;
6. the contributions which each of the parties has made or is likely in the foreseeable future to make to the welfare of the family, including any contribution made by looking after the home or caring for the family;
7. the conduct of each of the parties, if that conduct is such that it would in the opinion of the court be inequitable to disregard it;
8. in the case of proceedings for divorce or nullity of marriage, the value to each of the parties to the marriage of any benefit (for example, a pension) which by reason of the dissolution or annulment of the marriage, that party will lose the chance of acquiring[3].

Having considered these matters in relation to the party against whom an order is being made, the court must then move on to consider in relation to each child of the family in relation to whom it may exercise its powers under the Act, the following matters:

1. the financial needs of the child;
2. the income, earning capacity (if any) property and other financial resources of the child;
3. any physical or mental disability of the child;
4. the manner in which he was being and in which the parties to the marriage expect him to be educated or trained;

5. the considerations mentioned in relation to the parties to the marriage in the paragraphs set out above[4].

As can be seen, factors to which the court must have regard under this Act are virtually identical to those to which the court is directed under the provisions of the Children Act 1989, except in so far as these relate specifically to issues arising from or as a result of the proceedings for divorce or nullity of marriage[5].

Where the court is being asked to make an order against a party to a marriage who is not a parent of the child in question the court is directed[6] to have regard to whether that party assumed any responsibility for the child's maintenance and, if so, to what extent, and to whether in assuming such responsibility that party did so knowing the child was not his or her own, and for the liability of any other person to maintain that child[7]. Again as was the case with the Children Act, an order for secured or unsecured periodical payments in respect of a child will not in the first instance extend beyond his seventeenth birthday, unless the court considers in the circumstances of the case that the welfare of the child requires that it should be extended to a later date[8]. Orders for such payments will not extend beyond the child's eighteenth birthday unless he is, or would be if an order were made, be receiving instruction at an educational establishment or undergoing training for a trade, profession or vocation whether or not he is also gainfully employed, or where there are special circumstances which justify the making of an order[9].

1   Matrimonial Causes Act 1973 s 25 (1).
2   When the court is exercising its powers under the Matrimonial Causes Act 1973 ss 23, 24 and 24A.
3   Ibid s 25 (2).
4   Ibid s 25 (3).
5   For example ibid s 25 (2)(d), (g), (h).
6   Ibid s 25 (4).
7   Ibid s 25 (4).
8   Ibid s 29 (2).
9   Ibid s 29 (3).

152. Failure to provide reasonable maintenance. As well as being able to make application for periodical payments under the regime associated with divorce, nullity or judicial separation, the Matrimonial Causes Act further provides that either party to a marriage may apply to the court for an order for periodical payments or lump sum provision on the ground that the other party to the marriage has failed to provide or to make a proper contribution towards reasonable maintenance of any child of the family[1] who is not a qualifying child under the terms of the Child Support Act 1991. In order to be able to make an application it must be shown that either the applicant or the respondent have been domiciled or habitually resident for one year in England and Wales on the date of the application[2].

In determining whether or not the respondent has failed to provide or make a proper contribution towards the reasonable maintenance of any child of the family who is not a qualifying child the court must have regard to all the circumstances of the case, including the criteria set out in the previous paragraph. Again, first consideration must be given to the welfare of any child while a minor[3], and where the child of the family to whom the application relates is not a child of the respondent then again attention must be given to the issue of whether the party had assumed any responsibility for the child's maintenance and if so to what extent and to whether in assuming such responsibility that party did so knowing that the child was not his or her own, and the liability of any other person to maintain that child[4].

One or two amendments are made to the criteria laid down for guiding the court in its decision whether or not to make orders so that instead of references to the breakdown of a marriage there are instead references to the failure to provide or make a proper contribution towards reasonable maintenance for the child of the family to whom the application relates[5].

The range of provision which may be made on an application for failure to provide reasonable maintenance is restricted to orders for periodical payments, secured periodical payments or lump sum provision to or for the benefit of the child[6].

1 Matrimonial Causes Act 1973 s 27 (1). See Form 121 post.
2 Ibid s 27 (2).
3 See Paragraph 151 ante and Matrimonial Causes Act 1973 s 25 (1).
4 Ibid s 25 (4).
5 Ibid s 27 (1), (3).
6 Ibid s 27 (6).

153. Variation and discharge of orders for financial provision under Matrimonial Causes Act 1973. It is provided that where the court has made an order for financial provision then it shall further have the power to vary or discharge the order or to suspend any provision thereof temporarily and to revive the operation of any provision so suspended[1]. The court's powers are exercisable in relation to any orders for maintenance pending suit and any interim orders for maintenance, any periodical payments orders, secured periodical payments orders, lump sum provision, any order for settlement of property and any order made for the sale of property[2].

Where the court exercises its powers and varies or discharges a periodical payments or secured periodical payments order then the court has power to direct that the variation or discharge shall not take effect until the expiration of such period as may be specified in the order[3].

1 Matrimonial Causes Act 1973 s 31 (1).
2 Ibid s 31 (2).
3 Ibid s 31 (10).

154. Procedure. It should be noted that the procedure for making applications for financial relief under the Matrimonial Causes Act is now governed by the Family Proceedings Rules 1991 and corresponds with the provisions made for applications under the Children Act 1989[1]. Thus proceedings must commence by filing an application in the prescribed form[2] with sufficient copies for each respondent and must be accompanied by an affidavit of means[3]. The notice of application must be served within 4 days of filing[4] and the respondent must within 28 days (or such other time as the court may fix) after the service of the applicant's affidavit, file an affidavit of means in answer[5].

1 Children Act 1989. See ante Paragraphs 141-147.
2 See Forms M11 and M13 Family Proceedings Rules 1991 as amended by SI 1992/456
3 Family Proceedings Rules 1991, SI 1991/1247, r 2.58 (2).
4 Ibid r 2.55.
5 Ibid r 2.58 (3).

4: UNDER THE DOMESTIC PROCEEDINGS AND MAGISTRATES' COURTS ACT 1978

155. Grounds for making an application. An application for financial provision for children of the family not covered by the provisions of the Child Support Act 1991[1] may be made to the court and the court may order such financial provision in the following circumstances: where the applicant has proved one or more of the four grounds of application[2]; with the agreement of the other spouse[3]; or where the parties have been living apart by agreement for a continuous period exceeding three months and the respondent has been making periodical payments[4]. When the court is considering whether and how to exercise its jurisdiction to make an order under the Act it must give first consideration to the welfare of any child of the family and must have regard to the same criteria applicable in applications under the Matrimonial Causes Act 1973 when determining the level of such orders[5], and in deciding whether to make an order against the party to the marriage who is not a parent of the child the court must have regard again to the factors considered relevant under the Matrimonial Causes Act 1973[6].

Where the applicant has proved one of the grounds for financial provision[7], then the court may make an order that the respondent make to the applicant for the benefit of or to a child of the family such periodical payments and for such term as may be specified or such lump sum as may be specified[8]. It should be noted that either spouse may be ordered to make financial provision in favour of a parent who is not a party to the marriage if that parent has the child or children living with them.

Any lump sum provision which is ordered to be made in the magistrates' court may not exceed £1,000[9].

See ante para 141.

1 See ante para 141.
2 Domestic Proceedings and Magistrates Courts Act 1978 ss 1, 2.
3 Ibid s 6.
4 Ibid s 7.
5 Ibid s 3 (1).
6 Ibid s 3 (2), (4).
7 Ibid s 1 but note that orders may be made in favour of an applicant even where the court is not satisfied of any ground in ibid s 1.
8 Ibid s 2 (1).
9 Ibid s 2 (3).

156. Procedure. It should be noted that the procedure for making applications for financial relief under the Domestic Proceedings and Magistrates' Courts Act is now governed by the Family Proceedings Courts (Matrimonial Proceedings etc) Rules 1991 and corresponds with the provisions made for applications under the Children Act 1989[1]. Thus, proceedings must commence by filing an application in the prescribed form[2] with sufficient copies for each respondent and must be accompanied by a statement of means and notice of hearing. Service must be effected in accordance with the terms of the rules previously discussed and the respondent's answer and his statement of means filed within a period of fourteen days thereafter[3].

1 See Paragraphs 142-148 ante.
2 See Family Proceedings Courts (Matrimonial Proceedings) etc Rules 1991, SI 1991/1991 Sch1 Form 1.
3 See Paragraph 143 ante.

5: ENFORCEMENT OF ORDERS FOR FINANCIAL PROVISION

157. Enforcement of orders in the magistrates' courts. Under the provisions of the Children Act 1989[1] and the provisions of Part I of the Domestic Proceedings and Magistrates' Courts Act 1978[2], all orders for financial provision made in the magistrates' court are enforceable as magistrates' courts maintenance orders[3]. Any money due under Magistrates' Courts Maintenance Orders may be enforced by distress or committal to prison[4]. Such orders may also be enforced by the procedure relating to attachment of earnings[5], or by registration in the High Court under the Maintenance Orders Act 1958 and subsequent enforcement in that court[6].

It should be noted that under the Maintenance Enforcement Act 1991 magistrates' courts are required when making an order for periodical payments, and as long as the person against whom the order is made is ordinarily resident in England and Wales at the time that the order was made, to specify the method of payment. Under the provisions of the Act the specified method of payment must be one of the following: payments made directly by the debtor to the creditor; payments made to the clerk of the court or the clerk of any other magistrates' court; payment by standing order; or payment by any other method which requires one person to give his authority for payment of a specific amount to be made from an account of his to an account of another, on specific dates during the period of which the authority is in force and without the need for any further authority from him[7]. Under the provisions of the Act the magistrates' courts are empowered to make an attachment of earnings order to secure payments under the order[8]. Where the payment is ordered to be by standing order or some similar method the court is further empowered to require the debtor to open an account[9].

The Children Act makes further specific provision with regard to persons liable to make payment under that Act[10]. These provisions require any person liable to make payments to give notice of any change of address to such person if any as may be specified in the order and any person failing without reasonable excuse to do so shall be guilty of an offence and liable on summary conviction to a fine[11].

1 Children Act 1989 Sch 1 para 12 (3).
2 Domestic Proceedings and Magistrates' Courts Act 1978 s 32 (1)(as substituted by the Family Law Reform Act 1987 s 33(1), Sch 2 para 88 (b)).
3 Children Act 1989 Sch 1 para 12 (3) and see Magistrates' Courts Act 1980 s 150 (1)(as amended by the Family Law Reform Act 1987 s 33 (1), Sch 2 para 70).
4 Magistrates' Courts Act 1980 s 76.
5 Attachment of Earnings Act 1971 s 1 (3)(a), 2, Sch 1 paras 4, 5.
6 See Maintenance Orders Act 1958 s 1 (1A) and note a lump sum order is also capable of being registered see ibid s 2 (3A).
7 Maintenance Enforcement Act 1991 s 2.
8 Magistrates' Courts Act 1980 s 59 (as substituted by the Maintenance Enforcement Act 1991 s 2).
9 Magistrates' Courts Act 1980 s 59 (4)(as substituted by Maintenance Enforcement Act 1991 s 2).
10 Children Act 1989 Sch 1 para 12 (1).
11 Ibid Sch 1 para 12 (2).

158. Enforcement of orders for financial provision in the county court and High Court. When steps are considered necessary to take proceedings for the enforcement of orders for financial provision in the county court or High Court then these must be done in the appropriate manner in accordance with the procedure applicable in those courts. These will include recovery of arrears which may be directed at the respondent's current income using a judgment summons or an attachment of earnings order or at the respondent's capital assets using garnishee proceedings, charging orders, fiere facias or warrants of execution or other similar remedies[1]. The relevant provisions of the rule which deal with the enforcement of an order for payment of money require an affidavit to be filed before any process for enforcement may be issued. In the affidavit the amount due must be verified and it must be shown how that amount due was arrived at[2].

1 See Family Proceedings Rules 1991, SI 1991/1247, rr 7.1-7.6.
2 See Family Proceedings Rules 1991, r 7.1 (1) and the request must be filed on Form M16.

6: MAINTENANCE AGREEMENTS

159. Meaning and effect of maintenance agreements. Maintenance agreements may be made and be legally enforceable under provisions in the Matrimonial Causes Act 1973[1] and the Children Act 1989[2] and are further not restricted by the provisions of the Child Support Act 1991[3]. But as a result of the Act, provided the child support officer has jurisdiction a parent with care can seek a maintenance assessmernt under the Child Support Act 1991 and courts will not be able to vary the agreement[4]. It would thus appear that such agreements would in future only be of utility in those cases not covered by the 1991 Act[5]. It should further be noted that any clause in an agreement purporting to restrict the right of any person to seek an assessment in respect of a qualifying child shall be void.

Under the provisions of the 1973 Act where the 1991 Act does not apply applications may be made by spouses or former spouses to have the agreement altered[6] and it is further provided that any term in any maintenance agreement which purports to restrict any right to apply to court for an order containing financial arrangements is void[7]. The Children Act 1989 provides that application can in certain circumstances be made to the court for the agreement to be altered by either parent but no express provision is made rendering any terms void although it seems likely in fact that such a term would be held to be unenforceable[8].

Under the terms of the 1973 Act a maintenance agreement must be in writing and made between spouses or future spouses[9]. It must further be an agreement containing financial arrangements whether made during the continuation of or after the dissolution or annulment of the marriage; or a separation agreement which contains no financial arrangements in a case where no other agreement in writing between the same parties contains such arrangements[10]. Financial arrangements for these purposes are defined as provisions governing the rights and liabilities towards one another when living separately of the parties to a marriage (including a marriage which has been dissolved or annulled) in respect of the making or securing of payments or the disposition or use of any property, including such rights and liabilities with respect to the maintenance or education of any child, whether or not a child of the family[11].

By contrast, an agreement under the Children Act 1989 does not have to have been made between spouses or former spouses although it must be in writing, and made with respect to a child between the father and mother and must contain provision with respect to the making or securing of payments or the disposition or use of any property, for the maintenance or education of the child[12].

1 Matrimonial Causes Act 1973 s 34.
2 Children Act 1989 Sch 1 para 10.
3 Child Support Act 1991, s 9(2).
4 Ibid, s 9(3) and (4).
5 See ante para 141
6 Matrimonial Causes Act 1973 s 35.
7 Ibid s 34 (1).
8 Children Act 1989 Sch 1 para 10 (2), (3) and see *Hyman v Hyman* [1929] AC 601, [1929] All ER Rep 245, HL.
9 Matrimonial Causes Act 1973 s 34 (2).
10 Ibid s 34 (2)(a), (b).
11 Ibid s 34 (2).
12 Children Act 1989 Sch 1 para 10 (1).

160. Alteration of maintenance agreements. A maintenance agreement made between spouses or former spouses under the provisions of the 1973 Act and not caught by the provisions of the Child Support Act 1991 may be made the subject of an application for alteration to the High Court or county court provided each of the parties is either domiciled or resident in England and Wales[1]. Where, however, an application is made to the magistrates' court each party though not the child must be resident in England and Wales at the date of the making of the application[2]. In determining whether or not to exercise its powers the court must be satisfied that the child support officer does not have jurisdiction and the agreement should be altered either because there has been a change in the circumstances in the light of which any financial arrangements contained in the agreement were made or, as the case may be, where omitted from it or because the agreement failed to contain proper financial arrangements with respect to any child of the family[3]. In this situation the courts may alter the agreement by varying or revoking any financial arrangements contained in it or by inserting in it financial arrangements for the benefit of any child of the family as may appear to the court to be just[4]. Where application is being made against a party in favour of a child who is not that person's natural or adoptive child, then the court must have regard to the criteria applied by the courts when making orders for financial provision generally[5].

Provided that the Child Support Act 1991 does not rule out the court having jurisdiction then as far as applications in respect of maintenance agreements between mothers and fathers in favour of their children under the Children Act 1989 are concerned, the application may be made by either parent, but in the case of an agreement intended to continue after the death of the parents, application may be made either by the surviving parent or the personal representative[6]. An application may not be made, save with leave of the High Court or county court, after the end of a period of six months from the day on which representation in regard to the estate of the deceased is first taken out[7].

Jurisdiction to hear an application for alteration is possessed by the High Court and county court provided the Child Support Act 1991 does not rule it out and each party is either domiciled or resident in England and Wales[8] but in respect of the magistrates' court jurisdiction only exists where both parties are resident in England and Wales and at least one of them is resident in the relevant commission area[9]. It should be pointed out that magistrates only possess a power to increase, reduce or terminate periodical payments and they have no power to alter arrangements made in connection with property[10].

Provided the Child Support Act does not apply then the criteria for alteration of an agreement under the Children Act are clearly laid down and the court may exercise its powers only where it is satisfied either that, by reason of a change in the circumstances in the light of which any financial arrangements contained in the agreement were made (including a change foreseen by the parties when making the agreement), the agreement should be altered so as to make different financial arrangements, or that the arrangement does not contain proper financial arrangements with respect to the child[11]. Where it is so satisfied the court may vary or revoke any financial arrangements as may appear just[12]. Any agreement which has altered provision for periodical payments should not in the first instance extend beyond the child's seventeenth birthday unless the child is undergoing full-time education or vocational training whether or not in paid employment, or there are special circumstances[13]. Finally it should be noted that the powers to alter such agreements are retrospective and thus apply to agreements made before as well as after 14th October 1991[14].

1 Matrimonial Causes Act 1973 s 35 (1).
2 Ibid s 35 (3).
3 Ibid s 35 (2).
4 Ibid s 35 (2)(b)(i), (ii).
5 Ibid s 25 (4), s 35 (2).
6 Children Act 1989 Sch 1 para 11 (1).
7 Ibid Sch 1 para 11 (3).
8 Ibid Sch 1 para 10 (2).
9 Ibid Sch 1 para 10 (6).
10 Ibid Sch 1 para 10 (6)(a), (b).
11 Ibid Sch 1 para 10 (3)(a), (b).
12 Ibid Sch 1 para 10 (3).
13 Ibid Sch 1 para 3 (1), (2).
14 Ibid Sch 1 para 10 (1).

CHAPTER 7: CHILD ABDUCTION

161. Introduction. A frequent and trenchant criticism of the Children Act 1989 was that it did not take any further[1] steps to solve the increasing problems caused by child abduction, the unilateral removal of a child by one parent without the consent of the other parent. Whatever the background reasons, child abduction represents an extremely traumatic experience for children and parents alike. It has been noted[2] that "frequently abductions occur because a separated parent feels excluded from the child's life and this is usually coupled with hostility and anger towards the carer. In some cases children are abducted because the separated parent has genuine concerns about the child's welfare and a lack of confidence in the legal system here or abroad to deal with the issues appropriately. Whatever the motivation for the abduction it represents a traumatic and possibly violent experience for a child resulting in sudden disturbance, removal from a settled home, familiar surroundings, school and friends and also from contact with the parent or settled carer." Inevitably due to an increase in the numbers of relationships between partners of different nationalisation and easier and cheaper international travel, child abduction is on the increase. The Child Abduction Unit at the Lord Chancellor's Department[3] estimates that there were over 200 foreign abductions in 1991 whilst practitioners in the field put the numbers at closer to 1000.[2] The figures are likely to increase much more with the free movement of persons within the European Community and the dissolution of border controls coming into effect from the beginning of 1993. Criminal liability for the abduction of a child who is under sixteen is governed by the provisions of the Child Abduction Act 1984. There is also the offence at common law of kidnapping a child[4]. The provisions of the Child Abduction Act 1984 distinguish between abduction by persons who are "connected with the child" and abduction by those persons who are not so connected[5]. Those persons who are deemed to be connected with the child include a parent (which, in the case of a child whose parents were not married to each other, includes any person in respect of whom there are reasonable grounds for believing that he is the father of the child; any person in whose favour a residence order is in force or who otherwise has custody of the child; and a guardian[6]). The Act provides that persons connected with the child only commit an offence where the child is wrongfully removed out of the United Kingdom, which is to be contrasted with those persons who are not connected with the child who may commit an offence whether the child is removed within or outside the United Kingdom[7]. An offence is actually committed under the Child Abduction Act 1984 where a person connected with the child takes or sends a child under the age of sixteen out of the United Kingdom without the appropriate consent[8]. The appropriate consent required is that of each of the following:

1. the child's mother;
2. the child's father if he has parental responsibility for him;
3. any guardian of the child;
4. any person in whose favour a residence order is in force with respect to the child and
5. any person who has custody of the child;

or with the leave of the court granted under or by virtue of any provision of Part II of the Children Act 1989 or of the court which granted custody[9]. The Act provides that no offence is committed by any person in whose favour a residence order is in force, removing a child from the United Kingdom without consent for periods of less than one month unless this is in breach of a prohibited steps order[10].

The offence of child abduction can be committed by other persons if they, without lawful authority or reasonable excuse, take or detain a child under the age of sixteen so as to remove him from the lawful control of any person having lawful control of him; or so as to keep him out of the lawful control of any person entitled to lawful control of the child[11]. The persons having lawful control are: where the father and mother of the child in question were married to each other at the time of his birth, the child's mother and father; where the father and mother of the child in question were not married to each other at the time of his birth, the child's mother, any person in whose favour a residence order is in force, or who has custody of the child or who is a guardian of the child. The Act makes a distinction between parents or other persons connected with the child who will only be guilty of an offence where the child is removed from the United Kingdom and other persons who may be guilty of an offence simply by removing or detaining the child[12]. The reason for such a distinction has been said to be that parties to family disputes in respect of children should seek to resolve their differences by making applications for orders under the Children Act 1989[13], and that where there is deemed to be an emergency or a risk of a child being removed from the jurisdiction, then this could be dealt with by an order being made ex parte[14]. Where, therefore, a child is removed out of the United Kingdom and an allegation is made that this has been wrongfully done then the parties must seek to sort out their disputes at civil law under the provisions of the Child Abduction and Custody Act 1985[15].

Whilst the main aim of the Child Abduction Act 1984 is to deter parents from abducting their children out of the country, it also provides the means by which parents can seek to prevent abduction. Since the act makes it an offence to attempt to remove a child from the United Kingdom, the police are able to arrest[16] any person whom they reasonably suspect of attempting to take a child out of the country contrary to the provisions of the 1984 Act. Guidance issued by the Home Office[17] gives guidance to chief police officers in relation to enforcement. The technologies that police intervention at the stage of the attempt will offer a particularly effective means of enforcement. An arrest can be made at this stage only if the test of reasonable suspicion is met and: "whether that test is met may often depend among other things on the nature of the information which the officer contemplating the arrest has received beforehand. Whether or not arrest should be resorted to would depend on the urgency of the situation (eg if a suspect is about to embark) and will have regard to the highly charged emotions of the case". The consent of the Director of Public Prosecutions is required to bring a prosecution but it is not envisaged that this should be obtained before an arrest or before charges are preferred. Because of the sensitive nature of child abduction within the family, the Circular advises "so far as is possible it will be important in such circumstances for those who receive the complaint to make what inquiries are practicable to satisfy themselves that the complaint is bona fide before any action is initiated". It is therefore extremely important that clear and detailed information is given to the police. In addition where the police decide to act they can through the port alert system alert immigration officers at ports and airports to the possibility of a child being taken out of the country unlawfully. Requests for port alerts should be made to the local police[18]. The port alert procedures can be invoked where the child is under the age of 16 and there is reason to believe that an offence has been committed under the Child Abduction Act 1984 or where an order has been made in wardship, matrimonial or children act proceedings containing a restriction on the child being removed from the jurisdiction[19]. The police will send out an all-ports message on the police national computer. There will be local arrangements at ports between the police and the immigration service and the child's name will be placed on an immigration "stop list" held by immigration officers at points of exit. A child's name will be placed on the stop list only where danger of removal is "real and imminent". In this context "imminent" means within 48 hours and "real" that the ports stop is not being used as an insurance policy. The police will want to know whether threats or removal have been made, whether the person has unsupervised contact and if so whether the child is with that person and whether the child has previously been returned on time. The child will remain on the "stop list" for four weeks unless a further port alert application is made. Immigration officers do not have legal powers to detain or hold the child but they will notify the police, who will be able to do so. Because of the large numbers of children travelling abroad and the limits on immigration officers' powers to detain, this whole system is by no means guaranteed to prevent unauthorised removal. The police have to be satisfied that an attempt to commit an offence under the Child Abduction Act has been made or must be shown evidence of the court orders. In situations of extreme emergency, a sealed copy of an originating summons in wardship will suffice. The police will need to know a certain amount of information concerning the case. Police will need to know details in relation to the child including name, sex, date of birth, description, nationality and passport number where known; persons likely to remove the child including name, age, description, nationality, passport number if known and relationship to the child and whether the child is likely to assist him or her; details of the persons applying for the port alert including names, relationship to child, nationality, telephone number, solicitor's name and telephone number where appropriate; the likely destination, time of travel and port of embarkation; the grounds for the port alert; and finally the details of the person to whom the child should be returned where interception takes place. Other means of preventing the child's removal from the jurisdiction would depend on action being taken in several proceedings. Thus a prohibited steps order could be obtained under Section 8 of the Children Act 1989[20]. An order such as this can restrain removal either from the United Kingdom as a whole or in certain situations from England and Wales alone. As has been noted earlier on a prohibition against removal from the United Kingdom for any period in excess of one month is automatically included in any residence order[21]. Alternatively action can be taken to make the child a ward of court in order to prevent the child's removal from the jurisdiction.[22] The advantage of this approach is that the prohibition on removal of the ward arises immediately the child is warded and there is no need for any additional relief[23]. Other advantages to making an application for an order in civil proceedings include the fact that a specific order prohibiting the child's removal can act as a deterrent in itself; official assistance to trace the alleged abductor can be obtained[24]; where the order is broken the applicant can invoke the court's contempt powers[25] and can seek to enforce the order in other parts of the United Kingdom[26], or in any country that is a party to the European Convention on Child Abduction. Finally where an order has been obtained prohibiting removal, steps can be taken to prevent the issue of a United Kingdom passport[28] or where one has already been issued the court can be requested to order its surrender[29]. In any of these situations, as the Child Abduction Unit's booklet[30] on child abduction stresses, speed is absolutely crucial if an attempted abduction is to be successfully frustrated but even where all the preventative measures have been taken this does not mean that a child cannot nevertheless be abducted.

The Child Abduction and Custody Act 1985 deals with children covered by two different conventions and gives effect to these in civil law[31]. Pursuant to ratification of the first convention which governs situations where children under the age of sixteen have been brought from or taken to those European countries which are signatories to the European Convention on Recognition and Enforcement of Decisions Concerning Custody of Children, Part II of the Act provides that proceedings may be taken pursuant to the effects of that convention[32]. The convention and this part of the 1985 Act therefore are concerned with the recognition and enforcement of Custody Orders, which is defined to include residence orders made under the Children Act 1989[33], and also with the enforcement of decisions relating to access which again is defined to include a contact order within the meaning of the Children Act 1989[34]. Part I of the 1985 Act is of much wider application since it gives effect to The Hague Convention on the Civil Aspects of International Child Abduction, which has a number of signatories all over the world and is concerned with the return of children under the age of sixteen who have been wrongfully removed or retained in breach of rights of custody and access as defined by the convention[35].

Where a parent or other person with whom a child is living fears that some attempts may be made to remove a child from the United Kingdom, then it may be appropriate to seek an order for the surrender of the passport of any child or of the passport which contains particulars of a child in respect of whom an order has been made prohibiting or restricting the removal of the child from the United Kingdom[36]. In order that no further passport be issued, the court will notify the passport office in every case in which the surrender of a passport has been ordered[37]. It should also be pointed out that where there is in force a residence order in respect of a child, then the holder of such a residence order may remove the child from the United Kingdom for periods of up to one month unless a prohibited steps order is further obtained to restrict specifically the child's removal even for periods allowed under the provisions of the Act[38].

Both conventions provide for an administrative agency referred to in the conventions as the "Central Authority", which has the duty of tracing the child and taking any necessary steps including court proceedings, to secure the child's return or to secure access to the child. The 1985 Act provides that in England and Wales the functions of the Central Authority are discharged by the Lord Chancellor[39] through the Child Abduction Unit. The unit is staffed by administrative officials, and there is access to a law division if required. The Central Authorities for Scotland and Northern Ireland are the Scottish Courts Administration and the Northern Ireland Court Service respectively. Her Majesty's Attorney General for the Isle of Man has responsibility for the administration of the Manx Central Authority. It is provided that a Central Authority may discharge its functions through judicial or administrative authorities of the State and in respect of England and Wales the judicial authority is the High Court[40]. It should be pointed out, however, that neither the Convention nor the Act gives specific guidance as to how a Central Authority is to make use of its authorities. The provisions of the Act provide for rules of court to be made[41] but none have been made, nor has any practice direction or advice been issued by the Lord Chancellor. It is suggested therefore that solicitors and counsel involved in any applications under the Act should seek advice from the Lord Chancellor's Child Abduction Unit before making any application since the Act provides that it is one of the functions of the Lord Chancellor, as the Central Authority "to initiate or facilitate the institution of judicial or administrative proceedings with a view to obtaining the return of the child and, in a proper case, to make arrangements for organising or securing the effective exercise of rights of access"[42].

1 Steps had already been taken by the Child Abduction Act 1984, the Child Abduction and Custody Act 1985 and the Family Law Act 1986.
2 See Childright "Children's Legal Centre Information Sheet on Child Abduction" Issue no 89 at p9.
3 Information including a free booklet entitled Child Abduction produced by the Lord Chancellor's Department in consultation with the Foreign and Commonwealth Office, the Home Office and Reunite (the National Council for Abducted Children) is available from The Child Abduction Unit, Lord Chancellor's Department, Trevelyan House, Great Peter Street, London SW1P 2BY
4 *R v D* [1984] AC 778, [1984] 2 All ER 449, HL in relation to kidnapping; and in respect of the offence of unlawful imprisonment, see *R v Rahman* (1985) 81 Cr App Rep 349, [1985] Crim LR 596, CA.
5 Child Abduction Act 1984, ss 1, 2 (as substituted by the Children Act 1989 s 108 (4), Sch 12 para 37).
6 Ibid s 1 (2)(as substituted).
7 Ibid s 1 (as substituted).
8 Ibid s 1 (5)(as substituted).
9 Ibid s 1 (3)(as substituted).
10 Ibid s 1 (4), (4A)(as substituted).
11 Ibid s 2.
12 Ibid ss 1, 2.
13 Children Act 1989 s 8 (1).
14 Family Proceedings Rules 1991, SI 1991/1247, r 4.4 and Family Proceedings Courts (Children Act 1989) Rules 1991, SI 1991/1395, r 4 and see *Re B (A Minor)* [1992] 2 FLR 1, CA.
15 Child Abduction and Custody Act 1985.
16 The police can arrest without a warrant since it is an arrestable offence. See Child Abduction Act 1984 s 1.
17 Home Office Circular no 75/1984.
18 *Practice Direction (Child:Removal from Jurisdiction)* [1986] 1 All ER 983 and see Home Office Circular no 21/1986.
19 It should be noted that the Family Law Act 1986 s 35 provides that orders restricting removal from the jurisdiction extend to the whole of the United Kingdom.
20 See for example *Re D (A Minor)* [1992] 1 All ER 892.
21 See ante para 123.
22 See post para 231.
23 The automatic prohibition is enforceable irrespective of the defendant's knowledge of the wardship: see *Re J (An Infant)* (1913) 108 LT 554.
24 There is an obligation on various government agencies to reveal the last known address of the alleged abductor: see *Practice Direction* [1989] 1 All ER 765.
25 The court's powers of contempt include committal to prison and sequestration. See

Richardson v Richardson [1989] 3 All ER 779, in which it was held that money raised by the sequestrators could be used to pay the innocent party's costs of instituting proceedings abroad to recover the child, and *Mir v Mir* [1992] 1 All ER 765 in which it was held that the court had power to order the sale of sequested property.

26 Under the provisions of the Family Law Act 1986.

27 See post para 167

28 See the Home Office's revised leaflet published at [1986] Fam Law 50. This procedure will not prevent a visitor's passport being issued at a passport office and the procedure is inapplicable to foreign passport holders. Where a solicitor agrees to hold a foreign passport he owes a duty of care to the other parent not to let it out of his possession: *Al-Kandari v J R Brown & Co* [1988] 1 All ER 833, CA

29 Under the Family Law Act 1986 s 37. In order to prevent the reissuing of a passport the court should notify the Passport Office that he has ordered a surrender of the passport: *Practice Direction* [1983] 2 All ER 253.

30 See booklet Child Abduction published by the Child Abduction Unit, the Lord Chancellor's Department, Trevelyan House, Great Peter Street, London SW1P 2BY which is available free.

31 The conventions to which the Act gives effect are the convention of 1980 on the Civil Aspects of International Child Abduction, and the European Convention of 1980 on the Recognition and Enforcement of Decisions concerning the Custody of Children and on Restoration of Custody of Children.

32 Child Abduction and Custody Act 1985 Parts I and II.

33 Ibid s 27 (1), Sch 3.

34 Ibid see s 27 (4)(as inserted by the Children Act 1989 s 108 (5), Sch 13 para 57(2)).

35 Hague Convention 1980 on the Civil Aspects of International Child Abduction Articles 3, 5 (a), 5 (b).

36 Family Law Act 1986, s 37.

37 See *Practice Direction (Minor: Passport)* [1983] 2 All ER 253.

38 Children Act 1989 s 13 (1)(b) and s 13 (2). Note where the child is a ward of court there is an automatic prohibition against removing the child from England and Wales unless the child is habitually resident in another part of the United Kingdom, when he can move there freely, see Family Law Act 1986 s 38. In such circumstances no other specific order will be necessary.

39 Child Abduction and Custody Act 1985, ss 3 (2), 14 (2).

40 Ibid s 4 (a).

41 Ibid s 10.

42 1980 Convention on Civil Aspects of International Child Abduction as included in Child Abduction and Custody Act 1985 Sch 1 art 7.

162. The Hague Convention: Part I of the Child Abduction and Custody Act 1985.

162. The Hague Convention: Part I of the Child Abduction and Custody Act 1985. Part I of the Child Abduction and Custody Act 1985 gives effect to those parts of the Hague Convention which have been ratified by the United Kingdom which are set out in the Schedule to the Act[1]. The Convention thus applies to wrongful removal or retention of a child under sixteen who immediately before the removal or retention was habitually resident in a Contracting State. Under the provisions of the Act a removal or retention is considered to be wrongful where it occurs: in breach of rights of custody attributed to a person, institution or any other body, either jointly or alone, under the law of the State in which the child was habitually resident immediately before the removal or retention; and at the time of removal of retention, those rights were actually exercised either jointly or alone or would have been so exercised but for the removal or retention[2]. It must be remembered that pursuant to the Children Act 1989 rights of custody should now be interpreted as referring to parental responsibility and custody orders can include orders made pursuant to Section 8[3].

It should be noted that under the Hague Convention it is not necessary for the applicant actually to have a court order in his favour, but the removal or retention of the child must be wrongful and thus effectively must be in breach of someone's rights. For this reason the unilateral removal or retention of a child by an unmarried mother may not be considered to be wrongful[4], although those seeking return of a child to England and Wales can apply to the High Court for a declaration that a removal was wrongful[5]. In such circumstances, however, unless the applicant already possesses rights of custody such an order would be of little utility where the child has already been removed and has become habitually resident in the territory of another contracting state[6]. It has been stated by the courts that wrongful removal or retention is to be treated as an event occurring on a specific date and not as a continuing state[7]. It has also been held that it is "wrongful" for a parent with interim custody in her favour to remove the child from the jurisdiction[8] as has the removal of a ward of court from the United Kingdom without express court permission by a person having care and control[9].

1 Child Abduction and Custody Act 1985 Sch 1. As to the meaning of habitual residence see *C v S (Minor: Abduction: Illegitimate Child)* [1990] 2 AC 562, [1990] 2 All ER 961, HL, and *Re S (a Minor: Abduction)* [1991] FCR 656, [1991] 2 FLR 1, CA.
2 Child Abduction and Custody Act 1985 Sch 1 arts 3, 4 for an interpretation of "wrongful removal" see *C v C* 1992 1 FLR 163 FD. See also *Re F (A Minor) (Child Abduction)* [1992] 1 FLR 548, CA.
3 Child Abduction and Custody Act 1985 Sch 3; Children Act 1989.
4 See *C v S (Minor: Abduction: Illegitimate Child)* (supra).
5 Child Abduction and Custody Act 1985 s 8.
6 See further *C v S (Minor: Abduction: Illegitimate Child)* (supra), see note 1 supra.
7 See *Re H (Minors: Abduction: Custody Rights), Re S (Minors)(Abduction: Custody Rights)* [1991] 2 AC 476, [1991] 3 All ER 230, HL.
8 See *Re H (A Minor: Abduction)*, [1990] 2 FLR 439, [1990] FCR 990.
9 Child Abduction and Custody Act 1985 Sch 1 art 3 and note that a parent of a ward who has been granted access is entitled to obtain a declaration under ibid s 8, see *Re J (Minor: Abduction: Ward of Court)* [1989] Fam 85, [1989] 3 All ER 590.

163. Taking steps for the return of the child. Any person wishing to secure the return of a child who has been wrongfully removed or detained to or in a foreign contracting State, may seek assistance from the Lord Chancellor where the child is habitually resident in this country or from the Central Authority of the State to which the child has been taken. In most cases application will be made to the Lord Chancellor who directs that the application should be made through the High Court. Where an application is made it must contain the following details[1]:

1. information concerning the identity of the applicant, of the child and of the person alleged to have removed or retained the child;
2. where available the date of birth of the child;
3. the grounds on which the applicant's claim for return of the child is based; and
4. all available information relating to the whereabouts of the child and the identity of the person with whom the child is presumed to be.

Such an application may also be accompanied by an authenticated copy of any decision or agreement, such as a residence or custody order, a certificate or affidavit concerning the relevant law of England and Wales[2], and any other relevant document, and it should be noted that the application and any accompanying documents should be in English as the "original language"[3]. On receipt of the application the Central Authority of the Contracting State to which the child has been removed or is being detained must take all appropriate steps to obtain the voluntary return of the child[4].

Where proceedings have to be taken, the judicial or administrative authorities must act expeditiously. Where no decision has been reached within six weeks of commencement of proceedings, the requesting Central Authority or the applicant has the right to request a statement of the reasons for the delay[5]. Where the child has been wrongfully removed or detained and at the date of the commencement of the proceedings less than twelve months has elapsed since the wrongful removal, then the authority concerned "shall order the return of the child forthwith". In situations where more than twelve months has elapsed, the return of the child should still be ordered "unless it is demonstrated that the child is now settled in its new environment"[6]. As to the interpretation of the word "now", it has been held that this refers to the date of the commencement of the proceedings and not the date of the hearing. It has also been stated that "settled" involves both a physical element in the sense of relating to or being established in a community and an emotional state indicative of security, and further that "new environment" encompasses place, home, school, people, friends, activities and opportunities but not of itself the relationship with the parent[7]. However, where the court has reason to believe that the child has been taken to another state, it may stay the proceedings or dismiss the application for the return of the child[8].

Where the return of the child is opposed by any person then the foreign court is not bound to make an order for the return of the child where, it is shown that either the person having the care of the child was not actually exercising his right to custody at the time of removal or retention or had consented to or acquiesced in the removal or retention[9], or that there is a grave risk that the child, if returned, would be exposed to physical or psychological harm[10] or would otherwise be placed in an intolerable situation[11] or where the child objects to being returned and has attained an age and degree of maturity at which it is appropriate to take account of the child's views[12]. The foreign court in considering these issues must take into account any information relating to the social background of the child provided by the Lord Chancellor or on his behalf by the High Court[13]. The information can be obtained by the Lord Chancellor or the High Court requesting a local authority or probation officer's written report to be prepared or from any court from which a written report relating to the child has already been made[14].

Before the foreign court makes any order for the return of the child it may request that the applicant should obtain a decision or other determination from the court in England and Wales that the removal of the child was wrongful[15]. This may be done by the applicant making application to the High Court and obtaining a declaration to this effect[16], but in terms of possible delay at this stage it would obviously be preferable to seek such a declaration before the applicant submits his application for the return of the child to the High Court for transmission onwards to the foreign contracting State[17].

Any decision concerning the return of the child must not, under the provisions of the Act, be taken to be a determination on the merits of any custody issue[18] and the foreign court must not decide on the merits of any rights of custody until it has been determined that the child is not to be returned or unless the application for return of the child has not been lodged within a reasonable time following receipt of the notice that there has been a wrongful removal[19]. However, where that court or any other court or administrative authority within the requested Contracting State before the application for return made a decision relating to custody, that in itself does not justify refusing the return of the child to England and Wales, but the court in deciding whether to order such a return may take account of any reasons for the earlier decision[20].

1 Child Abduction and Custody Act 1985 Sch 1 art 8.
2 See ibid art 7 (e) which provides that it shall be the duty of the Lord Chancellor to take all appropriate measures to provide information of a general character as to the law of the United Kingdom in connection with the application of the Hague Convention.
3 Ibid art 24 states that where translation into the official language of the required state is not feasible, there must be a translation into French or English, but it seems clear that an alternative translation is unnecessary if the original language is French or English.
4 Ibid art 10.
5 Ibid art 11.
6 Ibid art 12.
7 See *Re N (Minors: Abduction)* [1991] FCR 765, [1991] 1 FLR 413.
8 Child Abduction and Custody Act 1985 Sch 1 art 12.
9 Note that acquiescence is a question of fact but where an applicant has actually sought custody in the State of the child's habitual residence, this is a strong indication that there has been no such acquiescence: see *Re A (Minors: Abduction)* [1991] FCR 460, [1991] 2 FLR 241, CA.
10 The risk of physical or psychological harm must be substantial and not trivial. See *Re A (A Minor: Abduction)* [1988] 1 FLR 365; *Re E (Minor: Abduction)* [1989] 1 FLR 135; *C v C (Minor: Abduction: Rights of Custody Abroad)* [1989] 2 All ER 465, [1989] 1 FLR 403.
11 See *Re N (Minors: Abduction)* (supra).
12 See *Re R (A Minor: Abduction)* [1992] 1 FLR 105, [1991] Fam Law 475, CA.
13 Child Abduction and Custody Act 1985 Sch 1 art 13.
14 Ibid s 6, Sch 1 arts 7 (d), 13.
15 Ibid Sch 1 art 15.
16 Ibid s 8.
17 Ibid s 8.
18 Ibid Sch 1 art 19.
19 Ibid Sch 1 art 16.
20 Ibid Sch 1 art 17.

164. Applications for access. An application to make arrangements for organising or securing the effective exercise of rights of access may be made in exactly the same way as an application for the return of a child[1]. It is also provided that those rights include that of taking a child for a limited period of time to a place other than the child's habitual residence[2]. For these purposes a decision relating to access includes a decision as to the contact which a child may or may not have with any person[3]. Under the convention the Central Authority is required to promote peaceful enjoyment of access rights and the fulfilment of any conditions to which the exercise of those rights may be subject. The Central Authority is further required to "take steps to remove so far as possible, all obstacles to the exercise of such rights", and may initiate or assist in the institution of proceedings with a view to organising or protecting these rights and securing respect for the conditions to which the exercise of those rights may be subject[4].

Whilst it is useful that the convention underlines the importance of abiding by decisions with regard to access or contact, it nevertheless has to be admitted that foreign courts find it equally difficult to enforce such orders within their own jurisdictions as do English courts. It should be noted that there are no specific provisions relating to the enforcement of access and thus it may be that wardship will be as effective as an application under the terms of the convention[5].

1 Child Abduction and Custody Act 1985 Sch 1 art 21. See *C v C* [1992] 1 FLR 163, FD.
2 Ibid Sch 1 art 5.
3 Ibid s 27 (4)(as inserted by the Children Act 1989 s 108 (5), Sch 13 para 57 (2)).
4 Ibid Sch 1 art 21.
5 See *B v B (Minors: Enforcement of Access Abroad)* [1988] 1 All ER 652, [1988] 1 WLR 526.

165. Implementation dates. The Hague Convention does not have retrospective effect[1] and thus the dates upon which contracting states implemented the convention are of crucial importance. Appendix 1[2] sets out the parties to the Hague Convention on International Child Abduction and the dates of coming into force as between the United Kingdom and the State or territory concerned.

1 See *Re H (Minors: Abduction: Custody Rights), Re S (Minors: Abduction: Custody Rights)* [1991] 2 AC 476, [1991] 3 All ER 230, HL.
2 See Appendix 1 post.

166. Removal of a child to England and Wales. Where a child is wrongfully removed to England and Wales from a contracting state, the obligations imposed on the foreign central authority and foreign court as previously discussed will instead be discharged in this country by the Lord Chancellor and the High Court, assisted where appropriate by the relevant administrative authorities[1]. Where an application is referred to the High Court, the court may before determining it give such interim directions as it thinks fit for the purpose of securing the welfare of the child or of preventing changes in the circumstances relevant to the determination of the application[2]. Since the primary reason for the convention is to provide a means for the prompt return of a child to the country of his habitual residence, there is an onerous burden on the person who has allegedly wrongfully removed the child to persuade the High Court that he has not in fact done so[3]. It would appear that where a person has custody pursuant to an interim order made by a foreign court, this does not in itself justify the child's removal from the foreign jurisdiction on the ground that the custody order empowers the person to choose the child's place of residence, and this is more particularly the case where any other person has been granted access to the child pursuant to the order[4].

As with applications in respect of children wrongfully removed from England and Wales, applications in respect of those wrongfully removed to this country should be accompanied by the appropriate documents[5]. As soon as it receives an application, the Lord Chancellor's Department will check that the application meets the criteria laid down under the convention and that it is accompanied by the necessary documentation. Where the application is in order, a firm of solicitors selected from a list drawn up by the Lord Chancellor's department in consultation with the Law Society, will be instructed by the department on behalf of the applicant. Where any documentation is not in English, it may be necessary to obtain a translation, the cost of which will be borne by the legal aid fund which will be free for the applicant[6].

An application must be brought in the High Court[7] and should be initiated by originating summons[8] and in an emergency an application may be made ex parte[9]. The application will be heard by a judge in chambers unless the court otherwise directs[10] and interim directions may be given[11]. Where an application has been made under the convention it freezes any other application including wardship proceedings[12]. In those situations where there is not sufficient information as to where the child is, the court may order any person whom it has reason to believe may have relevant information to disclose it to the court, and such person shall not be excused from complying with the order on the grounds of self-incrimination, although any statement which is made is not admissible in evidence in proceedings for any offence other than perjury[13]. The court cannot, however, compel a defendant to give evidence once the child has been surrendered to the authorities[14].

Due consideration must be given in child abduction cases to the provisions which allow the court a discretion to decline to order an abducted child to be returned. Thus where a child of sufficient maturity seeks to remain in this country and expresses her views most strongly, and such views have not resulted from undue influence and are more than simply a preference for staying with the abducting parent then this would be sufficient to confer a discretion upon the court. In the case of *Re R*[15] the girl had objected strongly to being returned and had been suicidal at the thought of it. Bracewell J found that the girl's objection justified allowing her to remain in England despite the fact that she found that there was no grave risk of harm in her going back. Similarly in *Re S*[16] the Court of Appeal confirmed Ewbank J's refusal to order the return of a ten year old girl to France because her mental age had been assessed as twelve and she had advanced mature and cogent reasons for her wish to remain in England. it was thus only right to take proper account of her views.

1 See Paragraph 161 ante.
2 Child Abduction and Custody Act 1985, s 5. The court may direct that the child is to reside with a specified person or at a specified place pending the hearing of the application.
3 See *Re E (A Minor: Abduction)* [1989] 1 FLR 135, (1989) Fam Law 105, CA. *Re A (Minor: Wrongful Removal of a Child)* [1988] Fam Law 383; see also *Re G (Minor: Abduction)* [1989] 2 FLR 475, [1990] FCR 189, CA.
4 See *Re E (Minor Abduction)* (supra).
5 Child Abduction and Custody Act 1985 Sch 1 arts 8, 13.
6 Ibid Sch 1 art 26, and see Civil Legal Aid (General) Regulations 1989, SI 1989/339, reg.14. Applications should be directed to Legal Aid Area No.1 and should then receive immediate attention.
7 Child Abduction and Custody Act 1985 s 4.
8 Family Proceedings Rules 1991, SI 1991/1247, r 6.3.
9 Ibid r 6.13.
10 Ibid r 6.8.
11 Ibid r 6.13.
12 Child Abduction and Custody Act 1985, ss 9, 27.
13 Ibid s 24A (as inserted by the Family Law Act 1986 s 67 (4)).
14 See *Re D (A Minor)(Child Abduction)* [1988] FCR 585, [1989] 1 FLR 97n.
15 [1992] 1 FLR 105
16 (1992) Independent, 8 July CA. Ewbank J's decision reported at 1992 2 FLR 31 sub nom *S v S*.

167. The European Convention: Child Abduction and Custody Act 1985 Part II. The provisions of Part II of the Child Abduction and Custody Act 1985 implement the 1980 European Convention on the Recognition and Enforcement of Decisions Concerning Custody of Children and the Restoration of Children[1]. As with the Hague Convention, the European Convention is also administered by the Central Authority of Contracting States and their judicial or administrative authorities. In relation to this Convention, the Central Authority is, again, the Lord

Chancellor[2]. The provisions of the Convention apply to the "improper removal" of any person of any nationality who is under the age of sixteen and who does not have the right to determine his own place of residence under the law of his habitual residence, the law of his nationality or the internal law of the State addressed[3].

Improper removal is defined under the terms of the convention as meaning: "the removal of a child across an international frontier in breach of a decision relating to his custody which has been given in a Contracting State and which is enforceable in such a State; the failure to return a child across an international frontier at the end of a period of the exercise of the right of access to this child or at the end of any other temporary stay in a territory other than that where the custody is exercised; and any removal which is subsequently declared to be unlawful"[4]. Thus the provisions of the convention can apply to a custody decision following removal where the English court can declare the removal to be unlawful, if it is satisfied that the applicant has an interest in the matter and that the child has been removed out of England without the consent of the person having the right to determine the child's place of residence under English law[5]. A decision relating to custody includes a decision of a judicial or administrative authority relating to the care of the person of the child, including the right to decide on his place of residence, or to the right of access to him[6]. A decision relating to custody therefore includes residence and contact orders made under the provision of the Children Act[7].

1 Child Abduction and Custody Act 1985 Sch 2.
2 Ibid s 14.
3 Ibid Sch 2 art 1. It should be noted that the child does not only have to be under sixteen but also must not have the right to decide on his own place of residence under the relevant law. As a result of the result in *Gillick v West Norfolk and Wisbech Area Health Authority* [1986] AC 112, [1985] 3 All ER 402, HL. It would appear that a child under sixteen may well have that right in England and Wales where he is deemed to be sufficiently mature to choose his own place of residence. See also *Re R (Minor: Abduction)* [1992] 1 FLR 105, [1991] Fam Law 475.
4 Child Abduction and Custody Act 1985 Sch 2 art 1.
5 Ibid s 23 (2) and see Family Proceedings Rules 1991, SI 1991/1247, r 6.5 and Magistrates' Courts (Child Abduction and Custody) Rules 1986, SI 1986/1141, r 9.
6 Child Abduction and Custody Act 1985 Sch 2 art 1 (b).
7 Child Abduction and Custody Act 1985 Sch 3 para 1 (6) and s 27 (4)(as amended by the Children Act 1989 s 108 (5) Sch 13 para 57 (2)).

168. Recognition and enforcement of decisions. Any person who has obtained a decision in a Contracting State relating to the custody of a child and who wishes to have that decision recognised or enforced in another Contracting State may submit an application for this purpose to the Central Authority in any Contracting State[1]. Under the provisions of section 16 of the Act recognition and enforcement is achieved by registering the court order in a court of the Contracting State to which the child has been taken. In England and Wales such applications to register must be made to the High Court. Under Section 18 of the Act once the order is registered the court has the same power of enforcement as if it had made the original order and it is by this means that the return of the child will be ordered. An application for recognition or enforcement must be accompanied by the appropriate documents[2], and the Central Authority receiving the application may refuse to intervene where it is manifestly clear that the conditions of the convention are not satisfied[3].

The receiving authority must send the documents without delay to the Central Authority of the State in which the child is thought to be, termed the State addressed and must keep the applicant informed without delay of the progress of his application[4]. The Central Authority must take or cause to be taken without delay all steps which are considered to be appropriate, if necessary by instituting proceedings before its competent authorities, in order: to discover the whereabouts of the child; to avoid, in particular by any necessary provisional measures, prejudice to the interests of the child or of the applicant; to secure the recognition or enforcement of the decision; to secure the delivery of the child to the applicant where enforcement is granted; and to inform the requesting authority of the measures taken and their results[5]. With the exception of the expenses of repatriation, the cost of any steps taken by the Central Authority, including the costs of the proceedings and, where applicable, costs incurred by engaging a lawyer are to be borne by the contracting state[6].

Decisions on rights of access or contact are recognised and enforced in exactly the same way as decisions relating to custody, but the competent authority of the State addressed may fix the conditions for the implementation and exercise of the right of access taking into account, in particular, undertakings given by the parties on this matter[7]. It is provided that where no decision on the right of access has been taken or where recognition or enforcement of the decision relating to custody is refused, the Central Authority of the State addressed may apply to its competent authorities for a decision on the right of access if the person claiming the right of access so requests[8].

It has been held in the case of *Re L*[9] that recognition must be given to an order even where it was made before the two countries, in this case Ireland and England, had mutually ratified the European Convention. The European Convention therefore unlike the Hague Convention[10] is taken to have retrospective effect.

1 Child Abduction and Custody Act 1985 Sch 2 art 4.
2 Ibid arts 4 (2), 13.
3 Ibid art 4 (4).
4 Ibid art 4 (3), (5).
5 Ibid art 5 (1).
6 Ibid art 5 (3).
7 Ibid art 11 (2).
8 Ibid art 11 (3).
9 [1992] Fam Law 379 FD.
10 See *Re H* [1991] 3 All ER 230.

169. Refusal of recognition or enforcement. Under the provisions of the Act and the Convention, recognition and enforcement of decisions may be refused if:

1. in the case of a decision made in the absence of the defendant or his legal representative, the defendant was not duly served with the document which instituted the proceedings or an equivalent document in sufficient time to enable him to arrange his defence; but such a failure to effect service cannot constitute a ground for refusing recognition or enforcement where service was not effected because the defendant had concealed his whereabouts from the person who instituted the proceedings in the State of origin;
2. in the case of a decision given in the absence of the defendant or his legal representative, the competence of the authority giving the decision was not founded:
   2.1. on the habitual residence of the defendant;
   2.2. on the last common habitual residence of the child's parents, at least one parent still being habitually resident there; or
   2.3. the child's habitual residence; or

3. the decision is incompatible with the decision relating to custody which became enforceable in the State addressed before the removal of the child, unless the child has had his habitual residence in the territory of the requesting State for one year before his removal[2]. It is further provided that in no circumstances may a foreign decision be reviewed as to its substance[3].

Recognition and enforcement may also be refused on any of the following grounds:

1. if it is found that the effects of the decision are manifestly incompatible with the fundamental principles of the law relating to family and children in the State addressed;
2. if it is found that by reason of a change in the circumstances, including the passage of time but not including a mere change in the residence of the child after an improper removal, the effects of the original decision are manifestly no longer in accordance with the welfare of the child[4];
3. if at the time when the proceedings were instituted in the State of origin:
    3.1. the child was a national of the State addressed or was habitually resident there and no such connection existed with the State of origin;
    3.2. the child was a national both of the State of origin and of the State addressed and was habitually resident in the State addressed;
4. if the decision is incompatible with the decision given in the State addressed or enforceable in that State after being given in a third State, pursuant to proceedings begun before submission of the request for recognition or enforcement, and if the refusal is in accordance with the welfare of the child[5].

1   Child Abduction and Custody Act 1985 Sch 2 art 9 (1)(a).
2   Ibid art 9 (1)(b).
3   Ibid art 9 (3).
4   See *F v F (Minors)(Custody: Foreign Order)* [1989] Fam 1, [1988] 3 WLR 959; but see *Re G (Minor: Abduction: Enforcement)* [1990] FCR 973, [1990] 2 FLR 325 and *Re K (A Minor: Abduction)* [1990] 1 FLR 387, (1990) FCR 524. Contrast with *F v F (Minors) (Custody: Foreign Order)* [1988] WLR 959 where recognition was refused.
5   Child Abduction and Custody Act 1985 Sch 2 art 10 (1).

170. Parties to the European Convention. The parties to the European Convention are set out in Appendix 2[1] although a constant check should be made as to those countries which have implemented the Convention[2].

1   See Appendix 2 post.
2   See the Child Abduction and Custody (Parties to Conventions) Order 1986, SI 1986/1159 (as amended).

171. Procedure in the magistrates' court. Special rules have been made governing procedure in the magistrates courts[1] and separate provision is made in the Family Proceedings Rules to govern procedure in applications under the Child Abduction and Custody Act 1985 in the High Court[2]. Where in magistrates' courts proceedings a decision falls to be made on the merits of rights of custody pending in a magistrates' court and the court receives notice from the High Court or the Court of Session that an application in respect of the child concerned has been made under the Hague Convention, the magistrates' court should order that all further proceedings and the proceedings pending before it shall be stayed and shall cause notice to be given to the parties to the proceedings accordingly[3]. Where a magistrates' court has stayed such proceedings and received notice from the High Court or the Court of Session that an order has been made under the Hague Convention for the return of the child concerned, the court shall dismiss the complaint and cause notice to be given to the parties to the proceedings accordingly[4]. Where a magistrates' court which has stayed any proceedings receives notice from the High Court or Court of Session that an order for the return of the child concerned has been refused[5], the court shall order that the stay be lifted and shall notify the parties to the proceedings, and then shall proceed to deal with the complaint in the normal way[6]. Where a magistrates' court which has stayed any proceedings receives notice from the High Court or Court of Session that an order has been made staying or dismissing the application because there is reason to believe that the child has been taken to another State, then the court shall continue the stay on the proceedings pending before it or, in a case where the High Court or Court of Session has dismissed the application, dismiss the complaint and shall cause notice to be given to the parties accordingly[7].

Any person who wishes to make an application under the Hague Convention in a Contracting State other than the United Kingdom and who wishes to obtain from a magistrates' court an authenticated copy of a decision of that court relating to the child in respect of whom the application is to be made, must apply in writing to the justices' clerk of that court[8]. The application must specify:

1. the name and date or approximate date of birth of the child concerned;
2. the date or approximate date of the proceedings in which the decision of the court was given, and the nature of those proceedings;
3. the Contracting State in which the application in respect of the child is to be made;
4. the relationship of the applicant to the child concerned;
5. the postal address of the applicant[9].

A justices' clerk who receives an application for an authenticated copy of a decision in this way shall send by post to the applicant at the address indicated in the application an authenticated copy of the decision concerned[10]. For these purposes a copy of a decision shall be deemed to be authenticated if it is accompanied by a statement signed by the justices' clerk that it is a true copy of the decision concerned[11]. Finally an application to a magistrates' court for a declaration that the removal of a child from the United Kingdom has been unlawful[12] may be made orally or in writing in the course of the custody proceedings[13].

1 The Magistrates' Courts (Child Abduction and Custody) Rules 1986, SI 1986/1141.
2 Family Proceedings Rules 1991, SI 1991/1247, Pt VI.
3 The Magistrates' Courts (Child Abduction and Custody) Rules 1986, r 3.
4 Ibid r 4.
5 Ibid r 5.
6 Ibid r 5.
7 Ibid r 6.
8 Ibid r 8 (1).
9 Ibid r 8 (2).
10 Ibid r 8 (3).
11 Ibid r 8 (4).
12 Under Child Abduction and Custody Act 1985 s 23 (2).
13 Magistrates' Courts (Child Abduction and Custody) Rules 1986, r 9 and see Child Abduction and Custody Act 1985 s 27 for the definition of "custody proceedings" as amended.

172. Procedure in the High Court. Except where an application is being made for a declaration that the removal of a child from the United Kingdom has been unlawful, every application under the Hague Convention and the European Convention must be made by originating summons which must be in the prescribed form[1]. The originating summons must state:

1. the name and date of birth of the child in respect of whom the application is made;
2. the names of the child's parents or guardians;
3. the whereabouts or suspected whereabouts of the child;
4. the interest of the plaintiff in the matter and the grounds of the application;
5. particulars of any proceedings (including proceedings out of the jurisdiction and concluded proceedings) relating to the child, and shall be accompanied by all relevant documents including but not limited to the documents specified in the relevant articles of the Hague Convention[2] and the European Convention[3].

In addition, applications under the Hague Convention must also state the identity of the person alleged to have removed or retained the child[4] and where the application is being made under Article 15 of the Hague Convention for a declaration, the proceedings in which the request that such a declaration be obtained was made[5]. Applications under the European Convention shall also identify the decision relating to custody or rights of access which is sought to be enforced or registered[6].

The defendants to an application shall be:

1. the person alleged to have brought into the United Kingdom the child in respect of whom an application under the Hague Convention was made;
2. the person with whom the child is alleged to be;
3. any parent or guardian of the child who is within the United Kingdom and is not otherwise a party;
4. the person in whose favour a decision relating to custody has been made if he is not otherwise a party;
5. any other person who appears to the court to have a sufficient interest in the welfare of the child[7].

The time limited for acknowledging service of an originating summons by which an application is made under the Hague Convention or the European Convention shall be 7 days after the service of the originating summons including the day of service or in the case of those defendants referred to in 4. or 5. such further time as the court may direct[8].

The plaintiff, on issuing an originating summons under the Hague Convention or the European Convention, may lodge affidavit evidence in the Principal Registry in support of his application and serve a copy of the same on the defendant with the originating summons and the defendant may reply again lodging affidavit evidence if he so desires in the Principal Registry and serve a copy of the same on the plaintiff within 7 days after service of the originating summons upon him[9]. The plaintiff in an application may within 7 days thereafter lodge in the Principal Registry a statement in reply and serve a copy thereof on the defendant[10].

Any application shall be heard and determined by a judge and be dealt with in chambers unless the court otherwise directs[11]. The court may dispense with service of any summons (whether originating or ordinary) in any proceedings under the Child Abduction and Custody Act 1985[12]. The hearing of the originating summons under which an application under the Hague Convention or the European Convention is made may be adjourned for a period not exceeding 21 days at a time[13].

A party to proceedings under the Hague Convention shall, where he knows that an application relating to the merits of rights of custody is pending in or before a relevant authority, file in the Principal Registry a concise statement of the nature of the application which is pending, including the authority before which it is pending[14]. Any party to proceedings for the registration of custody decisions under Section 16 of the 1985 Act or to proceedings as a result of which a decision relating to custody has been registered under those provisions, shall where he knows that such an application is pending in or before a relevant authority, file a concise statement of the nature of the application which is pending[15].

The proper officer shall on receipt of either such statement notify the relevant authority in which or before whom the application is pending and shall subsequently notify it or him of the result of the proceedings[16]. Where the court receives such notification under these provisions or equivalent notification from the Court of Session or the High Court in Northern Ireland then where the application relates to the merits of custody, all further proceedings in the action shall be stayed until the other proceedings are dismissed, and the parties to the action shall be notified by the proper officer of the stay and of any such dismissal accordingly; or where the application is otherwise to be treated as pending, then the proper officer shall notify the parties to the action[17].

The court may at any stage in the proceedings of its own motion or on the application by summons of any party to the proceedings issued on two days' notice order that the proceedings be transferred to the Court of Session or the High Court in Northern Ireland. Where such an order is made the proper officer shall send a copy of the order which shall state the grounds together with the originating summons, the documents accompanying it and any evidence, to the Court of Session or the High Court in Northern Ireland as the case may be, and where such proceedings are transferred then the cost of the whole proceedings shall be at the discretion of the court to which the proceedings are transferred[18]. Where proceedings are transferred to the High Court from the Court of Session or the High Court in Northern Ireland, the proper officer shall notify the parties of the transfer and the proceedings shall continue as if they had been begun by originating summons[19].

Any application for interim directions[20] may where the case is one of urgency be made ex parte on affidavit but shall otherwise be made by summons[21].

Any person who intends to make an application under the Hague Convention in a Contracting State other than the United Kingdom shall on satisfying the court as to that intention be entitled to obtain an office copy sealed with the seal of the Supreme Court of any order made in the High Court relating to the child in respect of whom the application is to be made[22].

Where any decision has been registered under the provisions of the European Convention[23] and is subsequently varied or revoked by an authority in the Contracting State in which it was made, then the court shall on cancelling the registration of a decision which has been revoked notify:

1. the person appearing to the court to have care of the child;
2. the person on whose behalf the application for registration of the decision was made; and
3. any other party to the application, of the cancellation[24].

The court shall on being notified of the variation of the decision notify the person appearing to the court to have the care of the child and any other party to the application for registration of the decision, of the variation and any such person may apply by summons in the proceedings for the registration of the decision, for the purpose of making representations to the court before the registration is varied[25]. Any person appearing to the court to have an interest in the matter may apply by summons in the proceedings for the registration of a decision for the cancellation or variation of the registration[26].

Finally at any stage in proceedings under the European Convention the court may if it has reason to believe that any person may have relevant information about the child who is the subject of those proceedings, order that person to disclose such information and may for that purpose order that the person attend before it or file affidavit evidence[27].

1 Family Proceedings Rules 1991, SI 1991/1247, r 6.2. See Form 2 post and form of affidavit see Form 3 and for application for declaration of unlawful removal see Form 5 post.
2 Hague Convention art 8.
3 European Convention art 13.
4 Family Proceedings Rules 1991 r 6.4 (1)(b).
5 Hague Convention art 15.
6 Family Proceedings Rules 1991 r 6.4 (2).
7 Ibid r 6.5.
8 Ibid r 6.6.
9 Ibid r 6.7 (1), (2). See Form 3 post.
10 Ibid r 6.7 (3).
11 Ibid r 6.8.
12 Ibid r 6.9.
13 Ibid r 6.10.
14 Ibid r 6.11 (1).
15 Child Abduction Act and Custody Act 1985 s 16; Family Proceedings Rules 1991 r 6.11 (2).
16 Family Proceedings Rules 1991 r 6.11 (3).
17 Ibid r 6.11 (4).
18 Ibid r 6.12 (1), (2), (3).
19 Ibid r 6.12 (4).
20 Under s 5 or s 19 of the Child Abduction and Custody Act 1985.
21 Family Proceedings Rules 1991, r 6.13.
22 Ibid r 6.14. For the form of an order see Form 4 post.
23 Ibid r 6.15 (1).
24 Ibid r 6.15 (2).
25 Ibid r 6.15 (3).
26 Ibid r 6.15 (4).
27 Ibid r 6.16.

CHAPTER 8: CARE AND ASSOCIATED PROCEEDINGS

1: GENERAL

173. Generally. The Children Act 1989 which came into force on 14th October 1991 effected radical reforms to the public law governing state intervention in children's lives and in the lives of their families. Prior to that date the courts had possessed a bewilderingly wide and complex range of statutory powers[1] to effect the compulsory removal of children into or detention in the care of a local authority. As a result it had become extremely difficult to understand the different responsibilities which might fall upon the holder of a care order determined as it was by any one of a range of over seventeen statutory routes into care. If the law was difficult for professionals to understand, it presented even greater problems for those most affected by its complexity, children and their parents. Increasingly, this area of public law was subjected to attack[2] and criticism especially in the area of wardship which was being used to plug any gaps in the statutory scheme particularly in favour of local authorities[3]. The availability of wardship to local authorities was not, however, matched by its availability to parents or other members of a child's family who might have felt aggrieved by the actions of a local authority in respect of a child in its care[4].

The complexities of the system were attacked in a series of official reports, and far reaching proposals for reform were set out in a Government White Paper[5]. At the same time the private law relating to children who were the subject of disputes between their parents, or their parents and third parties, was being subjected to close scrutiny by the Law Commission. Aware of the recommendations for reform outlined in the White Paper, it acknowledged the need for a much closer alignment of the public and private law systems for dealing with children and their families and published its final Report[6] containing a draft Bill in July 1988. The report was primarily concerned with the law governing the adjustment of family relationships with children upon family breakdown and upon the acquisition and transfer of parental responsibility for children. It also dealt with the rationalisation of the private law governing maintenance of children. The draft bill in the Law Commission's report also and inevitably reflected these concerns.

It seemed however that the Government needed some added impetus to press forward with new legislation and this coincidentally occurred, also in July 1988, with the publication of the Report of the Inquiry into Child Abuse in Cleveland[7]. This report highlighted previously exposed inadequacies in the child care law system and called for the reforms proposed in the White Paper of 1987 to be brought forward in legislation without delay. The controversy surrounding the Cleveland Report encouraged the Government to move quickly and a Children Bill was published on 24 November 1988. The Bill, on being introduced by the Lord Chancellor in the House of Lords, was described as the most fundamental reform of child law in England and Wales this century, bringing together as it did both the public and private law relating to children. The opportunity was also taken during the bill's one year passage through Parliament to reform the jurisdiction of the courts in children's cases[8], the law on evidence in civil cases involving children[9], and the law governing procedure in all civil cases involving children[10].

Amongst the most important of the changes introduced by the Children Act 1989 was the reduction of the number of routes into the care of the local authority from over seventeen to just one[11]. The Act abolished the criminal care order with effect as to any continuing orders from 14th April 1992[12] and no new criminal care orders could be made after implementation of the Children Act 1989 on 14th October 1991[13]. The only way in which a child can now be committed into the care of the local authority is by a care order made under Section 31 of the Act on an application made either by the local authority or very rarely by the NSPCC[14]. The Act provided that wardship cannot be used as a backdoor route into care by repealing Section 7 of the Family Law Reform Act 1969[15].

The power of the High Court to exercise inherent jurisdiction over children is further restricted by Section 100 so that no court can exercise it so as to: require a child to be placed in the care, or put under the supervision, of a local authority; require a child to be accommodated by or on behalf of a local authority; make a child who is the subject of a care order a ward of court; or confer on any local authority power to determine any question which has arisen or which may arise, in connection with any aspect of parental responsibility for a child[16]. The former power of courts hearing matrimonial cases to commit children into the care of the local authority has also been abolished[17]. In family proceedings now where the magistrates or judges are concerned about whether a child is suffering or likely to suffer significant harm, the local authority can be ordered to investigate the situation in order to determine whether it is necessary for an application to be made for a care order under Section 31[18].

The making of a care order in civil care proceedings under Section 31 is the only situation in which a child can technically be described as being in care[19]. Other children who may be being "looked after"[20] by the local authority are described under the Act as being "provided with accommodation"[21]. These children include those who have been deemed to be in need of the service of accommodation because their parents cannot (whether or not permanently, and for whatever reason) provide them with suitable accommodation or care, or those for whom there is no-one with parental responsibility, or those who are lost or who have been abandoned. "Accommodated children" can also include those who have been removed from home on an emergency protection order or child assessment order[22]; those in police protection[23]; those on remand or being detained under the Police and Criminal Evidence Act 1984[24] or those subject to a supervision order with residence requirements where the order was made in criminal proceedings in accordance with the Children and Young Persons Act 1969[25].

The differences between children described as "in care" and those who are "accommodated" under the Children Act 1989 are not merely those of nomenclature but reflect the differing powers and responsibility exercisable in respect of such children.

Local authorities have a number of duties and responsibilities common to all "looked after" children such as the duty to safeguard and promote the children's welfare[26], to involve them in decision-making processes[27] and to pay special attention to the children's race, language, religion and culture[28]. Where children are accommodated, however, parental responsibility generally rests more with their parents[29], whereas local authorities exercise much greater powers and responsibilities over children who are "in care"[30].

Further, whenever resort has to be made to court proceedings it must be remembered that the general principles laid down in Section 1 (1) of the Act will be applied to all cases[31]. Thus, every decision in respect of a child must be based on the child's welfare being the court's paramount consideration[32], and it is presumed that any delay in determining cases is likely to prejudice the welfare of the child[33]. Where a court is considering whether or not to make any orders under the Children Act 1989 with respect to a child, Section 1 (5) provides that the court shall not do so unless it considers that doing so would be better for the child than making no order at all.

Where the court is considering whether to make, vary or discharge any orders under Part IV of the Act, or any Section 8 orders where this is opposed by any party to the proceedings, then the court must take into account all the factors listed in the welfare checklist in Section 1 (3) of the Children Act 1989[34]. It should be noted that Section 31 (3) of the Children Act 1989 provides that neither a care order nor a supervision order may be made with respect to an unmarried child who has reached the age of seventeen or a married child who has reached the age of sixteen. It is also provided by Section 100 (2) of the Children Act 1989 that the local authority will not be able to invoke the inherent jurisdiction of the High Court where there are concerns about the child. In addition the nearer the child is to the particular age limit laid down in the Act, the less it is likely that the court would deem an order to be in the paramount interest of the child, bearing in mind that the order would expire on the child attaining majority. The Act prevents any application being made in respect of unborn children because the definition of a child for the purposes of the Act is any "person" under the age of eighteen.

1 See Children and Young Persons Act 1969 ss 1, 7 (as amended), the Matrimonial Causes Act 1973 s 43, the Family Law Reform Act 1969 s 7 (2) and the Guardianship Act 1973 s 2 (2).
2 DHSS, *Review of Child Care Law* (1985); DHSS, *A Child in Mind; Protection of Children in a Responsible Society* (1987).
3 See for example *Re C (Minor) (Justices' Decisions: Review)* [1979] 2 FLR 62; *Re D (Minor) (Justices' Decision: Review)* [1977] Fam 158, [1977] 3 All ER 481; *Re J (A Minor)* [1984] 1 All ER 29, [1984] 1 WLR 81.
4 *A v Liverpool City Council* [1981] 2 FLR 222; *Re W (A Minor)(Wardship: Jurisdiction)* [1985] 2 All ER 301, [1985] 2 WLR 892, HL; *Re T D (a Minor)(Wardship: Jurisdiction)* [1985] 6 Fam Law 18.
5 The Law relating to Child Care and Family Services (Cmnd 62, 1987).
6 Guardianship and Custody (Law Com No 172).
7 Child Abuse in Cleveland (1988) (Cmnd 412).
8 Children Act 1989 s 92 and Sch 11.
9 Ibid s 96.
10 Ibid ss 93 (as amended by the Courts and Legal Services Act 1990 s 116, Sch 16 para 22), 95 and 100.
11 Ibid s 31.
12 Ibid Sch 14 para 36.
13 Ibid s 90.
14 Ibid s 31 (1)(a).
15 Ibid s 100 (1).
16 Ibid s 100 (2).

17 Ibid Sch 15.
18 Ibid s 37.
19 Ibid s 105.
20 Ibid s 22 (1).
21 Ibid s 22 (1) and see ibid s 20 (1).
22 Ibid s 21 (1).
23 Ibid s 21 (2)(a).
24 Ibid s 21 (2)(a), (b) and (c)(i).
25 Ibid s 21 (c)(ii).
26 Ibid s 22 (3).
27 Ibid s 22 (4).
28 Ibid s 22 (5) and see *R v Lancashire County Council ex parte M* [1992] 1 FCR 283.
29 Ibid s 20.
30 Ibid s 33.
31 See Paragraph 177 post.
32 Children Act 1989 s 1(1) although it should be noted that an application by a foster parent seeking leave to apply for a s 8 residence order is not such a decision, see *Re A (Minors)(Residence Orders: (Leave to Apply)* [1992] 3 All ER 872, [1992] 3 WLR 422, CA.
33 Ibid s 1 (2).
34 Ibid s 1 (4).

2: PROTECTION OF CHILDREN

174. Protecting children. The Children Act 1989 gives local authorities[1] and authorised persons, currently only the NSPCC[2], new powers to intervene at an early stage where there are merely suspicions[3] that a child is being ill-treated or is failing to develop properly, extended powers to remove children from their homes if certain criteria are satisfied[4], and gives the police the right to exercise new powers of police protection[5]. In addition, a new recovery order[6] is provided in order to protect children who may have been abducted or run away from any place where they were being looked after whilst subject to a care or emergency protection order, or in police protection. Moreover provision is made for refuges[7] for children at risk of harm, and a system of certification exempting those who run such a refuge from liability to prosecution for certain offences.

Where powers are given to apply to court for a child assessment order or emergency protection order, or for the police to exercise their powers of protection, the condition precedent for the exercise of such powers is that the child is, or is believed to be suffering, or at risk of suffering, significant harm. These terms are defined in Section 31 of the Children Act 1989 although the Court of Appeal has already emphasised that it is to be hoped that in approaching cases under the Children Act 1989 courts will not be invited to perform in every case a strict legalistic analysis of the statutory meaning of Section 31. According to the Court of Appeal the words of the statute must be considered but they were not intended to be unduly restrictive when the evidence clearly indicated that a certain course should be taken in order to protect a child[8]. Thus, harm is defined as meaning ill-treatment or the impairment of health or development; development as meaning physical, intellectual, emotional, social or behavioural development; health as meaning physical or mental health; and ill-treatment as including sexual abuse and forms of ill-treatment which are not physical. Where the question of whether harm suffered by a child is significant turns on the child's health or development it must be compared with that which could reasonably be expected of a similar child.

In circumstances where the local authority or the NSPCC are merely suspicious about whether or not a child is suffering or likely to suffer significant harm they may now seek an order usually from the magistrates' family proceedings court known as a child assessment order[9]. Before granting a child assessment order the court must be satisfied that the applicant has reasonable cause to suspect that: the child is suffering or is likely to suffer significant harm; an assessment of the state of the child's health or development or of the way in which he has been treated is required to enable the applicant to determine whether or not the child is suffering or is likely to suffer significant harm; and it is unlikely that such an assessment will be made, or be satisfactory in the absence of a child assessment order[10].

An application for a child assessment order must be made by filing an application in respect of each child in the appropriate form and providing sufficient copies for service on each respondent[11]. The period of notice which must be given in respect of a child assessment order application is seven days[12] and this underlines the fact that the order should not be used in emergencies. It should be seen instead as a planned response to concerns about a child's health or development. Where it is intended to restrict contact with a child or to provide for medical examination, psychiatric or other assessment of the child, the application should include a request for such directions from the court[13], and such directions requests can include a request that a particular doctor, or one of a particular sex should conduct a medical examination. It should be noted that whilst the court may give a direction that a medical examination, psychiatric or other assessment should take place the Act provides that where the child is of sufficient understanding to make an informed decision, he may refuse to submit to such examination or assessment[14].

The child assessment order must specify the date by which the assessment is to begin, and it has effect for such period not exceeding seven days beginning with that date as may be specified in the order[15]. In some courts this is being interpreted so as to allow assessment to take place on one day a week for up to seven weeks. The child assessment order can provide that the child live away from home for a period or periods not in total exceeding seven days[16]. There is no provision for extending a child assessment order, although the child, his parents and anyone with parental responsibility, and any person with whom the child was living immediately before the making of the order, may apply for the discharge of the order[17] and provisions on contact may be challenged by these people and also anyone in whose favour the courts had previously made a contact order under Section 8 or Section 34 which is still in force[18].

As soon as is practicable after the commencement of proceedings for a child assessment order, the court is required by Section 41 (1) of the Children Act 1989 to appoint a guardian ad litem for the child concerned unless satisfied that it is not necessary to do so in order to safeguard the child's interests. The court (or the guardian if one has already been appointed) may appoint a solicitor under Section 41 (3) to represent the child where it is of the view that the child has sufficient understanding to instruct a solicitor and wishes to do so, or it appears to the court that it would be in the child's best interests for him to be represented by a solicitor, or no guardian ad litem has in fact been appointed.

Any person may apply to the court, usually a single justice in the magistrates' court, for an order authorising a child's removal to accommodation provided by or on behalf of the applicant, or authorising the child remaining in the place in which he is being accommodated provided that the court is satisfied that there is reasonable cause to believe that to do otherwise would mean that the child would be likely to suffer significant harm[19]. This order is called an emergency protection order[20].

An emergency protection order application can be made either ex parte or on notice. Given the urgent nature of the grounds for making an order it is understood that most magistrates' clerks are giving leave for such an application to be made ex parte[21]. The application is made by filing the appropriate form (one for each child) at the time the application is made or as directed by the justices' clerk[22]. A local authority, in addition to being able to rely on the more general grounds, can apply for such an order where inquiries are being made in the course of a local authority investigation under Section 47 of the Children Act 1989 and those inquiries are being frustrated by access to the child being unreasonably refused and the applicant has reasonable cause to believe that access to the child is required as a matter of urgency[23]. A similar power is vested in any authorised person under the Act which at the moment only extends to the NSPCC[24].

When an application is made for an emergency protection order it may already be known or suspected that gaining access to premises on which the child is believed to be may be difficult. Provision is therefore made to enable the applicant to obtain a warrant authorising a police constable to obtain entry to such premises, if need be by force, and to remove the child[25]. The applicant may accompany the police officer and where relevant may also have an order that the police officer be accompanied by a registered medical practitioner, health visitor or registered nurse[26]. Where the applicant wishes to restrict contact between the child and anyone else for the duration of the order[27] or intends that the child should be medically examined, or subject to psychiatric or other assessment[28] then directions on these matters should be sought at the stage of applying for the order although it can be done later[29]. Provision is also made under Section 41 (6) for the court to appoint a guardian ad litem even at this early stage and where the court believes the child should have a solicitor then by Section 41 (3) of the Children Act 1989 the court can appoint one. If the applicant, the child, or parents or those with parental responsibility are dissatisfied with any directions issued, they can apply to court for a variation of the directions[30]. Where a direction is sought and obtained with regard to a medical examination, psychiatric or other assessment of the child, the child may nevertheless overrule the court's direction where he is deemed to be of sufficient understanding to make an informed decision[31]. The emergency protection order will last for eight days[32] with the provision for one extension of seven days[33] in exceptional circumstances. After 72 hours the child, any parent or other person with parental responsibility or any person with whom the child was living immediately before the making of the order may apply to the court for an order discharging the emergency protection order[34]. If an emergency protection order is extended there is no further right to apply for discharge of the order[35].

In some situations it may be that the police are the first to discover that a child is suffering or likely to suffer significant harm and the Children Act 1989 provides the police with powers of protection to remove a child or to authorise his remaining in a particular place such as a hospital[36]. This power can be exercised by the police for up to 72 hours but where the police believe this period should be extended they should either have contacted social services with a view to the local authority applying for an emergency protection order[37] or for an interim care order[38] or they should have applied for and obtained an emergency protection order on behalf of the local authority[39]. Whilst the police are exercising their powers of protection they must notify parents and those with parental responsibility or with whom the child was living of what is happening[40], and must afford such people reasonable contact with the child unless that would not be in the child's interests[41].

The Act provides for a recovery order to be obtained where a child has been abducted, is missing or has run away from a person who is responsible for him under an emergency protection order, or a care order, or who is responsible for the exercise of police powers of protection[42]. Those who remove or keep children away, or assist or induce a child to run away or stay away from the responsible person may be guilty of an offence under Section 49 or under Section 50 of the Act[43].

An application for a recovery order is made by filing the appropriate form with the court and may be heard either ex parte or on one day's notice[44]. An order will be issued by the court in the appropriate form as provided for in the rules[45] and is effective in Scotland[46].

Children may, however, be justified in seeking to leave a threatening or abusive environment and in recognition of this, Section 51 of the Act provides for refuges for children at risk of harm[47]. It should be noted that the word significant is not used in this context. A system of certification provided by the Secretary of State ensures that persons running such refuges will be exempted from liability to prosecution for offences under the Act relating to the abduction or absconding of a child[48].

1   Children Act 1989 ss 43 (1), 44 (1).
2   Ibid s 31 (9).
3   Ibid s 43 (1). See ibid s 31 (9).
4   Ibid s 44 (1)(a), (b), (c).
5   Ibid s 46.
6   Ibid s 50.
7   Ibid s 51.
8   Ibid s 31 (9), (10) per Sir Stephen Brown P in *Newham London Borough v A G* [1992] 2 FCR 119 at 120.
9   Ibid s 43. The order will usually be requested from the magistrates' court in accordance with the Children (Allocation of Proceedings) Order 1991, SI 1991/1677, art 3 (1) except in those circumstances referred to in art 3 (2). It should be noted that in the first twelve months of the operation of the Act most courts were reporting little or no use of child assessment orders, see DICKENS J — Applications for Child Assessment Orders [1993] JSWFL 47 and see First Report of Children Act Advisory Committee 1991/92 (LCD 1992).
10 Ibid s 43 (1).
11 Family Proceedings Courts (Children Act 1989) Rules 1991, SI 1991/1395, r 4 (1). See CHA Form 33.
12 Ibid Sch 2 col (ii).
13 Children Act 1989 s 43 (9).
14 Ibid s 43 (8).
15 Ibid s 43 (5).
16 Ibid s 43 (5), (9).
17 Ibid s 43 (11), (12).
18 Family Proceedings Courts (Children Act 1989) Rules 1991, Sch 2 col (iii).
19 Children Act 1989 s 44 (4), and see note 9 supra and CHA Form 34.
20 Ibid s 44 and see CHA Form 35.
21 Family Proceedings Courts (Children Act 1989) Rules 1991, r 4 (4). Again it should be noted that magistrates' courts all over the country have noted that fewer applications are being made for emergency protection orders with the local authorities appearing to treat it very much as an "emergency" order and only to be used when there is no other alternative.
22 Ibid r 4 (1)(a).
23 Children Act 1989 s 44 (1)(b).

24 Ibid s 44 (1)(c).
25 Ibid s 48 (9) and see CHA Forms 43 and 44.
26 Ibid s 48 (11).
27 Ibid s 44 (6)(a).
28 Ibid s 44 (6)(b).
29 Ibid s 44 (9)(a), (b).
30 Ibid s 44 (9)(b).
31 Ibid s 44 (7).
32 Ibid s 45 (1).
33 Ibid s 45 (4), (5) and see CHA Form 38.
34 Ibid s 45 (8), (9).
35 Ibid s 45 (8), (9).
36 Ibid s 46 (1), (6).
37 Under ibid s 44.
38 Ibid s 38.
39 Ibid s 46 (7).
40 Ibid s 46 (4).
41 Ibid s 46 (10).
42 Ibid s 50.
43 Ibid see s 49 (1), (3) and s 50 (9).
44 Family Proceedings Courts (Children Act 1989) Rules 1991, r 4 (1)(a) and Sch 2 col (ii); and Family Proceedings Rules 1991, r 4.4 (4)(d) and App 3 col (ii) and see CHA Form 45.
45 See CHA Form 46.
46 Children Act 1989 s 50 (13).
47 Ibid s 51 (1), (2).
48 Ibid s 51 (5).

3: CARE OR SUPERVISION ORDER PROCEEDINGS

175. Care or supervision order proceedings. A local authority or a person authorised[1] by the Secretary of State to do so may make an application to the court for a care order or supervision order where it is believed that the criteria for the making of such orders is met[2].

Care or supervision order proceedings must generally be commenced in the magistrates' family proceedings court[3] for the area in which the child ordinarily resides[4] or for the area in which the incident occurred if a child is visiting[5]. Where an order is eventually made it must be made in favour of the authority in whose area the child ordinarily resides, unless the child is from outside the jurisdiction in which case the order must be made to the local authority in whose area the incidents or neglect occurred[6].

Care proceedings may be started in a higher court if they have arisen out of a direction by a higher court under Section 37 of the Children Act 1989 or where other proceedings are pending in another court[7]. Where an application is commenced in a county court it must be commenced in a care centre[8].

Where any party to proceedings is not happy for the application to proceed in the magistrates' court, or where the clerk and or magistrates believe the case should be transferred, the position will be considered by the court according to specified criteria[9] and the case may then be allocated to a higher court. If the magistrates' court refuses to transfer the case an application can be made to a district judge in the relevant care centre[10] to determine whether the case merits transfer under the transfer criteria and if so to which court the case should be transferred[11]. The Children (Allocation of Proceedings) Order 1991 also provides for the transfer of cases from one magistrates'[12] or county court[13] to another and for the transfer down to a magistrates' or county court where the higher court deems it appropriate under the terms of the Order[14].

1 Only the NSPCC currently authorised under the Children Act 1989, see ibid s 31 (9).
2 Children Act 1989 s 31 (2). *See Re O (A Minor) (Care Order: Education Procedure)* [1992] 2 FLR T. See *Newham London Borough v AG* [1992] 2 FCR 119 and CHA Form 49.
3 Children (Allocation of Proceedings) Order 1991, SI 1991/1677, art 3.
4 Children Act 1989 s 31 (8).
5 Ibid s 31 (8).
6 Ibid s 31 (8)(a), (b).
7 Children (Allocation of Proceedings) Order 1991, art 3 (2), (3).
8 Ibid art 18 (1). Care centres are listed in Sch 2 col (ii) of the Order.
9 Ibid art 7, and Paragraph 20 ante. See CHA Forms 64 and 65, for Certificate of Transfer and Refusal of Transfer. It should be noted that the higher courts have indicated that they believe certain types of cases must be transferred eg. in *Re C (A Minor) (Care Proceedings)* [1992] 2 FCR 341, WARD J stated that the issue of returning a battered baby to parents was exceptionally grave and important and should be transferred from the magistrates' court; and in *L v Berkshire CC* [1992] 1 FCR 481 the President indicated that "cases requiring a lengthy hearing (in this case 8 days) should be transferred from the magistrates' court. This would then avoid the difficulty of having to assemble the magistrates on a number of days". It should be noted however that if such a transfer would result in the case not being heard in the county or High Court for a long time due to pressure on s 1(2) that the case should stay with the magistrates. See also comments of THORPE J in *Re H (A Minor)* (1992) Times, 5 June, FD and see the comments of CONNELL J in *S v Oxfordshire County Council* [1993] Fam Law 74 that cases involving contested issues of non-accidental injury *should* be transferred using art 7.
10 Ibid art 9.
11 Ibid art 9 (2), (3).
12 Ibid art 6.
13 Ibid art 10.
14 Ibid arts 11, 12, 13.

176. Procedure in care and supervision order proceedings. An application for a care or supervision order may have been preceded by the granting of a child assessment order[1] or an emergency protection order[2], or by the exercise of police powers of protection[3] or as a result of a court directed investigation[4] under Section 37 of the Children Act 1989. Equally the applicant may be applying to court for an order where no previous action has been taken in respect of the child[5].

An applicant proposing to bring proceedings for a care or supervision order must file an application in respect of each child in the appropriate form laid down in the rules[6], together with sufficient copies for one to be served on each respondent and anyone else to whom notice must be given[7]. The notice for service which is part of the form must notify each respondent and anyone else to whom notice is required to be given of the date, time and place fixed for the hearing and give three full days notice of the hearing[8]. Those persons who are respondents[9] are the child, and anyone with parental responsibility for the child and the local authority if it is not the applicant, and the persons to whom notice must be given are[10] the persons caring for the child at the time proceedings were commenced, every person whom the applicant believes to be a parent without parental responsibility, a refuge provider if the child is staying in a refuge and every person whom the applicant believes to be a party to pending relevant proceedings in respect of the same child.

Upon receipt of the application the justices' clerk in the family proceedings court or the clerk in the higher court will fix the date, time and place for a hearing or a directions appointment, allowing sufficient time for the applicant to comply with the rules as to service of notice, indorse the date, time and place so fixed upon the copies of the application filed by the applicant and return the copies to the applicant for service[11]. In many cases where there has been no preceding legal action the justices' clerk or the court may feel it appropriate to deal with a number of matters at a directions appointment prior to a first full hearing of an application.

In the case of an application for a care or supervision order, no provision is made in the rules for the filing of an answer in contrast to the position with regard to applications for Section 8 orders or financial orders under Schedule 1[12].

If a directions hearing is held first then the justices' clerk in the family proceedings court or the court (be it magistrates', county or High Court if a case has been transferred or consolidated), may consider giving, varying or revoking directions for the conduct of the proceedings including the timetable for the proceedings, the attendance of a child, the appointment of a guardian ad litem under Section 41 or of a solicitor under Section 41 (3) or the submission of evidence including experts' reports, the possibility of transferring proceedings to another court and the consolidation with other proceedings[13].

In proceedings for care and supervision orders the child is a party and the court or, in the case of the family proceedings court, the justices' clerk must consider the appointment of a guardian ad litem unless it is satisfied that it is not necessary in order to safeguard the child's interests[14], and the appointment of a solicitor where it would appear to be in the child's best interests, where the child has sufficient understanding to instruct a solicitor, or where no guardian ad litem has in fact been appointed[15].

The court's duty to appoint a guardian ad litem arises only in relation to specified proceedings which include those governing state intervention in the family but do not include private law disputes between individuals with the major exception of adoption and wardship for which entirely separate provision is made. The Children Act 1989 Section 41 (6) defines "specified proceedings" as meaning:

1. proceedings on applications for care or supervision orders;
2. proceedings in which the court has given a direction under Section 37 (1) and has made or is considering whether to make, an interim care order;
3. proceedings on an application for the discharge of a care order or for variation or discharge of a supervision order;
4. proceedings on an application to substitute a supervision order for a care order;
5. proceedings in which the court is considering whether to make a residence order with respect to a child who is the subject of a care order; proceedings with respect to contact between a child who is the subject of a care order and any other person;
6. any proceedings relating to child assessment orders, emergency protection orders or recovery orders;
7. on appeals against the making of orders in any of the preceding applications or proceedings;
8. in any proceedings which are specified for the time being by rules of court[16].

These in fact provide that the Section shall be extended to cover: proceedings under Section 25 for a secure accommodation order, applications under Section 33 (7) for the leave of the court to the proposed change of surname for a child who is the subject of a care order or the proposed removal of such a child from the United Kingdom; applications under paragraph 19 (1) of Schedule 2 for the arranging or assistance in arranging for a child in the care of the local authority to live outside England and Wales; applications under paragraph 6 (3) of Schedule 3 for the extension, or further extension of a supervision order originally made under Section 31; and to any appeals arising from these proceedings[17]. No attempt has been made, therefore, in the Children Act 1989 to provide for a system of separate representation of a child by a guardian ad litem in all private law disputes comparable to that which exists for children who are the subject of state intervention in their family life. The power of the court to appoint a guardian ad litem or a solicitor is exercisable at any stage in the proceedings either on application being made by any party[18] or by the court or by a justices' clerk, and whether or not an application has actually been made[19]. As soon as an appointment has been made the court clerk or the justices' clerk should notify any other parties to the proceedings of such appointments[20].

The duties of the guardian ad litem are laid down in the Rules and, unless excused by the court, the guardian ad litem must attend all directions, appointments and hearings in the proceedings and must appoint a solicitor to represent the child unless one has already been appointed and must give such advice to the child as is appropriate and, subject to the child wanting to instruct a solicitor and being capable of so doing, instruct a solicitor on the child's behalf. The guardian ad litem must also advise the court on:

1. whether the child is of sufficient understanding for any purpose including the child's refusal to submit to a medical or psychiatric examination or other assessment that the court has power to direct or order;
2. the wishes of the child on any relevant matter including his attendance at court;
3. the appropriate forum for the proceedings; the appropriate timing of the proceedings or any part of them; the options available to the court and the suitability of each option including what order should be made in each determination and any other matter upon which the court wishes for advice[21].

The advice so given may be given orally or in writing[22] but before a final hearing the guardian must not less than 7 days previously file a written report in court advising on the interests of the child copies of which will be served by the court on all parties[23]. Where at any stage it appears to the guardian ad litem that the child is instructing his solicitor direct or the child intends to and is capable of conducting proceedings on his own behalf, he must inform the court of the situation and thereafter perform his other duties and take such part in the proceedings as the court may direct and may with the leave of the court have legal representation in his conduct of those duties[24]. Legal aid continues for the child but is not additionally available for the guardian ad litem.

Where a solicitor for the child is appointed the Rules provide that he shall accept service of documents and represent the child in accordance with instructions received from the guardian ad litem unless the solicitor considers, having taken into account the views of the guardian ad litem, that the child wishes and is capable of giving instructions which conflict with the guardian ad litem in which case he must conduct the proceedings in accordance with instructions given by the child[25]. Where no guardian ad litem for the child has been appointed then the solicitor must, if the child has sufficient understanding, act according to the child's instructions or in the absence of such instructions in furtherance of the child's best interests[26]. In common with other parties to the proceedings the child may apply through his solicitor, or if he is not of sufficient understanding the solicitor may apply on the child's behalf for a guardian ad litem to be appointed at any stage in the proceedings[27]. In addition to his other duties the guardian ad litem must notify any person who should be joined to the proceedings to safeguard the interests of the child and shall inform the court of anyone whom he has attempted to notify or of anyone else whom he believes wishes to be joined to the proceedings[28]. Where no solicitor has been appointed for the child and there is no-one to accept or serve documents on his behalf the guardian shall do so and shall advise the child of the contents of such documents where the child is of sufficient understanding[29].

At any stage in the proceedings any party may apply for, or the court may of its own volition hold, directions appointments and issue the directions earlier discussed[30]. Any party seeking directions must do so by written request specifying the direction sought which must be filed and served on the other parties, or to which the other parties have consented and they or their representative have agreed in writing. Where the directions sought are not agreed, all parties, having been served, must be given the opportunity to attend and be heard or to make written representations. Experience of the first twelve months operation of the Act seems to be showing that the presumptive 12 week timetable is not working out in practice. Considerable reservations have been expressed about directions appointments which seem to offer greater opportunity for delaying tactics and magistrates' clerks report cases taking longer than under the old law. Solicitors and guardians acting for children should be aware of their duty to attempt to speed up proceedings in accordance with section 1(2) of the Act.

Thus one of the most important matters which the court will have to address early on and probably in a directions hearing is the issue of the timetabling of the case[31]. Guidance has been issued to the courts that in public law proceedings 12 weeks is the approximate period after which the full hearing should take place. Clearly this guidance ties in with the delay principle in Section 1 (2) of the Children Act 1989 but the presumption should be capable of rebuttal on the basis of the paramountcy of the child's welfare. Where the child is undergoing assessment for the purpose of a psychiatric report then it may not be possible for a specialist assessment to be done within what may be left of a 12 week period. Where any party realises there may be problems about the submission of expert evidence due to the nature of the assessment then they should return to court and seek directions on re-timetabling at the earliest opportunity[32].

Under the Rules, each party to a case must file and serve on the other parties, any welfare officer appointed and any guardian ad litem: any written statements of the substance of the oral evidence which the party intends to adduce at a hearing of or a directions appointment in those proceedings, which must be signed and dated and contain a declaration by the person making the statement that he believes it to be true and understands that it may be placed before the court. There must also be filed and served copies of any documents including subject to rule 18 (3) experts' reports upon which the party intends to rely at any hearing or directions appointment[33].

It should be noted that no person can without the leave of the justices' clerk or the court cause a child to be medically or psychiatrically examined or otherwise assessed for the purpose of the preparation of expert evidence for use in the proceedings[34]. All parties and the guardian ad litem must be served with notice of the application unless the justices' clerk or the court otherwise directs and where there is a hearing it will be treated as a directions hearing[35]. Where a court orders that such a medical, psychiatric or other examination or assessment should take place, such a direction is mandatory and does not merely give the local authority a discretion as to whether or not it should be carried out.[37] Where the leave of the justices' clerk or the court has not been given, no evidence arising out of an examination or assessment can be adduced without the leave of the court[37]. Service of all statements and reports must take place by such time as the justices' clerk or court directs or in the absence of a direction, before the hearing or appointment.

Supplementary statements may be filed and served[38] subject to any direction of the justices' clerk or court about the timing of such statements. Amendments to documents which have been filed or served can only be achieved after serving all parties with notice of such a request for amendment with the court's leave and then the court may either grant leave or invite the parties to make representations regarding the application to amend[39].

Parties who have not filed and served copies of their statement, documents or reports upon which they intend to rely may not adduce such evidence without the leave of the justices' clerk in the case of a directions appointment in the family proceedings court, or in any other directions appointment or hearing, of the court[40].

The rules specifically provide that all documents lodged with the court, other than a record of any orders made, relating to the proceeding are confidential and will not be disclosed except to any party to the proceedings or his legal representative, the guardian ad litem, the Legal Aid Board or a welfare officer without the leave of the court[41].

The court may give directions as to the order of speeches and evidence at a hearing or directions appointment in the course of the proceedings. In the absence of such directions the parties and the guardian ad litem should adduce their evidence in the following order:

1. the applicant,
2. any party with parental responsibility for the child,
3. other respondents,
4. the guardian ad litem,
5. the child, if he is a party to the proceedings and there is no guardian ad litem[42].

The justices' clerk, a proper officer of the court or the court itself must keep a note of the substance of the oral evidence given during the course of proceedings on a directions appointment or any hearing[43].

After hearing all the evidence the court must make its decision as soon as practicable[44]. When making any order or refusing any application the court must state any findings of fact and the reasons for any decision[45]. Any order which is made must be recorded by the court or proper officer either in the appropriate form laid down in the Rules or, where there is no such form, in writing, and it must be served on all parties[46].

When the court has finally disposed of the case, the guardian ad litem, in conjunction with the solicitor in a case in which the infant is represented, must consider whether it would be in the infant's best interests to appeal to a higher court[47].

Where the case is heard in the magistrates' family proceedings court the appeal will lie to the High Court Family Division, and where the case is heard in the county court or in the High Court the appeal lies to the Court of Appeal, Civil Division[48].

1   Children Act 1989 s 43.
2   Ibid s 44.
3   Ibid s 46.

4 Ibid s 37 (2)(a).
5 In which case the full application form for a care or supervision order must be completed and filed in court.
6 Family Proceedings Rules 1991, SI 1991/1247, r 4.4 (1)(a) and Family Proceedings Courts (Children Act 1989) Rules 1991, SI 1991/1395, r 4 (1)(a).
7 Ibid r 4.4 (3) and r 4 (3) respectively.
8 Ibid App 3 col (ii) and Sch 2 col (ii) respectively.
9 Ibid App 3 col (iv) and Sch 2 col (iii).
10 Ibid App 3 col (iii) and Sch 2 col (iv).
11 Ibid rr 4.4 (2) and 4 (2) respectively.
12 Ibid rr 4.9 and 9 respectively.
13 All provided for in Family Proceedings Rules 1991, r 4.14 (2) and Family Proceedings Courts (Children Act 1989) Rules 1991, r 14 (2).
14 Ibid rr 4.10 and 10 respectively.
15 Ibid rr 4.11 and 11 respectively.
16 Children Act 1989 s 41 (6).
17 Family Proceedings Rules 1991 r 4.2 (2) and Family Proceedings Courts (Children Act 1989) Rules 1991 r 2 (2). The duties of the guardian ad litem, how they should conduct themselves and what matters their reports should address are fully analysed in *Manual of Practice Guidance for Guardians Ad Litem and Reporting Officers* by J Timms for DOH, 1992 HMSO.
18 Ibid rr 4.10 (2) and 10 (2) respectively.
19 Ibid rr 4.10 (4) and 10 (4) respectively and see CHA Form 30.
20 Ibid rr 4.10 (5) and 10 (5) respectively.
21 Ibid rr 4.11.(2)(4) and 11 (2)(4) respectively.
22 Ibid rr 4.11 (5) and 11 (5) respectively.
23 Ibid rr 4.11 (7) and 11 (7) respectively.
24 Ibid rr 4.11 (3) and 11 (3) respectively.
25 Ibid rr 4.12 and 12 respectively and it should be noted that capability to instruct a solicitor is less than that required to give valid refusal to medical treatment. See comments of THORPE J in *Re H (A Minor)* (1992) Times, 5 June, FD.
26 Ibid rr 4.12 (b), (c), and 12(b) and (c) respectively.
27 Ibid rr 4.10 (2) and 10 (2) respectively
28 Ibid rr 4.11 (6) and 11 (6) respectively.
29 Ibid rr 4.11 (8) and 11 (8) respectively.
30 Ibid rr 4.14 (3) and 14 (3) respectively.
31 Ibid rr 4.14 (2)(a) and 14 (2)(a) respectively.
32 See Form 158 post.
33 Ibid rr 4.17 (1) and 17 (1) respectively.
34 Ibid rr 4.18 (1) and 18 (1) respectively.
35 Ibid rr 4.18 (2) and 18 (2) respectively.
36 See *Re O* 1992 2 FCR 394
37 Ibid rr 4.18 (3) and 18 (3) respectively and Children Act 1989 s 32.
38 Ibid rr 4.18 (2) and 18 (2) respectively.
39 Ibid rr 4.19 and 19 respectively.
40 Ibid rr 4.17 (3) and 17 (3) respectively.
41 Ibid rr 4.23 and 23 respectively.
42 Ibid rr 4.21 (1)(2) and 23 (1)(3) respectively.
43 Ibid rr 4.20 and 20 respectively.
44 Ibid rr 4.20 (3) and 20 (4) respectively.
45 Ibid rr 4.20 (4) and 20 (6) respectively.

46 Ibid rr 4.20 (5), (6) and 20 (7) respectively and see CHA Form 20.
47 Children Act 1989 s 94.
48 Ibid rr 4.11 (2) and 11 (2) respectively and see CHA Form 30.

4: ORDERS

177. Care and supervision orders. On the application of any local authority or authorised person the court can make an order placing the child in the care of a designated local authority or putting him under the supervision of a designated local authority or of a probation officer[1]. The court can only make a care or supervision order if it is satisfied on the balance of probabilities that:

1. the child concerned is suffering or is likely to suffer significant harm; and
2. that the harm or likelihood of harm, is attributable to:
    2.1 the care given to the child or likely to be given to him if the order were not made, not being what it would be reasonable to expect a parent to give him; or
    2.2 the child's being beyond parental control[2].

In addition to the court being satisfied that these two conditions are met, it must further be satisfied that making an order on the child will be better for the child than making no order at all[3]. The court must satisfy itself that such is the case by applying[4] the welfare principle[5] as informed by the welfare checklist[6].

The condition as to significant harm is drawn with reference to the child concerned and so the court must look at the position, characteristics and needs of each particular child. This is reflected in the requirement that separate forms of application must be completed for each child[7] and the criteria met before an order will be made in respect of each individual child[8].

The new criteria cover situations both where the child is suffering or is likely to suffer significant harm. The use of the term "is suffering" is intended to concentrate attention on present or continuing conditions but problems which have temporarily been ameliorated since the commencement of proceedings could still found an application[9]. Applications relating solely to past events could thus not found an application unless linked in some way to the present evidenced by some harm continuing, or being likely to continue[10]. As to relying on the future possibility of harm as indicated by "likely to suffer significant harm" the applicant must seek to show that there would be a greater risk to the child in leaving him with his family than by seeking his removal. When balancing these risks the court will have to decide on all the evidence, including experts' reports and guardian ad litem reports, which constituted the greater. In this context the view has been expressed that in cases of emotional or psychological harm the approach taken will be that which will prevent unwarranted intervention[11], but courts may take a robust view regardless of the species of the apprehended harm[12].

The harm suffered or apprehended must be "significant" and where this turns on the child's health or development then his health or development shall be compared with that which could be expected of a similar child[13]. As far as the word significant is concerned, the DHSS Review of Child Care Law stated that minor shortcomings in the health care provided, or minor deficits in physical, psychological or social development, should not give rise to compulsory intervention unless they are having, or likely to have, serious and lasting effects upon the child[14]. The Lord

Chancellor has also said that "unless there is evidence that a child is being, or is likely to be, positively harmed because of a failure in the family, the state whether in the guise of a local authority or a court should not interfere"[15]. In the early days of the operation of the Act however there were widespread signs that both local authorities and the courts were placing an over-emphasis on the words "significant" and were failing to make care or supervision orders in situations in which they were obviously required.

Interpretation of significant harm — The interpretation of the phrase "likely to suffer significant harm" has already come up for consideration in the higher courts attracting in its wake a criticism of the dangers of excessive legalism in the area of Section 31. In *Newham London Borough Council v AG*[16] a baby boy had been made the subject of wardship proceedings in February 1990 as a result of possible threats to the child's life arising out of the mother's acute psychiatric condition. The evidence showed that the mother had already had thoughts of killing the child and expert psychiatric evidence had disclosed that the mother was unstable and unpredictably violent. For this reason, the mother's parents' application for the child to be placed with them would not ensure sufficient protection for the child since if the child was living with the grandparents it would be impossible to prevent the mother having contact. The Judge at first instance had also found that "with a person in the mother's condition, a swift move by her and the harm would be done, and no amount of supervision, even in social work offices, could ensure that there would be no risk to the child." For this and other reasons to do with the grandparents' care of the child's mother and her brothers, the judge applied Section 31 of the Children Act 1989 and made an order committing the child to the care of the local authority, whose plan was to place the child for adoption. The grandmother appealed and the Court of Appeal dismissed her appeal holding that when interpreting and giving effect to the phrase "likely to suffer significant harm" in Section 31(2)(a) of the Children Act 1989 it would be wrong to equate "likely to suffer" with "on the balance of probabilities". The court was not applying a test to events which had happened and deciding on the evidence, on the balance of probabilities whether an event had in fact happened. In considering the phrase "likely to suffer" the court was looking to the future and had to assess the risk. When looking to the future, all the court could do was to evaluate the chance. On the facts of this case the Judge had had to make an assessment of the future risk to the child in the light of the evidence before him. He had found that there was a real significant risk of the child suffering significant harm if he did not make a care order and his conclusion was amply supported by the evidence. The President of the Family Division sitting in the Court of Appeal took the opportunity to emphasise that he hoped that, in approaching cases under the Act, "courts would not be invited in every case to perform a strict legalistic analysis of the statutory meaning of section 31. The words of the statute must be considered, but they were not intended to be to be unduly restrictive when evidence clearly indicated that a certain course should be taken in order to protect the child."[17]

Interpretation of "similar child"— The comparison to be made with a similar child is not without problems, since it is required that one compare this subjective child with that hypothetically similar child[16]. This issue came up for consideration by the courts in the case of *Re O*[19] which concerned a girl aged 15 years 4 months who had persistently truanted from school for over three years. Ewbank J had supported magistrates who had made a care order on the basis that the girl's intellectual and social development was suffering and was likely to suffer, and that the harm which she was suffering from, or was likely to suffer from, was significant. It was further urged on behalf of the girl that, in determining whether the harm was "significant", the comparison which had to be made was with a "similar child", and there was no evidence that she had suffered harm compared with a similar child. Ewbank J took a very robust view of what constituted a similar child in such circumstances. He stated that in his view "similar child" means "a child of equivalent intellectual and social development, who has gone to school, and not merely an average child who may or may not be at school."[20] Clearly however, if the child is disabled in some way, and that has affected his health and development then the court must ask itself what state of health or development could be expected of a child with a similar disability. As to whether "similar" connotes any consideration being given to the child's background, this is doubtful since, according to the Lord Chancellor "the care that a parent gives to his child must relate to the circumstances attributable to that child in the sense of physical, mental and emotional characteristics"[21]. The child's background, how-ever, may be considered relevant once the care conditions are satisfied when the court is considering whether or not to make an order[22].

Merely satisfying the court that the child is suffering or likely to suffer significant harm is not sufficient of itself. It must further be proved that the harm or likelihood of harm is attributable to an absence of an objectively reasonable standard of care being offered to the child or that the child is beyond parental control[23].

When looking at whether the care given to the child, or likely to be given to him if an order were not made, is not what it would be reasonable to expect a parent to give, the type of care is not further defined. Clearly, if harm can encompass the impairment of mental, physical, emotional, intellectual and social development[24], then "care" can be defined in the same way and may include the lack of emotional care demonstrated by a complete disregard for the child's feelings. This condition also has a prospective element so that even where the child is being provided with accommo-dation at the time any proceedings are instituted, the court can look to a previous lack of care and at the likelihood of this being repeated if the child is returned to the parent's care. Furthermore, if other children have remained in the family setting and there are now concerns about them, the care of the child dealt with in earlier proceedings may become relevant when considering the likelihood of harm to them and the standard of care which they may have received. It is, however, important to remember that each child's case must be considered individually.

Whilst the test is subjective in looking at the child, it is clearly objective in looking at the standard of care offered by the parent. Thus it must be an objectively reasonable standard of care offered by the hypothetical reasonable parent[25]. The parent cannot rely on his or her personal inadequacies to argue that he or she could not have provided a better standard of care because they are expected to seek assistance from the local authority to provide the requisite degree of care[26]. Where the parent has failed to avail himself of such services and the child has suffered harm then the local authority would be justified in intervening through care or supervision order proceedings.

The second limb in Section 31 (2)(b) refers to the child being beyond parental control which is a matter of fact on which evidence can be presented much as it was under the old law. Whilst roughly 10% of all care orders made under the old law were based on the child being beyond parental control, a local authority will be reluctant to take action on this ground unless the breakdown is so serious that court interven-tion is warranted, and parents will not easily be able to avoid responsibility for their troublesome teenagers. Where, however, a parent has done all in their power to offer good quality care and advice to a child, which the child rejects by opting at an early age for a life of crime, or of sexual exploitation, the child will be deemed to be beyond parental control[27] and the quality of care limb will not be in issue.

The case of *Re O*[19] is again of relevance when considering the second limb and is further interesting in its reference back to the law applicable under the Children and

Young Persons Act 1969. Ewbank J held that, in his judgment, "where a child is suffering harm in not going to school and is living at home, it will follow that either the child is beyond her parents' control or that they are not giving the child the care that it would be reasonable to expect a parent to give."[20] He then quoted with approval the judgment of Denning MR in *Re S*[28] to the effect that "if a child was not being sent to school or receiving a proper education then he was in need of care."

Once the court is satisfied that the care criteria are met, it must next satisfy itself that making an order is better for the child than not making an order at all[29]. In considering this it will regard the child's welfare as its paramount consideration[30] and since these are proceedings under Part IV it must be bound by the welfare checklist[31]. A very important item on the checklist for these purposes is the range of orders available in the proceedings[32], which can include for the first time the mixing of private law with public law orders[33]. Thus, whilst the court could determine on making a care or supervision order alone[34], it could equally determine on making a residence order in favour of some member of the child's family other than a parent, with a contact order in favour of the mother, a prohibited steps order preventing the father having contact and a supervision order in favour of the local authority. The court has available to it not only the orders set out in Section 31 (1) and Section 35 but also the full range of the Section 8 orders and if necessary the family assistance order under Section 16. It is thus open to the court to make a residence order subject to certain conditions in favour of the parents, combined perhaps with a supervision order. This was indeed the solution adopted in *Re C*[35] by Ward J. In this case there had been an application for a care order but the magistrates had made a supervision order. Neither order was appropriate in Ward J's view since, in the absence of a final assessment, it would be better to make a residence order in favour of parents subject to conditions, and an interim supervision order also subject to conditions. The conditions to be attached to the residence order were that the parents would undertake a programme of assessment and access to the child and the condition attaching to the interim supervision order were that the child be subject to various medical assessments. Although the effect of Section 9(5) of the Act is to prevent local authorities from applying for prohibited steps orders or specific issues orders where the result of such applications would achieve the result of a residence or contact order by the back door[36], this does not prevent the court from making such orders where the local authority has correctly used Part IV of the Act. Precisely which orders if any are to be made will depend upon the court's view of what is in the paramount interests of the child, having received experts' reports and the report of the guardian ad litem[37].

Before making a care order with respect to any child, the court shall consider the arrangements which the authority has made or proposes to make, for affording any person contact with a child to whom this section applies; and invite the parties to the proceedings to comment on those arrangements[38]. Where the court feels that the proposed contact arrangements should be reconsidered after a period of time then the court in *Chesire CC v B*[39] emphasised that the court can make a care order together with an interim contact order with a view to reviewing the progress of contact at a slightly later date.

Where the court decides to make a care order then the local authority designated in a care order must be the authority within whose area the child is ordinarily resident[40] or, where the child does not reside in a local authority's area, then the authority within whose area any circumstances arose in consequence of which the order has been made[41]. The care order places the designated authority under a duty to receive the child into their care and to continue to keep him in their care whilst the order remains in force[42], and gives the authority parental responsibility for the child. It was noted by the courts in *R v Kirklees MBC ex parte C* that the care order in conferring parental responsibility confers on the local authority the power to consent to a child being admitted to a hospital for the mentally ill in order to be assessed.[43] It is not necessary to go through the procedures for compulsory admission under the Mental Health Act 1983. Thus the local authority exercises parental power to consent to health care acquired by virtue of the care order. The parents also retain considerably attenuated parental responsibility[44]. Indeed it is the local authority which has the power to determine the extent to which a parent or guardian of the child may meet his responsibility for him[45].

The making of a care order will operate to extinguish a residence order or any Section 8 order[46] and any wardship ceases to be of effect[47]. The making of a care order will also bring to an end a supervision order under Section 35[48] and a school attendance order[49]. The care order will continue in force until the child reaches the age of eighteen unless brought to an end earlier[50]. It should be noticed that no care or supervision order can be made with respect to a child who has reached the age of seventeen (or sixteen in the case of a child who is married)[51]. Where the court makes a care order it has no power to add any direction. The responsibiliity for the child is firmly with the local authority and it was emphasised in *Re CN*[52] that the court cannot as happened in that case direct that a guardian ad litem be allowed to have continuing involvement in order to investigate the rehabilitation process and apply to have contact terminated if appropriate. The question was however left open in this case as to whether a guardian has power under Section 34(2) to apply for an order to contact.

Where the court determines that a residence order under Section 8 should be made, then no care order can be made or continue. If it is thought appropriate to involve the local authority in some way, it will have to be done by the making of a supervision order[53] in addition to the residence order. The new supervision order which is governed by Section 35 and Schedule 3 has a great deal more teeth than the old supervision order[54]. While the supervision order is in force it is the duty of the supervisor to advise, assist and befriend the supervised child, to take such steps as are reasonably necessary to give effect to the order and where the order has not been fully complied with, or the supervisor considers that the order may no longer be necessary consider whether or not to apply for the discharge of the order[55]. Whilst the order is in force the supervisor can direct that the child participate in certain activities[56], undergo medical or psychiatric assessment[57] or can ask the court to direct that the child undergo medical or psychiatric treatment[58]. The supervisor can also now direct with the consent of any responsible person that he takes all reasonable steps to ensure that the supervised child complies with any direction for activities, medical and psychiatric examinations or with any directions as to medical and psychiatric treatment, and that the responsible person participates in certain activities[59].

A supervision order has a limited life ending one year from the date on which it was made[60] and the total number of days in respect of which, for example, a residence condition might be included is now without limitation following an amendment effected by the Courts and Legal Services Act 1990[61]. The supervision order can be extended or further extended for such period as the court thinks fit[62] except that it cannot be extended to run beyond the end of the 3 years beginning with the date on which it was made[63].

One of the factors which might influence either a guardian ad litem in making a report to the court, or the court itself in considering a supervision order, is the availability to the court of the range of private law orders in Section 8 and Section 16 of the Children Act 1989 to complement the supervision order. Thus the court might wish to make a residence order to a grandparent whilst recognising the risk to the child and may thus decide to make a supervision order alongside the residence order. Contact could be controlled if necessary so that one might have an order for contact with the mother in the grandparent's home and a prohibited steps order forbidding the father from having contact with the child.

The precise nature of the Section 8 and Section 16 family assistance orders which the court might make in conjunction with a supervision order are considered elsewhere[64].

In *Devon CC v S*[65], Thorpe J considered the proper approach to proceedings under section 31 where all the parties were agreed on the resolution of the case. The child in this case had been sexually abused by her father and placed in the care of the local authority on an interim order with contact to the mother but none to the father. Before the final hearing all the parties had accepted that it was appropriate to continue this arrangement and a full care order in those terms was proposed. The justices made an order which provided for contact in substantially different terms without warning the parties that they planned to do so. The local authority appealed and Thorpe J held that although there was an overriding duty on the court to investigate non-contested proposals, nevertheless the depth of that investigation should reflect the fact that there was concensus amongst the parties. It was inappropriate in such a situation to hear full oral evidence. Where the court reaches a conclusion which differs from that suggested by the parties. this should be communicated to the parties and they should be given an opportunity to comment upon the magistrates' proposals. Thorpe J allowed the local authority's appeal and contact was ordered in the terms originally agreed between the parties. He further suggested that it would be helpful for family proceedings courts to adopt the practice used in the Family Division for agreed proposals to be presented in the form of a draft order. This would have the effect of reducing the risk of disagreement over the precise terms of an order where there was concensus on its substance.

1 Children Act 1989 s 31 (1) and see CHA Form 20.
2 Children Act 1989 s 31 (2).
3 Ibid s 1 (5).
4 Ibid s 1 (4).
5 Ibid s 1 (1).
6 Ibid s 1 (3).
7 Family Proceedings Courts (Children Act 1989) Rules 1991, SI 1991/1395, r 4 (1)(a) and Family Proceedings Rules 1991, SI 1991/1247, r 4.4 (1)(a).
8 Children Act 1989 s 32 (1)(a).
9 Such was the case under the old law criteria: see *M v Westminster City Council* [1985] FLR 325, [1985] Fam Law 93 and the same approach has been adopted with the new criteria: see *Northamptonshire County Council v S* [1992] 3 WLR 1010.
10 As was the case in *Re D (A Minor)* [1987] AC 317, [1987] 1 All ER 20, HL.
11 DHSS Review of Child Care Law at para 15.18.
12 *F v Suffolk County Council* (1981) 2 FLR 208 and see now comments of Scott Baker J in Re H noted at [1993] Fam Law 62 that "the likelihood of harm is not confined to present or near future but applies to the ability of a parent or carer to meet the emotional needs of a child years ahead"..
13 Children Act 1989 s 31 (10).
14 DHSS *Review of Child Care Law* para 15.15.
15 In the Joseph Jackson Memorial Lecture (139) WLJ 505 at 508.
16 [1992] 2 FCR 119
17 Sir Stephen Brown P in *Newham London Borough Council v AG* [1992] 2 FCR 119 at 128
18 Children Act 1989 s 31 (10).
19 *Re O (A Minor)(Care Order: Education: Procedure)* [1992] 2 FLR 7.
20 Ibid at p 12.
21 Children Bill LH Deb Committee Vol 503, 19 January 1989, col 355.

22 See Children Act 1989 s 1 (3)(d).

23 Ibid s 31 (2).

24 Ibid s 31 (9).

25 Ibid s 31 (2)(a).

26 See ibid Pt III generally and Sch 2 Part I.

27 Ibid s 31 (2)(b).

28 [1978] QB 120 at 140F.

29 Ibid s 1 (5) and see *Humberside County Council v B* [1993] Fam Law 61..

30 Ibid s 1 (1).

31 Ibid s 1 (3), (4) and see *Re O (Minors)(Medical Examination)* [1992] 2 FCR 394.

32 Ibid s 1 (3)(g).

33 Family proceedings in which Section 8 orders can be made include proceedings under Part IV of the Act, see Children Act 1989 s 8 (4).

34 Including a care order when a supervision order had been requested in the application, or a supervision order when a care order had been applied for: Children Act 1989 s 31 (5).

35 *Re C* [1992] 2 FCR 341, FD.

36 *Nottinghamshire CC v P* (1992) Independent, 2 November, FD.

37 Family Proceedings Rules 1991 r 4.21 and Family Proceedings Courts (Children Act 1989) Rules 1991 r 21.

38 Children Act 1989 s 34 (11).

39 [1992] 2 FCR 572

40 Ibid s 31 (8)(a) and see CHA Form 20.

41 Ibid s 31 (8)(b).

42 Ibid s 33 (1) and (2). Note once a guardian has been appointed it is pointless to seek an order under s 7 for a welfare report to be prepared. This would simply duplicate functions — *Re S* [1992] 2 FCR 554 CA per Butler-Sloss LJ at p 558.

43 Ibid s 33 (3)(a) and see *R v Kirklees MBC, ex parte C* [1992] 2 FLR 117.

44 Ibid s 2 (6) subject to ibid s 33.

45 Ibid s 33 (3)(b).

46 Ibid s 91 (2).

47 Ibid s 91 (4).

48 Ibid s 91 (3).

49 Ibid s 91 (5).

50 Ibid s 91 (12).

51 Ibid s 31 (3).

52 *Re C N* [1992] 2 FCR 401, FD.

53 Ibid s 35 and see CHA Form 20.

54 See particularly Children Act 1989 Sch 3 paras 2, 3.

55 Ibid s 35 and see CHA Form 20.

56 Ibid Sch 3 para 2.

57 Ibid Sch 3 para 4.

58 Ibid Sch 3 para 5.

59 Ibid Sch 3 para 3.

60 Ibid Sch 3 para 6 (1).

61 Ibid Sch 3 para 7 (1) as amended by Courts and Legal Services Act 1990. Sch 16, para 27 deleting para 7 from Children Act 1989, Sch 3..

62 Ibid Sch 3 para 6 (3).

63 Ibid Sch 3 para 6 (4).

64 See Paragraphs 120-140 ante.

65 *Devon CC v S* [1992] 3 WLR 273 FD; [1992] 3 All ER 793 FD; [1992] 2 FLR 244 [1992] 1 FCR 550

178. Interim orders. The court has the power under Section 38 of the Children Act 1989 to make either an interim care order or an interim supervision order[1]. Interim orders can be made on the adjournment of proceedings for a care or supervision order[2], or in any family proceedings in which the court has given a direction[3], that a local authority should investigate a child's circumstances with a view to considering whether or not it should commence proceedings for a care or supervision order[4]. Where in any proceedings for a care or supervision order the court exercises its discretion to choose from the range of orders available[5] and makes a residence order, it must also make an interim supervision order with respect to the child[6], unless the child's welfare would be satisfactorily safeguarded without an interim order being made. It should be noted that it is not possible to make an interim residence order[7]. This course of action was actually adopted in *Re C*[8] when on appeal Ward J substituted a residence order in favour of the child's parents subject to conditions together with an interim supervision order subject to conditions.

The court cannot make an interim care or supervision order unless it is satisfied that there are reasonable grounds for believing that the criteria set out in Section 31 (2) of the Children Act are satisfied[9], and that the welfare principles in Section 1 are adhered to[10], in particular that making an order must be better for the child than making no order at all[10]. Since at a first hearing it is most unlikely that all the evidence which a local authority might ultimately wish to rely on will be available, the proceedings in which a first interim order is made will not be as lengthy as for a full order but may nevertheless be hotly contested.

It is already apparent that first hearings are taking considerably longer to deal with than was the case under the old law, because of the requirement to satisfy the care conditions and to convince the court that the particular order sought is the best one in the circumstances and better for the child than making no order at all. Even where the making of a first interim order is unopposed, the court is still bound by the no order principle and must therefore consider all the alternatives[12]. In such circumstances the guardian ad litem should be able to advise whether any such alternatives are viable and what options have already been examined and to what effect. The magistrate or other court hearing an application for an interim care order have a mandatory duty to comply with the Rules of court which require them to read any documents filed before the commencement of the hearing.

Since a number of problems have arisen in practice in relation to hearings for interim orders Cazalet J took the opportunity in *Hampshire CC v S*[13] to lay down a number of guidelines for courts hearing applications for interim care or supervision orders:

1. An interim care order is a holding order but the court should nevertheless consider all relevant risks pending the substantive hearing and should ensure perhaps by giving directions that the final hearing takes place at the earliest possible date.
2. If there is insufficient court time in that court the case should be transferred laterally.
3. In an interim order hearing the court should only rarely make findings on disputed facts.
4. Courts should be cautious about changing a child's residence on an interim order.
5. Where an interim care order would lead to a substantial change in the child's position then the court should permit the hearing of limited and evidence but must ensure that there is not a dress rehearsal of the full hearing.
6. The court should ensure that it has the written advice of the guardian ad

litem but any party opposed to the guardian's recommendations should be given an opportunity to put questions to the guardian.

7. Justices hearing a case must comply with the mandatory requirements of Rules.

8. When granting interim relief, justices should state their findings and reasons concisely and summarise briefly the essential factual issues between the parties. The justices will not however be able to make findings on disputed facts since they will not have heard the evidence in full.

Where the court makes a first interim care or supervision order it may last up to 8 weeks from the date on which it was made[14], although the Department of Health has issued guidance that this should not become the standard duration of a first order[15]. A second or subsequent order may last up to four weeks beginning with the date on which it was made[16] or, where the first order was for less than four weeks, the second or late order may last for more than four weeks but cannot expire more than eight weeks from the beginning of the first order[17]. Thus in many cases the sequence of orders may be a first order for eight weeks followed by one subsequent order for four weeks especially bearing in mind the guidance from the Lord Chancellor's department on timetabling in public law proceedings[18], the no delay principle[19] and the guidelines laid down in *Hampshire CC v S.*[13].

In some cases the first order may only be for two weeks in which case a second order could last for up to six weeks provided that the total period does not exceed eight weeks from the making of the first order[20]. In that situation third and subsequent orders could be for up to four weeks at a time[21]. There is no limit to the number of interim orders which may be made but again special attention must focus on the requirements of Section 32 and Section 1 (1) and 1 (2) of the Act. As the Department of Health points out: "Although there is no limit to the number of interim orders which can be made under the Act a balance will have to be struck between allowing sufficient time for inquiries, reports and statements and risking allowing the child to continue in interim care or supervision for so long that the balance of advantage is distorted in favour of continued intervention"[22]. It should be noted that the President of the Family Division took the opportunity in *Re S*[23] to emphasise that only *exceptionally* should care cases be held up to await the outcome of any criminal proceedings, since the welfare principle and the "no delay" principle would militate naturally against such postponement.

Pursuant to the courts' power to be able to give directions as to the medical or psychiatric examination or other assessment of a child in proceedings for child assessment orders[24] or emergency protection orders[25], similar power is given to the courts on the making of an interim care or supervision order[26]. The court must consider whether it should grant any request for such directions but, even where such are issued, if the child is of sufficient understanding to make an informed decision he may refuse to submit to the examination or assessment. It should be noted that if a local authority does not seek specific directions, decisions as to such examinations and assessments will be the local authority's responsibility[27], and if any person with parental responsibility objects then it is they who should seek a direction that no such examination or assessment should take place[28]. It should however be noted that following the decision of Rattee J in *Re O*[29] where the court gives a direction for medical tests to be carried out, the effect of such a direction is mandatory and does not merely give the local authority a discretion as to whether or not the tests should be performed. In the case of *Re O*[29] the magistrates had made an interim care order and as it was known that both parents were HIV positive, the magistrates also gave a direction that tests should be carried out on the children to determine whether or not they were HIV positive. The local authority appealed querying first whether they ever had the ability to appeal a decision to make directions under the section, because Department of Health Guidance indicated such directions were unappealable[30]. The local authority further contended that the power to give such directions was permissive only, and did not include a power to direct a local authority to subject a child to an examination or assessment if the local authority did not choose to have it carried out. The local authority also stated that the results of an HIV test were not relevant to the court's consideration of the local authority's application for a care order and that the magistrates had not allowed the local authority to call expert evidence as to the desirability of such tests. Rattee J held that directions as to medical, psychiatric or other assessments were appealable to the High Court and the statement in the Department of Health Guidance that such a direction was unappealable was wrong[31]. Directions once given in the form of an order[32] were however mandatory and not discretionary, and so a local authority was bound to comply with the directions. He went on to hold that the court's function was not limited to determining whether the threshold criteria were met. Once the court was satisfied as to the criteria having been met its function extended to considering whether, having regard to the welfare of the children concerned and in particular to the matters set out in the welfare checklist, it was appropriate to make a care order. In this case, said the judge, the question of whether these children were, or were not, HIV positive might have a real bearing on the particular choice of placement for their long term future.

Unlike the position with regard to emergency protection orders and child assessment orders, there is no power simply to give directions on contact where an interim care order is made since for these purposes the making of an interim care order is treated like the making of a full order[32]. Before making a care order the Act requires the court to consider any proposed contact arrangements and to invite the parties to the proceedings to comment on them[33]. Where any party is dissatisfied with the proposed contact arrangements they can seek a contact order under Section 34 of the Act[34] as can the child if he is unhappy about contact proposals[35]. The guardian ad litem would further be expected to advise the court in such situations, and if necessary to make a report.

Further it should be noted that the making of a residence order at any stage in the proceedings discharges an interim care order.

1   Children Act 1989 s 38 (1) and see CHA Form 27 and see also comments of HOLLINGS J in *Croydon London Borough Council v A (No 1)* [1992] 2 FLR 341.
2   Ibid s 38 (1)(a).
3   Ibid s 38 (1)(b).
4   Ibid s 37 (2) and see CHA Form 19.
5   Ibid s 1 (3)(g).
6   Ibid s 38 (3) and see CHA Form 27.
7   Ibid s 11.
8   *Re C* [1992] 2 FCR 341, FD.
9   Ibid s 38 (2). See ibid s 31 (2) and see *Re B (Care Proceedings: Threshold Criteria: Interim Order)* [1992] Fam Law 563, FD. Note also *Northamptonshire County Council v S* [1992] 3 WLR 1010, FD.
10 Ibid s 1 (1), (2), (3).
11 Ibid s 1 (5).
12 Ibid s 1 (4) and see *The Children Act 1989 Guidance and Regulations*, Vol 1 Court Orders, para 3.42 (Department of Health, HMSO 1991).

13 (1992) Times, 3 November, FD.

14 Ibid s 38 (4) and see CHA Form 27.

15 See *The Children Act 1989 Guidance and Regulations*, Vol 1 Court Orders para 3.44 (Department of Health, HMSO 1991) and Children Act 1989 s 32 (1), (2).

16 Ibid s 38 (4)(b), (5)(a) and see CHA Form 27.

17 Ibid s 38 (4)(b), (5)(b).

18 See Guidance issued by the Lord Chancellor's Department October 1991.

19 Children Act 1989 s 1 (2).

20 Ibid s 38 (4)(b) and (5)(b).

21 Ibid s 38 (4)(b) and (5)(a).

22 *The Children Act 1989 Guidance and Regulations*, Vol 1 Court Orders para 3.46 (Department of Health, HMSO 1991).

23 [1992] FCR 31.

24 Children Act 1989 s 43(7) and see CHA Form 32.

25 Ibid s 44 (6) and see CHA Form 34

26 Ibid s 38 (6) and see CHA Form 27.

27 Ibid ss 31 (11), 33 (3)(a).

28 Ibid s 38 (7).

29 *Re O (Minors)(Medical Examination)*[1992] 2 FCR 394.

30 The Children Act 1989: Guidance and Regulations, Vol 1 Court Orders para 3.47.

31 Under Children Act 1989, s 38(6).

32 Ibid s 31 (11).

33 Ibid s 34 (11) and see CHA Form 20.

34 Ibid s 34 (3) and see CHA Form 28.

35 Ibid s 34 (2).

179. Variation, discharge and termination of care and supervision orders.

Under the Children Act 1989 the court does not possess any power to vary a care order, but can, on the application of any person entitled to apply for the discharge of a care order[1], substitute a supervision order for a care order[2]. Before the court can order such a substitution it must be able to satisfy itself that the welfare principles have been adhered to[3], but in making a substitution it does not have to be satisfied again that the care conditions are met[4]. The rationale for this must be that the conditions were obviously met at the time the original order was made and rather than redirecting the court to go over conditions, which have already been satisfied, it is better to focus on whether the substituted order will be in the child's paramount interests[5] and will be better for the child than not ordering such a substitution[6].

A care order including an interim care order can be discharged by the court on the application of the child himself, the local authority designated in the care order or any person with parental responsibility for the child[7]. It should be noted that this will include parents since the making of a care order does not operate to terminate their responsibility but would exclude grandparents or former foster parents with whom the child had lived under a residence order and who had previously held parental responsibility because the making of the care order will have discharged the residence order[8]. This means therefore that they cannot apply for discharge of the care order.

The conditions which must be satisfied before the court can grant an order discharging the care order are the welfare principles in Section 1 of the Children Act 1989. The court must determine that a discharge is in the paramount interests of the child[9] and since the order is an order under Part IV of the Act the welfare checklist comes into operation[10], and thus the court has to look at the likelihood of harm occurring to the child[11]. Finally, the court has to consider whether granting an order for discharge will be better for the child than not so doing[12]. A phased return home may be achieved by substituting a supervision order with residence requirements. Technically, as seen above, an application would have to be made by the local authority for such a variation, so that the court may be dealing with an application by a parent for discharge of a care order countered by the local authority applying for a substituted supervision order in order to achieve the phased return.

Where the court refuses an application for the discharge of a care order or the substitution of a supervision order for a care order, no further application can be made within six months of the determination of such an application unless the court grants leave[13].

A care order will terminate when the child reaches the age of eighteen, unless it is brought to an end earlier[14]. It will also be terminated by the making of a residence order[15] since application can be made for such an order even though the child is on a care order[16]. The child can also make an application for a residence order to be made in favour of a particular person if for some reason they are unable or unwilling to make application themselves, and provided the child is of sufficient understanding[17]. The care order will also terminate where the child is lawfully taken to live in Northern Ireland, the Isle of Man, or any of the Channel Islands provided the court's prior permission for such removal had been obtained, and the relevant authorities in those jurisdictions have indicated their willingness to take over the care of any such child, and the court has since been notified of their willingness[18].

As far as supervision orders are concerned these can be varied or discharged on an application being made by the child, the supervisor or any person who has parental responsibility for the child[19].

The conditions to be satisfied before ordering variation or discharge of the terms of a supervision order are again those contained in Section 1 of the Children Act 1989. Where the variation sought is the substitution of the supervision order by a care order then the requirement of Section 31 (2) would again have to be met as Section 39 (5) only applies to the substitution of a care order by a supervision order and not vice versa[20]. Where such an application is made the court must consider whether it is necessary to appoint a guardian ad litem[21]. The supervisor may seek variation of the terms of the supervision order where the earlier order is not being complied with, which may include a requirement that the child live in a specified place for a period or periods so specified, participate in certain activities[22], undergo a medical or psychiatric examination[23] or psychiatric or medical treatment[24]. No court should include a requirement that the child undergo such assessment or treatment unless it is satisfied that where the child has sufficient understanding to make an informed decision, he consents to its inclusion[25]. Where a supervision order has imposed requirements on a "responsible person" not being a person with parental responsibility, that person can also apply for variation of the order as it relates to him[26].

No further application can be made for the discharge of a supervision order within six months of the previous application except with the leave of the court[27].

Moreover it should be noted that a supervision order terminates on the child reaching the age of 18[28] or when a care order is made[29] when an adoption order is made[30], or when the court takes action under Section 25 (1)(a) and (b) of the Child Abduction and Custody Act 1985[31].

1 Children Act 1989 s 39.
2 Ibid s 39 (4).

3 Ibid s 1 (4).
4 Ibid s 39 (5).
5 Ibid s 1 (1), (3).
6 Ibid s 1 (5).
7 Ibid s 39 (1).
8 Ibid s 91 (2).
9 Ibid s 1 (1).
10 Ibid s 1 (4).
11 Ibid s 1 (1)(e).
12 Ibid s 1 (5).
13 Ibid s 91 (15)(a).
14 Ibid s 91 (12).
15 Ibid s 91 (1).
16 Ibid s 9 (1).
17 Ibid s 10 (8).
18 Ibid s 101 (4) and for the conditions see the Children (Prescribed Orders: Northern Ireland, Guernsey and Isle of Man) Regulations 1991, SI 1991/2032.
19 Children Act 1989 s 39 (2).
20 Ibid s 39 (5).
21 Ibid s 41 (6)(d)
22 Ibid Sch 3 Pt I para 2 (1)(c).
23 Ibid para 4.
24 Ibid para 5.
25 Ibid para 5 (5)(a).
26 Ibid s 39 (3).
27 Ibid s 91 (15)(b).
28 Ibid s 91 (13).
29 Ibid s 91 (3).
30 Adoption Act 1976 s 12 (3)(aa)(as inserted by Children Act 1989 Sch 10 para 3 (3)).
31 Children Act 1989 Sch 3 Pt II Para 6 (2).

180. Contact with children subject to care orders. As has already been noted[1], before a court makes a care order the Act requires the court to consider any proposed contact arrangements and to invite the parties to the proceedings to comment on them[2]. Since local authorities looking after children subject to care orders are now required actively to promote contact between the child and his family[3], the Act underlines this by providing that contact between child and any parent, guardian, or any other person in whose favour a residence or contact order under Section 8 had been made must be reasonable[4]. The Act does not further define what is meant by reasonable in this context, but quite detailed and illuminating guidance can be found in the Department of Health Guidance to the Children Act 1989 in Volumes 3 and 4 of that series[5]. Especially where it is proposed that children are to be swiftly rehabilitated with their parents, it is stated that "contact should be in the family home at the earliest possible stage[6]. Such visits have the advantage of maintaining links with the neighbourhood to which the child will be returning[7]." The Guidance goes on to state that "if possible parents should be encouraged to participate in some way in the child's daily life, by preparing tea for example, or by shopping for clothes, or putting a young child to bed[8]." One should be keenly aware that this Guidance marks a considerable departure from much previously accepted local authority practice in relation to contact with children subject to care orders, and many may now be open to challenge using the procedures laid down in Section 34 of the Act.

Care and associated proceedings

Where therefore any party to care proceedings is dissatisfied with the proposed contact arrangements, they can seek a contact order under Section 34 of the Act, and this includes the child where he is unhappy about contact proposals[9]. Where this occurs the guardian ad litem would be expected to give further advice to the court, and, if necessary, furnish a further report or an addendum to the original dealing with the contact issues[10].

Where, however, contact arrangements are agreed at the time of the making of the care order, and a party or some other person becomes dissatisfied with the arrangements for contact, an application can be made for a contact order under the Act[11]. Such an application may be made by the local authority to terminate or reduce contact with a named individual[12], or by the child to terminate, reduce or increase contact with a particular person[13], and the court may make such order as it considers appropriate[14]. Parents, guardians, the holders of prior residence orders, or any person who had prior care of the child as the result of the exercise of the High Court's inherent jurisdiction may make an application for a contact order[15], as may any person who has obtained the leave of the court[16]. Thus grandparents, aunts, uncles, godparents or any significant person in the child's life including a brother or sister could seek the leave of the court to make an application under Section 34.

On an application made by the local authority or the child, the court may make an order authorising the authority to refuse to allow contact between the child, and a parent or guardian, and the holder of a prior residence order or a person who had care of the child under an order made pursuant to the exercise of the High Court's inherent jurisdiction[17]. Where an application for a contact order is made, the court must appoint a guardian ad litem for the child concerned unless satisfied that it is not necessary to do so in order to safeguard the child's interests[18]. In most applications for contact orders a guardian will be appointed and his duties will be the same as those which he performs in proceedings for a care and supervision order[19]. The focus of his work in this situation will, however, be on whether there should or should not be contact with a specific named individual, and whether or not this is in the paramount interests of the child[20]. In *West Glamorgan CC v P*[21] the Family Division court stated that the court has power, where a child is the subject of a care order, to make an interim order refusing contact under Section 34(4). In the later substantive hearing styled *West Glamorgan CC v P(No 2)*[22] the magistrates refused the local authority's application for an order for no contact and made an order that there should be weekly supervised contact. On appeal the Family Division ruled that the magistrates should not have done this. It was stated that once a care order is made, the decision as to the long term future of the child was entirely a matter for the local authority during the subsistence of the care order. Thus when considering an application under Section 34(4) it was suggested that the court is bound to consider the effects of refusing or making any such order on the long term plans of the local authority for the child's future. The basis upon which the court approached the matter was that the local authority has reached an "unimpeachable" decision. This it was suggested could only be impeached by demonstrating that there is cogent evidence that the local authority had acted contrary to the interests of the child or capriciously. The reasoning in this case followed that in the case of *Re S*[23] determined before implementation of the Children Act 1989. The Court of Appeal's judgment in the case of *Re B* gives clear guidance on the approach to be taken in applications under Section 34 and indicated that the approach taken in the case of *Re S* and *West Glamorgan County Council v P* should *not* be followed. In *Re B* two girls aged 4 and 2 were the subject of care orders and the local authority's plans for adoption of the girls had been approved by the adoption panel. The children's mother had had a third child, her parenting skills were much improved and she had had frequent and regular contact with the two older children. Despite these improvements the local authority applied for an order under Section 34(4) to terminate contact and the mother instead applied for discharge of the care order or an increase in contact supported by the guardian ad litem, with the ultimate view of rehabilitation. The judge at first instance followed the line taken in the *West Glamorgan* case and said it would not be right directly or indirectly to force the local authority's hand and put pressure on for rehabilitation because he had to consider the application for contact in the context of the plan for adoption and thus determine whether the welfare of the children required that contact be refused. He allowed the authority's application, and on the guardian ad litem's appeal supported by the mother, the authority relied on the principle established in *A v Liverpool City Council* that courts would not generally interfere with a local authority's decision to refuse access by a parent to a child in its care under a care order where the challenge was based solely on the merits of the decision. In her judgment in *Re B*, however, Butler Sloss LJ declared: "I do not, however, believe that the important principle set out in *A v Liverpool City Council*. . . applies to the intervention of the court in response to an application which is properly made, or fetters the exercise of the judicial discretion on an application under the Children Act." She considered her own judgment in *Re S* which Rattee J had followed in *West Glamorgan* even though *Re S* had been decided under the old law and concluded: "I do not consider that my judgment in *Re S* adapts felicitously into the philosophy of the Children Act." The court therefore held that the approach adopted in *Re S* and in the *West Glamorgan* case should not be followed when considering applications under Section 34. The Court of Appeal went on to elaborate in considerable detail the approach which should be taken now in applications under Section 34 and this guidance should be followed carefully. In her very important judgment Butler-Sloss LJ went on to emphasise that "the local authority's plan has to be given the greatest possible consideration by the court and it is only in the most unusual case that a parent will be able to convince the court, the onus being firmly on the parent, that there has been such a change of circumstancesas to require further investigation and reconsideration of the local authority's plan. If, however, a court was unable to intervene it would make a nonsense of the paramountcy of the welfare of the child which is the bedrock of the Act and would subordinate it to the administrative decision of the local authority in a situation where the court is seised of the contact issue. That cannot be right." The court went on to allow the mother's appeal.

Where a contact order is made under Section 34, then a local authority cannot depart from the terms of that order unless this is done by agreement with the person in relation to whom the order was made and in accordance with regulations made by the Secretary of State[24], or in an emergency, where the situation does not last for more than seven days[25], by which time if the authority wishes to continue to stop contact, it must bring the matter to court and only where it can be shown to be necessary in order to safeguard or promote the child's welfare[26]. Where the court makes a contact order allowing contact between the child and any named person, the order may impose such conditions as the court considers appropriate[27]. The court may further vary or discharge any order made under this Section on the application of the authority, the child concerned or the person named in the order[28].

Where the court is concerned about repeated or vexatious applications for contact with a child subject to a care order, it may take the step of issuing a direction under Section 91 (14) that no further application for contact be made with respect to the child by any named person without the leave of the court. In the case of *F v Kent CC*[29] the President of the Family Division held that the power under section 91(14) of the Act should be used sparingly and only after hearing representations. In this case a father had applied for contact with his children, who were in care. The justices made a consent order granting him contact but went on to make an order under Section 91(14) restricting his right to apply again although they acknowledged that his application had been proper. The President upheld the father's appeal finding that the justices had acted improperly in making such an order against a father who had not been vexatious, frivolous or unreasonable in making his application. The President stated that the power to make such a direction would be desirable where applications were being made too often and the other party and the child were suffering from them. The order might appropriately be used following the reasoning of Butler Sloss LJ in *Re H*[30] where contact had been refused after a full substantive hearing and where a subsequent application for contact would have no prospect of success.

1　See Paragraph 177 ante.
2　Children Act 1989 s 34 (11).
3　Ibid Sch 2 Pt II para 15.
4　Ibid s 34 (1).
5　See *The Children Act 1989 Guidance and Regulations*, Vol 3 Family Placements, and Vol 4, Residential Homes (Department of Health, HMSO) 1991.
6　See Vol 3 para 6.18.
7　Ibid para 6.18.
8　Ibid para 6.18.
9　Children Act 1989 s 34 (2); see CHA Form 21.
10 Ibid s 41.
11 Ibid s 34 (3).
12 Ibid s 34 (2),(4).
13 Ibid s 34 (2), (4).
14 Ibid s 34 (3).
15 Ibid s 34 (3)(a).
16 Ibid s 34 (3)(b).
17 Ibid s 34 (4).
18 Ibid s 41 (1).
19 See Paragraph 176 ante.
20 Children Act 1989 s 1 (1).
21 [1992] 2 FCR 378, FD
22 [1992] 2 FCR 406, FD
23 [1991] 1 FLR 161.
24 Ibid s 34 (8). See also Contact with Children Regulations 1991, SI 1991/891.
25 Children Act 1989 s 34 (6)(b).
26 Ibid s 34 (6) (a).
27 Ibid s 34 (7).
28 Ibid s 34 (9).
29 [1992] 2 FCR 433, FD
30 [1991] FCR 896 at 899.

181. Education supervision orders. Under the Children Act 1989 an entirely separate order exists to enable local education authorities to deal with children, who are not receiving an appropriate and efficient full-time education for whatever reason, and this is termed an education supervision order[1].

An application for a supervision order must be made in the first instance to a magistrates' family proceedings court and must be made by filing the appropriate form of application, and the period of notice required for such proceedings is seven days, which is longer than that required for supervision orders made under Section 35. It will be rare for such cases to be transferred to any higher court[2]. The court may only make an order where it is satisfied on the balance of probabilities that the child concerned is of compulsory school age and is not being properly educated[3], which means that he is not receiving efficient full-time education suitable to his age, ability and aptitude and any special educational needs he may have[4]. It is assumed under the Act that a child who is the subject of a current school attendance order which is not being complied with, or who is a registered pupil at a school which he is not attending regularly, is not being properly educated[5] and any respondent denying this would be expected to produce evidence in rebuttal.

Whilst it had been though that failure to receive an efficient full-time education would no longer be sufficient on its own to ground an application for a care order[6], and would be dealt with instead in serious cases by an application for the education supervision order, the Children Act clearly envisages close co-operation between education authorities and social services. Before considering making an application for an education supervision order, the local education authority must consult the social services committee of the appropriate local authority[7]. Such consultation will focus attention particularly upon those children, who may be causing concern to different agencies in different ways or to alert social services that their concern over one child is mirrored by the education authority's concern about another child in the same family[8]. Such liaison may however reveal that there is agreement between education and social services order and this was the case in *Re O*[9]. A girl aged 15 years 4 months had been truanting from school for over three years and the education welfare officer had tried every approach which would have been achieved by the making of an education supervision order. In the circumstances therefore the magistrates had made a care order which was upheld on appeal with Ewbank J stating that in his judgment, where a child is suffering harm in not going to school and is living at home, it will follow that either the child is beyond her parents' control or that they are not giving the child the care it would be reasonable to expect a parent to give. He went on to quote with approval the judgment of Denning MR in *Re S*, a pre Children Act case to the effect that "if a child was not being sent to school or receiving a proper education then he was in need of care".

Furthermore, where an education supervision order has been made on a child who persistently fails to comply with any direction given under the order then the education authority must notify social services who will then be under a duty to investigate the child's circumstances with a view to further action[10]. Such action may include discussion of further services being provided to the child under Part III of the Act or the bringing of proceedings for a care or supervision order based on the child's intellectual development being impaired[11] and the child thus suffering or likely to suffer significant harm[12]. Social services officers would clearly need to discuss this in depth with education officials, but if an education supervision order has already been tried and failed, or as in *Re O*[9] what could be achieved by the making of an education supervision order has already been tried, the local authority will be in a stronger position to succeed in getting a care or supervision order.

Whilst the basic criteria for making an order are laid down in Section 36, the order, if made, would be under Part IV of the Act and thus all three limbs of the welfare test come into play[13]. The court is bound by the principle that the child's welfare is paramount[14], and in considering this must look to the welfare checklist[15], and it must be convinced that making an education supervision order is better for the child than not making an order at all[16].

An education supervision order may not be made with respect to a child who is in the care of the local authority[17], since it is presumed that the local authority will be able to deal with the problem of truancy, if necessary by education on the premises of its own children's homes. An education supervision order could be made coexistent with a supervision order under Section 35, or even with one made in criminal proceedings under Section 7 (7)(b) of the Children and Young Persons Act 1969[18].

Any education supervision order made must designate a local education authority as responsible for the order[19], and this must be either the local education authority within whose area the child concerned is living or will live[20] or where the child is a registered pupil at a school outside his own education authority area and the education authority responsible for his school agrees, then that authority can be designated[21].

Further more detailed provision relating to the powers and duties of supervisors are set out in Part III of Schedule 3 of the Act. The supervisor is under a duty to advise, assist, befriend and give directions to the supervised child and his parents in such a way as will in the opinion of the supervisor secure that he is properly educated[22]. Before issuing and settling the terms of any such directions the supervisor must so far as is reasonably practicable ascertain the wishes and feelings of the child[23] and his parents[24] including in particular their wishes as to the place at which the child should be educated and give due consideration to them. Such directions may be given at any time while the education order is in force[25].

Where an education supervision order is in force with respect to a child, the duties of the child's parents to secure education of their children and regular attendance of registered pupils is superseded by their duty to comply with any direction issued and the local education authority's taking over responsibility for securing the child's education[26]. Where an education supervision order is made it further operates so as to terminate automatically any school attendance order[27], and while the order remains in force certain provisions of the Education Act 1980 with respect to parental wishes[28], references and appeals will not apply[29]. While the education supervision order is in force any education requirement which would otherwise have been included in a supervision order made in criminal proceedings shall not be included[30], or where one was already in force it shall cease to have effect[31].

The terms of the education supervision order may require the child to keep the supervisor informed of any change in his address and to allow the supervisor to visit him at the place where he is living[32]. The parent of a child subject to an education supervision order is required if asked by the supervisor to inform him of the child's address if he knows it, and if he is living with the child to allow the supervisor reasonable contact with the child[33].

Where either the parent or child fail to comply with the terms of the supervision order, the supervisor must first consider what further steps to take in the exercise of his powers[34]. The supervisor may issue new directions[35] but where there has been a persistent failure by the child to comply with directions the local education authority must notify the local authority social services who must investigate the child's circumstances[36] to determine the need for further action under Part III or Part IV of the Children Act 1989. Where the parent of the child has persistently failed to comply with any directions given by the supervisor he will be guilty of an offence under the Act and if convicted will be liable to a fine[37]. Where the parent can prove that he took all reasonable steps to ensure that the direction was complied with, or it was unreasonable, or it was not reasonably practicable to comply with the direction in the education supervision order and the requirements of a supervision order, then he shall have a defence to any charges[38].

An education supervision order can last for a period of one year[39] unless it is further extended in the last three months of the initial order by application being made to court for an extension[40]. The period of extension cannot be greater than three years[41], but there is no limit to the number of extensions which may be granted[42]. The education supervision order differs therefore in this important respect from a supervision order under Section 35, which has a maximum duration of three years[43].

In theory an education supervision order could be made and extended to last throughout a child's schooling up to the age of sixteen. The education supervision order ceases to have effect on the child ceasing to be of compulsory school age[44] or on the making of a care order with respect to the child[45].

The child, his parent or the local education authority designated in the order may apply for the education supervision order to be discharged[46]. In making such a determination the court would have to apply the welfare principles, and may, if it discharges the order, direct the local authority in whose area the child lives or will live to investigate the child's circumstances[47] in order to determine whether services could be provided under Part III of the Act or further action such as care proceedings taken under Part IV. Where an application to discharge the order is not granted no further application may be made within six months of the previous application unless the court grants leave[48].

1 Children Act 1989 s 36 and see CHA Form 25.
2 Family Proceedings Courts (Children Act 1989) Rules 1991, SI 1991/1395, Sch 2. See Children (Allocation of Proceedings) Order 1991, SI 1991/1677, art 3 (1)(e). For the exceptions see ibid art 3 (2), (3).
3 Children Act 1989 s 36 (3).
4 Ibid s 36 (4).
5 Ibid s 36 (5).
6 See the Children and Young Persons Act 1969 s 1 (2)(e) (repealed).
7 Children Act 1989 s 36 (8).
8 See *Working Together under the Children Act 1989* (Department of Health, HMSO 1991).
9 [1992] 2 FLR 7
10 Children Act 1989 Sch 3 Pt III para 19 (1).
11 Ibid s 31 (9).
12 Ibid s 31 (2)(a).
13 Ibid s 1 (4).
14 Ibid s 1 (1).
15 Ibid s 1 (3).
16 Ibid s 1 (5).
17 Ibid s 36 (6).
18 Ibid Sch 3 Pt III para 14 (1).
19 Ibid s 36 (1) and see CHA Form 26.
20 Ibid s 36 (7)(a).
21 Ibid s 36 (7)(b).
22 Ibid Sch 3 Pt III para 12.
23 Ibid Sch 3 Pt III para 12 (2)(a).
24 Ibid Sch 3 Pt III para 12 (2)(b), (3).
25 Ibid Sch 3 Pt III para 12 (4).
26 Ibid Sch 3 Pt III para 13.
27 Ibid Sch 3 Pt III para 13 (2)(a).
28 Ibid Sch 3 Pt III para 13 (2)(b) and Education Act 1944 s 76 .
29 Children Act 1989 Sch 3 Pt III para 13 (2)(b) and Education Act 1980 ss 6 and 7.
30 Children Act 1989 Sch 3 Pt III para 13 (2)(c).
31 Ibid Sch 3 Pt III para 13 (2)(d).
32 Ibid Sch 3 Pt III para 16 (1).
33 Ibid Sch 3 Pt III para 16 (2).
34 Ibid Sch 3 Pt III para 12 (1).
35 Ibid Sch 3 Pt III para 12 (4).

36 Ibid Sch 3 Pt III para 19.
37 Ibid Sch 3 Pt III para 18 (1), (3).
38 Ibid Sch 3 Pt III para 18 (2).
39 Ibid Sch 3 Pt III para 15 (1).
40 Ibid Sch 3 Pt III para 15 (2), (3). See CHA Form 51.
41 Ibid Sch 3 Pt III para 15 (5).
42 Ibid Sch 3 Pt III para 15 (4).
43 Ibid Sch 3 Part II para 6 (4).
44 Ibid Sch 3 Part III para 15 (6)(a).
45 Ibid Sch 3 Pt III para 15 (6)(b).
46 Ibid Sch 3 Pt III para 17 (1) and see CHA Form 53.
47 Ibid Sch 3 Pt III para 17 (2) and see CHA Form 54.
48 Ibid s 91 (15)(c).

5: APPEALS AND ORDERS PENDING APPEALS

182. Appeals in general. Any party to proceedings for a care or supervision order (including interim orders) or for an education supervision order has a right of appeal under the Children Act 1989[1]. The appeal lies to the High Court Family Division against the making or refusal to make any such order by a magistrates' court[2]. An appeal against the making or refusal to make any such orders by a judge in the county court[3] or in the High Court[4] lies to the Court of Appeal Civil Division. This means that children, parents, local authorities and anyone else who attained party status in the proceedings now have equal rights to appeal against decisions made by the courts with which they are dissatisfied.

1 Children Act 1989 s 94 (1) and Paragraph 176 ante.
2 Children Act 1989 s 94 (1) and see the Family Proceedings Rules 1991, SI 1991/1247, r 4.22 (1).
3 County Courts Act 1984 s 77 (1).
4 Supreme Court Act 1989 s 16.

183. Procedure. An appeal against the making, varying or discharging or the refusal to make, vary or discharge any care or supervision orders (including interim orders) or any education supervision order[1] is lodged by filing in the court in which the appeal is to be heard and serving on the parties to the proceedings and any guardian ad litem a notice of appeal in writing setting out the grounds upon which the appellant relies[2]. Accompanying this there must be filed a certified copy of the summons or application and of the order appealed against and of any order staying its execution[3], a copy of the notes of evidence[4], and a copy of any reasons given for the decision[5]. It has been emphasised in the form of a Direction from the President of the Family Division that these documents must be filed in the registry (which is also a care centre) nearest to the court in which the order appealed from was made.[6]

The notice of appeal must be filed and served within 14 days after the determination against which an appeal is brought[7], unless it is an appeal against an interim care or supervision order in which case it must be within seven days[8], or with the leave of the court to which, or judge to whom, the appeal is to be brought, within such other time as that court or judge may direct[9].

A respondent who wishes to contend on appeal that the decision of the lower court should be varied, either in any event or in the event of the appeal being allowed in whole or in part[10], or that the decision of the lower court should be affirmed in whole or in part[11], or by way of cross-appeal that the decision of the lower court was wrong in whole or in part[12], must within 14 days of receipt of the notice of appeal, file and serve on all other parties to the appeal a notice in writing, setting out the grounds upon which he relies[13]. No such right exists in respect of an appeal against an interim care or supervision order made under Section 38 of the Children Act 1989[14].

An appeal to the High Court will be heard and determined by a single judge[15] who will normally sit in open court, and an application to that court to withdraw the appeal, have it dismissed with the consent of all the parties or to amend the grounds of appeal may be heard by a district judge[16].

1   Children Act 1989 s 94 (1).
2   Family Proceedings Rules 1991, SI 1991/1247, r 4.22 (2)(a), and see Paragraph 176 ante.
3   Ibid r 4.22 (2)(b).
4   Ibid r 4.22 (2)(c).
5   Ibid r 4.22 (2)(d).
6   President's Direction [1992] 1 FLR 463; [1992] 1 FCR 432.
7   Ibid r 4.22 (3)(a).
8   Ibid r 4.22 (3)(b).
9   Ibid r 4.22 (3)(c).
10 Ibid r 4.22 (5)(a).
11 Ibid r 4.22 (5)(b).
12 Ibid r 4.22 (5)(c).
13 Ibid r 4.22 (5).
14 Ibid r 4.22 (6).
15 Ibid r 4.22 (8).
16 Ibid r 4.22 (7).

184. Orders pending appeal. The Children Act 1989 provides for the first time the court's powers to make orders pending appeals in certain situations in care or supervision order proceedings[1]. The powers given by the Act represent an attempt to ensure some continuity in the child's life and since such orders come within Part IV of the Act they are again subject to the application of the three limbs of the welfare principle[2]. The criteria which must be met are that there must have been some intervention already in the child's life in the proceedings represented by the making of a care or supervision order, or an interim order[3]. There is, however, a lacuna if the intention is to appeal against a refusal to make a first interim order, since an earlier emergency protection order would not seem to qualify as an order being made pending such an appeal to provide for the child to remain in the care of the local authority[4].

The Act provides therefore that where the court dismisses an application for a care order and the child is at that time subject to an interim care order, the court may make a care order pending the appeal[5]. If it dismisses an application for a care order or an application for a supervision order and the child is at the time subject to an interim supervision order, the court may make a supervision order pending the appeal[6]. The court has the power in each case to include such directions in the order on any matter to do with the child's welfare as it sees fit[7]. Where the court grants an application to discharge a care or supervision order it can order that pending the appeal the decision is not to have effect[8], or that the order should remain in force subject to any directions it gives[9].

The appellate court may extend these orders where an appeal is lodged against a decision of another court with respect to an order pending appeal[10]. Orders made pursuant to this provision can only have effect until the date upon which the appeal is determined[11], or where no appeal is made the period during which an appeal could have been made[12]. Where the court has made a residence order together with any other Section 8 orders in care or supervision proceedings, it has the power to postpone the coming into effect of the order or impose temporary requirements pending an appeal[13].

Under no circumstances should the power to make these orders pending the outcome of the appeals lead to unnecessary delay or contribute to adverse effects on the child's welfare due to lingering uncertainty. Appeals should generally be heard by the High Court Family Division within 28 days[14], and the Court of Appeal is equally bound in children's cases by the no delay principle[15].

1   Children Act 1989 s 40.
2   Ibid s 1 (4).
3   Ibid s 40.
4   Ibid s 40 (1)(b), (2)(b).
5   Ibid s 40 (1).
6   Ibid s 40 (2).
7   Ibid s 40 (1), (2).
8   Ibid s 40 (3)(a).
9   Ibid s 40 (3)(b).
10 Ibid s 40 (5).
11 Ibid s 40 (6)(a).
12 Ibid s 40 (6)(b).
13 Ibid s 11 (7).
14 *Practice Note* [1984] 1 WLR 1125.
15 Children Act 1989 s 1 (2).

CHAPTER 9: CHILDREN IN THE PUBLIC CARE

185. Introduction. Under the provisions of the Children Act 1989 local authorities are now placed under a heavy duty to safeguard and promote the welfare of children within their area who are in need and, so far as is consistent with that duty, to promote the upbringing of such children by their families, by providing a range of the level of services appropriate to those children's needs[1]. In order to enable the local authority to discharge their general duty under this provision, further specific duties and powers are laid down in the Act and the full extent of the services which could be made available under these provisions is set out in a number of the Volumes of Guidance issued by the Department of Health in relation to the Children Act[2]. Before determining whether there is any necessity to provide services under the provisions of the Act, the local authority must decide whether any particular child is to be taken as being a child in need[3]. A child is taken to be in need if:

1. he is unlikely to achieve or maintain or to have the opportunity of achieving or maintaining, a reasonable standard of health or development without the provision for him of services by a local authority; or
2. his health or development is likely to be significantly impaired, or further impaired, without the provision for him of such services; or
3. he is disabled[4].

For the purposes of the Act a child is disabled if he is blind, deaf or dumb or suffers from a mental disorder of any kind or is substantially and permanently handicapped by illness, injury or congenital deformity or such other disability as may be prescribed; and in the Act "development" means physical, intellectual, emotional, social or behavioural developments; and "health" means physical or mental health[5]. The Act provides that local authorities must take steps to identify the extent to which there are children in need within their area and to identify what services could be provided to meet the requirements of those children in need[6]. To facilitate the provision of services to children with disabilities the local authority is encouraged to open and maintain a Register of Disability[7] which may be kept by means of a computer and where a number of statutory assessments have to be done to identify the needs of particular children then the Act provides that these wherever possible should be done together[8].

One of the most frequently used services which local authorities provide for children who can be described as being in need is that of day care[9]. Indeed under the provisions of the Children Act every local authority is required to provide such day care for children in need within their area who are aged 5 or under and not attending school as is appropriate[10]. There is a further duty upon local authorities to provide for children in need within their area who are attending school, such care or supervised activities as is appropriate outside school hours or during school holidays[11]. The Act goes on to provide that every local authority shall review the provision of day care which they make under Section 18 together with the extent to which there are services available in the locality of child-minders and day nurseries[12]. A review of the provision of daycare and childminding for the under eights must be conducted with the local education authority within one year of the date of the implementation of the Act and then once in every subsequent period of three years[13]. A great many other services may be offered to children in need in a family by a local authority[14], and one local authority may be in a position to provide everything. There are, however, many circumstances in which local authority services are not provided under the umbrella of any one local authority and where this is the case the Act makes a specific provision to enable cooperation between authorities[15]. Thus the Act provides that where it appears to a local authority that another local authority, any local education authority, any local housing authority, any health authority or National Health Service Trust or any authorities authorised by the Secretary of State, could, by taking any specified action, help in the exercise of any local authority functions under Part III of the Act then the local authority may request the help of that other authority specifying the action in question 1[16]. An authority whose help is requested shall comply with the request if it is compatible with their own statutory or other duties and obligations and does not unduly prejudice the discharge of any of their other functions[17].

Despite a local authority providing services to a family or perhaps because of a range of other circumstances affecting the family, situations may arise where the local authority may instead have to offer to the child in need and the family the provision of accommodation[18]. Thus every local authority must provide accommodation for any child in need within their area who appears to them to require accommodation as a result of:

1. there being no person who has parental responsibility for him;
2. his being lost or having been abandoned;
3. the person who has been caring for him being prevented (whether or not permanently, and for whatever reason) from providing him with suitable accommodation or care[19].

The nature of this new provision of accommodation is voluntary and there is no intention that it should be a backdoor route into care[20]. Nevertheless in the first year of working with the Act many local authorities were using the provision of accommodation for 1-2 weeks as a way of avoiding the necessity to take emergency protection orders. This practice seemed to have become fairly widespread by November 1992 and must account in large part for the courts' experience of few applications for emergency protection orders. A child who is accommodated under this provision of the Children Act is described as an accommodated child, and his condition should be compared with those children who are looked after by a local authority where a care order has been made[21]. Both groups of children are nevertheless described as "looked after children"[22].

Where a local authority is looking after a child it has a number of duties towards the child. The duty of any local authority looking after a child is to safeguard and promote the child's welfare and to make use of such services available for children cared for by their own parents as appears to the authority to be reasonable in the child's case[23]. Before making any decision with respect to a child not here qualified by any reference to understanding whom they are looking after, or proposing to look after, the local authority must, so far as is practicable, ascertain the wishes and feelings of the child, his parents including unmarried fathers,, any person who is not a parent of his but who has parental responsibility for him, and any other person whose wishes and feelings the authority considers to be relevant, regarding a matter to be decided[24]. Other persons in this context includes persons who have looked after the child, or been in close contact with the child. This category also includes all the relevant statutory agencies who might have been involved with the child and the local authority may contact the child's school or G P.[25] Where the child has a guardian ad litem then he or she must also be consulted [26] and may be of considerable use to the local authority in helping to ascertain the child's wishes and feeling. In making any such decision a local authority is required to give due consideration to such wishes and feelings of the child as they have been able to ascertain and having regard to his age and understanding, to such wishes and feelings of any parent or person with parental responsibility or other relevant persons and to the child's religious persuasion, racial origin and cultural and linguistic background[27]. Where it appears to the local authority that it is necessary for the purpose of protecting members of the public from serious injury, to exercise their powers with respect to the child whom they are looking after in a manner which may not be consistent with their duties to the child, they may do so.

When a local authority is trying to determine where a child who is being accommodated by them or who is in their care is to live, then the local authority may provide accommodation and maintenance for any child by placing the child in one of a wide range of living situations[28]. Thus a local authority can provide accommodation and maintenance for any child whom they are looking after by placing him with a family, a relative of his or any other suitable person on such terms as to payment by the authority and otherwise as the authority may determine; by maintaining him in a community home, voluntary home or registered children's home; by maintaining him in a home provided in accordance with arrangements made by the Secretary of State; or by making such other arrangements as appear appropriate to the authority and comply with any regulations made by the Secretary of State[29]. There is thus an extremely wide range of provisions which can be made to cater for a child, whilst he is being looked after by a local authority. In addition it should be pointed out that a child, whilst he is being looked after by a local authority, may be placed in accommodation provided for the purpose of restricting his liberty[30] in certain circumstances. Where the child or young person is being kept in secure accommodation for more than seventy-two hours in any twenty-eight day period, then application must be made to a court for an order to keep the child in secure accommodation[31].

In order to cater for a large number of difficult situations with regard to the standard of care exercised in respect of children being looked after by a local authority, the Children Act provides for a system of reviews of cases to enable the child complainant's voice to be heard[32]. In addition the new representations procedures must be made available to:

1. any child who is being looked after by the local authority or who is not being looked after by them but is in need;
2. any parent of his;
3. any person who is not a parent of his but who has parental responsibility for him;

    4. any local authority foster parent, and

    5. such a person as the authority consider has a sufficient interest in the child's welfare to warrant his representations being considered by them, or at the discharge by the authority of any of their powers, duties and responsibilities under the provisions of Part III of the Children Act[33].

1 Children Act 1989 s 17 (1).

2 Ibid s 17 (2).

3 Ibid s 17 (10).

4 Ibid s 17 (10)(a)-(c).

5 Ibid s 17 (11).

6 Ibid Sch 2 Pt I para 1.

7 Ibid Sch 2 Pt I para 2.

8 Ibid Sch 2 Pt I para 3.

9 Ibid Sch 2 Pt I paras 4, 7.

10 Ibid s 18.

11 Ibid s 18 (5).

12 Ibid s 19 (1).

13 Ibid s 19 (5).

14 Ibid s 27.

15 Ibid s 27 (1).

16 Ibid s 27 (3)(as amended by the Courts and Legal Services Act 1990 s 116 Sch 16 para 14(b)).

17 Ibid s 27 (2).

18 Ibid s 20 (1).

19 Ibid s 20 (1)(a)-(c).

20 Ibid s 20 (8).

21 Ibid s 22 (1).

22 Ibid s 22 (1)(b).

23 Ibid s 22 (3).

24 Ibid s 22 (4).

25 See the Children Act 1989; Guidance and Regulations 1989 Volume 4 Residential Care HMSO London 1991 para 2.51.

26 See *R v North Yorkshire CC, ex parte M* [1989] 1 All ER 143, and see further Guidance sup cit n25 at para 2.51.

27 Ibid s 22 (5).

28 Ibid s 23 (2).

29 Ibid s 23 (2)(as amended by the Courts and Legal Services Act 1990 s 116 Sch 16 para 12(1)).

30 Ibid s 25 (1).

31 Ibid s 25 (2); Children (Secure Accommodation) Regulations 1991, SI 1991/1505, rr 10-12 as amended by Children (Secure Accommodation) Amendment Regulations 1992 SI 1992/2117.

32 Ibid s 26 (2) (3).

33 Ibid s 26 (3).

186. Local authority duties in respect of childminding and day care facilities.
One of the most important services for families with children in need will be the provision of day care either through a placement in a local authority day nursery, or by the local authority paying for the services of a child minder or the provision of a private day nursery place. Under the provisions of the Children Act local authorities are required to provide such day care for children under 5 in need in their area as is

appropriate[1]. There is thus no guarantee of a right to a day nursery or childminding place in respect of any children in need, but clearly where a child is determined to be a child in need under the provisions of the Act and the provision of such a place would relieve that need, local authorities would be expected to provide it[2]. It should be remembered, however, that a large number of children are placed with childminders or in day care facilities by their parents who are going out to work and who wish to be satisfied that their children are adequately protected for such period of time as they are not being looked after by them. Such children will not be placed via local authorities but under the provisions of the Children Act parents are entitled to look to the local authority registration and certification processes as a means of guaranteeing their children's welfare and protection[3]. When looking at the available range of day care provision in their locality local authorities are now required to consider the extent to which such facilities reflect the needs of racial groups within the community[4].

Every local authority is required to keep a register of persons who act as childminders on domestic premises within the authority's area and further of those persons who provide day care for children under the age of eight other than on domestic premises within their area.

For the purposes of the Children Act 1989 a person acts as a child-minder where she looks after one or more children under the age of eight for reward and the period or the total of periods which she spends so looking after children in any day exceeds two hours[5]. Where day care is being provided for children under eight on premises other than domestic premises then the person providing day care who needs to be registered may be providing sessional day care[6] or full day care[7] under the terms of the Act and any limitations which the local authority may lay down under a registration process may reflect requirements drawn up in response to these levels of care[8].

Any person receiving or proposing to receive children under the age of eight on to premises which are not domestic premises for full day care or sessional day care and whether or not for reward is required to apply for registration with the relevant local authority[9]. Day care facilities which are used for less than six days in a year are exempt from the registration requirement[10]. Registration is also required where the day care provider or child minder is offering a service for children aged under eight for a period or total period of more than two hours in any one day. Therefore, this means that facilities such as day nurseries and creches in shopping centres, leisure centres or colleges which are open throughout the day are registrable, even though individual children are likely to attend for less than two hours[11] and no charge is actually made.

The legislation on registration looks to two major issues in connection with the quality of care being provided and these are the issues of whether the persons providing childminding or day care facilities are fit persons and secondly whether the premises on which such care is to be provided are suitable premises[12]. Registration may thus be refused where the local authority is satisfied that any person looking after the children at the premises is not a fit person to look after children, or where the premises in which the children are received or proposed to be received are not fit (whether because of the condition thereof or the equipment thereon or for any reason connected with the situation, construction or size thereof) to be used for the purpose[13].

With regard to the issue of whether someone is a fit person or not, the provisions of the legislation look at two categories of persons. Thus where the person is proposing to look after children under eight the Social Services Department of the local authority must be satisfied that he is fit and that any person who will be looking after or likely to be looking after any children on the premises is also fit[14]. In addition the local authority must be satisfied that any person who is, or is likely to be, living or employed on the premises is fit to be in the proximity of children under the age of eight[15]. Where the application is made for a person to act as a child-minder then the local authority must again be satisfied not only that the person providing care is fit but also that any person living or likely to be living at the premises is also a fit person[16].

Guidance issued by the Department of Health suggests that when local authorities are considering the issue of whether someone is fit to look after children aged under eight then they should take into account the following matters:

1. previous experience of looking after or working with young children or people with disabilities or the elderly;
2. qualification and or training in a relevant field such as child care, early years education, health visiting, nursing or other caring activities;
3. ability to provide warm and consistent care;
4. knowledge of and attitude to multicultural issues and people of different racial origins;
5. commitments and knowledge to treat all children as individuals and with equal concern;
6. physical health;
7. mental stability, integrity and flexibility;
8. known involvement in criminal cases involving abuse of children[17].

Police checks will therefore be done on all those people who propose to provide day care on premises within the area of the local authority and in addition the local authority must check the previous criminal record of any persons living or working on such premises and also any known involvement which such persons might have in criminal cases involving abuse of children[18]. Certain persons are disqualified under regulations from looking after children in the capacity of childminders or providing day care[19] but local authorities have a discretion to overrule such disqualification, if in their view the person can be deemed to be safe and suitable and thus a fit person to look after children[20].

The local authority is further required to satisfy itself about fitness, basically the suitability, of any premises whether domestic or non-domestic which are to be used for the provision of day care or childminding facilities. The authority must have regard to the issue of fitness before granting registration and in considering suitability the local authority must look to situation, construction and size[21]. The type of premises used will vary considerably and each authority will have to decide for itself whether particular premises satisfy their criteria for suitability having regard to location, type of building and size. Guidance issued by the Department of Health lists a large number of points to which local authorities should have regard when determining on the suitability of premises for caring for children under the age of eight. The guidance further provides that persons applying for registration should know what factors are being considered when assessing the suitability of premises.

Once the local authority has determined that a day care facility or child-minder should be registered, then they may in granting a certificate of registration impose such requirements as to the numbers of children, security and equipment on the premises, as to the keeping of relevant records, and as to the requirement to notify the authority of any changes in personnel, as the authority thinks fit[22].

An application to register day care or child minding facilities may be refused and an existing registration cancelled in those circumstances where the authority are of the opinion that the circumstances of the case are such that they would be justified in refusing to register or in cancelling the registration of any person or premises[23]; or where the care provided by any persons on the relevant premises is seriously inadequate having regard to the needs of the children concerned[24]; or where the person acting as child-minder or running the day care facility has contravened or failed to comply with any requirements imposed on him at the time of registration or where such person has failed to pay an annual fee for registration[25].

In order to enable local authorities to determine whether registration should be cancelled at any stage, the Act provides that persons authorised to do so by the local authority may at any time enter the premises of childminders or premises on which day care is being provided in order to be able to inspect the premises, any children being looked after on the premises, the arrangements made for their welfare, and any records relating to them which are kept as a result of the requirements of registration[26].

Notice of intention to make an order refusing or cancelling any registration or imposing, removing or varying any requirements as to registration or refusing to grant any application for the variation or removal of such requirements must be sent to the child-minder or day care provider not less than fourteen days before taking such a step. The local authority concerned must in their notice to the relevant person or applicant inform the person of the authority's reasons for proposing to take the step and inform the person concerned of his rights[27]. Where the recipient of such a notice informs the authority in writing of his desire to object to the step being taken, then the authority must afford him an opportunity to do so either in person or by means of a representative[28]. Where the authority having given the person concerned an opportunity to object to the step being taken, decide nevertheless to take it they must send him written notice of their decision[29]. A person aggrieved by the taking of any step may appeal against it to the magistrates' court and such appeal will be treated as an application under the rules in the normal way[30]. Any such appeal to the court must be brought within twenty-one days from the date of the step to which the appeal relates[31]. Any such application must be made on the prescribed form and where the court makes an order this too must be in the form prescribed by the relevant rules of court[32].

1 Children Act 1989 s 18.
2 Ibid s 17 (1), (10).
3 Ibid s 71.
4 Ibid Sch 2 para 11.
5 Ibid s 71 (2).
6 Sessional day care is defined by the Child Minding and Day Care (Applications for Registration and Registration and Inspection Fees) (Amendment) Regulations 1991, SI 1991/2129, as care of a child for a continuous period of less than four hours in any day. See ibid reg 2B.
7 Full day care is defined as a continuous period of four hours or more in any day; see ibid reg 2A.
8 Ibid reg 2B.
9 Children Act 1989 s 71 (1).
10 Ibid Sch 9 para 5.
11 Ibid s 1 (2).
12 Ibid s 71 (7), (8) and (11).
13 Ibid s 71 (8), (11).
14 Ibid s 71 (7)(a), (b).
15 Ibid s 71 (8).
16 See *The Children Act 1989 Guidance and Regulations*, Vol 2 Family Support: Day Care and Education for Young Children, (Department Of Health, HMSO 1991), para 7.32.
17 Ibid para 7.32.
18 See the Disqualification for Caring for Children Regulations 1991, SI 1991/2094.

19 Children Act 1989 Sch 9 para 2 (1).

20 Ibid Sch 9 para 2 (4).

21 See *The Children Act 1989 Guidance and Regulations*, Vol 2 Family Support: Day Care and Education for Young Children, (Department Of Health, HMSO 1991), para 7.33.

22 Children Act 1989 s 72 (2).

23 Ibid s 74 (1)(a), (2)(a).

24 See s 74 (1)(b), (2)(b).

25 Ibid s 74 (1)(c), (2)(c).

26 Ibid s 76.

27 Ibid s 77 (2).

28 Ibid s 77 (3), (4).

29 Ibid s 77 (5).

30 Ibid s 77 (6) and see the Family Proceedings Courts (Children Act 1989) Rules 1991, SI 1991/1395, r 29.

31 Ibid r 29 (2).

32 See CHA Forms 60 and 61.

187. Looked after children. As previously noted, the term "looked after children" describes children who are both provided with accommodation under the provisions of the Act[1] and who are being looked after as a result of a care order made under the Act[2]. The local authority has a number of duties to children whom they are looking after which have been previously identified and they also have duties of after care towards the children where a child ceases to be looked after by a local authority[3].

It is the duty of the local authority where a child has been looked after by them to advise, assist and befriend the child with a view to promoting his welfare when he ceases to be looked after by the local authority[4]. Where a child reaches the age of sixteen and then ceases to be looked after by the local authority at any stage after the age of sixteen the local authority is under a duty to provide the child with advice and assistance where it appears to the local authority that the young person is in need of such assistance[5]. Assistance may be given in kind or in exceptional circumstances in cash, and such contribution to the expenses of the young person may be paid where these are being incurred in connection with him seeking employment or being employed or receiving education or training. Assistance may be given through the provision of a grant to enable the young person to meet expenses connected with his education or training[6]. Where a local authority is assisting a young person by making a contribution or grant with respect to a course of education or training they may continue to do so even though he reaches the age of twenty-one before completing the course. They may also disregard any interruption in his attendance on the course if he resumes it as soon as is reasonably practicable.

1   Children Act 1989 s 20.
2   Ibid s 31.
3   See Paragraph 185 ante.
4   Children Act 1989 s 24 (1).
5   Ibid s 24 (4), (5).
6   Ibid s 24 (8).

188. Accommodation of children with foster parents. As was noted in the introduction[1] it is possible for a local authority looking after children to provide for the child's accommodation and maintenance by placing the child whom they are looking after with a family, a relative of the child or any other suitable person, on such terms as to payment by the authority and otherwise as the authority may determine[2]. Where a child is placed under these provisions then the person with whom the child is placed will be deemed to be a local authority foster parent[3] unless he is a parent of the child, someone with parental responsibility or where the child is in care under a care order and there was a residence order in force, then the person in whose favour the residence order was made[4]. It should be noted that the obligation upon local authorities generally under Section 17 of the Children Act 1989 is to safeguard and promote the welfare of children and so far as possible promote the upbringing of children by their families. This principle has been extended into the provision of foster care so that under the provisions of the Act[5] a local authority must now follow a list of priorities laid down which dictates that all attempts should first be made to place the child with a relative, friend or other person connected with him, unless that would not be reasonably practicable or consistent with the child's welfare[6]. Thus the emphasis under the Children Act 1989 is very much on placing the child within the extended family wherever this is possible.

The local authority is also under a duty to ensure that where they are placing a child with a foster family they do so with a family living near to the child's home and where the authority are also providing for a sibling of the child that the child and the sibling are accommodated together[7]. Where a child is placed with a foster family then he will be so placed subject to regulations which have been made by the Secretary of State[8].

There are two sets of regulations, the first concerning arrangements for placement of children which focus primarily on the child[9] and the second set of regulations which focus primarily on the foster placement itself and also provide for the approvals of placements with foster parents, the provisions regarding keeping of records of foster parents and the duties of the local authorities to make visits to the foster parents' home to see the child[10].

Both sets of regulations provide for the local authority to enter into agreements. Under the Placement of Children (General) Regulations, the authority looking after the child must make any arrangement, generally in practice referred to as an agreement with the parents of the child, concerning a number of matters[11]. Unless it would not be consistent with the child's welfare to do so, the agreement would indicate the type of accommodation to be provided for the child together with the address and the name of the person who will be responsible for the child on behalf of the local authority[12]. The agreement should further detail any services to be provided for the child and should identify the respective responsibilities of the local authority and the child, any parent of his and any person who is not a parent but who has parental responsibility for him[13]. The agreement should further record what delegation has been made by parents or others with parental responsibility to the local authority of the exercise of parental responsibility in respect of the child's day to day care[14]. The agreement must record any arrangements for involving parents and those with parental responsibility as well as the child in decision-making processes having regard to the differing duties of local authorities, voluntary organisations and registered children's homes which may be providing the actual accommodation[15].

The agreement must also set out the arrangements of contact between the child and his parents; any person who is not a parent but who has parental responsibility for the child; and any relative, friend or other person connected with the child unless such contact is being denied, when the regulations require that the local authority set out the reasons why contact with any such person would not be reasonably practicable or would be inconsistent with the child's welfare[16]. The agreement must further provide for the arrangements for notifying changes in arrangements in respect of contact, and in the case of a child aged 16 or over, whether accommodation is being offered to the child against the parents' wishes[17]. Finally, the agreement should reflect the expected duration of the arrangements and the steps which should apply to bring the arrangements to an end, including arrangements for rehabilitation of the child with the person with whom he was living before the voluntary arrangements were made, or some other suitable person, having regard in particular, in the case of the local authority looking after a child, to the requirement under the Act that wherever possible children should be placed with their parents and to the requirement under the Act that local authorities positively promote contact between the child and his or her family[18]. These are the matters to be covered in agreements reached between local authorities and the child's parents and anyone else with parental responsibility and generally they are separate from agreements reached with foster parents[19]. In some authorities, however, it is clear that both parents and foster parents are being included in the same agreements. Yet where this is the case then the requirements of both sets of regulations must be met[20].

Those matters which must be included in foster care agreements reached with foster parents include provision as to the support and training to be given to the foster parents, procedure for the review of approval of a foster parent, the procedure in connection with the placement of foster children including the respective obligations under such agreements of the authority and the foster parent, the authority's arrangements for meeting any legal liabilities of the foster parents arising by reason of the placement, and the procedure available to the foster parents for making representations to the local authority in whose area that child is placed[21]. The foster parent must undertake to give certain information by written notice to the local authority, must undertake not to administer corporal punishment to any child placed with him, must ensure that any information about the child is kept confidential, must comply with the terms of any foster placement agreement which requires the child to be treated as if he were a member of the foster parent's family and to notify the responsible authority immediately of any serious illness of the child or of any other serious occurrence affecting the child[22]. The agreement should further provide the foster carers with information concerning all important aspects relating to the child, must provide for the responsible authority's arrangements for the financial support of the child and any arrangements for delegation of responsibility for consent to medical or dental examination or treatment of the child[23]. The agreement should set out clearly the circumstances in which it is necessary to obtain in advance the approval of the responsible authority for the child to live, even temporarily, away from the foster parents' home. It should also deal with arrangements for visits to the child by local authority social workers and the frequency of such visits and should also set out clearly the terms relating to the reviews to be held on children[24]. Finally the agreement should set out the arrangements for the child to have contact with his parents and any other persons including where the child is the subject of a care order any arrangements made in pursuance of a contact order under Part IV of the Act, or where the child is accommodated any orders made under the provisions of Section 8 of the Children Act 1989[25].

It should be noted that foster parents have a right themselves to apply for a Section 8 residence order in respect of a child where he has been living with them for more than three years[26], and they may also apply for a residence order to be made where the child has been living with them for less than three years where the local authority gives the foster parent leave to make such an application[27]. Where the local authority is refusing to give consent to an application being made in respect of the child then the only other alternative would be for the foster parent to encourage the child to apply for a residence order under the provisions of Sections 8 and 10 of the

Act[28]. Where a foster parent applies for a residence order, under the provisions of the Children Act the local authority is given discretion to pay a residence order allowance and that this is not limited to stranger foster parents and could thus be used to make an allowance in favour of a relative who has indicated a willingness to apply for a residence order[29]. Foster parents have a right to be involved in decision making processes involving the children since they will be persons who under the legislation have an interest in the child and whose views ought to be considered to be relevant by the local authority[30]. They should also be invited to attend reviews on the child's case[31]. Finally it should be pointed out that in respect of both the children and the foster parents each have a right to use the local authority representations procedure and thus, where the child has a complaint to make about the foster placement or the foster parents wish to complain about some service not being continued to a child whilst in their care[32], then they can each use the local authority representations procedure provided for under the Act[33].

1 See Paragraph 185 ante.
2 Children Act 1989 s 23 (2)(a).
3 Ibid s 23 (3).
4 Ibid s 23 (4).
5 Ibid s 23 (6).
6 Ibid s 23 (7).
7 Ibid s 23 (7)(a).
8 See the Arrangements for Placement of Children (General) Regulations 1991, Sl 1991/890 and the Foster Placement (Children) Regulations 1991, Sl 1991/910.
9 See the Arrangements for Placement of Children (General) Regulations 1991.
10 See the Foster Placement (Children) Regulations 1991 Part II dealing with approvals, Pt III dealing with records, and Pt IV dealing with local authority duties in respect of visits.
11 Ibid Sch 4.
12 Ibid Sch 4 para 1.
13 Ibid Sch 4 paras 2, 3.
14 Ibid Sch 4 para 5.
15 Ibid Sch 4 para 5.
16 Ibid Sch 4 para 6.
17 Ibid Sch 4 paras 7, 8.
18 Ibid Sch 4 para 9.
19 See the Foster Placement (Children) Regulations 1991.
20 See the Arrangements for Placement of Children (General) Regulations 1991, Sch 4 , and the Foster Placement (Children) Regulations 1991 Sch 2.
21 See the Foster Placement (Children) Regulations 1991 Sch 2 paras 13. As to representation procedures see Paragraph 185 ante.
22 Ibid Sch 3 paras 1-3.
23 Ibid Sch 3 para 3.
24 Ibid Sch 3 para 4, 5. See Paragraph 192 ante.
25 Children Act 1989 s 9 (3)(b).
26 Ibid s 9 (3)(c).
27 Ibid s 9 (3)(a).
28 Ibid s 10 (8). See Paragraphs 120-140 ante on Children and Residence Order applications.
29 Children Act 1989 Sch 1 para 15.
30 Ibid s 22 (4) and (5).
31 Review of Children's Cases Regulations 1991, SI 1991/895, r 7.
32 Children Act 1989 s 22 (3)(b).
33 Ibid s 26 (3).

189. Provision of accommodation in community homes. The Children Act 1989 provides that where a local authority is looking after a child, then it may provide for the child's accommodation and maintenance by placing him in a community home[1]. The Act goes on to provide that every local authority has a duty to make such arrangements as they think appropriate for securing that community homes are available for the care and accommodation of children looked after by them[2]. In making arrangements for the provision of such accommodation, the local authority should have regard to the need for ensuring that accommodation of different descriptions is available and which is suitable for different purposes and the requirements of different descriptions of children[3]. A community home may be provided, managed, equipped and maintained by a local authority or it may be provided by a voluntary organisation[4], in which case, if the management, equipment and maintenance of the home is the responsibility of the local authority, or where the responsibility for management remains that of the voluntary organisation, it is designated an assisted community home[5]. The arrangements between a voluntary organisation and a local authority in respect of a controlled or assisted community home are further detailed in the Act which also provides for the Secretary of State to make regulations governing the placement of children in community homes, the conduct of such homes and the processes for promoting the welfare of children in such homes[6].

The Act also provides that a local authority may provide accommodation for the child by placing the child in a children's home run by a voluntary organisation[7], and listed in a register kept for the purpose by the Secretary of State[8].

A child may also be cared for and provided with accommodation by a children's home which is referred to as a registered children's home[9]. Such homes are provided by private parties or institutions and are subject to a registration process with local authorities[10].

Children in all three types of children's homes are, as a result of the Children Act, treated in a very similar fashion and are subject to the same provisions of the Children's Homes Regulations 1991[11], and to the Guidance issued by the Department of Health.[12]

1 Children Act 1989 s 23 (2)(b).
2 Ibid s 53 (1).
3 Ibid s 53 (2).
4 Ibid s 53 (4).
5 Ibid s 53 (5).
6 Ibid Sch 4, and see the Children's Homes Regulations 1991 SI 1991/1506.
7 Ibid s 23 (2)(c).
8 Ibid s 60.
9 Ibid s 63.
10 Ibid s 63 (1).
11 Children's Homes Regulations 1991, SI 1991/1506.
12 See The Children Act 1989: Guidance and Regulations Volume 4 Residential Care.

190. Duties towards children looked after in children's homes. The general duties of a local authority looking after a child which placed that child in a children's home are clearly set down and are common to children being accommodated both by foster parents and those being accommodated by being placed in a children's home[1]. Where a child is being looked after in a voluntary home then it is the duty of the voluntary organisation to safeguard and promote the child's welfare; to make such use of the services and facilities available for children cared for by their own parents as appears to the organisation reasonable in his case; and to advise, assist and befriend him with a view to promoting his welfare when he ceases to be so accommodated[2]. Exactly the same provisions apply to a child who is being accommodated in a registered children's home and the duty in this case falls upon the proprietor in the children's home[3]. Local authorities, voluntary organisations and the proprietors of registered children's homes are similarly bound by corresponding duties to consult the child, the parents, any person with parental responsibility and any other relevant person before making any decision with respect to the child, and in making any such decision the local authority, voluntary organisation or registered children's home proprietor is required to give due consideration having regard to the child's age and understanding to such wishes and feelings of his as they have been able to ascertain; to such other wishes and feelings of relevant persons, parents, those with parental responsibility as they have been able to ascertain; and to the child's religious persuasion, racial origin and cultural and linguistic background[4]. Substantial provisions exist both in relation to the running and regulation of voluntary homes and for the running and regulation of registered children's homes[5].

1 Children Act 1989 ss 22, 23.
2 Ibid s 61 (1).
3 Ibid s 64 (1).
4 Ibid ss 22 (3), 61 (3), 64 (2), (3).
5 Ibid Schs 5, 6 and see also The Children Act 1989 Guidance and Regulations Volume 4, Residential Care DOH 1992 HMSO Lords.

191. Regulation of children's homes. Social Services staff running local authority community homes or voluntary organisation staff running voluntary homes or the proprietor and staff of a registered children's home are required to abide not only by the provisions contained in the Children Act 1989 but also to be bound and controlled by the provisions of the Children's Homes Regulations 1991[1]. Where the child, parent or any other person with parental responsibility or with sufficient interest in the child is concerned about the level of service which is being provided to a child in a children's home or about the quality of the care which is being received then they should be given adequate information to enable them to use the local authority representations procedure[2]. Those responsible for running children's homes must draw up a written statement of purpose for the unit and the way in which it is to be run which must be kept in the unit and which, together with a copy of the Children's Homes Regulations, must be made available to residents and to parents or those with parental responsibility for residents[3].

The Guidance states that "The overall purpose of the statement is to describe what the home sets out to do for children and the manner in which care is provided".[4] The Utting Report on Children in the Public Care further recommended that individual homes should include programmes of health education and health care in the statements of objectives.[5] The Regulations further interrelate with the Act with regard to the management and staffing of homes.[6] The managers of the homes are to act as agents of the responsible body which is the authority or organisation.[7] The responsible body is responsible for the submission of annual accounts and the employment of staff is a matter wholly reserved for the responsible body under the Act and the Regulations state that it must also ensure that number of staff at each children's home and their experience and qualifications are adequate to ensure that the welfare of children accommodated there is safe-guarded and promoted at all times.[8] The Guidance emphasises that it is not appropriate to specify one set of staff ratios for the differing kinds of children catered for.[9] Given the recent examples of pindown, regression therapy and the experience of children in the care of Frank Beck, the advice that homes should not attempt to use methods of care beyond the competence, experience and qualifications of the staff seems particularly to the point.[10] It is also stated in the Guidance that "those responsible for recruiting staff to children's homes should seek to ensure that the composition of the staff group reflects the racial, cultural and linguistic background of the children being care for".[11] It continues that is "important that black children should have positive experiences of being cared for by black care givers",[11] and that "it is usually possible to involve the genuine occupational qualification exemption to the Race Relations legislation[12] in order to recruit staff from a particular racial background".[11] Similarly there should be a proper balance of male and female staff and again it may be appropriate to use the exemptions in the Sex Discrimination Act 1975[13] to take positive steps in recruitment to ensure the appropriate balance, where it would be in the children's interest to do so.[12] Regulations include provision as to the state and nature of the building including the accommodation, personal space, provision of private pay phones and disability adaptations as well as dealing with provisions on fire precautions[14]. Strict provisions are laid down with regard to the administration of control and discipline within the homes so that staff are able to take immediate action to prevent any injury or serious damage to property but they are not able to take any steps which could be deemed to be prejudicial[15]. Other provisions in the regulations deal with such issues as the employment and education of young persons[16], religious observance[17], purchase of clothes[18], and the provision of food and cooking facilities[19].

The regulations also provide for the adequate and proper recording of vital information concerning the child[20], and provide for the circumstances in which local authorities will make regular visits to children's homes either as part of their inspection unit process or as part of a regular investigatory process[21]. Finally it should be noted that application must be made to a local authority for registration of the home be it a voluntary home or a registered children's home and such applications must include the particulars relating to persons who will be running or in any way assisting in running the relevant homes[22]. Where a registered home fails to comply with any of the provisions of the regulations or the authority is satisfied that it is no longer fit to carry on as a children's home then the authority may move to cancel the registration of a home and any appeal against a decision of a local authority under the Children Act[23] shall lie to a registered homes tribunal[24]. An appeal is brought by a notice in writing given to the local authority brought within twenty-eight days of service of the notice on him of the decision of the local authority[25]. On an appeal the tribunal may confirm the local authority's decision or direct that it shall not have effect or may decide to vary any condition, direct that any particular conditions cease to have effect or direct that any such condition as it thinks fit shall have effect with respect to the home[26]. It should further be noted that the procedure relating to appeals not only applies to steps being taken by the local authority to cancel registration but is further applicable to those situations in which application has been made for registration and that registration has been refused by the authority[27].

1 See the Children's Homes Regulations 1991, SI 1991/1506 and see Children Act 1989 Part VI and Schedule 4.
2 See Paragraph 185 ante and 192 post.
3 See Children's Homes Regulations 1991 reg 4.
4 The Children Act 1989 Guidance and Regulations Volume 4 Residential Care DOH 1991, para 1.18.
5 Children in the Public Care Report by Sir William Utting DOH 1991 para 3.24.
6 See Children Act 1989, Sch 4 and Children's Homes Regulations 1991, reg. 2,3 and 5-7.

7 Children Act 1989, Sch 4 para 3.
8 Children's Homes Regulations 1991, reg 5.
9 Guidance sup cit n.4 at para 1.29.
10 Ibid para 1.30
11 Ibid para 1.36
12 Race Relations Act 1976, s 5(2)(d).
13 Sex Discrimination Act, s 7(2)(e).
14 Ibid see regs 6, 7, 14.
15 Ibid see regs 8.
16 Ibid see regs 10.
17 Ibid see regs 11.
18 Ibid see regs 13.
19 Ibid see regs 12.
20 Ibid see regs 15, 17.
21 Children's Homes Regulations 1991 reg 28.
22 Children Act 1989 Sch 6 (6 Halsbury's Statutes (4th Edn) CHILDREN).
23 Children Act 1989 Pt VIII ss 63-65.
24 Children Act 1989 Sch 6, para 8 (1).
25 Ibid Sch 6 para 8 (2), (3).
26 Ibid Sch 6 para 8 (4), (5).
27 Ibid Sch 6 para 8.

192. Reviews. All children who are being looked after by a local authority must have their situations reviewed in accordance with regulations laid down under the Children Act 1989[1]. The reviews provide that each child's case must first be reviewed within four weeks of the date upon which the child begins to be looked after by a local authority and the second review shall be carried out not more than three months after the first[2]. Subsequent reviews are to be carried out not more than six months after the date of the previous review[3]. Each responsible authority must set out in writing their arrangements governing the manner in which the case of each child is to be reviewed and must draw the written arrangements to the attention of the child, his parents, anyone with parental responsibility and any other person whose views the authority consider to be relevant[4]. When conducting the review the local authority must have regard to a whole range of issues set out in the regulations including:

1. whether an application should be made to discharge the care order;
2. whether there should be any change sought in the child's status;
3. whether there is any need for changes in the arrangements to promote contact with the child's family;
4. any special arrangements regarding the child's education;
5. the authority's immediate and long-term arrangements for looking after the child and whether a change in those arrangements is necessary and;
6. whether plans need to be made to find a permanent substitute family for the child[5].

The local authority is also required under the review procedure to explain to the child any steps which the child may take under the Act including where appropriate[6]:

1. his right to apply with leave for a Section 8 order[7];
2. where he is in care, the child's right to apply for the discharge of the care order;
3. the availability of the procedure established under the Act for considering representations.

1 See the Review of Children's Cases Regulations 1991, SI 1991/895 (as amended by Children (Representations, Placements and Reviews) (Miscellaneous Amendments) Regulations 1991, SI 1991/2033).
2 Ibid reg 3 (1), (2).
3 Ibid reg 3 (2).
4 Ibid regs 4 (1), 7.
5 Ibid reg 5 and Sch 2.
6 Ibid Sch 1 para 5(a)(c).
7 Ibid see the Children Act 1989 s 8 (1).

193. Representations. The Children Act 1989 provides for the first time a means whereby children, parents, anyone with parental responsibility, any local authority foster parent and any such person as the authority considers to have a sufficient interest in the child's welfare, to have the right to make representations (including any complaints) to a local authority about the provision of any services including accommodation under the Act or the failure to provide any such services[1] and also where relevant to a voluntary organisation or to a registered children's home. The local authority ʿand where relevant the voluntary organisation or registered children's hon   is required to establish a procedure for considering any representations and this procedure is a two stage process. The local authority must ensure that at least one person who is not a member of the authority takes part in the first stage consideration and discussions about any action which should be taken in relation to the child in the light of the representation which has been made. The local authority and independent person involved must consider the representations and formulate a response within twenty- eight days of their receipt[2]. This first stage is very much a paper consideration followed up with a written notification of the local authority and independent person's response.

The response must be sent to the person from whom the complaint was received and where different to the person on whose behalf the representation was made and to any other persons who appears to have a sufficient interest or who are otherwise affected or involved.[3] The response should also advise the person making the original representation as to what further action may be taken.[4] Where such notification is then made to the complainant the complainant then has a right to inform the authority in writing within twenty-eight days of the date upon which notice has been given to him of the response that he is dissatisfied with the proposed result and wishes the matter to be referred to a Representations Panel appointed by the local authority for that purpose[5]. The panel must include at least one independent person and must meet within twenty-eight days of the receipt by the local authority of the complainant's request that the matter be referred to a panel[6].

Where the person making the representation before the panel wishes to be accompanied by another person of his or her choice to speak on his or her behalf then the Regulations permit this.[7] In certain circumstances, by analogy with the decision to allow legal aid to be used to finance a lawyer accompanying parents or children in a case conference, the Legal Aid Board may, if an appropriate case is made by legal representatives, be prepared to allow legal aid to finance the the payment of a lawyer to assist the child in the hearing before the panel. It could be argued that providing assistance at this stage could prevent the bringing of possible actions for judicial review or breach of statutory duty, or the possible taking of care linked proceeedings.

At the meeting of the panel the panel must consider any oral or written submissions the complainant or the local authority wish to make and where the independent person appointed to the panel is different from the person who considered the original complaint, then the panel must also consider any oral or written submissions from the previous independent person[8]. When a panel has heard the representations they must determine on their own recommendations and record them with their reasons in writing within twenty-four hours of the end of the meeting[9]. The panel must give notice of their recommendations to the local authority; the complainant; the independent person first involved in their considerations if different from the independent person on the Representations Panel; and any other person whom the local authority considers has sufficient interest in the case[10]. Finally, the local authority must together with the independent person on the panel consider what action if any should be taken in relation to the child in the light of the representation, and that independent person shall take part in any decisions about any such actions[11].

Where any complainant remains dissatisfied as a result of the determination of the panel then they must consider taking an action against the local authority possibly for breach of statutory duty or for judicial review.

1   Children Act 1989 s 26(3) and see the Representations Procedure (Children) Regulations 1991, SI 1991/894 (as amended by the Children (Representations, Placements and Reviews) (Miscellaneous Amendments) Regulations 1991, SI 1991/2033) cf the provisions of National Health Service and Community Care Act 1990, s 50. The idea is that the two schemes are broadly compatible so that local authorities wishing to do so will be able to use common structures for handling representations including complaints. The main difference is that the Children Act requires that involvement of an indpendent person. See The Children Act 1989 Guidance and Regulations, vol 3 (Department of Health, HMSO 1991) para 10.1.
2   Ibid reg 6.
3   Ibid reg 8(1).
4   Ibid
5   Ibid reg 8 (2).
6   Ibid reg 8 (4).
7   Ibid reg 8 (6).
8   Ibid reg 8 (5).
9   Ibid reg 9 (1).
10 Ibid reg 9 (2).
11 Ibid reg 9 (3).

194. Appointment of an independent visitor. Where a local authority is looking after a child who has infrequent communication with a parent or a person with parental responsibility, or has not visited or been visited by any such person within the previous twelve months, the authority is required to appoint an independent visitor if this would be in the child's best interests[1]. The visitor is under a duty to visit, advise and befriend the child[2]. The appointment may be terminated if the child, having sufficient understanding, objects to the appointment of an independent visitor[3]. Regulations have further provided for the circumstances in which a person may be appointed to the position of independent visitor for a child and as to the circumstances in which that person is to be regarded as independent[4].

1   Children Act 1989 Sch 2 Pt II para 17 (1).
2   Ibid Sch 2 Pt II para 17 (2).
3   Ibid Sch 2 Pt II para 17 (5).
4   See the definition in the Independent Visitors (Children) Regulations 1991, SI 1991/892.

195. Secure accommodation: definition. Secure Accommodation is defined in the Children Act as accommodation provided for the purpose of restricting liberty[1]. The Department of Health Guidance stresses that "restricting the liberty of children is a serious step which must be taken only when there is no appropriate alternative. It must be a "last resort" in the sense that all else must first have been comprehensively considered and rejected — never because no other placement was available at the relevant time, because of inadequacies in staffing, because the child is simply being a nuisance or runs away from his accommodation and is not likely to suffer significant harm in doing so, and never as a form of punishment".[2] The Department of Health guidance goes on to state clearly that a restriction of liberty is ultimately a matter to be determined by the court but states that it is important to recognise that any practice which prevents a child from leaving a room or building of its own free will may be deemed by the court to constitute a "restriction of liberty". For example, states the guidance, whilst it is clear that the locking of a child in a room, or part of a building to prevent him leaving voluntarily is caught by the statutory definition, other practices which place restrictions on freedom of mobility (for example, creating a human barrier) are not so clear cut[3]. When considering those children who may be placed in secure accommodation it would appear from the provisions of the Act that any child who has been provided with accommodation by a local authority, a local education authority, a health authority, a national health service trust, a residential care home, a nursing home or a mental nursing home might find himself in secure accommodation or subject to secure accommodation proceedings provided the relevant criteria are satisfied[4]. It should be noted, therefore, that children who are merely being provided with the service of accommodation may be subjected to secure accommodation proceedings or placed in secure accommodation just as much as children who are the subject of a care order[5].

There are certain conditions which must be fulfilled before a child can be placed in secure accommodation. These conditions are that the child:

(a) has a history of absconding and is likely to abscond from any other description of accommodation; and if he absconds, he is likely to suffer significant harm; or

(b) if he is kept in any other description of accommodation he is likely to injure himself or other persons[6].

As soon as the conditions cease to be met, the child should no longer be kept in secure accommodation, but there is some evidence to suggest that children are being detained in secure accommodation for longer than is necessary[7]. Between 1984 and 1990 the percentage of those children detained in secure accommodation rose from 20% to 26%[7].

The Act, combined with the relevant regulations, provide that a child may be kept in secure accommodation without the authority of a court for up to a maximum period of 72 hours, whether consecutive or not in any period of 28 consecutive days[8]. Where the period is likely to exceed 72 hours then the local authority, health authority or other relevant holding body[9] must seek the authority of the court to do so[10]. No child under thirteen may be kept in secure accommodation in a community home without the prior approval of the Secretary of State to the placement[11]. Where the local authority wish to restrict the liberty of a child under thirteen, the Guidance issued by the Department of Health recommends that the case should first be discussed with the Social Services Inspectorate[12]. The Guidance goes on to state that subject to the Inspectorate's advice a formal written submission should then be sent to the Secretary of State for his consideration, providing details of why restriction of liberty is considered the only appropriate way of dealing with the child.

There are four groups of children who are not covered by the provisions of secure accommodation in the Children Act 1989. These groups are listed in the relevant regulations and consist of two groups of children and young people who can be detained against their wishes but not using the secure accommodation provisions and the second group consisting of children and young people who simply cannot be detained at all[13]. The first two groups of children who can be detained against their wishes but not using secure accommodation are children who are detained under a provision of the Mental Health Act 1983. The detaining provisions of the Mental Health Act apply to children as well as adults and thus the powers and safeguards built into that Act are deemed to be sufficient without having recourse to the provisions of the Children Act 1989. Children who are detained because they have been convicted of certain grave crimes and whose detention is subject to the discretion of the Home Office are also not included in the group of children to whom secure accommodation is applied[14]. As to the second group of children who cannot be detained using the secure accommodation provisions, these include young people who are being provided with accommodation between the ages of 16 and 21 where the local authority considers that to do so would safeguard or promote the child's welfare[15]. In this second category of children who cannot be detained are those who are subject to a child assessment order and being kept away from home pursuant to that order[16].

1 Children Act 1989, s 25 (1) and see CHA Form 17.
2 Ibid para 8.10 and see *R v Northampton Juvenile Court, ex parte London Borough of Hammersmith and Fulham* [1985] FLR 193 where it was held that a behaviour modification unit in a hospital where the regime was designed to restrict liberty was secure accommodation.
3 *The Children Act 1989 Guidance and Regulations*, Vol 4 (Department of Health, HMSO)1991, para 8.5.
4 Children Act 1989 s 25 (3). For Form of order see CHA Form 17.
5 See the Children (Secure Accommodation) Regulations 1991, SI 1991/1505, reg 7.
6 Children Act 1989, s 25(1)(a) and (b)
7 See *Juvenile Offenders and the Use of Local Authority Secure Accommodation in England*, NACRO 1991.
8 Children Act 1989, s 25(2)(a) and the Children (Secure Accommodation) Regulations 1991 SI 1991/1505, reg 10.
9 Children Act 1989, s 25(1) and (2) as modified by Children Act (Secure Accommodation) Regulations 1991 SI 1991/1505, reg 7(3)(a) and (b) and see Children (Secure Accommodation) No 2 Regulations 1991 SI 1991/2034 reg 2.
10 Children Act 1989, s 25(2)
11 Children (Secure Accommodation) Regulations 1991 SI 1991/1505 reg 4.
12 The Children Act 1989 Guidance and Regulations, vol 4 (Department of Health HMSO) 1991 para 8.24.
13 See Mental Health Act 1983 ss 2-5 and see also *Mental Health Act Code of Practice*, para 29, (HMSO 1990).
14 Children Act 1989 s 21.
15 Children Act 1989 s 20 (5).
16 Children Act 1989 s 43.

196. Local authority responsibilities to children in secure accommodation. In addition to those responsibilities which the local authority has to children whom they are accommodating, there are two further specific responsibilities relating to children in secure accommodation[1]. The first concerns the establishment of a review panel and requires local authorities under the relevant regulations to appoint at least three persons, one at least of whom must not be employed by the local authority by or on behalf of which the child is being looked after, who shall review the keeping of the child in such accommodation for the purposes of securing his welfare within one month of the inception of the placement and then at intervals not exceeding three months where the child continues to be kept in such accommodation[2]. (This review is additional to the review required by Section 26 of the Act.) The duty to review the secure accommodation placement within one month is new as is the provision of the independent element in the review process. The regulations go on to provide for the conduct of the reviews. It is thus made clear that, within the general duty to have regard to the welfare of the child, those undertaking the review must satisfy themselves that the criteria for keeping the child in secure accommodation still apply, that the placement in secure accommodation in a community home continues to be necessary for the child; and whether there is any other kind of accommodation which would be appropriate[3]. It is further provided that those undertaking the review must, if practicable, ascertain and take into account the wishes and feelings of the child; any parent and anyone else with parental responsibility; at the discretion of the review anybody else who has had care of the child; any independent visitor; and the local authority managing the accommodation, where this is not the same authority as that which is looking after the child[4]. Once the review has been completed, the local authority is required to inform all of those people if practicable as to the outcome of the review[5]. The regulations further provide for the recording of important details relating to the child who is kept in secure accommodation pursuant to the Act[6].

Local authorities are of course under a number of other duties and liabilities in respect of children whom they are looking after[7]. It must be pointed out therefore that a secure accommodation order does not override the position of parents whose child is merely being provided with accommodation and who are able to bring such provisions to an end by simply removing the child from the accommodation[8]. The only way in which a local authority could prevent this from occurring would be to invoke the protective provisions of Part V of the Children Act 1989[9]. All other provisions relating to local authority care of children whom they are looking after apply as do the provisions with regard to after care[10].

1   The Children (Secure Accommodation) Regulations 1991, SI 1991/1505, rr 15, 16.
2   Ibid r 15 and see The Childrens Act 1989 Guidance and Regulations vol 4 paras 8.53-8.56.
3   Ibid r 16 (1).
4   Ibid r 16 (2).
5   Ibid r 16 (3).
6   Ibid r 17.
7   See Children Act 1989 s 22.
8   See Children Act 1989 s 20 (8).
9   Ibid s 24.
10 Ibid s 24.

197. Secure accommodation applications. Initially any application concerning secure accommodation must be made to the magistrates' court[1]. Thereafter the normal rules on transfer will apply if the magistrates' court thinks the case would more appropriately be heard by the county court or the High Court[2]. The regulations provide that an application to the court can only be made by the local authority which is looking after the child[3], although the Guidance document suggests that an application could be made on behalf of the local authority looking after the child by the local authority managing the secure accommodation in which the child is being accommodated where these are different.[4] Whilst is has already been noted[5] that a number of other agencies now have power to restrict the liberty of a child whom they are accommodating, where any such child is being looked after by a local authority, then responsibility for making the application remains with the local authority[6]. When lodging an application with the Family Proceedings Court the local authority or the other agency seeking an order completes the prescribed form[7] and lodges with the justices' clerk sufficient copies for service on all the respondents which for these purposes includes every person whom the applicant believes to have parental responsibility; in the case of a child subject to a care order everyone whom the applicant believes to have held parental responsibility immediately prior to the making of a care order; in the case of an application to extend, vary or discharge the secure accommodation order, the parties to the original proceedings; and the child[8]. The normal provisions apply with regard to fixing a date, time and place for the hearing or for directions appointment and the forms will then be indorsed and returned to the applicant who is responsible for service[9]. All respondents have to be given at least one day's notice of a hearing or directions appointment[10]. Under the provisions of the Act, the court is allowed to adjourn the proceedings and to make an interim secure accommodation order provided the criteria on which an order is sought appear to be satisfied[11]. Where the application is a first court hearing in the matter, the court will have to decide on the appointment of a guardian ad litem unless they are satisfied that to do so is not necessary in order to safeguard the child's interests[12]. The duties of the guardian ad litem in secure accommodation proceedings are exactly the same as they are in any other proceedings under the Children Act 1989[13]. The court hearing the secure accommodation application must determine whether the relevant criteria are met since the grounds for making the order must be set out in clear terms on the prescribed form for the order[14]. The powers of the court in secure accommodation proceedings are restricted in comparison with powers in other proceedings which are classified as family proceedings. None of the Section 8 orders are available in proceedings under Section 25 since these are not proceedings in which a Section 8 order can be made.[15] Applications for a child to be placed in secure accommodation are nevertheless to be treated as family proceedings when they involve a child who is being accommodated under the provisions of Section 20(1) or pursuant to a care order[16]. Since they are family proceedings pursuant to these provisions, the court in *Oxfordshire County Council v R*[17] therefore held that hearsay evidence which is admissible in "family proceedings" in the magistrates court would be admissible in secure accommodation proceedings involving a boy of nearly fifteen years of age. The justices had originally excluded psychiatric evidence contained in a report on the advice of their clerk as he had believed erroneously that secure accommodation proceedings did not fall within the scope of the Children (Admissibility of Hearsay Evidence) Order 1991 because they were not defined as "family proceedings" under s 8(3) of the Children Act 1989. The court, as indicated, found that these proceedings should be treated as family proceedings under Section 92(2) of the Act and also as a result of the amendment effected to that provision by the Criminal Justice Act 1991[16] ruled that the evidence contained in the report would certainly be admissible, although the weight to be attached to it would always be a matter for judicial discretion. The court hearing an application under Section 25 can only decide therefore whether or not to authorise the applicant to keep the child in secure accommodation but it should be noted that this order simply authorises detention, it does not require it[18]. The actual language used on the prescribed court order form[19] makes it clear that the order is permissive in form and this is further reinforced by the relevant guidance issued by the Department of Health which states: "the order is permissive: it enables but does not oblige the authority or person making the application to continue the placement for the duration of the order.

Neither does it empower the authority or person to continue the placement once the criteria under which the order was made ceased to apply"[20]. In the first instance the order can authorise the retention of a child in secure accommodation for a period of up to three months[21], and where the authority or person detaining the child wished to continue with the detention, further applications can be made for periods of up to six months at a time[22]. It was emphasised in *Oxfordshire County Council v R*[17] that magistrates hearing an application for a secure accommodation order should use the statutory criteria set out in Section 25 of the Act as a checklist and build their finds of fact and reasons around them. The court went on to quote from the Guidance to the effect that the court ought also "to have regard to the provisions and principles laid down in Section 1 of the Act. The court must therefore be satisfied that the order will positively contribute to the child's welfare and must not make an order unless it considers that doing so would be better for the child than making no order at all".

1 The Children (Allocation of Proceedings) Order 1991, SI 1991/1677, art 31(a).
2 See Paragraph 1828 ante.
3 The Children (Secure Accommodation) Regulations 1991 SI 1991/1505, reg 8.
4 The Children Act 1989 Guidance and Regulations vol 4 Residential Care para 8.38.
5 See ante para195.
6 The Children Act 1989 Guidance and Regulations vol 7 para 5.4 and see the Children (Secure Accommodation) (No 2) Regulations 1991.
7 See CHA Form 17.
8 Family Proceedings Courts (Children Act 1989) Rules 1991, SI 1991/1395, Sch 2 col (iii).
9 Ibid r 4.
10 Ibid Sch 2 col (ii).
11 Children Act 1989, s 25 (5).
12 Ibid s 41 (6) and s 41 (1).
13 Family Proceedings Courts (Children Act 1989) Rules 1991 r 11; and Family Proceedings Rules 1991, SI 1991/1247, r 4.11.
14 See CHA Form 18.
15 Children Act 1989 s 8 (4).
16 This is the effect of a combination of the provisions of Children Act 1989 s 90(2), and the Criminal Justice Act 1991 s 60(3). See further The Children Act 1989 Guidance and Regulations vol 7, Guardians ad Litem and Other Court Related Issues (Department of Health, 1991 HMSO) paras 5.5-5.6.
17 [1992] 1 FLR 648.
18 Ibid s 25 (2)(b).
19 See CHA Form 18.
20 *The Children Act 1989 Guidance and Regulations*, Vol IV, Residential Care, (Department of Health, HMSO) para 8.42.
21 Children (Secure Accommodation) Regulations 1991, SI 1991/1505, r 11.
22 Ibid r 12.

198. Secure accommodation applications: criteria for placing or keeping a child in secure accommodation. The Act provides that a child may neither be placed nor kept in secure accommodation unless it appears that the child has a history of absconding and is likely to abscond from any other description of accommodation; and if he absconds he is likely to suffer significant harm; or, that if he is kept in any other description of accommodation he is likely to injure himself or other persons[1]. These are the criteria which must be satisfied before resort can be made to secure accommodation but the guidance further sets out some of the circumstances in which secure accommodation should not be used. Thus it states that restricting the liberty of children is a serious step which must be taken only when there is no appropriate alternative. It must be a "last resort" in the sense that all else must first have been comprehensively considered and rejected — never because no other placement was available at the time, because of inadequacies in staffing, because the child is simply being a nuisance or runs away from his accommodation and is not likely to suffer significant harm in doing so, and never as a form of punishment[2]. The local authority decision to seek a secure placement must be taken at a senior level within the authority. The guidance to local authorities points out that this should be not less than at Assistant Director level and such a person should be accountable to the Director of Social Services for that decision[3]. Where a child has been provided with accommodation outside the local authority community home system, for example in a health authority establishment or private nursing home, the decision should be taken by equally senior personnel[4].

Where a child is placed in secure accommodation, he may not be kept there for more than a total of 72 hours (whether or not consecutive) in any period of 28 consecutive days without the authority of a court[5]. Where the court decides to make an order then it may authorise a placement in secure accommodation up to an initial maximum period of three months[6] and then in subsequent applications in respect of the same child may authorise further maximum periods of six months at a time[7]. It would seem in theory therefore that there is no limit apart from the young person's age to the number of times a local authority might seek an extension of a secure accommodation order.

Once the local authority or other agency concerned has decided to seek a secure accommodation order from the court, it has a duty to inform as soon as possible the child's parents, any persons with parental responsibility, any independent visitor who might have been appointed in respect of the child and any other person whom the authority considers should be informed[8]. The Act further makes it clear that a secure accommodation order cannot be made if the child concerned is not legally represented, unless the child has been informed of his right to apply for legal aid and having had the opportunity to do so has refused or failed to apply[9]. The guidance points out that the child's automatic entitlement to legal aid is guaranteed under the provisions of the Children Act[10].

1   Children Act 1989, s 25 (1)(a), (b).
2   *The Children Act 1989 Guidance and Regulations*, Vol IV Residential Care, (Department of Health, HMSO) para 8.5.
3   Ibid para 8.6.
4   Ibid para 8.16 and see the Children (Secure Accommodation) (No 2) Regulations 1991, SI 1991/2034, r 2.2.
5   See Children (Secure Accommodation) Regulations 1991, SI 1991/1505, r 10.1.
6   Ibid r 11.
7   Ibid r 12.
8   Ibid r 14.
9   Children Act 1989 s 25 (6).
10 *The Children Act 1989 Regulations and Guidance,* Vol IV Residential Care, (Department of Health, HMSO) para 8.40; and the Children Act 1989 s 99 amending Legal Aid Act 1988 s 15.

CHAPTER 10: ADOPTION PROCEEDINGS

199. Generally. The law relating to the legal adoption of minors (ie under the age of 18, who are not and have not been married)[1] is contained in the Adoption Act 1976 as amended and supplemented by the Children Act 1989[2], while the practice is set out in the rules made under those statutes[3].

Adoption applications may be made to either the High Court, a county court or a magistrates' court subject to certain statutory provisions[4]. The choice of court is up to the applicant, but considerations which may affect the choice are the greater cost of proceedings in the High Court, the complexity of the matter and the possibility that a greater degree of privacy may be obtained in the High Court or a county court than in a magistrates' court in, say, a remote locality.

Adoption proceedings have been designated as "family proceedings" by the Children Act 1989[5]. Thus, the court when hearing adoption proceedings may make any of the orders available to it in family proceedings under Section 8 or Section 16[6], and may also, where it is of the view that the child may be at risk of suffering significant harm, direct a local authority to undertake an investigation of the child's circumstances under Section 37 of the Children Act 1989[7].

It should also be noted that the Children Act 1989 provides the potential for members of a child's original birth family to seek the leave of the court to make an application for any of the orders under Section 8 even after the making of an adoption order or a freeing for adoption order[8]. Where such an application for leave is made, the court would have to have regard to the criteria laid down in the Act in deciding whether or not to grant leave[9]. It has been suggested that having regard to the criteria laid down in Section 10 (9), it is likely to be rarely, if ever, that such an application for leave would be granted[10].

1   Adoption Act 1976 ss 12 (5), 72 and see *Re A (A Minor) (Adoption: Parental Consent)* [1987] 2 All ER 81, [1987] 1 WLR 153, CA.
2   Children Act 1989 s 88 and Sch 10 Pt I.
3   Ie the Adoption Rules 1984, SI 1984/265; the Magistrates' Courts (Adoption) Rules 1984, SI 1984/611; the Adoption (Amendment) Rules 1991, SI 1991/1880 and the Family Proceedings Courts (Matrimonial Proceedings etc) Rules 1991, SI 1991/1991.
4   Only the High Court has jurisdiction in proceedings for a convention adoption order (see Paragraph 220 post) or where the child is living abroad: Adoption Act 1976 s 62 (3) and

(4). Thus the magistrates' court has no jurisdiction on an application to adopt a child abroad: Adoption Act 1976 s 62 (6). Where the child is a ward of court leave of the court is required to commence adoption proceedings, or freeing for adoption proceedings but application may be made before the foster parents are known; *F v S (Adoption: Ward)* [1973] Fam 203, [1973] 1 All ER 722, and *Practice Direction* [1985] 2 All ER 832 (as amended by *Practice Direction* [1986] 1 All ER 652). Adoption applications where the arrangements have not been made by an adoption agency or a relative must be made to the High Court: see Adoption Act 1976 s 11 and *Re S* (1984) Times, 2 November. As to the considerations where there have been previous proceedings in the High Court or a county court regarding the child and adoption proceedings are brought in the magistrates' court see *Re B (A Minor) (Adoption by Parent)* [1975] Fam 127, [1975] 2 All ER 449. The magistrates' court is not a suitable forum for hearing long contested applications: *Re Adoption Application No 118/1984* (1985) Times, 15 February.

5 Children Act 1989 s 8 (3), (4).
6 Ibid ss 8 (4)(d), 16 (1) thus overcoming problems under the old law where separate concurrent proceedings for adoption and access had arisen and giving statutory effect to the decisions in *Re G (A Minor) (Adoption and Access Applications)* [1980] FLR 109, FD and *Re G (A Minor) (Adoption and Access Applications)* [1992] 1 FLR 642. See now *G v G (Adoption Order: Contact)* (1992) Times, December 24, FD.
7 Ibid s 37 (1).
8 Ibid ss 8 (4)(d), 10 (1)(b).
9 Ibid s 10 (9).
10 For example by Douglas BROWN J and BRACEWELL J, Manchester, July 31 1991.

200. The effect of adoption: the welfare of the child. Adoption operates to extinguish parental responsibility[1] exercised by a parent[2] or guardian[3] or anyone else holding parental responsibility[4] and to vest that responsibility in the adopters[5].

Because of the serious and final nature of an adoption order, a court in reaching any decision must have regard to all the circumstances, first consideration being given to the need to safeguard and promote the welfare of the child throughout his childhood; and must so far as practicable ascertain the wishes and feelings of the child regarding the decision and give due consideration to them, having regard to his age and understanding[6].

The court must also be satisfied that the various statutory requirements discussed below have been complied with[7].

1 For the definition of parental responsibility see Children Act 1989 s 3 (1).
2 Parents where they are or have been married have joint parental responsibility but the mother only of an illegitimate child has automatic parental responsibility. The putative father may acquire parental responsibility through the making of a parental responsibility agreement with the mother or by obtaining an order of the court under Children Act 1989 s 4 (1)(a) or (b) or under ibid ss 8 and 12 (1).
3 A guardian appointed in accordance with Children Act 1989 s 5.
4 Ie the holder of a residence order who is neither a parent or guardian: Children Act 1989 s 12 (2).
5 Adoption Act 1976 s 12 (1), (3).
6 Ibid s 6. For the extent to which this section applies to the withholding of parental consent see Paragraph 206 post. The section also applies to the decisions of adoption agencies as to which see Paragraph 204 post. The moral and religious welfare of the child and any ties of affection must be considered, as well as his physical well-being. See *Re McGrath*

(Infants) [1893] 1 Ch 143 at 148, CA, per LINDLEY LJ and *Re E (An Infant)* [1963] 3 All ER 874. As to the court's duty in connection with the requirement to give due consideration to the wishes and feelings of the child see *Re G (T J) (An Infant)* [1963] 1 All ER 20, CA; *Re D (Minors) (Adoption by Step-Parent)* [1980] 2 FLR 102; and *Re B (A Minor) (Adoption)* [1988] 18 Fam Law 172.

7 See Paragraphs 202-208 post. Where applicants proceed with an adoption application knowing they have breached the law's requirements, the High Court will have to decide whether to exercise its discretion and allow the adoption to go ahead. Examples include cases where payments in respect of the adoptions have been made, which are illegal. See *Re An Adoption Application* [1992] 1 FLR 341; *Re A W (Adoption Application)* [1992] Fam Law 539; and *Re C (A Minor) (Adoption Application)* [1992] Fam Law 538.

201. Placing children for adoption. Provision is made for local authorities[1] and approved adoption societies[2] to act as adoption agencies, responsible, inter alia, for placing children for adoption[3]. They have other statutory duties and responsibilities[4].

Once a child under sixteen has been placed for adoption he normally becomes a protected child[5] and once an application to free for adoption or for an adoption order has been commenced, he may not be removed from the surroundings in which he is placed without the leave of the court[6].   •

A local authority has a duty to visit protected children and to satisfy itself as to their well-being and give such advice as to their care and maintenance as may be needed[7].

A person with whom a protected child is living has no insurable interest in his life[8].

Where there are concerns about the health or welfare of a protected child, then the range of powers available to protect all children may be used as appropriate[9], and the special provisions which used to exist in the Adoption Act 1976 have been repealed by the Children Act 1989[10].

1 Ie the council of a county (other than a metropolitan county), a metropolitan district or a London Borough, or the Common Council of the City of London: Adoption Act 1976 s 72 (as amended by the Children Act 1989 s 108 (7), Sch 15), and for certain provisions namely ibid ss 13, 22, 28-31, 35 (1) and 51 includes a regional or islands council. Each council has a duty to establish an adoption service: Adoption Act 1976 s 1; and act as an adoption agency under the Adoption Agencies Regulations 1983, SI 1983/1964, reg 1(1).
2 Adoption Act 1976 s 3 and Adoption Agencies Regulations 1983 regs 2, 3.
3 For the agencies' duties in relation to such placements see ibid regs 7-9, 12.
4 These include a duty to provide counselling services for parents (ibid reg 7); a duty to keep and preserve the confidentiality of case records (ibid reg 14) and to provide the prospective adopters with written information about the child.
5 Adoption Act 1976 s 32.
6 See Paragraph 204 post.
7 Adoption Act 1976 s 33.
8 Ibid s 37 (2).
9 Ie child assessment order under Children Act 1989 s 43; emergency protection order ibid: s 44; police powers of protection: ibid s 46; instituting proceedings under ibid s 31 for a care or supervision order. See further Paragraphs 174180 ante.
10 See the Children Act 1989 Sch 15, repealing Adoption Act 1976 s 34.

202. Who may adopt. The court may, on application made in the prescribed manner[1] make an adoption order vesting parental responsibility for the child in the applicant[2]. A joint application may be made only by a married couple[3], who have each attained the age of twenty-one years[4] unless one of them is the father or mother[5] of the child, in which case they must have attained the age of eighteen years[6] but the spouse must still be at least twenty-one[7]. Where an application is made by a married couple, at least one of them must be domiciled in a part of the United Kingdom, or in the Channel Islands or the Isle of Man[8], unless the application is for a convention adoption order[9].

Where the application is made to a court in England or Wales by a married couple consisting of a parent and step-parent of the child, or where the sole applicant is a step-parent of the child, the court or the guardian ad litem may consider that the matter might be better dealt with by an application for a residence order under Section 8 of the Children Act 1989[10]. This would have the effect of conferring legal status on the applicant because it confers parental responsibility[11] whilst not denigrating from or depriving the other parent from being able to exercise the parental responsibility held by that other parent[12].

An adoption order may be made on the application of one person only if he is over twenty-one and (unless the application is for a convention adoption order) is domiciled in a part of the United Kingdom, or in the Channel Islands or the Isle of Man[13]. Where a sole applicant is married, an adoption order may not be made unless the court is satisfied that:

1. his spouse cannot be found[14]; or
2. the spouses have separated and are living apart and the separation is likely to be permanent[15]; or
3. his spouse is by reason of ill health, whether physical or mental, incapable of making an application for an adoption order[16].

An adoption order will not be made on the application of the mother or father of the child alone[17] unless the court is satisfied that:

1. the other natural parent is dead or cannot be found or by reason of Section 28 of the Human Fertilisation and Embryology Act 1990, there is no parent[18]; or
2. there is "some other reason" justifying the exclusion of the other natural parent[19].

This "other reason" justifying exclusion must relate to the welfare of the child[20], and where such an order is made, the reason justifying the exclusion of the other parent is recorded by the court[21].

There are not otherwise any further prohibitions on who may apply to adopt a child, but, where an adoption is not deemed to be for the welfare of the child, the court can decline to make an order on that ground[22].

1 See Table 5 post (High Court and county court) and Adoption Rules 1984, SI 1984/265, Sch 1 Form 6 as amended by Adoption (Amendment) Rules 1991, SI 1991/1880, r 41 and see also Form FD 725 as used in the Family Division.
2 Adoption Act 1976 s 12 (1).
3 Ibid s 14.
4 Ibid s 14 (1A).
5 Ibid s 14 (1B)(a).
6 Ibid s 14 (1B)(a).
7 Ibid s 14 (1B)(b).
8 Ibid s 14 (2)(a).
9 Ibid s 14 (2)(b).
10 By the Children Act 1989 s 8 (4), adoption proceedings under the Adoption Act 1976 are

family proceedings and thus the court is empowered in such proceedings to make any of the Section 8 orders including a residence order.

11 Children Act 1989 s 12 (2).

12 Ibid s 2 (5), (6).

13 Adoption Act 1976 s 15 (1)(a).

14 Ibid s 15 (1)(b)(i), ie all reasonable steps have been taken to trace him: *Re C (An Infant)* (1957) Times, 2 April; or there are no practical nor safe means of communication with him *Re R (Adoption)* [1966] 3 All ER 613, [1967] 1 WLR 34.

15 Ibid s 15 (1)(b)(ii). The meaning of living apart in this context is the same as that which pertains in matrimonial causes and such decisions would herein be applicable.

16 Ibid s 15 (1)(b)(iii).

17 Ibid s 15 (3). An order may be made authorising an unmarried mother to adopt her illegitimate child: see *Re D (An Infant)* [1959] 1 QB 229, [1958] 3 All ER 716. The natural father of an illegitimate child may adopt him (see also *F v S* [1973] Fam 203 at 207, [1973] 1 All ER 722 at 725, CA.

18 Ie where the husband has not consented to the in vitro fertilisation or artificial insemination of his wife by an anonymous sperm donor.

19 Adoption Act 1976 s 15 (3)(b).

20 An approach confirmed by *Re C (A Minor) (Adoption by a Parent)* [1986] Fam Law 360.

21 Adoption Act 1976 s 15 (3).

22 Ibid s 6.

203. Who may be adopted. Any child[1] who has not been married[2] may be adopted. The child need not be a British subject and his domicile is irrelevant, but if he is a foreign national, or was until recently resident abroad, the court will consider whether an English adoption order will be recognised abroad and, if not, whether such an order will still be for the child's benefit[3].

Where the effect of the order is to circumvent the provisions of the immigration legislation, the order may be refused on policy grounds even though the court is satisfied that the order would be for the benefit of the child. The test is whether the applicants are really in loco parentis to the child[4].

Where the child is a ward of court[5], application must first be made in the wardship proceedings for leave to make an adoption application[6]. An adoption order may be made in respect of a child who has already been adopted[7].

1 Ie under the age of 18: Adoption Act 1976 s 72. An order can be made even where the period of childhood remaining is short: see *Re D (A Minor)(Adoption Order: Injunction)* [1991] Fam 137, [1991] 3 All ER 461, CA.

2 Adoption Act 1976 s 12 (5).

3 *Re B (S) (An Infant)* [1968] Ch 204, [1967] 3 All ER 629. See similar provisions regarding convention and foreign adoptions: Adoption Rules 1984, SI 1984/265, rr 33, 48 (3).

4 *Re A (An Infant)* [1963] 1 All ER 531, [1963] 1 WLR 231; *Re R (Adoption)* [1966] 3 All ER 613, [1967] 1 WLR 34; *Re H (A Minor) (Non Patrial)* [1982] Fam 121, per HOLLINGS J. See also *Re Kamal Pravin Bhatt* [1984] CLY 2196.

5 As to wards of court see Paragraphs 228-238 post. The test is whether the proposed adoption might reasonably succeed, not whether adoption is in the best interests of the child: *F v S* [1973] Fam 203, [1973] 1 All ER 722. For the procedure see Family Proceedings Rules 1991, SI 1991/1247, r 5.4.

6 For the procedure on obtaining access to the wardship-file by the prospective adopters see *Practice Direction* [1989] 1 All ER 169, [1989] 1 WLR 136.

7 Adoption Act 1976 s 12 (7).

204. Freeing for adoption. *Applications for freeing* —Where on an application by an adoption agency[1] the court[2] is satisfied in the case of each parent or guardian[3] that he freely, and with full understanding of what is involved, agrees generally and unconditionally to the making of an adoption order[4], or that his agreement should be dispensed with on one of the grounds specified in Section 16 (2) of the Adoption Act 1976[5], the court shall make an order declaring the child free for adoption[6]. This is subject to the first consideration being given to the need to safeguard and promote the welfare of the child throughout his childhood[7]. The agreement of the mother is ineffective if given within six weeks of the birth[8]. The court may not dispense with the required consents unless the child is already placed for adoption or the court is satisfied that he will be adopted[9].

An application may not be made except with the consent of a parent or guardian[10]; or unless the adoption agency is applying for dispensation with the consent of each parent or guardian and the child is the subject of a care order[11] in favour of the adoption agency, which will therefore have to be a local authority. Where a child is merely being accommodated by a local authority[12], there can be no application for freeing unless either the parents or guardian agree or the local authority has obtained a care order[13].

Declarations and the effects of freeing order —Before making an order, the court must satisfy itself that each parent or guardian who can be found has been given the opportunity of making, if he so wishes, a declaration that he prefers not to be involved in any future questions concerning the adoption of the child, and any such declaration must be recorded by the court[14]. If he does not do so then the adoption agency has a duty to notify him of the progress of the adoption[15]. The parents in such cases must also be informed when the child ceases to have his home with a person with whom he has been placed for adoption[16]. If the first planned placement breaks down, a decision by the adoption agency to place the child with a new set of adoptive parents can be challenged by means of judicial review and an order be granted quashing the decision[17].

The effect of the order is to extinguish the parental responsibility held by the parent or guardian relating to the child to vest those parental responsibilities in the adoption agency[18].

If, twelve months after the making of the freeing order, no adoption order has been made and the child does not have his home with a person with whom he has been placed for adoption, a parent or guardian may apply to the court to revoke the order on the grounds that he wishes to resume parental responsibility[19]. While the application is pending the adoption agency must not place the child for adoption without the leave of the court[20].

As a result of a change effected by the Children Act 1989, Section 20 (3) of the Adoption Act 1976 now makes it clear that a revocation order operates

1. to extinguish the parental responsibility given to the adoption agency by the freeing order;
2. to give that responsibility back to the child's parents; and
3. to revive any parental responsibility agreement or order and any appointment of a guardian previously extinguished by a freeing order[21].

A revocation order does not revive any previous Section 8 orders or care orders extinguished by the making of the original freeing order[22], nor (reversing previous law) does it revive a duty to make payments for the child arising from a court order or agreement which was extinguished by the making of a freeing order[23]. Where an application to revoke the freeing order is dismissed on the ground that it would not promote the welfare of the child, the former parent who made the application will not be entitled to make any further application unless the court grants leave[24].

1 Adoption Agencies Regulations 1983, SI 1983/1964, reg 1 (3): see Paragraph 204 ante. For the procedure see the Adoption Rules 1984, SI 1984/265, rr 4-11 (as amended by the Adoption (Amendment) Rules 1991, SI 1991/1880 and the Magistrates' Courts (Adoption) Rules 1984, SI 1984/611), rr 4-11 (as amended by the Family Proceedings Courts (Matrimonial Proceedings etc) Rules 1991, SI 1991/1991).
2 Ie the High Court, county court or magistrates' court, any of these courts are authorised courts under Adoption Act 1976 s 62 (2).
3 For new definition see Adoption Act 1976 s 72 (as amended by Children Act 1989).
4 Adoption Act 1976 s 18 (1)(a).
5 Ibid s 18 (1)(b).
6 Ibid s 18 (1).
7 Ibid s 6.
8 Ibid s 18 (4).
9 Ibid s 18 (3).
10 Ibid s 18 (2)(a).
11 Ibid ss 18 (2)(b), 18 (2A) (as inserted by the Children Act 1989 s 88 (1) Sch 10 Pt I para 6(1)) and which refers to a child in the care of the adoption agency. Under Children Act 1989 s 105 a child can only be described as being in care where he is the subject of a care order.
12 Under the provisions of Children Act 1989 s 20.
13 Adoption Act 1976 s 18 (2A).
14 Adoption Act 1976 s 18 (6) and note that by ibid s 18 (7) where the child's mother and father were not married to each other and the father does not have parental responsibility, the court must also satisfy itself in relation to any person claiming to be the father that either he has no intention of making an application under the Children Act 1989 s 4 (1) for a parental responsibility order or of making an application under ibid s 10 or, if he did make any such application, it would be likely to be refused.
15 Ibid s 19.
16 Ibid s 19 (3).
17 See *R v Derbyshire County Council, ex p T* [1990] Fam 164, [1990] 1 All ER 792, [1989] FCR 713, CA.
18 Adoption Act 1976 s 18 (5).
19 Ibid s 20 (1).
20 Ibid s 20 (2).
21 Ibid s 20 (3)(a).
22 Ibid s 20 (3A).
23 Ibid s 20 (3A)(a)(ii).
24 Ibid s 20 (4).

205. Agreements. Unless the child has been freed for adoption[1], before an adoption order or interim order[2] can be made, the court must be satisfied that, in the case of each parent holding parental responsibility[3] or guardian[4] of the child, he freely and with full understanding of what is involved agrees unconditionally to the making of the adoption order (whether or not he knows the identity of the applicant)[5]. Where the father of a child, who is not or has not been married to the child's mother, does not hold parental responsibility by virtue of an agreement with the child's mother or an order of the court[6], his agreement will not be necessary. The only other circumstance under which his agreement may be required is where the father has been appointed guardian of the child by the mother in her will or by a duly witnessed document[7] and she has died[8] or in the absence of such an appointment by the mother, the father is appointed guardian by court order[9] after her death.

Where the unmarried father is neither a parent or guardian as set out above nor liable by virtue of an order or agreement to maintain the child, the local authority which is involved in the adoption process has a discretion whether or not to include the father in that process[10]. Where the local authority decides not to name or interview him its decision cannot be challenged unless it has improperly exercised its discretion[11].

1 See Paragraph 204 ante and the Adoption Act 1976 s 18.
2 Ibid s 25.
3 For definition of parent see Adoption Act 1976 s 72 and see also *Re C (Minors) (Adoption)* [1992] 1 FLR 115, CA.
4 Ibid s 72.
5 Ibid s 16 (1)(b). For a case on the validity of the agreement of a parent, see *Re P (An Infant)* (1954) 118 JP 139, CA. Agreement must be operative at the time the adoption order is made: *Re Hollyman* [1945] 1 All ER 290, CA; *Re F (An Infant)* [1957] 1 All ER 819; although it is not mandatory to use the prescribed Form: *Re W (A Minor)* (1991) [1992] Fam 64, where the Court of Appeal accepted that a document signed by the child's mother agreeing to adoption by the grandparents was, in the absence of other evidence, material on which the court could find that she had agreed to the adoption. A mother who is a minor can agree to an order: *Re K (An Infant)* [1953] 1 QB 117, [1952] 2 All ER 877, CA. Although a consent may be withdrawn at any time the longer the child remains where he is, the more likely it is that the court will hold that consent is being unreasonably withheld: see *Re H (Infants) (Adoption: Parental Consent) (Note)* [1977] 2 All ER 339, CA, per ORMROD LJ. As soon as is practicable after the originating process has been filed or at any stage thereafter, if it appears that a parent or guardian is willing to consent, the court may appoint a reporting officer to ensure that consent is freely given, to witness the signature on a written agreement, investigate all the circumstances and prepare a written report to the court. Adoption Rules 1984, SI 1984/265, r 17 (as amended by the Adoption Amendment Rules 1991, SI 1991/1880); and Magistrates' Courts (Adoption) Rules 1984, SI 1984/611, r 17 (as amended by the Family Proceedings Courts (Matrimonial Proceedings etc Rules) 1991, SI 1991/1991).
6 An agreement made under Children Act 1989 s 4 in the prescribed form or an order of the court under ibid s 4 or s 8 giving him parental responsibility.
7 See Children Act 1989 s 5 (5).
8 Ibid s 5 (7)(a).
9 See ibid s 5 (1).
10 See Adoption Act Rules 1984, SI 1984/265, r 15 (2)(h) or Magistrates Courts (Adoption) Rules 1984, SI 1984/611, r 15 (2)(h).
11 See *Re L (A Minor) (Adoption Procedure)* [1991] 1 FLR 171, CA.

206. Dispensing with agreements. Where the parents are or a parent is withholding agreement to the making of an adoption order, then agreement can be dispensed with on one or more of six grounds[1] which are now examined in detail in turn:

1. *The parent cannot be found or is incapable of giving his agreement*[2] — Agreement may be dispensed with if the court is satisfied that every reasonable step by every reasonable means has been taken to trace the parent or guardian and he or she cannot be found by such means[3]. It may be deemed impossible to "find" the parents or they may be deemed "incapable" of giving agreement if there are no practical means of communicating with them and

they are unable to give their agreement as they cannot be made aware of the occasion for consenting and would not be permitted freely to give agreement if they were so aware[4]. Where an adoption order is made without all reasonable steps having been taken and the parent or guardian later comes forward he may be given leave to appeal out of time[5] but if he delays in making such an application it is less likely to be granted given that it may not after the passage of a certain period of time be in the child's interest to have the order set aside[6]. In such circumstances a parent might seek a contact order under Section 8 of the Children Act 1989[7]. Incapacity to give agreement on the grounds of mental illness or incapacity would come within this ground but only where the parent or guardian has attempted to give his agreement. Where, as is more often the case, he has refused to give agreement then the more appropriate ground would be Section 16 (2)(b) below, and his mental state may then be relevant in determining whether his refusal could be deemed to be reasonable[8].

2. *The parent or guardian is withholding his agreement unreasonably* — Although this ground has given rise to far more reported cases than all the others, it actually only arises in a very small number of applications. The court in such applications must first of all consider whether an adoption (or freeing for adoption) order would promote the child's welfare as required by Section 6 of the Adoption Act 1976[9] for although reasonableness should be viewed in the context of the totality of the circumstances a reasonable parent would view the child's welfare as being very important and would take it into account[10]. If adoption is deemed by the court to meet the child's welfare, it must then determine whether the parent is withholding that agreement unreasonably. The test is an objective one to be made in the light of all the circumstances but there is a broad range of reasonable decisions which a parent may reach[11]. Within this broad band differences of emphasis as to the reasonableness of withholding agreement are to be found in three groups of cases:

   2.1. *Cases involving babies or young children* —Many of the cases are those in which the natural parent, usually the mother, originally agreed and then withdrew her agreement. Time runs against the natural parent in such cases and the court most readily dispenses with agreement in such cases[12]. A mother has been deemed to be unreasonable in withholding agreement: in the face of medical evidence that the child would be harmed by removal from the applicants[13]; in a situation in which she admitted she could not give the child a home but to give agreement would break the natural bond with her child and give the impression that she had abandoned it[14]; and in a situation in which she repeatedly vacillated between giving and withholding agreement[15]. Fathers of young children may also be deemed to be withholding agreement unreasonably particularly where, as in one case, he had been convicted of murdering the mother. Whether a parent is withholding agreement reasonably does not depend on any question of the parent's culpability but solely on whether a reasonable parent acting reasonably would in all the circumstances of the case have granted or withheld agreement[17].

   2.2. *Those involving older children where long term foster parents have applied to adopt the child* — In those cases where there has been contact and the natural parent is known to the child the parent may not be withholding agreement unreasonably even where adoption may be in the child's best interests[18]. A possible remedy here however would be to make a Section 8 contact order in favour of the parent although there may be difficulties of enforcement where the adoptive applicants are opposed. Alternatively the court may have to consider the issue of contact with a sibling quite separately and could now make a Section 8 contact order in his favour[19]. Where there has been a strong bond between child and natural parent and continuing contact it may be better for all concerned if the court were instead to make a Section 8 residence order in favour of the adoptive applicants[20].

2.3. *Step-parent adoptions* — These tend to be the cases where the natural parent's refusal will most readily be upheld[21]. Where there are concerns that the natural parent's desire to remain a parent is both honest and reasonable the court is entitled to ask whether the decision made by the father in his individual circumstances was by an objective standard reasonable or unreasonable[22]. The court may also decide that such cases may be better dealt with by the step-parent applying for a residence order under Section 8 of the Children Act 1989 although this approach is no longer mandatory.

3. *The parent or guardian has persistently failed without reasonable cause to discharge his parental responsibility*[23] *for the child* — Parental responsibility has the meaning assigned to it by Section 3 (1) of the Children Act 1989, but it was held in *Re P*[24] that the previous term "parental duties" encompassed the natural and moral duty of a parent to show affection, care and interest towards the child; and the common law or statutory duty of a parent to maintain his child in the financial or economic sense. The term "parental responsibility" includes all duties which by law a mother and father have[25], and so would include the duty to protect the child from harm, not to harm the child nor to expose him to risk. Thus, where a child has been made the subject of a care order this may tend to show that the parent has neglected to exercise his responsibility responsibly and thus failed to discharge his parental responsibility to the child. Whether a parent has persistently failed to discharge his parental responsibility is a question of fact and degree, but in order to establish the failure it must be shown that the failure has been so grave and complete that the child will derive no benefit from maintaining contact with his natural parent[26]. Furthermore persistently means permanently and it has been suggested that the parent has virtually washed their hands of the child[27]. Prolonged failure to visit a child or show any interest in him by such means as sending birthday or Christmas cards would constitute persistent failure[28].

4. *The parent or guardian has abandoned or neglected the child* — As far as both conditions are concerned the nature of the abandonment or neglect must be such as to render the parent or guardian liable to prosecution under the criminal law[29].

5. *The parent or guardian has persistently ill-treated the child* — This would again appear to be behaviour of such a nature as would give rise to criminal prosecution and engaged in over a period of time[30] and not the result of a sudden act of violence or a sudden quarrel.

6. *The parent or guardian has seriously ill-treated the child* — It would again seem that this ground also requires conduct of a criminal nature, although one act of serious ill-treatment will suffice. By Section 16 (2) of the Adoption Act 1976 however this ground cannot be used unless it can further be shown that rehabilitation of the child within the household of the parent or guardian is unlikely either because of the ill-treatment or for some other reason, such as the imprisonment of the parent or the child being the subject of a care order. It has been held that the question of rehabilitation should be interpreted in the light of the welfare principle in Section 6[31].

1 As set out in Adoption Act 1976 s 16 (2).
2 Ibid s 16 (2)(a).
3 *Re C (An Infant)* (1957) Times, 2 April.
4 *Re R (Adoption)* [1966] 3 All ER 613, [1967] 1 WLR 34.
5 *Re F (R) (An Infant)* [1970] 1 QB 385, [1969] 3 All ER 1101, CA.
6 Adoption Act 1976 s 6.
7 Applications for contact orders can be made in all family proceedings: Children Act 1989 s 8. Adoption proceedings are classified as family proceedings by ibid s 8 (4).
8 *Re L (A Minor) (Adoption: Parental Agreement)* [1988] FCR 92, [1987] 1 FLR 400.
9 See *Re D* [1990] FCR 615, [1991] 1 FLR 48, CA.
10 Per LORD HAILSHAM LC in *Re W (An Infant)* [1971] 2 All ER 49 at 55, HL.
11 Per LORD REID in *O'Connor v A and B* [1971] 2 All ER 1230, [1971] 1 WLR 1227, HL.
12 See *Re K (An Infant)* [1953] 1 QB 117; *Re F (A Minor)* [1982] 1 All ER 321, CA; *Re V (adoption: parental agreement)* [1985] FLR 45; *Re M (Minors) (Adoption : Parent's Agreement)* [1985] FLR 921 CA.
13 *Re C (L) (An Infant)* [1965] 2 QB 449, [1964] 3 All ER 483 CA. See also *Re W (Infants)* [1965] 3 All ER 231.
14 *Re H (Adoption: Parental Agreement)* (1981) 3 FLR 386.
15 See *Re Adoption Act 1950* (1958) Times 29 July; *Re P* [1985] FLR 635 CA.
16 *Re F (An Infant)* [1970] 1 All ER 344.
17 *Re B (C H O) (An Infant)* [1971] 1 QB 437; See also *Re P A (An Infant)* [1971] 3 All ER 522; *Re W (An Infant)* [1971] AC 682, [1971] 2 All ER 49, HL.
18 *Re F* [1982] 1 All ER 321; *Re H Re W (Adoption: Parental Agreement)* [1983] 4 FLR 614.
19 Children Act 1989 s 8 (1) and (4). See also *Re E (Adoption)* [1989] FCR 118, [1989]1 FLR 126.
20 Ibid s 8 (1), (4).
21 See especially *Re P (Minors) (Adoption)* [1988] FCR 401, [1989] 1 FLR 1; *Re B (A Minor) (Adoption by Parent)* [1975] Fam. 127, [1975] 2 All ER 449.
22 See *Re B* note 21 supra and *Re H* (1974) Times, 25 November, although see also *Re D (An Infant)* [1977] AC 602, [1977] 1 All ER 145 HL, where it was held that the decision actually made by the father in his individual circumstances was, by an objective standard reasonable or unreasonable; the fact that the father was a self-confessed practising homosexual was one but not the only factor to which regard had to be had in weighing both the claim of the father and the welfare of the child.
23 Words "parental responsibility" substituted to replace "parental duties" by Children Act 1989 Sch 10 para 5, Sch 14 para 1.
24 *Re P (Infants)* [1962] 3 All ER 789, [1962] 1 WLR 1296.
25 Children Act 1989 s 3 (1).
26 *Re D (Minors) (Adoption by Parent)* [1973] Fam 209, [1973] 3 All ER 1001.
27 *Re D (Minors) (Adoption by Parent)* (supra).
28 See *Re P (Infants)* (supra); *Re B (S) (An Infant)* [1968] Ch. 204, [1967] 3 All ER 629.
29 See *Watson v Nikolaisen* [1955] 2 QB 286, [1955] 2 All ER 427; *Re W (unreported)* cited in *Re P* [1962] 3 All ER 789 at 793.
30 Requires a series of acts but they could occur over a short period of time, see *Re A (Adoption: Dispensing with Agreement)* [1979] 2 FLR 173, CA, severe and repeated assaults over three weeks is sufficient.
31 See *Re P B (A Minor) (Application to Free for Adoption)* [1985] FLR 394, 405, per Sheldon J.

207. Procedure to request dispensing with agreement. A request to dispense with any necessary agreement must be made, unless otherwise directed, in the High Court or county court in the originating application, or subsequently on notice to the proper officer[1]; and in the magistrates' court in the application[2] itself. The request must be accompanied by three copies of the statement of the facts upon which it is sought to dispense with consent[3]. Notice of the request is, where practicable, given to the person with whose agreement it is sought to dispense. Such a person should also be sent a copy of the statement of facts[4].

1 Adoption Rules 1984, SI 1984/265, r 19 (1) (as amended by Adoption Amendment Rules 1991, SI 1991/1880) and see Forms 187, 193, 197 post.
2 Magistrates' Courts (Adoption) Rules 1984, SI 1984/611, r 19 (1) (as amended by Family Proceedings Courts (Matrimonial Proceedings etc) Rules 1991, SI 1991/1991).
3 Ibid r 19 (1).
4 Adoption Rules 1984, SI 1984/265, r 19 (3); Magistrates' Courts (Adoption) Rules 1984, SI 1984/611, r 19 (3).

208. Other conditions precedent. Before a full adoption order can be made, the child must be at least nineteen weeks old and have had his home with the applicant for at least 13 consecutive weeks immediately preceding the making of the order, where one of the applicants is a parent or relative of the child or the child was placed by an adoption agency[1]. In other cases the period is twelve months and the child must be twelve months old[2].

The court must not make an adoption order unless it is satisfied that the applicants have not received a payment or reward in relation to the adoption[3].

The court must not proceed to hear an adoption application where a previous application for a British adoption order has been refused[4], unless the previous court has directed that this provision should not apply[5] or, because of a change of circumstances, it appears to the court that it is proper to proceed with the application[6].

Unless the child was placed by an adoption agency, an adoption order must not be made unless the applicant has, at least three months before the date of the order, given to the appropriate local authority written notice of his intention to apply[7].

1 Adoption Act 1976 s 13 (1). By ibid s 72 (1A), references to the person with whom a child has his home are to the person who, disregarding absence of the child at a hospital or boarding school and any other temporary absence, has the child living with him. See *Re C S C (An Infant)* [1960] 1 All ER 711, [1960] 1 WLR 304, *Re W (An Infant)* [1962] Ch 918, [1962] 2 All ER 875, *Re A (An Infant)* [1963] 1 All ER 531, [1963] 1 WLR 231 and *Re B (G A) (An Infant)* [1964] Ch 1, [1963] 3 All ER 125.
2 Adoption Act 1976 s 13 (2).
3 Ibid s 57.
4 Ibid s 24 (1).
5 Ibid s 24 (1)(a).
6 Ibid s 24 (1)(b).
7 Ibid s 22 (1). The day on which the order is made to be excluded in the calculation of the period, and thirteen consecutive weeks must be counted backwards to arrive at the last day on which notice can be given: see *Dodds v Walker* [1980] 2 All ER 507, [1980] 1 WLR 1061 CA. The appropriate local authority is the authority within whose area the applicant is resident. On receipt of the notice, the local authority must investigate, so far as practicable, the suitability of the applicants and any other matters relevant to the operation of the Adoption Act 1976 s 6 and whether the child has been placed in breach of ibid s 11 (unlawful placements for adoption), and must submit a report to the court: ibid s 23.

209. Adoption application to High Court. Application for an adoption order is made to the Principal Registry of the Family Division of the High Court, where it will be dealt with in chambers[1]. The application is made by originating summons[2], in which the adopter is the applicant and the respondents are:

1. each parent or guardian (not being an applicant) of the child, unless the child is free for adoption;
2. any adoption agency having parental responsibility relating to the child by virtue of Section 18 or 21 of the Adoption Act 1976;
3. any adoption agency named in the application or in any form of agreement to the making of the adoption order as having taken part in the arrangements for the adoption of the child;
4. any local authority to whom the applicant has given notice under Section 22 of the Adoption Act 1976 of his intention to apply for an adoption order;
5. any person liable by virtue of any order or agreement to contribute to the maintenance of the child;
6. where the applicant proposes to rely on Section 15 (1)(b)(ii) of the Adoption Act 1976, the spouse of the applicant; and
7. in the High Court, the child[3].

The court may at any time direct that any other person or body, save in a county court the child, be made a respondent to the process. The procedure is detailed in a procedural table[4]. The proceedings are in chambers[5].

Directions may be made by the judge or a district judge of the Family Division[6].

An applicant who desires confidentiality can apply to the proper officer to have a serial number assigned to the case to the case to keep his or her identity secret[7].

1 Adoptions Rules 1984, SI 1984/265, r 15 (1)(a). These rules also apply to the county court.
2 See the Adoption Rules 1984, SI 1984/265, r 15 (2). This is an example of a class of originating summons to which "special provisions" apply in place of the "general provisions" of RSC Ord 7: see the Adoption Rules 1984, SI 1984/265, r 1. Thus the parties are not described as plaintiff and defendant. The summons must be issued out of the Principal Registry.
3 Ibid r 15 (2) (as substantially amended by the Adoption (Amendment) Rules 1991, SI 1991/1880).
4 See Table 5 post. Any information obtained by any person in proceedings relating to adoption are treated as confidential and are not disclosed except in particular circumstances, for which see Adoption Rules 1984, SI 1984/265, r 53 (3).
5 Adoption Act 1976 s 64.
6 Adoption Rules 1984, SI 1984/265, r 2 (1) (as amended by the Adoption (Amendment) Rules 1991, SI 1991/1880, r 3) and ibid r 21 (5).
7 Ibid r 14.

210. Adoption application to county court. Application for an adoption order may be made, in accordance with the provisions of the Adoption Rules 1984[1] as amended in 1991, to the county court within the jurisdiction of which the child resides at the date of the application[2]. The application is made by originating application[3], and subject to the special procedural provisions of the Adoption Rules, the County Court Rules apply[4]. The procedure is detailed in a procedural table[5]. The hearing takes place in camera[6] before the judge[7].

Where an application has been made to a county court, the High Court may, at the instance of any party to the application, order it to be removed to the High Court[8].

Directions may be made by the judge or a district judge[9].

An applicant who desires confidentiality can apply to the proper officer to have a serial number assigned to the case to keep his or her identity secret[10].

1 Adoption Rules 1984, SI 1984/265 (as amended by the Adoption (Amendment) Rules 1991, SI 1991/1880).
2 Adoption Act 1976 s 62 (2)(b).
3 For the prescribed form see Form 193 post.
4 Adoption Rules 1984, SI 1984/265, r 3 (2) as amended by Adoption (Amendment) Rules 1991, SI 1991/1880.
5 See Table 5 post.
6 Adoption Act 1976 s 64.
7 Adoption Rules 1984, r 23 (4).
8 For the procedure see Family Proceedings Rules 1991, SI 1991/1247, r 10.10, Practice Direction [1978] 3 All ER 960, [1978] 1 WLR 1456.
9 See Paragraph 209 note 6 ante and Family Proceedings (Allocation to Judiciary) Direction 1991 Sch 1 paras (e) and (f). Whilst these paragraphs suggest that the district judge can also deal with unopposed adoption this is not the case as the Adoption Rules do not give him the power.
10 Adoption Rules 1984, r 14.

211. Adoption application to magistrates' court. An application to a magistrates' court for a freeing order or for an adoption order will be treated as family proceedings[1] and must be made in the appropriate form laid down by the relevant rules of court[2]. An application for an adoption order must be made to the magistrates' court within the jurisdiction of which the child resides at the date of the application[3], whilst for a freeing order the application could also be heard by a magistrates' court within whose area a parent or guardian of the child resides[4].

An applicant for adoption who wishes to keep his identity secret can apply to the justices' clerk for a serial number to be assigned to him for the purpose of the proceedings[5].

Except where the child is already freed for adoption, the rules provide that each parent or guardian must be made a respondent[6] to the proceedings and depending on the child's circumstances, so must other persons or bodies[7]. Other respondents will generally be adoption agencies and local authorities.

Notice of the hearing must be served on all the parties and on the reporting officer and the guardian ad litem[8]. Where the applicant has had to give the local authority notice of his application, he must also provide the local authority with copies of the application papers[9]. The local authority or adoption agency, as the case may be, must submit what is termed a Schedule 2 report to the court within 6 weeks of receipt of the notice of hearing, with a copy also being sent to the guardian ad litem and the reporting officer[10]. Where an unmarried father is not a parent or a guardian of the child nor liable under any court order or by agreement to pay maintenance for the child, then it would appear that a local authority has a discretion whether or not to tell him that an adoption application has been made[11].

Provision is made in the court rules for a preliminary examination of the adoption application where it appears that there may have been a previous unsuccessful application in respect of the same child[12]. Where there has been an earlier refusal then, unless the first court directed otherwise when refusing the previous application or there has been a change in circumstances or some other reason, it will not be possible to proceed with the application[13]. The matter could only proceed after examination by the justices in order to determine whether one of the conditions precedent is satisfied[14].

Where it appears to the magistrates' court that the application would be more conveniently dealt with by the High Court, the magistrates' court shall refuse to make an order, and in that case no appeal lies to the High Court[15].

1   Children Act 1989 s 8 (4). Applications must be made in accordance with the Magistrates' Courts (Adoption) Rules 1984, SI 1984/611 (as amended by the Family Proceedings Courts (Matrimonial Proceedings etc) Rules 1991, SI 1991/1991).
2   Ibid, Forms 1, 6.
3   Adoption Act 1976 s 62 (2)(d).
4   Ibid s 62 (2)(d).
5   Magistrates' Courts (Adoption) Rules 1984, SI 1984/611, r 14.
6   Ibid r 4 (2)(a).
7   Ibid r 4 (2)(b) and (3).
8   Ibid r 21 and the notice must be in ibid Form 8. Note the notice need not include the precise date of the hearing see *Re G* (1990) 2 FLR 436.
9   Adoption Act 1976 s 22.
10 Magistrates' Courts (Adoption) Rules 1984, SI 1984/611, r 22.
11 See *Re L (A Minor)(Adoption Proceedings)* [1991] FCR 297, [1991] 1 FLR 171, CA.
12 Magistrates' Courts (Adoption) Rules 1984, SI 1984/611, r 16 and see ibid Form 6 para 19.
13 Ibid Form 6 para 19.
14 Ibid r 16.
15 Adoption Act 1976 s 63 (3).

212. Appointment of a reporting officer. Whenever a child is being considered for adoption, the adoption agency is under a duty to ensure that the parents or guardians are provided with full information about the consequences of adoption and the process of freeing for adoption[1]. The provisions in the Rules for keeping parents informed of the progress of a child freed for adoption have already been noted[2] but where parents or guardians indicate their willingness to agree to freeing or to an adoption application then the court must appoint a reporting officer[3]. In the magistrates' court the reporting officer can be appointed by a single justice or the justices' clerk[4], whereas in the High Court and county court the reporting officer must be appointed by a proper officer[5].

The appointment of a reporting officer must be made from a panel established under the Guardians ad Litem and Reporting Officers (Panels) Regulations 1991[6] but the officer must not have been involved in making arrangements for the adoption of the child[7]. The same person may be appointed as reporting officer in respect of two or more parents or guardians of the child[8].

1   Adoption Agencies Regulations 1983, SI 1983/1964, reg 7.
2   See Paragraph 204 ante.
3   Adoption Rules 1984, SI 1984/265, r 5 (1) and Magistrates' Court (Adoption) Rules 1984, SI 1984/611.
4   It will normally be the justices' clerk.
5   In the High Court, a district judge of the Principal Registry of the Family Division will be the proper officer and in the county court it will also be a district judge for an action of this nature. See Adoption Rules 1984 r 2.
6   Guardians ad Litem and Reporting Officers (Panels) Regulations 1991, SI 1991/2051.
7   Adoption Act 1976 s 65 (2) and Adoption Rules 1984, r 5 (3) and Magistrates' Court (Adoption) Rules 1984 r 5 (3).
8   Ibid r 5 (2).

213. Particular duties of a reporting officer. As soon as the reporting officer has been appointed the court must send to him a copy of the application and any relevant document and of the report supplied by the applicant[1]. The relevant court rules provide that the reporting officer has a number of duties and these are:

1. to ensure that any agreement to adoption has been given freely, unconditionally and with full understanding of what is involved;
2. to witness the signature by the parent or guardian to his agreement;
3. to ensure that the parent or guardian in an application for a freeing order has been given an opportunity to make a declaration of no further involvement;
4. to investigate all the circumstances relevant to the agreement and any such declaration;
5. where it is proposed to free for adoption a child whose mother and father were not married at the time of his birth for adoption and his father is not his guardian, to interview any person claiming to be the father in order to be able to advise the court on the matters listed in Section 18 (7) of the Adoption Act 1976, but if more than one reporting officer has been appointed, the court shall nominate one of them to conduct the interview; and
6. upon completing his investigation to make a written report to the court drawing attention to any matters which in his opinion, may be of assistance to the court in considering the application[2].

The reporting officer may find it necessary to provide an interim report to the court for the purpose of obtaining the court's directions[3]. He is required to report to the court where a parent or guardian is unwilling to agree to adoption[4]. The court will then notify the adoption agency so that it can decide whether or not to dispense with agreement and on what grounds. A final or interim report submitted by a reporting officer is confidential[5].

The court has a further residual power to require the reporting officer to perform such other duties as it considers necessary[6], and it may require him to attend the hearing of the application[7].

1 Adoption Rules 1984, SI 1984/265, r 5 (1), Magistrates' Courts Adoption Rules 1984, SI 1984/611 r 5 (1) as amended by SI 1991/1350 and SI 1991/1991 respectively.
2 Ibid r 5 (4) and ibid r 5 (4) respectively.
3 Ibid r 5 (5) and ibid r 5 (5) respectively.
4 Ibid r 5 (5) and ibid r 5 (5) respectively.
5 Ibid r 5 (8) and ibid r 5 (8) respectively.
6 Ibid r 5 (6) and ibid r 5 (6) respectively.
7 Ibid r 5 (7) and ibid r 5 (7) respectively.

214. Appointment of a guardian ad litem. Whereas a reporting officer is appointed where a parent or guardian is willing to agree to adoption, a guardian ad litem is appointed where the parent or guardian is refusing their agreement either to an application for a freeing order or for an adoption order[1]. A guardian will not be appointed where the child has already been freed for adoption[2].

Both a reporting officer and a guardian ad litem will be necessary where one parent or guardian is agreeing but the other is not, although the same person can be appointed to fulfil both roles[3]. Where the proceedings are taking place in the High Court, the Official Solicitor may be appointed as guardian ad litem where the court so appoints[4]. In any other case either in the High Court or the county or magistrates' court an appointment is again made from a panel established under the Guardians ad

Litem and Reporting Officers (Panels) Regulations 1991[5]. As was the case with the appointment of reporting officers the guardian ad litem should not be a member of or employee of the applicant agency or of any respondent body nor have been involved in making arrangements for the adoption of the child[6].

1 Adoption Rules 1984, SI 1984/265, r 6 (1); Magistrates' Courts (Adoption) Rules 1984, SI 1984/611, r 6 (1).
2 See Paragraph 204 ante.
3 Adoption Rules 1984 r 6 (3) and Magistrates' Courts (Adoption) Rules 1984 r 6 (3).
4 See directions issued pursuant to Children Act 1989 s 41 (8).
5 Guardians ad Litem and Reporting Officers (Panels) Regulations 1991, SI 1991/2051.
6 Adoption Act 1976 s 65 and Adoption Rules 1984, r 6 (5) and Magistrates' Courts (Adoption) Rules 1984 r 6 (4).

215. Duties of a guardian ad litem. The guardian ad litem of the child is charged with the duty of safeguarding the child's interests before the court[1].

The guardian ad litem is under a duty so far as is reasonably practicable to:

1. investigate
    1.1. so far as he considers necessary, the matters alleged in the originating process or application, the report supplied by the applicant and, where appropriate, the statement of facts supplied under rule 19 of the Adoption Rules 1984, and
    1.2. any other matters which appear to him to be relevant to the making of an order freeing the child for adoption or the making of an adoption order;
2. advise whether, in his opinion, the child should be present at the hearing of the originating process or application; and
3. perform such other duties as appear to him to be necessary or as the court may direct[2].

On completing his inquiries, the guardian ad litem must make a report to the court, drawing attention to any of the matters which, in his opinion, may be of assistance to the court in considering the application[3]. He may, with a view to seeking further directions, make an interim report[4] or carry out such further duties as the court considers necessary[5]. He must attend the hearing unless the court orders otherwise[6].

The guardian ad litem's report is confidential[7]. An individual referred to in a confidential report may inspect, for the purposes of the hearing, that part of any report which refers to him, subject to any direction given by the court limiting the extent of such disclosure[8]. The court may allow additional parts of the report to be disclosed[9].

Information obtained by any person in connection with adoption proceedings is confidential and shall be disclosed by him if, but only if, necessary for the proper execution of his duties, or if requested by a court, a public authority empowered to authorise an adoption, the Registrar General, or a specially authorised person[10].

1 Adoption Act 1976 s 65 (1)(a); Adoption Rules 1984, SI 1984/265, r 18; Magistrates' Courts (Adoption) Rules 1984, SI 1984/611, r 18.
2 Adoption Rules 1984 r 18 (6) (as amended by SI 1991/1880) Magistrates' Courts (Adoption) Rules 1984 r 18 (5) (as amended by SI 1991/1991).
3 Adoption Rules 1984 r 18 (7), applying ibid r 6 (7); Magistrates' Courts (Adoption) Rules 1984 rr 18 (6), 6 (6). For the special responsibilities of a guardian ad litem in step-parent adoptions see *Re S* [1977] Fam 173, [1977] 3 All ER 456.
4 Adoption Rules 1984 r 6 (8); Magistrates' Courts (Adoption) Rules 1984 r 6 (7).

5 Adoption Rules 1984 r 6 (9); Magistrates' Courts (Adoption) Rules 1984 r 6 (8).
6 Adoption Rules 1984 r 6 (10); Magistrates' Courts (Adoption) Rules 1984 r 6 (9).
7 Adoption Rules 1984 r 6 (11); Magistrates' Courts (Adoption) Rules 1984 r 6 (10). See also *Re M* [1973] QB 108, [1972] 3 All ER 321 and *Re P A (An Infant)* [1971] 3 All ER 522.
8 Adoption Rules 1984 r 53 (2); Magistrates' Courts (Adoption) Rules 1984 r 32 (4).
9 Adoption Rules 1984 r 53 (2)(c); Magistrates' Courts (Adoption) Rules 1984 r 32 (4)(c).
10 Adoption Rules 1984 r 53 (3); Magistrates' Courts (Adoption) Rules 1984 r 32 (5).

216. Appeals. Appeals from the High Court or the county court in adoption proceedings lie to the Court of Appeal[1].

Where, on application made in England to a magistrates' court, the court makes or refuses to make an adoption order, appeal lies to a Divisional Court of the Family Division[2]. The notice of appeal must be served, and the appeal entered, within four weeks after the date of the order or refusal to make an order[3]. Related interlocutory applications may be heard and disposed of by a single judge[4].

The appeal is similar to an appeal under the Domestic Proceedings and Magistrates' Courts Act 1978[5]. The procedure is modified so that the notice of motion is served on the clerk to the justices whose order is appealed from and on the guardian ad litem appointed by the magistrates' court[6]. The appellant also lodges with the clerk to the justices sufficient copies of the notice of motion to be served on other parties affected by the appeal, including the proposed adopter, every person whose consent is required[7] and every person made a respondent to the application[8]. The copies of documents[9] lodged in the Principal Registry must be certified copies, and the appellant must request the clerk to the justices to forward to the principal clerk of the Contentious Department, Principal Registry of the Family Division, a certified copy of each of the following[10]:

1. the adoption application and any documents exhibited thereto;
2. the notice of determination or of the making of the adoption order[11];
3. the report by the guardian ad litem and any other reports from welfare agencies;
4. any other exhibits used at the hearing; and
5. a certificate of service of the notice of appeal on appropriate parties, specifying the parties.

It is an abuse of the wardship jurisdiction to use it as a way of trying to appeal against the refusal of an adoption order by a competent tribunal[12].

1 RSC Ord 59; County Courts Act 1984 s 77. The normal rules governing appeals apply: see Paragraphs 29 et seq ante.
2 Adoption Act 1976 s 63.
3 The former procedure under RSC Ord 90 r 9 has not been replaced in the new rules, but it is submitted that the procedure would be as herein set out by analogy with RSC Ord 55 r 4 (2) and the Family Proceedings Rules 1991, SI 1991/1247, r 8 (2). Inquiry should be made of the Principal Registry of the Family Division.
4 Cf ibid r 8.2 (8)
5 Cf ibid r 8.2.
6 *Practice Direction* [1973] 1 All ER 64, sub nom Practice Note [1973] 1 WLR 44.
7 Adoption Act 1976 s 16 (1).
8 Ie under the Magistrates' Courts (Adoption) Rules 1984, SI 1984/611, r 15 (2).
9 Cf Family Proceedings Rules 1991 r 8.2 (4) (a)(d); see *Re J S (An Infant)* [1959] 3 All ER 856, [1959] 1 WLR 1218.

10 *Practice Direction* [1973] 1 All ER 64, sub nom *Practice Note* [1973] 1 WLR 44.
11 Ie under the Magistrates' Courts (Adoption) Rules 1984, r 2.
12 *Re S (A Minor)* (1978) 122 Sol Jo 759.

217. Removal of child from applicant. While an application for an order freeing a child for adoption is pending[1] and the child is in the care of an adoption agency, and the application is not made with the consent of each parent or guardian[2], no parent or guardian[3] is entitled, against the will of the person with whom the child has his home to remove the child from the home of that person[4].

While an application for an adoption order is pending, a parent or guardian who has signified his agreement to the making of the order (whether or not he knows the identity of the applicant), is not entitled, except with the leave of the court, to remove the child from the home of the person with whom the child has his home, against the will of that person[5].

While an application for an adoption order in respect of a child made by the person with whom the child has had his home for the five years preceding the application is pending, no person is entitled, against the will of the applicant, to remove the child from the applicant's home except with the leave of the court or under authority conferred by an enactment or on the arrest of the child[6]. Similarly, if the prospective adopter gives notice in writing to the local authority that he intends to apply for an adoption order in respect of a child who for the preceding five years has had his home with him, no person is entitled to remove the child from the prospective adopter's home before the period of three months from the receipt of the notice by the local authority expires or the prospective adopter applies for the adoption order whichever is the sooner[7].

In the High Court or county court, if an application for an adoption order or an order to free a child for adoption is pending, application for leave is by process on notice in those proceedings and if no such application is pending, by originating process in the appropriate court[8], to a judge in chambers, served on the applicant. In the magistrates' court application must be made by complaint[9]. Where process is pending, the application must be served on all parties to the proceedings, and on the reporting officer and guardian ad litem, if any[10]. In any other case it must be served on any person against whom an order is sought on the applicant for adoption and the local authority upon whom notice has been served and on such other person or body (not being the child) as the court thinks fit[11]. Such persons may file answers within seven days, and the prospective adopter must file his process for adoption within fourteen days or at the hearing of the application, whichever is the sooner[12]. If leave is given the court may then and there refuse an adoption order[13].

After an application has been made for an adoption order in respect of a child placed with any person in pursuance of arrangements made by a registered adoption society or local authority for his adoption by that person, the society or authority must not remove the child from the placement with that person without the leave of the court[14]. Application for leave follows the procedure indicated above.

1 See Paragraph 204 ante.
2 See Paragraph 205.
3 Adoption Act 1976 s 27 (2).
4 Ibid s 27 (2).
5 Ibid s 27 (1).
6 Ibid s 28 (1).
7 Ibid s 28 (2).
8 Adoption Rules 1984, SI 1984/265, r 47 (2). The appropriate court is the High Court or

the county court in whose district the applicant lives, or in a case under the Adoption Act 1976 s 28 (2) in whose district the child lives or the Principal Registry as a county court. On an application under this rule, the applicant should lodge in the court two copies of the summons (or originating summons), indorsing thereon an estimate of the likely length of the hearing. No date of hearing is given by the registry until the summons has been considered by the district judge. After fixing a date for the hearing of the application by a judge in chambers, the district judge notifies the applicant and serves a copy of the summons on the persons prescribed by the rule: *Practice Direction* [1976] 3 All ER 864, [1976] 1 WLR 1267. For the procedure see Table 6 post.

9 Magistrates' Courts (Adoption) Rules 1984, SI 1984/611, r 27 (2) (as amended by the Family Proceedings Court (Matrimonial Proceedings etc) Rules 1991, SI 1991/1991).

10 Adoption Rules 1984 r 47 (5)(a) (as amended by SI 1991/1880); Magistrates' Courts (Adoption) Rules 1984 r 27 (3)(a), (5) (as amended by SI 1991/1991).

11 Adoption Rules 1984 r 47 (5)(b), (c); Magistrates' Courts (Adoption) Rules 1984 r 27 (3)(b), (c). In cases where a serial number has been assigned or is sought, the proceedings for leave will be conducted with a view to ensuring that the identity of the parties is not disclosed: Adoption Rules 1984 r 47 (6), Magistrates' Courts (Adoption) Rules 1984 r 27 (4).

12 Adoption Rules 1984 r 47 (7); Magistrates' Courts (Adoption) Rules 1984 r 27 (6).

13 Adoption Rules 1984 r 47 (9); Magistrates' Courts (Adoption) Rules 1984, SI 1984/611, r 27 (9).

14 Adoption Act 1976 s 30 (2).

218. Adoption where the child is a foreign national. Where the applicants[1] are domiciled in a part of the United Kingdom, or in the Channel Islands or the Isle of Man[2] they may apply to adopt a child living with them[3] who was born or has been resident abroad. Apart from additional considerations, such as whether the adoption is being done to circumvent the Immigration Acts[4] and whether it would be recognised in the child's own country[5], the procedure and matters to be taken into account are the same as for any other adoption. Such children may also be the subject of Convention adoption orders[6].

1 Or a single applicant: see the Adoption Act 1976 s 15.
2 Ibid s 15 (2)(a).
3 Ibid s 13 (2).
4 See Paragraph 203 ante.
5 *Re B (S) (An Infant)* [1968] Ch 204, [1967] 3 All ER 629. See now *Re An Adoption Application* [1992] 1 FLR 341
6 When the requirements of Adoption Act 1976 s 17 will have to be met.

219. Adoption where applicants wish to adopt a child abroad. It is unlawful to take or send a child who is a British subject[1] out of Great Britain with a view to the child's adoption by any person not his parent or guardian or relative[2] except with the authority of an order made in accordance with the following provisions[3].

Where, on the application of a person not domiciled in England and Wales, an authorised court[4] is satisfied that he intends to adopt the child under the law of or within the country in which the applicant is domiciled, the court may make an order giving him parental responsibility for the child[5].

The application is in the High Court by originating summons[6] issued out of the Principal Registry of the Family Division or by filing an originating application in the county court within whose district the child is[7]. The applicant must provide expert evidence of the law of adoption in the country in which he is domiciled and an affidavit as to the law sworn by a suitably qualified expert is admissible in evidence without notice[8]. Otherwise the procedure is the same as for an adoption order[9].

1 The question of whether a person is a British subject is governed by the British Nationality Act 1981. It includes, for this purpose, citizens of the Republic of Ireland: Adoption Act 1976 s 56 (1).
2 Adoption Act 1976 s 56 (1) (as amended by the Children Act 1989 s 88 (1), Sch 10 para 23 (1), (2)). The offence is punishable summarily with a fine not exceeding level 5 on the standard scale or three months' imprisonment. For the meaning of "parent or guardian" see Adoption Act 1976 s 72. For the meaning of "relative" see ibid s 72 (as amended).
3 Or a provisional adoption order made under the previous legislation.
4 Adoption Act 1976 s 62. The magistrates' court has no jurisdiction.
5 Ibid s 55 (1). For the meaning of "parental" responsibility see ibid s 72 and Children Act 1989 s 3 (1) and Paragraph 100 ante. Specific requirements of the Adoption Act 1976 relating to ordinary adoption applications regarding domicile and the registration of orders in England and Wales are excluded. The court also has no power on an application under this section to make an order freeing the child for adoption or for an interim order: ibid s 55 (2).
6 Ibid.
7 Adoption Rules 1984, SI 1984/265, r 48 (1). Where the child is not in England and Wales the application must be made to the High Court: Adoption Act 1976 s 62 (3).
8 Adoption Rules 1984 r 48 (3). See also the Civil Evidence Act 1972 s 4 (1).
9 Adoption Rules 1984 r 48 (2).

220. Convention adoption. Where a child is a United Kingdom national[1] or the national of a Convention country[2] and is habitually resident in British territory[3] or a Convention country and is not or has not been married[4], application may be made for a Convention[5] adoption order, unless the applicants and child are all United Kingdom nationals living in British territory[6].

The applicant, or, if married, both applicants, must be either United Kingdom nationals or nationals of a Convention country and both must be habitually resident in Great Britain, or they must both be United Kingdom nationals and each must be habitually resident in British territory or a Convention country[7]; and, if the applicants are nationals of the same Convention country, the adoption must not be prohibited by a specified provision of the internal law of that country[8].

If the child is not a United Kingdom national, an order will not be made except in accordance with the provisions, if any, relating to consents and consultations of the internal law relating to adoption of the Convention country of which the child is a national, and the court must be satisfied that each person who consents to the order in accordance with that internal law does so with full understanding of what is involved[9].

The application must be made to the High Court[10] in a modified version of the usual originating summons[11]. It must have attached to it any document which is to be used for the purposes of satisfying the court as to the nationality of the applicant or the child and, where the applicant claims that he or the child is a national of a Convention country, he must also attach a statement by an expert as to the law of that country relating to nationality applicable to that person[12].

Where the child is not a United Kingdom national, the rules are modified regarding proof of consent[13]. The applicant must file with the originating process a statement by an expert as to the provisions relating to consents and consultations of the internal law relating to adoption of the Convention country of which the child is a national[14]. Any document signifying consent must be in a form which complies with the internal law of the country of which the child is a national[15]. Any person whose consent is required or who has to be consulted under the relevant internal law must be served with notice of the hearing[16]. Otherwise, the procedure is the same as for ordinary adoptions.

1   Ie a citizen of the United Kingdom and Colonies who has a right of abode in the United Kingdom: Convention Adoption (Miscellaneous Provisions) Order 1978, SI 1978/1432, art 7.
2   The Hague Convention 1965. Austria and Switzerland are the only other two countries who have so far ratified the Convention.
3   For meaning see the Adoption Act 1976 s 72 (as amended). Only the United Kingdom has been designated British Territory: Convention Adoption (Miscellaneous Provisions) Order 1978, SI 1978/1432, art 5.
4   Adoption Act 1976 s 12 (5).
5   It must be so described in the originating process: Adoption Rules 1984, SI 1984/265, r 28.
6   Adoption Act 1976 s 17 (3). For annulment or revocation of such orders see Paragraph 224 post.
7   Ibid s 17 (4). For definitions see notes 1, 3 supra.
8   Ibid s 17 (4) and see also ibid s 17 (8) for definition of specified provision. In relation to Austria and Switzerland the prohibitions are set out in the Convention Adoption (Austria and Switzerland) Order 1978, SI 1978/1431, Schs 1 and 2 respectively.
9   Adoption Act 1976 s 17 (6)(b).
10 Ibid s 62 (2), (4).
11 Adoption Rules 1984, r 28; see further ibid sch 4 as amended by the Adoption (Amendment) Rules 1991 SI 1991/1880 r 52.
12 Adoption Rules 1984, r 29 (as amended by Adoption (Amendment) Rules 1991, SI 1991/ 1880).
13 Ibid r 32 (as amended by Adoption (Amendment) Rules 1991).
14 Ibid r 33.
15 Ibid r 34 (1). If sufficiently witnessed, the statement will be admissible without further proof of the signature of the person by whom it was executed: ibid r 34 (2).
16 Ibid r 35.

221. Adoption orders and conditions. The court may impose such terms and conditions in an adoption order[1] as it thinks fit[2] and may postpone the determination of the application and make an interim order[3] giving parental responsibility for the child to the applicant for a period not exceeding two years upon such terms as it thinks fit[4].

An adoption order must contain a direction to the Registrar-General to make an entry in the Adopted Children Register in such form as the Registrar-General may by regulations specify[5]. A shortened form of birth certificate, omitting particulars of parentage and adoption, may be obtained in respect of a person who has been adopted, by furnishing to the Registrar-General his name and surname, the date of his birth, the name and surname of his adopter or adopters and the date upon which and the name of the court by which the adoption order was made.

Any adopted child over the age of eighteen years may apply to the Registrar-General to have supplied to him such information as is necessary to enable him to obtain a certified copy of the record of his birth, but before supplying any such information the Registrar-General must inform the applicant that counselling services are available to him[7].

1 See eg Forms FD 73 used in the Family Division and make appropriate adaptions to orders made in the cases of *Re W* 24 October 1949 and *Re W (unreported)*)1952 W No 448).

2 Adoption Act 1976 s 12 (6) (6 Halsbury's Statutes (4th Edn) CHILDREN). There are no provisions for the enforcement of the conditions: see *Re G (T J) (An Infant)* [1963] 2 QB 73, [1963] 1 All ER 20, CA. Prior to the Children Act 1989 it was rare for courts to insert conditions preserving contact between the child and his birth family or members of his birth family but such cases did occur: See *Re B (MF)(an infant)* [1972] 1 All ER 898, CA, and *Re J (Adoption Order: Conditions)* [1973] Fam 106, [1973] 2 All ER 410. See also *Re S (A Minor) (Adoption Order: Access)* [1976] Fam 1, [1975] 1 All ER 109, CA (contact between adopted child and natural father continued). But see *Re H* (1984) Times, 21 November in which it was said that the court should impose such a condition only if there was agreement: See further *Re W (A Minor)* [1988] FCR 129, [1988] 1 FLR 175 and *Re C (A Minor)* [1989] AC 1, [1988] 2 WLR 474, HL. Since the implementation of the Children Act 1989 adoption proceedings have been designated "family proceedings", see ibid s 8 (4) and thus applications can be made in adoption proceedings or subsequently for any of the Section 8 orders including contact orders. While the adoption proceedings are still pending a parent would be entitled to apply for any of the section 8 orders whereas after an adoption order the parent is no longer a parent and must therefore apply to court for leave to make an application and satisfy the conditions in ibid s 10 (9). In virtually all cases it is unlikely that leave would be given to make an application given the fact that the court must specifically look to the risk of disruption to the child's life if leave to pursue an application was granted. See also *Re F (Infants) (Adoption Order: Validity)* [1977] Fam 165, [1977] 2 All ER 777, CA in which is set out the procedure for remedying an order which, though valid on its face, is of doubtful validity.

3 Adoption Act 1976 s 25 (1). See Form 200 post. An interim order may be made even though the child is in care under the Child Care Act 1980 and operates so as to restrict the local authority's powers: *S v Huddersfield Borough Council* [1975] Fam 113, [1974] 3 All ER 296, CA.

4 Adoption Act 1976 s 25 (1).

5 Ibid s 50 (1).

6 Births and Deaths Registration Act 1953 s 33 Birth Certificate (Shortened Form) Regulations 1968, SI 1968/2050.

7 Adoption Act 1976 s 51 (1). If persons were adopted before 12 November 1975 (ie the date of the coming into force of the Children Act 1975), they are bound to have an interview with a counsellor before the Registrar-General will give the information: Adoption Act 1976 s 51 (7). For the manner of application by an adopted person for (1) access to his birth records or (2) verification of any relationship in connection with intended marriage, see the Adopted Persons (Birth Records) Regulations 1976, SI 1976/1743.

222. Adoption Contact Register. A major development introduced by the Children Act 1989 is the establishment of the Adoption Contact Register[1]. The Register is maintained by a Registrar-General[2] and is made up of separate entries of adopted persons[3] and their relatives who wish to have contact with them[4]. In the absence of any contact orders having been made under Section 8 of the Children Act 1989 in the adoption proceedings[5], this will constitute the only possibility for establishing contact after the adoption. The decision whether or not to make contact however rests with the adoptee who must be over 18[6]. Relatives are defined as "any person (other than an adoptive relative) who is related to the adopted person by blood, half blood or by marriage''[7].

The Registrar on payment of a fee registers applicants (who must be over 18) in the relevant register[8], and is under a duty to forward to an adopted person on the register the name and address, which can be a contact address for any relative in respect of whom there is an entry in the register[9].

1 See new Adoption Act 1976 s 51A (inserted by Children Act 1989 Sch 10 para 21).
2 Whose offices are located in Southport.
3 Adoption Act 1976 s 51A (2)(a).
4 Ibid s 51A (2)(b).
5 See Paragraph 199 ante.
6 Adoption Act 1976 s 51A (4)(b)and s 51A (9).
7 Ibid s 51A (13)(a).
8 Ibid s 51A (3), (5).
9 Ibid s 51A (9).

223. Refusal of an adoption order. Where the child has been placed by an adoption agency and an adoption order is refused, the applicants must return the child to the adoption agency within seven days[1]. A local authority which has parental responsibility for the child[2] may decide to allow the child to continue to remain with the applicants as long-term foster parents[3]. In other cases, such as step-parent adoptions, the status quo will continue. A court refusing an adoption application has the power to make any of the orders under Section 8 of the Children Act 1989[4], thus a residence order would discharge a care order[5], and such an order could be used to ensure that the child lives with, say, a grandparent or other relative.

1 Adoption Act 1976 s 30 (3). The court may extend the time to six weeks: ibid s 30 (6).
2 Ie under a care order made under the Children Act 1989 or an order which is deemed to be a care order under that Act, see Children Act 1989 Sch 14.
3 See Paragraph 188 ante as to foster children generally.
4 See also Children Act 1989 s 8 (4). Where the local authority has parental responsibility for a child it may object to the court exercising jurisdiction under the Children Act 1989 s 8, in which case the parent would have to apply to the family proceedings court to revoke the care order under the Children Act 1989 or apply for a residence or contact order under ibid s 8.
5 Children Act 1989 s 91 (1).

224. Amendment and revocation of adoption order. The court by which an adoption order has been made may, on the application of the adopter or adopted person amend the order by correcting any error in the particulars contained in it[1]. If satisfied on such application that within a year from the date of the order any new name has been given to the adopted person, whether by baptism or otherwise or taken by him, either in lieu of or in addition to a name specified in the order, the court may amend the order accordingly[2]; and if satisfied on the application of any person concerned that a direction for the making of an entry in the appropriate Register of Births[3] or the Adopted Children Register included in the order was wrongly so included, it may revoke the direction[4].

If a person adopted by his father or mother alone or jointly has subsequently become a legitimated person on the marriage of his father and mother[5] the court which made the adoption order may, on the application of any of the parties concerned revoke that order[6].

Application may be made to the Principal Registry of the Family Division of the High Court[7] within two years of the order[8] to annul a Convention adoption order[9] on the ground that at the relevant time the adoption was prohibited by a provision of the relevant internal law[10] and the adoption could have been impugned on those grounds, or that the order contravened the relevant internal law relating to consents or on any other ground on which it could be impugned under the law for the time being in force in the country in which it was effected[11]. Similar provisions enable the court to declare an overseas adoption invalid on the grounds of public policy or that the authority which made the order was not competent to entertain the case[12].

1 Adoption Act 1976 Schedule 1 para 4. See Table 5 Steps 2531 post. This goes further than merely giving power to correct slips in drawing up the order: see *R v Chelsea Juvenile Court Justices (Re An Infant)* [1955] 1 All ER 38, [1955] 1 WLR 52. See also *Re F (Infants) (Adoption order: Validity)* [1977] Fam 165, [1977] 2 All ER 777.
2 For the form of such an order adapt the order made in *Re G (unreported)* (1966 G No 2034).
3 Ie the register kept in England or Scotland.
4 Adoption Act 1976 s 50.
5 See the Adoption Act 1976 s 52.
6 Adoption Act 1976 s 50 (1). For revocation of a Convention adoption order on the same ground: see the Adoption Act 1976 s 53.
7 Adoption Rules 1984, SI 1984/265, r 37 (1). Application is by originating summons supported by affidavit: ibid r 39. A guardian ad litem may be appointed in the same way as for an adoption application: ibid r 40.
8 Adoption Rules 1984, r 37 (2); except with leave of the court.
9 See Paragraph 220 ante.
10 See the Convention Adoption (Austria and Switzerland) Order 1978, SI 1978/1431, Schedules.
11 Adoption Act 1976 s 53 (1)(b), (c).
12 Ibid s 53 (2); Adoption Rules 1984 r 38.

CHAPTER 11: MINORS' PROPERTY

225. Minors' property generally. The property of a minor, whether in possession or reversion, is frequently vested in trustees or executors who, under the 1925 statutory powers, have the fullest powers of management. In regard to instruments coming into effect after 1925, they have wide powers of advancement and maintenance[1]. The range of cases in which a contingent gift carries intermediate income has been extended[2] and thus more funds are available for maintenance. The trustees may, however, apply to the court as to how these or any other discretionary powers should be exercised[3]. A minor cannot hold a legal estate in land[4].

The High Court has jurisdiction, with respect to income or property belonging to or held in trust for a minor, to take care of it, to apply it for maintenance or otherwise for his benefit, and to accumulate any surplus not required to be so applied[5]. Where, however, the property is vested in trustees upon whom a discretionary power to apply income for the maintenance, education or benefit of a minor has been expressly conferred, whether by statute or otherwise, the court will not override or interfere with that discretion if the trustees have actually exercised it[6] and are not manifestly doing so in a manner prejudicial to the minor's interests[7].

Where a minor is beneficially entitled to any property, the court may, with a view to the application of the capital or income thereof for the maintenance, education and benefit of the minor, make an order appointing a person to convey the property or, in the case of stock or a thing in action, vesting in any person the right to transfer or call for a transfer of the stock, or to receive the dividends or income thereof, or to sue for and recover the chose in action upon such terms as the court thinks fit[8].

The court also has wide powers to authorise dealings with trust property[9] and to approve on behalf of minors the variation of a trust[10].

It must be remembered that under the provisions of the Children Act 1989 when a court determines any question with respect to the administration of a child's property or the application of any income arising from it, the child's welfare must be the court's paramount consideration[11].

1   Trustee Act 1925 ss 31, 32 (as amended by the Family Law Reform Act 1969 s 1 (3), Sch 1 Pt I).
2   Ie by the Law of Property Act 1925 s 175.
3   RSC Ord 85 r 2.

4 Law of Property Act 1925 s 1 (6).
5 *Wellesley v Wellesley* (1828) 2 Bli NS 124, HL; *Coster v Coster* (1836) 1 Keen 199; *Havelock v Havelock, Re Allan* (1881) 17 Ch D 807; *Re Smeed, Archer v Prall* (1886) 54 LT 929.
6 *Wilson v Turner* (1883) 22 Ch D 521, CA; *Re Wells, Wells v Wells* (1889) 43 Ch D 281.
7 *Brophy v Bellamy* (1873) 8 Ch App 798; *Re Hodges, Davey v Ward* (1878) 7 Ch D 754; *Re Lofthouse (An Infant)* (1885) 29 Ch D 921, CA; *Re Bryant, Bryant v Hickley* [1894] 1 Ch 324; *Klug v Klug* [1918] 2 Ch 67.
8 Trustee Act 1925 s 53.
9 Trustee Act 1925 s 57.
10 Variation of Trusts Act 1958 s 1 (1)(a); and see also *Re Chapman's Settlement Trusts (No 2)* [1959] 2 All ER 47n, [1959] 1 WLR 372.
11 Children Act 1989 s 1 (1).

226. Maintenance and advancement. The court may be, and frequently is, concerned with questions of maintenance and advancement of minors in wardship proceedings coupled with applications under the Children Act 1989 where maintenance is sought[1]; in proceedings under the Children Act 1989 alone[2]; and in applications relating to the execution of trusts in which minors are concerned[3].

Where minors possess property[4], applications relating to their maintenance and advancement may also be made under the inherent jurisdiction of the court by originating summons[5] (intituled in the matter of the minor[6]) supported by factual evidence showing the minors' ages, the nature and amount of their fortunes and incomes, and what relations they have, and suggesting, where necessary, a scheme of maintenance. Where the application is made in existing proceedings an ordinary summons is used.

1 See Paragraph 228 post.
2 See Paragraph 228 post.
3 Eg applications under the Trustee Act 1925 s 31 (discretion to pay maintenance: see Paragraph 225 ante), or ibid s 57 (1) (Court's power to authorise transactions). The court's inherent jurisdiction cannot be invoked to compel trustees to make payments for maintenance; proceedings in the matter of the estate are necessary: see *Re Lofthouse (an Infant)* (1885) 29 Ch D 921.
4 *Re McGrath (Infants)* [1893] 1 Ch 143.
5 RSC Ord 5 r 3.
6 Where statutory relief is also claimed the summons should also be intituled in the matter of the appropriate Act, and the section relied on must be referred to in the body of the summons: see the Supreme Court Practice 1991 para 7/17/5.

CHAPTER 12: WARDSHIP AND THE INHERENT JURISDICTION OF THE HIGH COURT

1: IN GENERAL

227. Introduction. The jurisdiction to make infants wards of court derives from the sovereign's obligation as *parens patriae* to protect the person and property of his subjects, particularly those unable to look after themselves[1]. It is an ancient jurisdiction whose roots it has been argued go back to well before the Norman Conquest. Nevertheless the jurisdiction to make a child a ward of court can be said to stem from the sovereign's duty to protect all his subjects who were unable to protect themselves, the so- called parens patriae protection. Thus wardship can be seen as an aspect of the exercise of this wider parens patriae or inherent jurisdiction, but one that in the years leading up to the Childrens Act 1989 had assumed very considerable importance, arguably overshadowing the parent jurisdiction. The inherent jurisdiction of the High Court has, however, come up for consideration in a number of cases in recent years[2], the development of which has been given added impetus by the provisions on the separate inherent jurisdiction of the High Court contained in the Children Act 1989[3]. Applications have already been made under the Children Act invoking the inherent jurisdiction of the High Court in situations such as where a local authority needs to get the consent to a medical operation where the child is the subject of a care order and the parents are refusing to give consent. It remains to be seen how much further the construct of the inherent jurisdiction of the High Court will be developed under the Children Act. It would appear to be the case, however, that wardship is merely an example of the use which may be made of the inherent jurisdiction of the High Court, albeit one where the powers exercisable may be more extensive than those linked solely to the exercise of the inherent jurisdiction,[4] and are certainly more extensive than those of a parent. Thus the Lord Chancellor has commented that "in the government's view, wardship is only one use of the High Court's inherent *parens patriae* jurisdiction. We believe therefore that it is open to the High Court to make orders under its inherent jurisdiction in respect of children other than through wardship". It has also been made clear in guidance issued under the Act[5] that there may be a whole range of situations in which the court's inherent jurisdiction may be invoked.

What is clear, however, is that as a result of the Children Act the ability of local authorities to use wardship as a means of getting a child committed into the care of the local authority has now been abolished through the repeal of various statutory provisions and a clear message has gone out to local authorities that if its desire is to get the child committed into their care they can only do this by using care proceedings under the Children Act 1989[6]. The provisions of the Children Act further make it clear that it will not be possible for local authorities to seek to invoke the inherent jurisdiction of the High Court unless the remedy they seek is not available elsewhere and the court deems it to be necessary in the interests of protecting children to exercise the inherent jurisdiction in favour of granting a local authority an order[7].

The wardship and inherent jurisdictions of the High Court over children and exercised by the Family Division of the High Court[8] and are thus accessible in the provinces, through the district registries, as well as in London through the Principal Registry. It is also possible once the main issues in a case have been decided by the High Court to transfer cases to the county court.[9]

That the two jurisdictions are deemed to be separate has already been noted and it is therefore proposed to treat them separately here.

1 Whilst *parens patriae* jurisdiction exists with regard to infants, it has been established there is no such jurisdiction with regard to the incapacitated adult especially in the arena of mental handicap, see *Re F (Mental Patient: Sterilisation)*[1990] 2 AC 1, [1989] 2 All ER 545, HL.

2 For the unrestricted nature of the jurisdiction, see the comments of PENNYQUICK J in *Re X (A Minor)* [1975] 1 All ER 697 at 706; and for the restrictions on the exercise of aspects of this jurisdiction. See *Richards v Richards* [1984] AC 174, [1983] 2 All ER 807, HL. However in *Re W (A Minor) (Medical Treatment: Courts Jurisdiction)* [1992] 2 FCR 785 reported also as *Re J (A Minor)* 1992 Times 15th July CA the Court of Appeal, in emphasising that the inherent jurisdiction of the High Court was equally exercisable whether or not the child was a ward of court, stated that whilst the powers of the court in the exercise of the inherent jurisdiction were theoretically limitless, there were nevertheless far reaching limitations in principle on the exercise of that jurisdiction.

3 Children Act 1989 s 100.

4 See comments of Lord Mackay LC in the "Joseph Jackson Memorial Lecture" at (1989) 139 NLJ 505.

5 See *The Children Act 1989 Guidance and Regulations*, Vol I (Department of Health, HMSO) 1991, para 3.98.

6 Children Act 1989 s 31.

7 Ibid s 100.

8 Administration of Justice Act 1970, s1(2) and Schedule 1.

9 Matrimonial and Family Proceedings Act 1984, s 38 (2)(b).

2: WARDSHIP

228. Jurisdiction. The rules on jurisdiction in wardship have been substantially affected by the provisions of the Family Law Act 1986[1]. Thus, to the extent that any orders in wardship come within the definition of Part I orders under the Family Law Act 1986 they will be governed by the Act's uniform rules of jurisdiction,[2] whereas any other orders will still be governed by the common law rules of jurisdiction. Under the provisions of the Family Law Act 1986 the High Court does not have jurisdiction to make a Part I order in the exercise of its inherent jurisdiction unless,[3] on the relevant date being the date of a first application or the date upon which the court is considering whether to make an order,[4] the child is either habitually resident in England and Wales, or is present in England and Wales and is not habitually resident in any part of the United Kingdom or a specified dependent territory,[5] and no proceedings for divorce, nullity or judicial separation are continuing[6] in a court in Scotland, Northern Ireland or a specified dependent territory in respect of the child's parent's marriage.[7] Where any such proceedings are continuing, the High Court may still be able to exercise jurisdiction where the court in which proceedings are ongoing has made an order either waiving jurisdiction[8] or staying the proceedings so as to allow the proceedings involving the child to be heard in England or Wales,[9] or where the child is actually present in England and Wales on the relevant date and the court considers that the immediate exercise of its powers is necessary for his protection. Where the orders to be made do not come within the definition of Part I orders under the Family Law Act 1986,[10] then the High Court is able to exercise its inherent wardship jurisdiction over any child[11] under the age of 18, who is a British subject regardless of whether the child is in the country,[12] and exceptionally over a child who was not born and it not resident within the jurisdiction and is therefore a foreign student.[13] Where a child is the subject of a case order the court has no power to exercise its wardship jurisdiction[14] although the more general inherent jurisdiction may be invoked.[15] In the case of minors who become wards of court in the strict sense, the Family Division of the High Court is the appropriate division exercising control and jurisdiction[16]. The court exercises a very wide and special jurisdiction and control[17] which is both parental and administrative[18]. The wardship courts' powers are however more extensive than those possessed by parents.[19] Indeed Lord Donaldson MR in *Re R*[20] observed that "the practical jurisdiction of the court is wider than that of parents. The court can for example forbid the publication of information about the ward or the ward's family circumstances. It is also clear that this jurisdiction is not derivative from the parent's rights and responsibilities, but derives from, or is, the delegated performance of the duties of the Crown to protect its subjects." The court cannot exercise the jurisdiction in the case of a minor whose parent while retaining parental rights claims diplomatic immunity[21]. The court will not interfere with decisions in immigration proceedings by allowing wardship proceedings to intervene and prevent the minor's removal from the jurisdiction, but the wardship may continue to provide for the children's protection.[22]

Similarly the decision to prosecute or to administer a police caution in a particular case is a matter for the prosecuting authority alone and where the juvenile is a ward of court it would be contrary to public policy for the wardship court to intervene in the decision making process. In deciding to administer a caution, the prosecuting authority has to obtain the consent of the wardship court with regard to the administration of the caution[23].

Pursuant to powers given to him under the Children Act 1989[24], the Lord Chancellor has now provided that in any civil proceedings before the High Court (this includes wardship), county court and family proceedings court, any evidence given in connection with the upbringing, maintenance or welfare of the child shall be admissible notwithstanding any rule of law relating to hearsay[25].

1 See particularly ss 1-7 thereof.
2 Family Law Act 1986 Part I.
3 Family Law Act 1986 s 2(3).
4 Ibid s 7.

5   The Act does not define habitual residence but it is a phrase used also in the Adoption Act
    1976 and much debated in a variety of cases. See for example *Cruse v Chittum* [1974] 2
    All ER 940; *Shah v Barnet LBC ex p Nilish Shah* [1983] 2AC 309; *V v B (A Minor)
    (Abduction)* [1991] 1 FLR 266 and *Re W (A Minor) (Care Proceedings: Residence)* 1991
    Fam Law 265 where residence for 14 days was sufficient to found jurisdiction in care
    proceedings.

6   For definition of "continuing" see Family Law Act 1986 s 42(2) and (3).

7   Ibid, s 3(2), (7).

8   Ibid s 13(6).

9   So long as the order continues in force, ibid s 3(3).

10 Ibid s 2(3)(b)

11 There is no jurisdiction to make an unborn child a ward of court, see *Re F (in Utero)* [1988]
    2 All ER 193 CA

12 *Re P (GE) (An Infant)* [1964] 3 All ER 977 CA. *Harben v Harben* [1957] 1 All ER 379
    at 381; *Re Willoughby (An Infant)* [1885] 30 Ch D 324, CA; *Hope v Hope* (1854) 4 De
    GM & G 328.

13 See *Re Mohamed Arif* [1968] Ch 643; *Re F (A Minor)* [1989] 1 All ER 1155 CA

14 Children Act 1989 s 100(2)(c)

15 Ibid s 100(2)-(5)

16 Supreme Court Act 1981 s 61 (1), Sch 1 para 3 (b)(ii).

17 For example *ex p Whitfield* (1742) 2 Atk 315 at 316: *Clayton v Clarke* (1861) 7 Jur NS
    562 at 563. The jurisdiction continues although the infant becomes of unsound mind:
    Vane v Vane (1876) 2 Ch D 124; *Re Edwards* (1879) 10 Ch D 605, CA. See further post
    para 230

18 *Scott v Scott* [1913] AC 417 at 437, HL. See also *Re D* [1976] Fam 185, [1976] 1 All ER
    326 (where an 11 year old girl was made a ward of court in a successful attempt to prevent
    her from being permanently sterilised even though her mother had consented to the
    operation).

19 For further detailed consideration of these powers, see post para 230.

20 *Re R (A Minor) (Wardship: Medical Treatment)* [1992] Fam 11, at p 24 [1991] 4 All ER
    177, at p186 CA, and see also *Re J (A Minor) (Inherent Jurisdiction: Consent to
    Treatment)* [1992] 2 FLR 165, CA.

21 *Re C (An infant)* [1959] Ch 363, [1958] 2 All ER 656.

22 *Re Mohamed Arif* [1968] Ch 643, where an attempt was made to obtain a fresh hearing
    and decision as to an applicant's right to admission under the Commonwealth Immigrants
    Act 1962 by the use of wardship proceedings cf *Re K and S* [1991] 1 FLR 432 FD where
    HOLLIS J continued the wardship of children who were to be deposited with their parents
    as illegally resident in England.

23 See *Re A (A Minor: Wardship: Police Caution)* [1989] Fam 103, [1989] 3 All ER 610, and
    see *Re R (Wardship: Criminal Proceedings)* [1991] Fam 56, [1991] 2 All ER 193, CA,
    in which it was held that the consent of the wardship court was required as a pre-condition
    to the right of the police to interview a ward or for the prosecution to do so.

24 Children Act 1989 s 96 (3).

25 Children (Admissibility of Hearsay Evidence) Order 1991, SI 1991/1115.

229. Making a minor a ward of court. Before 1949 a minor could become a ward
of court in a number of ways[1]. Now the only way is to seek an order to that effect[2] by
issuing an originating summons[3] out of the principal registry or certain district
registries of the Family Division of the High Court[4]. The plaintiff is required under
the new rules of court to file an affidavit in support of the application when the
originating summons is issued[5]. Unless the court otherwise directs, the plaintiff must
state in the summons the whereabouts of the minor, or that the plaintiff is unaware

of his whereabouts[6]. He must give the minor's address, if he has it, the name and address of any person with whom the minor is living and any other relevant information[7].

Every defendant, apart from the minor, must forthwith, after being served with the summons, lodge in the registry out of which the summons was issued a notice stating the defendant's address and the whereabouts of the minor, or that the defendant is unaware of the minor's whereabouts[8]. Unless the court otherwise directs, the defendant must serve a copy of the notice on the plaintiff[9].

Where any party other than the minor changes his address or becomes aware of any change in the minor's whereabouts after the issue or service of the summons, he must, unless the court otherwise directs, forthwith lodge notice of the change in the registry out of which the summons issued and serve a copy of the notice on every party[10].

At or before the time of the first hearing of the originating summons, proof of the minor's date of birth should, whenever possible, be given by lodgment of a birth certificate. Failing this, directions as to proof of birth will be given by the district judge[11]. Particulars of any summons issued in a district registry must be sent by the proper officer to the principal registry for recording in the register of wards[12].

Every originating summons to make a child a ward of court must be indorsed with a notice to the effect that it is a contempt of court to take a ward of court out of England and Wales without leave[13].

The minor becomes a ward of court upon the issue of the summons but ceases to be a ward if an appointment for the hearing of the summons has not been obtained within 21 days after its issue[14]. When an application for such an appointment is made the return date must not, without the leave of the district judge be later than 28 days from the date on which the appointment is taken[15].

Virtually any person who has an interest in the minor may apply, although usually the application is by the father, mother or guardian; in rare cases the minor may apply by his next friend[16].

If there is no person other than the minor who is a suitable defendant, an application may be made ex parte to a district judge of the Family Division for leave to issue either an ex parte originating summons, or an originating summons with the minor as defendant to the summons[17]. Unless leave is granted, the minor must not be made a defendant in the first instance[18]. In cases in which the ward has formed an undesirable association with another person, that other person should not be made a party to the summons but should be made a defendant in a summons within the wardship proceedings for injunction or committal[19].

Information obtained by any person in connection with wardship is confidential, and must be disclosed by him if, but only if, it is necessary for the proper execution of his duties, or if requested by a court. Application may be made to the court for directions as to what records and information should be made available and whether it should be in the form of a confidential report[20]. If a party wishes to introduce the evidence of a welfare officer, a children's officer or similar local authority officer or a probation officer, directions should be sought from a district judge as to any inquiries such officer should make[21].

Although it is provided that no information regarding wardship and other proceedings in private relating to children may be published[22], the President of the Family Division considers that the parties to such proceedings may obtain transcripts of them without the court's leave. Those who are not parties may obtain a transcript only in special circumstances and by leave of the judge[23].

Disclosure of evidential documents to non parties in wardship without the leave of the court may be a contempt of court even if the disclosure was only to obtain the advice of an expert as to whether expert evidence would be forthcoming or helpful to the court[24].

The appointment of the Official Solicitor — the appointment of the Official Solicitor to act as guardian ad litem of a child who is the subject of wardship proceedings may be done either on the application of any party to the proceedings, or of the courts' own motion. The appointment of a guardian ad litem in wardship proceedings is entirely at the discretion of the court[25] and where the court deems it to be necessary then the Official Solicitor should be invited to act[26]. His consent is necessary but is usually granted, unless it would involve him in a conflict of duties. Where one of the parties believes that someone other than the Official Solicitor should be appointed to represent the child, or where the Official Solicitor believes the case is not appropriate for him to be involved then such issues need to be referred to a judge of the Family Division for resolution.[27] Unlike the system of dual representation by a lawyer and a guardian ad litem (drawn from the social work profession) in care and associated proceedings, the Official Solicitor's appointment in wardship proceedings combines both functions within the one office. Thus, he acts not only as guardian ad litem of the child but also as his own solicitor. He does not however act on the instructions of the child in the same way as the solicitor in care proceedings. He expects to put forward the views of what is in the best interests of the child, and to set out what the child's views are but not to act specifically on the child's instructions[28]. The Official Solicitor is an officer of the court and obviously cannot personally conduct all cases, but is assisted by a staff who where they appear in court to represent the child will be legally qualified and who otherwise will be civil service personnel. Thus, interviewing of the child and other parties may be delegated to a member of the civil service who does not necessarily have a social work or probation qualification, but who has been deemed suitable to conduct such work. Such staff will assist in the preparation of a report to the court, which is intended to be the material evidence in relation to the ward's interests. Where the staff in the Official Solicitor's department feel that the report of an expert should be obtained[29], or for example that a child should be blood tested[30] then the court must be approached for appropriate directions or orders. Because of sheer pressure of work the courts have increasingly sought the assistance of the court welfare service either additionally or as an alternative to the appointment of the Official Solicitor[31]. In determining whether to appoint a welfare officer[32] or the Official Solicitor, or both, the court is obliged to look at their different functions. The duty of the welfare officer is to prepare an objective report on the child, his background and what is perceived to be in the child's best interests.[33] The role of the Official Solicitor however embraces not only the preparation or use of a report but actually advocating, using all the relevant material, a course of action which he deems to be in the child's best interests[34]. Once the Official Solicitor has been appointed as guardian ad litem for the child, he remains an interested party and thus should be notified in any subsequent applications of his right to be heard on the application[35].

Costs and Legal Aid — One of the problems which has always been associated with wardship is the cost of the proceedings for the court has an unfettered discretion to make such order as it thinks fit[36]. Where parents have taken proceedings and both are acting in the child's best interests, an order for costs will normally be made between the parties or an order for security of costs[37] may be made after hearing the parties involved[38]. Where a local authority or other individual has instituted the proceedings an order for costs may be made against that body or person, but there are no fixed rules. Where a party is on legal aid his liability for costs should be restricted to that which is reasonable for him to pay having regard to all the circumstances[39]. Where it has been felt to be appropriate to appoint the Official Solicitor to act this should be done without regard to the effects of costs on the parties to the proceedings. If the Official Solicitor has been appointed by the court of its own motion it is possible for no order for costs to be made, although it may equally be just to order one of the parties to pay the Official Solicitor's costs depending on the circumstances of the case.[36] Where however the Official Solicitor's appointment was made on the application of one of the parties, the court may then consider it right to order either that that party bears the costs of the Official Solicitor or that the costs of the Official Solicitor be shared equally between the parties or in such proportions as the court deems equitable[40].

Legal aid is available for parties considering taking, or who are actually involved in wardship proceedings[41] provided the normal means and merits tests are satisfied[42]. However in view of the considerable costs of wardship and the availability of the range of orders generally made under the Children Act 1989[43], practitioners should exercise care in completing the legal aid application form in order to properly demonstrate the necessity for wardship in all the circumstances of the case. Where wardship is being considered in an emergency, practices of local Legal Aid Boards differ with some granting emergency certificates over the phone whilst others insist on submission of an application in writing. Once the final orders in the wardship case have been made and the work for which the legal aid certificate was granted has been completed the certificate is discharged. Where any further step such as an appeal[44] is being considered a fresh application for legal aid should be made[45].

1 Ie usually by the settlement of a small sum of money upon the minor, followed by an action for the administration of the trusts of the settlement.
2 Supreme Court Act 1981 s 41. See *Re E (An Infant)* [1956] Ch 23, [1955] 3 All ER 174.
3 Family Proceedings Rules 1991, SI 1991/1247, r 5.
4 Ibid 5, 1(1).
5 Ibid r 5.1 (1).
6 Ibid r 5.1 (7).
7 Ibid r 5.1 (11).
8 Ibid r 5.1 (8).
9 Ibid r 5.1 (8).
10 Ibid r 5.1 (9).
11 Ibid r 5.1 (5).
12 Ibid r 5.1 (4).
13 *Practice Direction* [1977] 3 All ER 122, [1977] 1 WLR 1018.
14 Supreme Court Act 1981 s 41 (2); Family Proceedings Rules 1991, r 5.3 (1).
15 *Practice Direction* [1966] 3 All ER 144, [1966] 1 WLR 1384.
16 The name of each party to the proceedings must be qualified by a brief description of his interest in or relationship to, the ward: Family Proceedings Rules 1991, r 5.1 (6).
17 Ibid r 5.1 (3).
18 Ibid r 5.1 (3).
19 *Practice Direction* [1983] 2 All ER 672, [1983] 1 WLR 790.
20 *Practice Direction* [1968] 1 All ER 762, [1968] 1 WLR 373.
21 See *C v C* (1972) Times 6 November, *Re C (A Minor)* (1983) Times, 2 December and *Practice Direction* [1983] 1 All ER 1097, [1983] 1 WLR 416. See also *Re C (Minors)* (1984) Times, 19 June.
22 Administration of Justice Act 1960 s 12. This prohibition extends to cover not only the proceedings but also any documents, which in the case of *Re F (Otherwise A) (A Minor)* [1977] 1 All ER 114, CA included the Official Solicitor's Report prepared for the court. Showing the papers to other interested personnel is also prohibited, for example: showing papers to an independent social worker, see *Practice Direction* [1983] 1 All ER 1097, and

Re C (Wardship: Independent Social Worker) [1985] FLR 56; to medical officers: *Practice Direction* [1987] 3 All ER 640; to intending adopters and their legal advisers: *Practice Direction* [1989] 1 All ER 169; and to using them in different legal proceedings: see *Re S (Minors)* [1987] 3 All ER 1076; *Re X, Y and Z* [1992] 2 All ER 595; and *Re M* (1992) Independent, 26 August CA.

23 *Practice Direction* [1972] 1 All ER 1056, sub nom *Practice Note* [1972] 1 WLR 443. This Practice Direction was considered in *Re R (M J) (An Infant) (Publication of Transcript)* [1975] Fam 89, [1975] 2 All ER 749. The court has discretion to give leave in a proper case to publish information relating to wardship and adoption proceedings held in private. Thus in the present case the interest of the minor was outweighed by the public interest in upholding the law by providing relevant evidence for use in other legitimate proceedings relating to the bankruptcy of the father of the child. Publication of information in proceedings about a ward is not a contempt without knowledge of the newspaper publishing the information see *Re F (Otherwise A) (A Minor)* [1977] Fam 58, [1977] 1 All ER 114, CA.

24 See *Practice Direction (Wardship: Evidence)* [1987] 3 All ER 640, [1987] 1 WLR 1421 and see further *W v Egdell* [1990] 1 All ER 835; *Re an ex p Originating Summons in an Adoptive Application* [1990] 1 All ER 639, *Practice Direction* [1990] 1 All ER 640, *Re M* [1990] 2 FLR 36; *B v M* 1990 2 All ER 155, *Re X, Y and Z* [1992] 2 All ER 595; and *Re M* (1992) Independent 26 August CA.

25 See for example, *Taylor v Taylor* (1975) Fam Law 151, CA.

26 See *Re A,B,C and D (Minors) (Wardship: Guardian ad litem)* [1988] 2 FLR 500

27 Ibid.

28 See the comments of GOFF J in *Re R (PM) (An Infant)* [1968] 1 All ER 691 at 692 and see Venables D. *The Official Solicitor: Outline and Aspects of his Work* (1990) Fam Law 53, Note also the very ambiguous wording of Family Proceedings Rules 1991, r 9.2(1).

29 See *Re S (Infants)* [1967] 1 All ER 202 *Re R P M (An Infant)* sup cit r 28 *B (M) v B (R)* [1968] 3 All ER 170;

30 *Practice Direction* [1988] 2 All ER 103.

31 An increase in business from 62 applications in 1950 to 4327 in 1989, Civil Judicial Statistics 1989 London HMSO.

32 An increased reliance on welfare officers also came about as a result of the power in the Matrimonial and Family Proceedings Act 1984 to transfer wardship proceedings to the county court, which was extended by Children Act 1989 to any other proceedings which relate to the exercise of the inherent jurisdiction of the High Court in respect of children.

33 See however *Practice Direction* [1984] 1 All ER 69.

34 Re *W and W (Minors)* (1975) 5 Fam Law 157 CA; *Re J D (Wardship: Guardian ad litem)* [1984] FLR 359.

35 *Re H (a Minor)* [1985] 3 All ER 1 CA.

36 *Re G (a Minor) (Wardship Costs)* [1982] 2 All ER 32; Supreme Court Act 1981 s 51(1).

37 *Re B (Infants)* [1965] 2 All ER 651 parents should be able to put their case concerning the child's welfare and ought not to be prevented from doing so by reason of an order for security for costs.

38 *H v H and C* [1969] 1 All ER 262.

39 Legal Aid Act 1988, s 17.

40 See *Re G* sup cit r 36 and also *Re P C (An Infant)* [1961] 2 All ER 308.

41 Legal Aid Act 1988 s 14 and Sch 2.

42 Ibid s 15.

43 Children Act 1989 s 8, 16

44 See ante paras 29-36.

45 *Practice Direction (Wardship Proceedings)* [1983] 1 All ER 1097.

230. Court's powers over ward. A ward of court may not be removed out of the jurisdiction of the court without the leave of the court[1], he may not marry without the court's consent[2], and his education and the religion in which he is to be brought up are in the court's control and subject to its direction. The person having the custody or care and control of the ward is, indeed, under a duty to obtain the court's directions on any major issue affecting the ward's welfare[3]. Indeed it can be said that as soon as a child has been made a ward of court "no important step in the child's life can be taken without the court's consent"[4]. As to what constitutes such an important step, reference must be made to the plethora of decided cases on this issue[5], as well as to the provisions of the Rules of Court[6], and statutes.[7] Thus, any move of a ward from one set of foster parents to another requires leave[8], whereas if the family with whom the ward is living changes their residence it would be sufficient to notify the relevant Registry[9]. Any change in the ward's education requires leave[10] and leave is also necessary to commence proceedings to adopt the ward[11] or have her declared free for adoption.[12] In the fields of medical decisions a *Practice Direction*[13] has made it clear that leave is not required for physical examinations, although it will be required for psychiatric or psychological examinations. Any procedure necessitating operative or invasive treatment will require leave[14] for example tonsilectomy, abortion[15], sterilisation[16] and treatment in a special unit.[17] It will also be necessary to seek directions from the court on other matters relating to the medical treatment of the ward, such as the giving of contraceptive or abortion advice or treatment. It would also appear from the decisions of the Court of Appeal in *Re R*[18] and later in *Re W*[17] that the wardship court's powers are even more extensive than those of parents since it has the right to override both a "Gillick competent" child's refusal to have treatment, as well as her consent to treatment, where it believes such action is necessary to protect the ward's interests, future and upbringing, including, in addition to the matters referred to above, contumacious interference with the ward, untoward events[19] or tendencies in his career, and any proceedings proposed to be brought on his behalf or against him.

The court is not limited to the dispute between the parties. It may look beyond such submissions and act in the manner which will serve the welfare of the ward[20].

1 See Paragraph 231 post.
2 Marriage Act 1949 s 3 (6). Wardship proceedings are occasionally instituted with a view to preventing undesirable associations and runaway marriages.
3 *Re J (A Minor)*[1984] FLR 535: the court refused an application that a ward who was a witness in a criminal matter, should undergo a psychiatric examination or that an existing report relating to the ward should be disclosed to assist in the criminal proceedings: see *Practice Direction* [1989] 1 All ER 169, [1989] 1 WLR 136. Also in *Re A* [1989] Fam 103, [1989] 3 All ER 610 the court made it clear that where it was proposed to caution a ward under the guidelines set out in Home Office Circular 1985/14 it was the court itself whose consent was required as parent or guardian under Clause 4. The presence of the parent at the formal cautioning would be satisfied by the court directing someone to represent them. In this case the court directed that the local authority should do so. No specific person was named, in case unforeseen circumstances prevented their attendance.
4 per CROSS J in *Re S (Infants)* [1967] 1 All ER 202, 209.
5 See for example *F v S (Adoption: Ward)* [1973] 1 All ER 722, CA; *Re CB (A Minor) (Wardship: Local Authority)* [1981] 1 All ER 16; Re C [1990 1 FLR 152.
6 For example Family Proceedings Rules 1991 SI 1991/1247 r 5.1(9).
7 For example Mental Health Act 1983, s 33.
8 See *Re C B (A Minor) (Wardship: Local Authority)* [1981] 1 All ER 16.
9 Family Proceedings Rules 1991, r 5.1(9).

10 Stated in the notice of wardship issued with the originating summons.

11 *F v S (Adoption: Ward)* [1973] 1 All ER 722, CA.

12 *Re F (Wardship: Adoption)* [1984] FLR 60, CA. Application can be made ex parte to a district judge, see Family Proceedings Rules 1991 r 5.4(1)(b).

13 [1985] 3 All ER 576.

14 Unless it is an emergency when generally the operation would proceed without consent.

15 *Re GU (A Minor) (Wardship)* [1984] FLR 811, and see *Re B* [1991] 2 FLR 426.

16 *Re B (A Minor) (Wardship: Sterilisation)* [1988] AC 199 but note the decision in *Re E (A Minor) (Medical Treatment)* [1991] 2 FLR 585 where the court held that its consent was not required to perform an operation for therapeutic purposes even where a side effect was to sterilise the child.

17 *Re W (A Minor) (Inherent Jurisdiction: Consent to Treatment)* (1992) Times, 15 July, CA reported as *Re W* [1992] FCR 785 and for an earlier example of the same approach see *Re E (A Minor) (Wardship: Medical Treatment)* [1992] 2 FCR 219, FD

18 [1991] 4 All ER 177 CA.

19 See *H v London Borough of Lambeth* (1984) Times, 5 April.

20 See *Re E (A Minor)* [1984] 1 All ER 21.

231. Removal from jurisdiction. The removal of a ward out of the jurisdiction or out of proper custody without the leave of the court is a contempt of court[1]. The court will not allow a ward to be removed from its jurisdiction, even for a short holiday or by the father[2], unless satisfied that it is for the ward's benefit[3]. Application for leave is by summons supported by factual evidence and an undertaking to return the ward[4]. The strict operation of the rules on removal are modified somewhat by the provisions of the Family Law Act 1986[5]. Pursuant to the Act a ward may now be removed to another part of the United Kingdom, ie Scotland or Northern Ireland[6] where divorce or other matrimonial proceedings relating to the ward's parents are continuing[7] or the child is habitually resident there[8]. Where in either situation the other part of the UK is Scotland then the ward must be under sixteen in order to be lawfully removed[9]. Removal to any other place is also permissible where it is made with the consent of the appropriate court in the other part of the United Kingdom[10] or with the consent of the court before which the matrimonial proceedings are pending[11].

Where the court is satisfied that a ward should be able to leave England and Wales for temporary visits abroad without the necessity for special leave, it may make an order giving general leave for such visits, subject to certain conditions. The party obtaining the order must lodge at the registry where the matter is proceeding, at least 7 days before each proposed departure:

1. written consent by the other party to the ward's leaving the country, and
2. a written statement giving the date of departure, the period of absence and the whereabouts of the minor during such absence.
3. further, unless the court otherwise directs, the applicant must give a written undertaking to return the ward at the end of the proposed period.

If these requirements are met, the party may obtain a certificate to that effect from the registry for production to the immigration authorities[12]. Application may be made by summons to stop the unauthorised removal of the ward out of the jurisdiction[13], or to compel the ward's return.

The court may grant an injunction restraining the removal of the ward from the court's jurisdiction and in cases where the apparent threat comes from a foreign passport holder this may be the only safe course. The court may further order the surrender of any British passport issued to, or which contains any particulars of, the ward[14].

Official requests may be made by the district judge for information from the National Health Service records, the Department of Social Security, the Passport Office, or the Ministry of Defence, to help trace the whereabouts of a missing ward or of the person with whom a missing ward is said to be[15].

1 *Hockly v Lukin* (1762) 1 Dick 353; *Long Wellesley's Case* (1831) 2 Russ & M 639; *Harrison v Goodall* (1852) Kay 310; *Re J (an Infant)* (1913) 108 LT 554. An order will be made even though it cannot be enforced owing to the person in contempt being out of the jurisdiction: *Re an Infant* (1954) Times, 13 January. See also *Practice Direction* [1984] 2 All ER 407.
2 *De Manneville v De Manneville* (1804) 10 Ves 52.
3 *Re Callaghan, Elliot v Lambert* (1884) 28 Ch D 186, CA; *Re Benner (Infants)* [1951] WN 436.
4 The court (ie judge or district judge) usually requires a written undertaking, given by the person who has care and control or custody of the ward, that the ward will return within the jurisdiction within a given time or when so ordered. Leave will be given if it is for the benefit of the ward that he be taken out of the jurisdiction, and if there is no reason to doubt that the ward will be returned within the jurisdiction before the expiry of the period stipulated by the order giving leave. See the Supreme Court Practice 1991 para 2113.
5 Ss 38, 42, 32 and 40.
6 Family Law Act 1986 s 42(1).
7 Ibid s 42(4).
8 Ibid s 38(1) and (2).
9 Ibid
10 Ibid ss 40 and 32.
11 Ibid s 38 (3)(b)
12 *Practice Direction* [1973] 2 All ER 512, sub nom *Practice Note* [1973] 1 WLR 690.
13 Eg, in the case of attempts at runaway marriages, which frequently gave rise to wardship proceedings. For an order see Form 236 post. In a matrimonial cause begun by petition either spouse may at any time apply ex parte for an order prohibiting the removal of any minor child of the family out of England and Wales without the leave of the court except on such terms as may be specified in the order; such an application may be made to a district judge: see *Practice Direction* [1973] 2 All ER 400, [1973] 1 WLR 657; *Practice Direction* [1973] 3 All ER 194, [1973] 1 WLR 1014.
14 *Practice Direction* [1983] 2 All ER 253, [1983] 1 WLR 558.
15 *Practice Direction* [1973] 1 All ER 61; sub nom *Practice Note* [1973] 1 WLR 60 as amended by *Practice Direction* [1979] 2 All ER 1106. For the port alert procedure see *Practice Direction* [1986] 1 All ER 983, [1986] 1 WLR 475.

232. Education. Directions of the court should be taken in relation to the education[1] or proposed changes in the education of a ward who is under the control of the court[2]. The court cannot give directions at variance with the Education Act 1944 and should not interfere with a local education authority's exercise of its statutory powers.[3] Nevertheless the jurisdiction in wardship remains,[4] but the court must observe the restrictions imposed by the Children Act 1989[5] and avoid clashes with local education authorities. Thus the assertion in *Tameside Metropolitan Borough Council v Shofield*[6] that the wardship court has a full and unfettered jurisdiction to decide a ward's educational future notwithstanding the statutory code[7] was described by Woolf J in *Re D (a Minor)*[4] as clearly going too far. He stated that "the court in wardship proceedings cannot prevent the local education authority from exercising their statutory jurisdiction if they decide to do so".[8] However in that case no conflict or other difficulty had arisen. The wardship proceedings supplemented any powers which the local authority wanted to exercise but did not purport to oust such powers or their exercise.[9]

1 "Education" includes where the minor was to be educated: see *Beale v Governors of Edgehill College* (1984) Times, 12 January, CA.
2 *Creuze (Cruise) v Hunter* (1790) 2 Cox Eq Cas 242; *Campbell v Mackay* (1837) 2 My & Cr 31 at 38; *Kay v Johnston* (1856) 21 Beav 536.
3 *Re B (Infants)* [1962] Ch 201, [1961] 3 All ER 276, CA.
3 *Re Baker (Infants)* [1961] 3 All ER 276 and see Pearson LJ at p286.
4 See *Re D (a Minor)* [1987] 3 All ER 717.
5 See Children Act 1989 s 100.
6 *Tameside Metropolitan Borough Council v Shoheld* [1987] 3 All ER 729.
7 Ibid per WAITE J at p736.
8 *Re D (A Minor)* [1987] 3 All ER 717 at p 730.
9 Ibid.

233. Religion. The court will decide the religion in which the ward is to be brought up in the circumstances of the case and with the ward's welfare as the paramount consideration[1]. Any attempt to make the ward change his religion will be restrained by the court by injunction[2].

1 *Talbot v Earl of Shrewsbury, Doyle v Wright* (1840) 4 My & Cr 672; *Re Lyons (An Infant)* (1869) 22 LT 770.
2 *Iredell v Iredell* (1885) 1 TLR 260.

234. Orders available in wardship proceedings. Wardship will continue provided the procedure laid down under the relevant court rules is followed, and where the case proceeds to a full hearing, the judge must make a decision as to whether to confirm or to discharge the wardship[1]. Wardship proceedings are regarded as family proceedings under the provisions of the Children Act and the court is thus empowered to make any Section 8 orders under the Act[2]. Whilst there have as yet been no reported cases on the inter-relationship between wardship and Section 8 orders, it would appear from a consideration of the nature of the orders that a residence order would not be inconsistent with the court's control over its ward and thus such an order could be made[3]. A relevant question may be, however, whether there is any necessity to continue a wardship once a residence order has been made. Where the wardship does continue, however, the parents will exercise parental responsibility subject to the general direction of the court and the need to obtain the court's consent with regard to any important step in the child's life[4].

Where someone seeks contact with the child in wardship proceedings it would again seem appropriate for the court to make a Section 8 contact order and if it is felt necessary to place before the court specific questions that the court could determine on making a specific issues order[5].

Similarly if an order is thought to be necessary to prevent some action being taken then a prohibited steps order could be issued. It should also be stressed that whilst it is no longer possible in wardship proceedings to commit a child into the care of the local authority, the wardship court when hearing a case can, since the hearing would be deemed to be family proceedings under the Children Act, decide whether or not to exercise its powers under Section 37 of the Act to direct the local authority to investigate a child's circumstances[6] and further to make an interim care order in the meantime[7].

1 Family Proceedings Rules 1991, SI 1991/1247, r 5.3 (1) and see *Re F (Minors: Wardship: Jurisdiction)* [1988] FCR 679, [1988] 2 FLR 123, CA.
2 See Children Act 1986 s 8 (3).
3 Children Act 1989 s 8 (1) and compare with *Re J (Abduction: Ward of Court)* [1989] Fam 85, [1989] 3 All ER 590.
4 Ibid s 8.
5 Ibid s 8.
6 Ibid s 37 court's powers to direct an investigation.
7 Ibid s 3.

235. Protection of wards. The power of the courts to impose restrictions on publication for the protection of children is derived from the inherent jurisdiction of the High Court exercising the powers of the Crown as *parens patriae*[1]. In proceedings involving children in care the court has jurisdiction to grant an injunction restraining the press from publishing any information of a sensitive nature concerning the proceedings. However, the court will not automatically grant an injunction in restraint of publication but will balance the freedom of the press to publish an article governing children in care against the protection of the children involved and any detriment which the publicity would thereby cause[2]. Where the court finds that an injunction is necessary the order restricting the publication must be in clear terms, the limits of the restraint must be defined and the persons against whom the order is made must be clearly identified.[3] Publication in breach of any such order is punishable as contempt where it amounts to contempt at common law[4] that is where the party in contempt had mens rea[5]. An order restraining publication by a newspaper is a prohibitory injunction and must be brought to the specific attention of the newspaper individually, rather than relying upon any sort of general notice having been given[6].

1 *Re M and N (Minors)(Wardship: Publication of Information)* [1990] Fam 211, [1990] 1 All ER 205, CA, per BUTLER-SLOSS LJ.
2 *Re M and N (Minors)(Wardship: Publication of Information)*(supra). In that case the direction for service on newspapers etc was worded as follows: "And it is directed that the Plaintiff do forthwith circulate copies of this order by post to the editors of all national newspapers, and of all local newspapers circulated in the Rutley area and in the Plaintiff's Local Authority area and to the news editors of the [BBC], [ITN], the Independent Television contractors, and all local radio stations in the [Rutley] area and in [London]".
3 *Re L (a Minor) (Wardship: Freedom of Publication)* [1988] 1 All ER 418; *Re M and N (Minors)* [1990] 1 All ER 205.
4 See *Re F (Otherwise A) (A Minor) (Publication of Information)* [1977] Fam 58; [1977] 1 All ER 114 CA; *Re L (a Minor) (Wardship: Freedom of Publication)* [1988] 1 All ER 418; *Pickering v Liverpool Daily Post and Echo Newspapers Plc* [1991] 1 All ER 622 HL at 633-634 per Lord Bridge.
5 Ibid.
6 See RSC Ord r 45-7(7) and *Re W (Wards) (Publication of Information)* [1989] 1 FLR 246.

236. Marriage. A ward may not marry without the consent of the court[1], even though all other consents have been obtained[2]. Marriage, or connivance at marriage[3] without such consent is a contempt[4], and the ward may be committed for marrying without it[5]. Where the court refuses its consent an injunction will be granted to restrain the marriage[6].

Application may be made to the court to restrain marriage or communication with or by a ward[7]. If the whereabouts of the man whom it is sought to restrain are not known, an application may be made to the court by summons addressed to and served upon any parties to the originating summons in the wardship proceedings other than the applicants, but including the ward. The person whom it is sought to restrain should not be made a party, but the summons should, if possible, be served on him[8]. One has thus the unusual position of an application for an injunction against a person who is not a party to the proceedings. If there are no persons who ought to be and can be served, the application can be made ex parte. An ex parte application can also be made where there are persons who ought to be and can be served but where some immediate relief is wanted before they can be served.

The judge frequently refrains from making an injunction against the ward herself, in order to avoid the risk of having to commit her in the event of a breach. If the order is made in the absence of the persons restrained they cannot be committed[9]: until the order has been served on them, except, perhaps, if they married with knowledge of the substantive proceedings and their result and effect.

1 *Eyre v Countess of Shaftesbury* (1725) 2 P Wms 102; *Jeffrys v Vanteswarstwarth* (1740) Barn Ch 141, *Tombes v Elers* (1747) 1 Dick 88. The consent of the father is not sufficient: *Wellesley v Duke of Beaufort* (1827) 2 Russ 1. This applies to both male and female wards.
2 Marriage Act 1949 s 3 (6); Where the minor is not a ward of court application may be made under ibid s 3 (1) provisos (a), (b). See Paragraph 95 ante.
3 *Long v Elways* (1729) Mos 249.
4 *Eyre v Countess of Shaftesbury* (supra); *Re Sampson and Wall (Infants)* (1888) 25 Ch D 482, CA.
5 *Re Leigh, Leigh v Leigh* (1888) 40 Ch D 290, CA, *Re H's Settlement, H v H* [1909] 2 Ch 260.
6 *Smith v Smith* (1745) 3 Atk 304. The order need not be confined to the minority of the ward: *Pearce v Crutchfield* (1807) 14 Ves 206. An undertaking to abide by the directions of the court will not enable an injunction to be granted to prevent marriage after the ward has attained 21 (now of course the age would be 18); *Bolton v Bolton* [1891] 3 Ch 270.
7 *Beard v Travers* (1749) 1 Ves Sen 313; *Pearce v Crutchfield* (supra); *Scott v Padwick* (1888) 4 TLR 569.
8 *Practice Direction* [1983] 2 All ER 672, [1983] 1 WLR 790. Such a person should not be added to the title of the proceedings nor allowed to see any documents other than those relating to the summons. The judges of the Family Division consider that any such person should be allowed time within which to obtain representation and any order for an injunction should extend over a few days only.
9 The court hearing an application for committal arising out of wardship proceedings (and indeed, proceedings relating to the adoption, guardianship, residence, maintenance or upbringing of a minor, or to issues of contact with a minor) may sit in private (RSC Ord 52 r 6 (1)(a)), but if it decides to make an order of committal it must state in open court the name of the person committed, in general terms the nature of the contempt of court, and, if the committal is for a fixed period, the length of the period (RSC Ord 52 r 6 (2)(a)(c)).

237. Termination of wardship. The minor remains a ward of court until he attains 18[1] or the court otherwise orders[2]. The court may at any time, either upon an application in that behalf or without such an application, order that a minor who is for the time being a ward shall cease to be a ward[3]. The court has no jurisdiction over a ward after he has attained full age; it cannot interfere with the marriage of a former ward, or compel a settlement of his property, unless the marriage involves a contempt of court[4].

1   Family Law Reform Act 1969 s 1.
2   Supreme Court Act 1981 s 41 (2).
3   Supreme Court Act 1981 s 41 (3).
4   *Ball v Coutts* (1812) 1 Ves & B 292; *Bolton v Bolton* [1891] 3 Ch 270, CA. The court cannot interfere with the marriage of a minor who is not a ward of court, or compel a settlement of his property: *Re Potter* (1869) LR 7 Eq 484.

238. Maintenance for ward of court. The court's powers to make financial provision for wards of court is governed by the same provisions which are common to all children under the provisions of the Children Act 1989. It has, however, been held that there is further an inherent power in court to make an order for maintenance in respect of the children[2]. Such a power is thus in addition to the provisions contained in the Children Act 1989.

1   See the Children Act 1989 Sch 1. See also Paragraphs 141-160 ante.
2   *W v Avon County Council* (1979) 9 Fam Law 33 and see *Calderdale Borough Council v H and P* [1991] 1 FLR 461.

3: THE INHERENT JURISDICTION

239. Jurisdiction. An application to invoke the inherent jurisdiction of the High Court under the provisions of the Children Act 1989 must be made to the Family Division of that court and although no procedure is laid down under the Family Proceedings Rules, it is submitted that an application be begun in the same way as for wardship with the originating summons being drawn to reflect the difference in the jurisdiction[1]. As is the case with wardship, it would appear to be appropriate that the plaintiff should, unless directed otherwise, file an affidavit in support of an application where the summons is issued[2]. Individuals seeking to invoke the inherent jurisdiction of the High Court do not need to seek leave whereas local authorities would have to obtain leave of the court before they can invoke the jurisdiction[3].

1   See the Supreme Court Act 1981 Sch 1 para 3 (b)(ii)and the Family Proceedings Rules 1991, SI 1991/1247 and see also *Re W (Minors) (Medical Treatment: Court's Jurisdiction)* [1992] FCR 785.
2   See Family Proceedings Rules 1991 r 5.1 (1).
3   See Children Act 1989 s 100 (2), (3); for other cases relying on the inherent jurisdiction see ante para 227.

240. Effects of involving the inherent jurisdiction. It would appear that the effect of invoking the High Court's inherent jurisdiction is to give the court the power to make any orders which may be deemed to be necessary for the child and it would have to be shown that making an order is in the best interests of the child[1]. Since proceedings under the inherent jurisdiction are family proceedings under the provisions of the Children Act[2] it would appear that the court would be able to make any Section 8 orders or indeed an order under Section 16. As to the precise extent of any further powers that the court has, it could be argued that the jurisdiction should be at least as wide as that of wardship since both jurisdictions can invoke inherent powers. Wardship, however, is likely to be considered the wider jurisdiction since the effect is that final responsibility for the child is vested in the court. It could be suggested, however, that the inherent jurisdiction powers are more analogous to those under the Supreme Court Act 1981[3] and thus the court, if asked to grant an injunction without the provisions of Section 8 orders, would be restricted to making injunctions to protect legal or equitable rights[4].

1 Children Act 1989 s 1 (1) and see *Re W (A Minor) (Medical Treatment: Court's Jurisdiction)* [1992] FCR 785 originally reported as *Re J* 1992 Times July 15 CA..
2 Ibid s 8 (3).
3 Supreme Court Act 1981 s 37.
4 See *Richards v Richards* [1984] AC 174, [1983] 2 All ER 807, HL and see *Re D (A Minor)(Adoption Order: Validity)* [1991] Fam 137, [1991] 3 All ER 461, CA.

241. Local authorities' use of the inherent jurisdiction. It has been clearly stated[1] that local authorities are not any longer able to seek any back door route of getting a child committed into their care. Thus the inherent jurisdiction of the High Court cannot be invoked if the purpose of the local authority is: to achieve the committal into care of a child or to place a child under the supervision of a local authority; so as to require a child to be accommodated by or on behalf of a local authority; so as to make a child who is the subject of a care order a ward of court or for the purpose of conferring on any local authority power to determine any question which has arisen, or which may arise in connection with any aspects of parental responsibility for a child[2]. Therefore whilst the authority may seek to obtain leave to invoke the inherent jurisdiction, the court may only grant such leave if it is satisfied that the result which the authority wished to achieve could not be achieved through the making of any order which the local authority would be entitled to apply for and that there is reasonable cause to believe that if the court's inherent jurisdiction is not exercised with respect to a child, he would be likely to suffer significant harm[3]. This was indeed the case in *Re W*[4] also known as *Re J*[4] in 1992. The case involved a girl of 16 who was in the care of the local authority and thus would not be made a ward of court. Authority was therefore sought from the High Court exercising its inherent jurisdiction to authorise treatment of a 16 year old girl with anorexia where she was refusing treatment. The Court of Appeal stressed that the inherent jurisdiction of the court was exercisable in this case and would have been equally exercisable had the child been a ward of court. The court's powers it was said were theoretically limitless but there were far-reaching limitations in principle on the exercise of the inherent jurisdiction. The child's welfare was however the court's paramount consideration and, whilst the court would have regard to the view of a child of sufficient understanding to make an informal decision, if the child's welfare was threatened by a serious risk to his life or irreparable damage to his health, then the court should intervene and override the child's refusal of treatment[5].

It has already become apparent that the local authorities have been successful in invoking the inherent jurisdiction of the High Court where it has been necessary to determine whether an operation should take place in respect of a child who is in the care of the local authority and the parents are not agreeing to the operation being performed[6]. Similarly in situations where a child may be put at risk by being approached by a violent parent or a sexually abusing sibling then the only way in which the local authority may be able to protect the child will be by seeking an injunction granted by the High Court in the exercise of its inherent jurisdiction[7].

As has already been pointed out individuals do not need to seek the court's leave in order to be able to make an application to invoke the inherent jurisdiction of the High Court. Given the stance previously taken by the High Court in relation to its reluctance to interfere in children's cases where the children are the subject of care orders, it is unlikely that individual parents would meet with much success in seeking to invoke the inherent jurisdiction in order to challenge the care being given to a child by a local authority[8]. It is suggested that the only situation in which the court may consider exercising its inherent jurisdiction will be where there is some allegation that the local authority is acting in some way in breach or disregard of its statutory duties[9]. Even in those situations, however, it has been pointed out in a number of cases that the more appropriate step for the parent to take is to look to the use of the process of judicial review as the proper means by which the court can exercise supervisory control over statutory bodies[10].

1 See Paragraph 173 ante.
2 See the Children Act 1989 s 100 (2).
3 Ibid s 100 (4).
4 Originally reported in Times as *Re J* (1992) Times, 15 July, CA and as *Re W* in [1992] 2 FCR 785, CA and FD.
5 [1992] 2 FCR 785 at p810-811.
6 See for example *Re C (A Minor)(Wardship: Medical Treatment)* [1990] Fam 26, [1989] 2 All ER 782, CA.
7 *Re JT (A Minor)(Wardship: Committal)* [1986] 2 FLR 107, [1986] Fam LR 213; and *Re B (A Minor: Wardship: Child in Care)* [1975] Fam 36, [1974] 3 All ER 915.
8 See *A v Liverpool City Council* [1982] AC 363, [1981] 2 All ER 385, HL; *Re W (A Minor)*, [1985] AC 791; and see *W v Nottinghamshire County Council (Wardship: Jurisdiction)* [1986] 1 FLR 565, [1986] Fam Law 185, and *W v Shropshire County Council* [1986] 1 FLR 359, CA.
9 See per LORD WILBERFORCE in *A v Liverpool City Council* (supra) at 395.
10 See *Re DM (A Minor)(Wardship Jurisdiction)* [1986] 2 FLR 122, [1986] Fam Law 296, CA and see further *Re R M and L M (Minors)(Wardship: Jurisdiction)* [1986] 2 FLR 205, [1986] Fam Law 297 and *R v Hertfordshire County Council ex p B* , *R v Bedfordshire County Council, ex p C* [1987] 1 FLR 239, [1987] Fam Law 55, . See *Re S (A Minor: Care: Wardship)* [1987] FCR 85, [1987] 1 FLR 479, CA.

APPENDIX 1

The following are the parties to the Hague Convention on International Child Abduction and the dates of coming into force as between the United Kingdom and the State or Territory concerned[1].

Contracting States to the Convention	Territories specified in Declarations under Article 39 or 40 of the Convention	Date of Coming into Force as between the United Kingdom and the State or Territory
The Argentine Republic	—	1st June 1991
Australia	Australian States and mainland Territories	1st January 1987
Austria	—	1st October 1988
Belize	—	1st October 1989
Burkina		
Canada	Ontario	1st August 1986
	New Brunswick	1st August 1986
	British Columbia	1st August 1986
	Manitoba	1st August 1986
	Nova Scotia	1st August 1986
	Newfoundland	1st August 1986
	Prince Edward Island	1st August 1986
	Quebec	1st August 1986
	Yukon Territory	1st August 1986
	Saskatchewan	1st November 1986
	Alberta	1st February 1987
	Northwest Territories	1st April 1988
The Kingdom of Denmark	—	1st July 1991
Ecuador	—	1st April 1992
The French Republic	—	1st August 1986
Germany	—	1st December 1990
The Hungarian People's Republic	—	1st September 1986
Ireland	—	1st October 1991
Israel	—	1st December 1991
The Grand Duchy of Luxembourg	—	1st January 1987
Mexico	—	1st September 1991
Monaco	—	1st February 1993
The Kingdom of the Netherlands	—	1st September 1990
New Zealand	—	1st August 1991
Norway	—	1st April 1989
Poland	—	1st November 1992
The Portuguese Republic	—	1st August 1986
Romania	—	1st February 1993
Spain	—	1st September 1987
Sweden	—	1st June 1989
The Swiss Confederation	—	1st August 1986
The United States of America	—	1st July 1988
The Socialist Federal Republic of Yugoslavia	—	1st December 1991

---

1 Child Abduction and Custody (Parties to Conventions) Order 1986, SI 1986/1159, Sch 1 (as substituted by SI 1992/3199).

APPENDIX 2

The parties to the European Convention are set out as follows although a constant check should be made as to those countries which have implemented the Convention[1].

Contracting States to the Convention	Territories specified in Declarations under Article 39 or 40 of the Convention	Date of Coming into Force as between the United Kingdom and the State or Territory
The Republic of Austria	—	1st August 1986
The Kingdom of Belgium	—	1st August 1986
The Republic of China	—	1st October 1986
The French Republic	—	1st August 1986
The Federal Republic of Germany	—	1st February 1991
The Grand Duchy of Luxembourg	—	1st August 1986
The Kingdom of the Netherlands	—	1st September 1986
Norway	—	1st May 1986
The Portuguese Republic	—	1st August 1986
Spain	—	1st August 1986
Sweden	—	1st July 1986
The Swiss Confederation	—	1st August 1986

1 Child Abduction and Custody (Parties to Conventions) Order 1986, SI 1986/1159, Sch 2 (as substituted by SI 1990/2289).

Procedural Tables

Table 1: Infant plaintiff: High Court

NOTE: *The procedure described in this table applies to High Court actions other than probate actions [1], and covers:*

1. *The commencement of an action by a minor (Steps 1–4);*
2. *Acknowledgment of service and dismissal where a minor has sued as an adult (Steps 5–11);*
3. *The appointment of a new next friend (Steps 12–15); and*
4. *Infant plaintiff coming of age (Steps 16–27).*

Compromise is covered in Table 3, post.

Steps to be Taken	RSC
Either:	
1. Solicitor to proposed Infant Plaintiff ascertains from minor's parent or guardian name of person who is prepared to act as next friend [1].	
Time: At or as soon as practicable after the consultation: strictly, a solicitor can only receive instructions from the next friend, and not from a parent or guardian unless he is the next friend.	
A minor may not bring, or make a claim in, any proceedings except by his next friend.	**80,** 2 (1)
A next friend must act by a solicitor.	**80,** 2 (3)
2. Next friend gives written consent to act.	**80,** 3 (8) (a)
3. Solicitor to Infant Plaintiff certifies in writing: (1) that he knows or believes the Plaintiff to be a minor; and	**80,** 3 (8) (c) (i)
(2) *except where the next friend is the Official Solicitor:* that the proposed next friend has no interest adverse to that of the minor.	**80,** 3 (8) (c) (iii)
The certificate is usually indorsed on the next friend's consent to act, but may be given separately.	
The certificate should be signed by the solicitor personally, but he will be effectively committed by a certificate made and signed in the firm's name.	
4. Solicitor to Infant Plaintiff lodges in Central Office, Chancery Chambers or district registry:	**80,** 3 (7)
1. Next friend's consent to act; and	
2. Solicitor's certificate.	**80,** 3 (6)
Time: When issuing writ or originating summons.	**80,** 3 (6)
Or, *if Infant Plaintiff sues as an adult without a next friend:*	
5. Infant Plaintiff issues and serves on Defendant writ or originating summons.	
6. Defendant who wishes to challenge the issue of the writ or originating summons should file	

Steps to be Taken	RSC
acknowledgment of service containing notice of intention to defend, and then issue a summons for relief under RSC Ord 12 r 8. (*see step 8 infra*)	**12,** 1 **12,** 8
7. Defendant applies to court ex parte for stay of further proceedings until next friend is added.	**80,** 2 (1)
8. Defendant applies to court by summons or motion (*as the case may be*) to set aside writ or originating summons. *Time:* within the time limited for service of defence.	**12,** 8

9. Defendant issues summons and files supporting affidavit applying for order:
     1. That next friend be added; *or*
     2. Setting aside writ or originating summons; and
     3. That solicitor pay costs to Plaintiff.
     Time: Within time limited for service of defence or as directed by court[2].
	12, 8 (4)

10. Defendant serves summons and copy affidavit on Infant Plaintiff.	

11. Master hears summons and makes order either:
     1. Dismissing action with costs; or
     2. Directing addition of next friend.	

In any case, *if it becomes necessary to appoint a new next friend*[3]*:*	

12. Plaintiff by his present next friend or "next friend for the purposes of the application" applies to court for order appointing new next friend *either:*
     (1) by summons; *or*
 	
     (2) by notice under the summons for directions; *or*
     (3) *if the application arises because of the death of the former next friend:* by ex parte application.
     Time: As soon as circumstances necessitate the appointment.
     The application must be supported by:
     1. Consent to act of new next friend; and
     2. Affidavit as to facts.
 	
     If, for any reason other than death, the summons is not issued by the present next friend, it should be addressed to him.
     A new next friend cannot act until appointed by Court order.
	25, 7 (3)
	
	 80, 3 (4)

13. Plaintiff serves summons on Defendant and, unless the application is made by him or he is dead, on the present next friend.	

Steps to be Taken	RSC

14. Master hears application and makes order.

15. Plaintiff produces order at Central Office, Chancery Chambers or district registry (*as the case may be*) for noting in the Cause Book.

In any case, *if Infant Plaintiff comes of age[4] during course of action[5]:*

Either, *if Plaintiff adopts action:*

16. Plaintiff files in the Central Office, Chancery Chambers or district registry (*as the case may be*) for noting in the Cause Book notice that he is of full age and adopts the action.
  Time: As soon as practicable after he comes of age and gives the necessary instructions.
  He may at the same time file notice of change of solicitors.

17. Plaintiff serves notice of adoption of proceedings (and any notice of change of solicitors) on other parties (and, in the case of a change of solicitors, on former solicitor).
  Time: Immediately after filing.

18. Plaintiff intitules all subsequent proceedings "A. B. (formerly a Minor but now of full age), Plaintiff", and conducts subsequent proceedings as an adult.

Or, *if Plaintiff repudiates action:*

19. Plaintiff (by separate solicitor if there are other Plaintiffs) issues summons for order that action be dismissed or, if there are other Plaintiffs, that his name be struck out as a Plaintiff[6].
  Time: As soon as practicable after he comes of age and gives the necessary instructions.
  It is suggested that no evidence is necessary in the first place, but supporting and opposing affidavits may be required in some cases.
  Where appropriate, notice of change of solicitors will be required[7].

20. Plaintiff serves summons and affidavit on Defendant and on any other Plaintiffs.

21. Master or District Judge hears summons and may by order:
  1. Strike out former Infant Plaintiff as Plaintiff; *or*
  2. *On application of other Plaintiffs:* direct that former Infant Plaintiff be made a Defendant[8].

22. Former Infant Plaintiff has order drawn up, entered, served and produced to the appropriate court office for noting on the court record.

Steps to be Taken	RSC
23. *If order directs that former Infant Plaintiff be added as Defendant:* Former Infant Plaintiff acknowledges service.	
Or, *if Plaintiff does not either adopt or repudiate action within a reasonable time after coming of age:*	
24. Next friend may issue summons for order that he be discharged as next friend.	
25. Next friend serves summons on former Infant Plaintiff and on all other parties.	
26. Master or District Judge hears summons and may make order, which may be conditional on the next friend's giving security for past costs.	
27. Order is drawn up and noted on court record.	

1 As to who may be the next friend see Paragraph 38 ante.
2 See Step 7 supra.
3 Eg by reason of death, adverse interest appearing or any other cause. See Paragraph 40 ante.
4 See Paragraph 2 ante.
5 See Paragraph 41 ante.
6 See Paragraph 41 ante. Whilst there is no settled procedure it is suggested that the proper procedure is as here suggested. See also the Supreme Court Practice 1991 para 80/2/6.
7 See Steps 16, 17 supra.
8 See *Bicknell v Bicknell* (1863) 32 Beav 381.

Table 2: Infant defendant: High Court

NOTE: *The procedure described in this table applies to High Court actions other than probate actions, and covers:*
  1. *Service and acknowledgment of service of infant defendant (Steps 1–6);*
  2. *The appointment of a guardian ad litem (Steps 7–14);*
  3. *The appointment of a new guardian ad litem (Steps 15–18); and*
  4. *Infant defendant coming of age (Steps 19–22).*
Compromise is covered in Table 3, post.

Steps to be Taken	RSC
1. Plaintiff serves writ or other originating process personally on either:	
1. Minor's father or guardian[1] or, if he has no father or guardian, on the person with whom he resides or in whose care he is, or	**80,** 16 (2) (a)
2. *With the approval of the Court, obtained on summons, supported by affidavit, either before or, if necessary, after service:* the Minor.	**80,** 16 (3)
Service may be accepted by the minor's solicitor.	**10,** 1
2. Solicitor to Infant Defendant ascertains from Defendant's parent or guardian details of person who is prepared to act as guardian ad litem of minor for the purposes of the action[2].	

Steps to be Taken	RSC
Time: At or as soon as practicable after the consultation: strictly a solicitor can only receive instructions from the guardian ad litem.	
A minor may not defend, counterclaim or intervene in any proceedings, or appear in any proceedings under a judgment or order notice of which has been served on him, except by his guardian ad litem.	**80,** 2 (1)
A guardian ad litem must act by a solicitor.	**80,** 2 (3)
3. Guardian ad litem gives written consent to act.	**80,** 3 (8) (a)
4. Solicitor to Infant Defendant certifies in writing:	
(1) that he knows or believes the Defendant to be a minor; and	**80,** 3 (8) (c) (i)
(2) *except where the guardian ad litem is the Official Solicitor:* that the proposed guardian ad litem has no interest adverse to that of the Defendant.	**80,** 3 (8) (c) (iii)
The certificate is usually indorsed on the guardian ad litem's consent to act, but may be given separately.	
The certificate should be signed by the solicitor personally, but he will be effectively committed by a certificate made and signed in the firm's name.	
5. Solicitor to Infant Defendant lodges in Central Office, Chancery Chambers or in district registry:	
1. Guardian ad litem's consent to act;	**80,** 3 (6)
2. Solicitor's certificate; and	**80,** 3 (6)
3. Acknowledgment of service[3].	**12,** 1 (1), (3)
Time for filing acknowledgment of service: Within 14 days after service of the writ or originating summons, including the day of service.	**12,** 5 (a)
A Defendant may file acknowledgment of service at any time before judgment but the time limited for serving the defence continues to run.	**12,** 6 (2)
Then:	
Either, *if defendant acknowledges service:*	
6. Officer of the appropriate court office on receiving acknowledgment of service affixes stamp showing date, enters acknowledgment of service in the cause book and posts copy to Plaintiff or Plaintiff's solicitor.	**12,** 4
Time: On the day on which acknowledgment of service is filed.	
Or, *if Defendant fails to file acknowledgment of service:*	
7. Plaintiff issues summons for order appointing guardian ad litem.	**80,** 6 (1) (a)
Time: After the expiry of time limited for filing acknowledgment of service and before proceeding further with the action.	**12,** 5

Steps to be Taken	RSC
Application may also be made in appropriate cases by notice under the summons for directions.	
8. *Unless court otherwise directs:* Plaintiff serves summons on Infant Defendant's parent or guardian.	**80,** 6 (1), (6)
Time: at least 7 days before day named for hearing.	**80,** 6 (5) (d)
9. Plaintiff files Affidavit supporting summons.	**80,** 6 (5)
The affidavit must prove:	
(1) that the Defendant is a minor:	**80,** 6 (5) (a)
(2) that the proposed guardian ad litem is willing to act (exhibiting his consent to act);	**80,** 6 (5) (b)
(3) that the proposed guardian ad litem is a proper person to act and that he has no interest in the proceedings adverse to that of the minor;	**80,** 6 (5) (b)
(4) That the writ or other originating process was duly served on the minor (proof of this will normally be by a separate affidavit of service); and	**80,** 6 (5) (c)
(5) that (unless service was dispensed with) the summons or other notice of the application was duly served.	**80,** 6 (5) (d)
10. Master or District Judge hears application and may make order appointing guardian ad litem.	**80,** 6 (1)
11. Plaintiff has order drawn up, and entered.	
12. Guardian ad litem files acknowledgment of service.	
Time: Within any time limited by the order.	
The guardian ad litem must act by a solicitor.	**80,** 2 (3)
13. Defendant serves sealed copy of acknowledgment of service on Plaintiff [4].	
Then:	
14. Parties continue action in usual way.	
In any case, *if it becomes necessary to appoint a new guardian ad litem* [5]*:*	
15. Defendant by his present guardian ad litem (or, if that person has died, by his proposed guardian ad litem) applies to Master or District Judge for order appointing new guardian ad litem either:	
(1) by summons; or	**25,** 7 (3)
(2) by notice under the summons for directions; or	
(3) *if the application arises because of the death of the former guardian ad litem:* by ex parte application* [6].	
Time: As soon as circumstances necessitate the appointment.	
The application must be supported by:	
1. Consent to act of new guardian ad litem,	
2. Affidavit as to facts.	

Steps to be Taken	RSC
If, for any reason other than death, the summons is not issued by the present guardian ad litem it should be directed to him. A new guardian ad litem cannot act until appointed by court order.	**80,** 3 (4)
16. Defendant serves summons on Plaintiff and, unless the application is made by him or he is dead, on the present guardian ad litem.	
17. Master or District Judge hears application and makes order.	
18. Defendant produces duplicate order at Central Office, Chancery Chambers or district registry for noting on record.	
In any case, *if Infant Defendant comes of age during course of action*[7]:	
19. Defendant files in appropriate court office notice that he is of full age and adopts the action. *Time:* As soon as practicable after he comes of age and gives the necessary instructions. He may at the same time file notice of change of solicitors[10].	
20. Defendant serves notice of adoption of defence (and any notice of change of solicitors) on other parties (and, in the case of a change of solicitors, on former solicitor). *Time:* Immediately after filing.	
21. All subsequent proceedings are intituled "C. D. (formerly a Minor but now of full age), Defendant".	
22. Defendant may issue summons for leave to serve new defence.	

1 For the appointment of guardians see Paragraph 44 ante.
2 As to who may be a guardian ad litem see Paragraph 44 ante.
3 RSC Ord 12 rr 1 (1), 10.
4 Step 6 ante.
5 Eg by reason of death, adverse interest appearing or any other cause. See Paragraph 47 ante.
6 Practice Direction [1955] 1 All ER 30, [1955] 1 WLR 36.
7 See Paragraphs 2, 48 ante.

**Table 3: Compromise and settlement of claims and
actions involving minors: High Court**

NOTE: *This table deals with:*
  1. *Settlement of money claim before action brought (Steps 1–10);*
  2. *Compromise of action after action brought (Steps 11–15);*
  3. *Approval of arrangements involving minors (Step 16).*
The table gives only those steps necessitated by the fact that a minor is involved

Steps to be Taken	RSC
Either, if a money claim[1] is settled before proceedings are begun:	
1. Party seeking court's approval issues originating summons asking for approval of the settlement and for appropriate directions.	**80,** 11 (4)
	80, 11 (1)
Time: When agreement is reached.	**80,** 11 (1)
Fee on issuing summons: £10[2]	
The summons may be issued in any division and, if desired, out of a district registry, notwithstanding RSC Ord 7 r 5.	**80,** 11 (3)
The acknowledgment of service must be returned to the appropriate court office.	**80,** 11 (4)
The summons should be addressed to all other interested parties.	
The minor must act by his next friend or guardian ad litem, who must in turn act by a solicitor.	**80,** 2 (1), (3)
Where the claim is made under the Fatal Accidents Acts the summons must include the prescribed statutory particulars[3] as to the persons for whom and on whose behalf the action is brought and of the nature of the claim.	**80,** 11 (2)
The directions sought will be, as appropriate:	
(1) as to payment into court of money recovered by the minor[4]; *or*	**80,** 11, 12 (2)
(2) as to the manner in which money recovered by or on behalf of, or adjudged or ordered or agreed to be paid to or for the benefit of, a minor is to be dealt with; *or*	**80,** 12 (3)
(3) such as may be necessary to give effect to the Court's approval; *or*	**80,** 11 (1) (a)
(4) as to the further prosecution of the claim.	**80,** 11 (1) (b)
2. Plaintiff takes originating summons and copy summons to Central Office, Chancery Chambers or District Registry to fix day and time for attendance of parties.	**28,** 2 (2)
Time: Immediately after issue of summons.	
Fee: None.	
3. Central Office, Chancery Chambers or District Registry gives appointment.	**28,** 2 (2)
4. Plaintiff swears and files affidavits supporting originating summons.	**28,** 1A
In the Chancery and Family Divisions: an affidavit as to the facts is usually necessary, and in any event an affidavit by the minor's next	

Steps to be Taken	RSC
friend or guardian ad litem should be filed, showing that the deponent believes the settlement to be beneficial to the minor and exhibiting the case to and opinion of counsel that he considers it to be so[5].	
In the Queen's Bench Division: an affidavit is not usually required, but in rare cases the Master may require an affidavit on the lines of the Chancery procedure.	

5. Plaintiff serves on Defendants:
    1. Copy originating summons and notice of date fixed for hearing;
    2. Copy affidavit in support of summons[6].
    Time: Not less than 4 clear days before the day fixed for the attendance of the parties.
	28, 3 (2)
	28, 1A (3)
	
	28, 1A (3), 3 (2)

Either, *in the Chancery Division:*	
6. Master hears summons and makes order which is drawn up and entered, *or* if the claim exceeds £30,000 adjourns summons to Judge in Chambers[7].	
7. Judge in Chambers hears summons and makes order, which is drawn up, and entered. The minor will be separately represented.	
Or, *in the Queen's Bench Division:*	
8. Master hears summons and makes order[8].	
Or, *in the Family Division:*	
9. District Judge hears summons and makes order[9].	
Then, *in all divisions:*	
10. Parties take appropriate action in pursuance of the directions contained in the order. For example, if the settlement is approved the Defendants may be directed to pay money into court; if it is not approved the parties may be given directions as to the further prosecution of the action.	
Or, if an action is compromised after it has been brought:	

11. Plaintiff applies by summons in the action (or, in the case of an action begun by originating summons, sometimes under the originating summons itself[10]) for:
    1. Approval of the compromise;
    2. Directions to deal with any fund recovered.
    Time: When agreement is reached.
    Fee on summons: £10[11].
    He should obtain an appointment, as in Steps 2 and 3.
	
	see **80,** 12
	
	see **80,** 12

12. Plaintiff serves summons on Defendants.	
13. Plaintiff swears and files affidavits in support.	

Steps to be Taken	RSC

14. Judge, Master or District Judge hears summons and makes order.

Or, if settlement is agreed during trial:

15. Parties mention agreed terms to Judge and ask for his approval.

Minutes of the proposed order (which may be in the "Tomlin" form[12]) may be handed up to the Judge.

Or, if the court's approval is sought to arrangements[13] where minors are involved:

16. Person seeking approval issues originating summons in Chancery Division and follows the procedure above indicated[14].

The order will recite the Judge's opinion that the arrangement is for the benefit of the minors.

The arrangements can then be carried into effect.

---

1 This procedure is limited to cases in which a claim for money is made by or on behalf of a person under disability: RSC Ord 80 r 12 (1).

2 Supreme Court Fees Order 1980, SI 1980/821 Schedule Fee 2 (a) (as amended).

3 Ie those required by the Fatal Accidents Act 1976 s 2 (4).

4 See Paragraph 53 ante.

5 See *Re Birchall, Wilson v Birchall* (1880) 16 Ch D 41, CA, and *Re Barbour's Settlement, National Westminster Bank Ltd v Barbour* [1974] 1 All ER 1188, [1974] 1 WLR 1198.

6 Usually the guardian should lodge an affidavit exhibiting counsel's opinion and agreeing thereto. In some cases the master or district judge may dispense with the affidavit if counsel attends before him to uphold the settlement.

7 Masters do not in general have power to approve compromises on behalf of a minor where the amount of the claim does not exceed £30,000: Chancery Division Practice Directions No 13 B.

8 An appointment is normally taken by the master in his private room. The amount of the compromise must not be stated in the summons. On the return date the solicitors, and in exceptional cases counsel, attend before the master. Generally the master does not require an affidavit, but requires to be told: (a) whether the question of liability is resolved; (b) medical reports (when considering quantum of damages); and (c) whether the settlement is reasonable and for the benefit of the minor.

9 If the summons has been adjourned to the judge by the district judge, he should indicate whether the matter is to be heard in open court: see *Re F (deceased)* (1985) Times 11 February.

10 Eg in an application under the Inheritance (Provision for Family and Dependants) Act 1975 s 1. The masters of the Chancery Division and the District Judges of the Family Division will not require the issue of a separate summons where the terms of the order meet the relief claimed by the originating summons. Minutes of the proposed order must be lodged in such cases.

11 See Supreme Court Fees Order 1980, SI 1980/821, fee 5A (as amended).

12 Practice Note [1927] WN 290.

13 Where minors are involved in arrangements (eg, deeds of family arrangement) which have the approval of all interested parties who are sui juris, the court's approval must be sought on behalf of the minors.

14 See Steps 1–10.

Table 4: Freeing for adoption in the High Court and county court[1]

Steps to be Taken	Adoption Rules 1984[2]
1. Applicant prepares originating summons (in High Court), originating application (in county court) for application to free for adoption; Applicant is the adoption agency[3], the Respondents are each parent or guardian of the child; any local authority or voluntary organisation which has parental responsibility for, is looking after, or is caring for the child; any person liable by virtue of any order or agreement to contribute to the maintenance of the child; and *in the High Court* the child[4].	r 4 (1) (a) r 4 (1) (b) r 4 (2) r 4 (2)
2. Applicant files originating summons/application with appropriate fee together with 3 copies of summons/application[5], and a report in writing from adoption agency setting out details of the child, his parents, guardians and generally[6].	
3. As soon as practicable after originating process has been filed Court appoints a reporting officer[8] in respect of each parent of child, if it appears that parent is willing to agree to an adoption order. The same person may be appointed if both parents agree to adoption. The duties of the reporting officer are to ascertain that parental agreement is given freely and witness and investigate the circumstances of such agreement, and report to the Court, which report will be confidential.	r 5 (1) r 5 (2) r 5 (4), (8)
4. As soon as originating process is filed or after statement of facts has been filed Court appoints Guardian ad litem[9] if it appears that a parent or guardian is unwilling to agree to an adoption order being made; or if there are special circumstances and the Court considers such appointment is for the welfare of the child.	r 6 (11) r 6 (2)
5. *Applicant having filed originating process and accompanying documents (Step 1)*, Court serves Reporting Officer and Guardian ad litem with originating process and report supplied by Applicant. **[It is prohibited for the originating process to be served upon any other than the above persons.]**	r 9 (2)
6. Applicant files statement of facts[10] attached to originating process or notice if Court is requested to dispense with agreement of parent or guardian[11].	r 7 (1)
7. Court, as soon as practicable after originating process has been filed, lists the case for hearing by Judge[12], and serves notice of the hearing on all parties and Reporting Officer and, if any, Guardian ad litem.	r 9 (1)

Steps to be Taken	Adoption Rules 1984[2]
8. Proper officer informs parent or Guardian of request to dispense with his consent and sends copy of statement of facts[13] to him and Reporting Officer and Guardian ad litem (if any).	r 7 (3) r 7 (4)
9. District Judge before hearing may give directions for hearing and not less than four weeks before the date fixed for hearing, considers documents and gives such further directions as appear necessary[14].	r 9 (3) r 6 (8)
10. Court receives report of Reporting Officer and/or Guardian ad litem. Court considers directions (e.g. if child should be present at the hearing). Report is confidential.	r 9 (3) r 6 (6) (b), (11)
11. The hearing: attendance. Any person[15] served with notice may attend and be heard on question whether an order freeing child should be made.	r 10 (1)
1. Guardian ad litem attends unless Court otherwise directs.	r 6 (10)
2. A duly authorised representative of the Applicant attends in person.	r 10 (4)
3. Child attends unless Court otherwise directs.	r 10 (4), (5)
4. Court may direct that any other party do attend.	r 10 (6)
12. The hearing: special procedures.	
1. Any member or employee of a party which is a local authority or other body may address Court if authorised to do so by that body.	r 10 (2)
2. Any person with whom child has been placed for adoption who wishes his identity to remain confidential should request that proceedings be conducted in a manner to secure he is not seen or identified by any respondent.	r 10 (3) r 11 (1)
3. Proof of identity, age and place of birth of the child are deemed as proved under Rule 11.	r 11 (4)

13. Judge hears application and either
     1. Refuses application, or
     2. **Makes order freeing child for adoption.**
 Hearing is in chambers.
 Court serves notice of refusal order or freeing order on all parties who were not present when order was refused or made.	

14. Former parent[16] may apply for revocation of order to Court which made the original order freeing child for adoption, by application in prescribed Form 4. *Time:* not earlier than 12 months from date of original order[17].	r 12 (1)
15. Application states reasons relied upon for revocation of order.	Note to Sch 1 Form 4
16. Proper officer serves notice on all parties and on	

Steps to be Taken	Adoption Rules 1984[2]
any adoption agency in which parental rights and duties are vested[18].	r 12 (2)
17. Proper officer appoints Guardian ad litem and sends him a copy of application and any documents attached thereto.	r 12 (3)
18. Proper officer lists case for hearing. *Time:* as soon as practicable after receipt of the application. (*The procedure then progresses as in Steps 8–12*).	r 12 (3)
19. Judge hears application and either: (a) **Refuses application**[19] and child remains free for adoption, or (b) **Grants application** and parent takes over parental responsibility and child returns to parent's custody[20].	r 12 (3)

1 This is the procedure under the Adoption Act 1976 s 18 (as amended). For the similar procedure in the Magistrates' Court see the Magistrates' Courts (Adoption) Rules 1984, SI 1984/611, rr 4–13 (as amended by the Family Proceedings Courts (Matrimonial Proceedings) Rules 1991, SI 1991/1991).
2 See the Adoption Rules 1984, SI 1984/265 (as amended by the Adoption (Amendment) Rules 1991, SI 1991/1880).
3 Ie the local authority or approved adoption society: Adoption Act 1976 s 2 (1).
4 The child must be a party in the High Court, but may not be even at the court's discretion in the county court: Adoption Rules 1984 r 4 (2), (3).
5 Ibid Sch 1 Form 1.
6 The matters to be covered are set out in ibid r 4 (4) and Sch 2.
7 Family Proceedings Fees Order 1991, SI 1991/2114, Fee 3 (a).
8 The reporting officer is appointed from a panel established under the Guardians ad Litem and Reporting Officers (Panels) Regulations 1991, SI 1991/2051.
9 In the High Court the official solicitor will be the guardian ad litem unless the applicant desires some other person to be appointed or the official solicitor does not consent: Adoption Rules 1984 r 6 (4). In any other case the guardian ad litem is appointed from the panel: ibid r 6 (5). The guardian ad litem may be the reporting officer appointed under ibid r 5 (1): ibid r 6 (3).
10 A statement of facts should set out the material facts upon which the applicant intends to rely when requesting the court to dispense with parents' or guardian's consent to freeing the child for adoption: ibid r 7 (1)–(3).
11 Grounds for dispensing with a parent or guardian's consent are set out in the Adoption Act 1976 s 16 (2).
12 Court is defined by the Adoption Rules 1984 r 2 (1) as amended.
13 Where the applicant has been informed by a person with whom the child is placed that he wishes his identity to remain confidential the statement of facts must not disclose his identity: ibid r 7 (2).
14 The guardian ad litem may submit an interim report with a view to obtaining such directions as appear necessary.
15 Adoption Rules 1984 r 9 (1), (3). Such persons are the parties the reporting officer and the guardian ad litem and any person directed by the court to be served with notice.
16 This includes a former guardian, but a parent or guardian of the child who has made a declaration under the Adoption Act 1976 s 18 (6), that he prefers not to be involved in further questions concerning the adoption of the child may not make an application to revoke the order.
17 Ibid s 18 (1).
18 This does not include the parties set out in the Adoption Rules 1984 r 4 (2) (b) (as amended by SI 1991/1880) but all other parties to the original process: ibid r 12 (2).
19 See the Adoption Act 1976 s 18 (4). A former parent who made application is not entitled to make further application to revoke unless the court gives leave under ibid s 18 (5).

20 Ie the person in whom parental responsibility was vested prior to the making of the order see
    ibid s 18 (3).

Table 5: Adoption application: High Court and county court

Steps to be Taken	Adoption Rules 1984[1]
1. Proposed adopter as Applicant prepares originating summons (in High Court) originating application (in county court[2]).	
2. Before the summons/application is filed if the Applicant wishes his identity to be kept confidential, he should apply to proper officer[3] for a confidential serial number. *Time:* before filing originating process.	r 14
3. **Either:** Applicant issues originating summons out of the Principal Registry of the Family Division. *Fee on issuing the summons £30[4].*	r 15 (1) (a)
or:	
Applicant files originating application in office of county court. *Fee on filing the application £30[4].*	r 15 (1) (b)
4. Parties (a) the proposed adopters shall be the Applicants; (b) the Respondents shall be	r 15 (2)
(i) each parent or guardian (not being an applicant) of the child, unless the child is free for adoption;	
(ii) any adoption agency having parental responsibility for the child by virtue of sections 18 or 21 or the Adoption Act 1976;	
(iii) any adoption agency named in the application or in any form of agreement to the making of the adoption order as having taken part in the arrangements for the adoption of the child;	
(iv) any local authority to whom the applicant has given notice under section 22 of the Adoption Act 1976 of his intention to apply for an adoption order;	
(v) any local authority or voluntary organisation which has parental responsibility for, is looking after, or is caring for, the child;	
(vi) any person liable by virtue of any order or agreement to contribute to the maintenance of the child;	
(vii) where the applicant proposes to rely on section 15 (1) (b) (ii) of the Adoption Act 1976, the spouse of the applicant; and	
(viii) *in the High Court*, the child.	r 15 (2)

Steps to be Taken	Adoption Rules 1984[1]
The Court may at any time direct that any other person or body may be made respondent.	r 15 (3)
5. Documents to be filed with originating process: (a) 3 copies of originating process; (b) marriage certificate (if Applicants are married and in case of married, sole Applicant)[5]; (c) medical certificates as to health of Applicants made within 3 months of date of filing[6]; (d) medical certificate as to the health of the child unless placed by adoption agency or child of one of the Applicants[6]; (e) agreement of child's parents, or order freeing child for adoption; (f) statement of facts if application to dispense with parental consent; (g) birth certificate of child or if previously adopted certified copy of the entry in the Adopted Children Register.	r 15 (4)
6. If it appears to the Proper Officer that Court may be precluded from hearing application[7] or Court may not have jurisdiction to make an adoption order, he refers process to Judge for directions.	r 16
7. As soon as practicable after the originating process has been filed Court appoints reporting officer[8] in respect of each parent of child, if it appears that parent is willing to agree to adoption order. The same person may be appointed if both parents agree to the adoption. The duties of the reporting officer are to ascertain that parental agreement is given freely and witness and investigate circumstances of such agreement, and report to Court, which report is confidential.	r 17 (1) r 17 (2) r 17 (4), (5)
8. As soon as the originating process is filed or after the statement of facts has been filed the Court shall appoint a Guardian ad litem[9] if it appears that a parent or guardian is unwilling to agree to an adoption order being made; or if there are special circumstances and the Court considers such appointment is for the welfare of the child.	r 18 (1) r 18 (2)
9. Court serves reporting officer and the Guardian ad litem with originating process and reports (if any supplied) under rule 15 (4)[10] and, where Section 18 of the Children Act 1975[11] applies, local authority to whom notice has been given.	r 21 (3) r 21 (2)
10. Applicant files statement of facts[12] attached to the originating process or notice if Court is requested to dispense with agreement of a parent or guardian[13]. The Proper Officer informs parent or guardian of request to dispense with his consent and sends copy of statement of facts[14] to him and reporting officer and Guardian ad litem if any.	r 19 (1) r 19 (3), (4)

Steps to be Taken	Adoption Rules 1984[1]
11. (*As for Table 4 Step 7*)	
12. District Judge may give directions for hearing and not less than 4 weeks before the date fixed for hearing, consider documents; and ensures case is not listed for hearing less than 3 months from date of notice given to a local authority pursuant to Section 22 of Adoption Act 1976; and gives such further directions as appear necessary[15].	r 21 (4), (5)
13. Court receives report of Reporting Officer and/or Guardian ad litem. Adoption agency which placed child supplies 3 copies of report[16] within 6 weeks of receipt of notice of hearing covering matters set out in Schedule 2 to the Rules. Court sends report to Reporting Officer and/or Guardian ad litem.	r 22 (1), (3) r 22 (4)

14. **Hearing: attendance.**
    Any person[17] served with notice may attend and be heard on question whether an adoption order should be made.
        1. Guardian ad litem attends unless Court otherwise directs;
        2. Representative of the Applicant duly authorised, attends personally;
        3. Child attends unless the court otherwise directs;
        4. Court may direct that any other party do attend.
	r 23 (1)
	rr 18 (7), 6 (10), 23 (1)
	
	r 23 (2)
	
	r 23 (4), (5)
	
	r 23 (6)

15. **Special procedures.**
        1. Any member or employee of a party which is a local authority or other body may address the court if authorised to do so by that body.
        2. If Applicant has been assigned a serial number, the proceedings must be conducted in a manner to secure he is not seen or identified by any Respondent.
        3. Proof of identity, age and place of birth of child are deemed as proved under Rule 24.
	r 23 (2)
	
	r 23 (3)
	
	r 24 (1)–(5)

16. Judge hears Application in Chambers with special provision to secure that Applicant who has sought a confidential serial number is not seen by other parties.
Judge makes Order: *either*
        1. refuses Application; *or*
        2. postpones determination of Application and makes interim Order giving parental responsibility for the child to Applicant for a specified period not exceeding 2 years or an interim order, on such terms as to maintenance, education etc. as he thinks fit[18]; *or*
        3. makes adoption Order.
	r 23 (3)

17. Proper Officer serves notice of refusal of Order, or	

Steps to be Taken	Adoption Rules 1984[1]
of making of interim or final Order, on all parties who were not present when Order was refused or made. *If interim order is made:*	r 52 (5)
18. *Unless date has been fixed for further hearing of application:* District Judge fixes date for further hearing. *Time:* At least 1 month before expiration of period specified in interim order.	r 25
19. District Judge serves notice of appointment on Guardian ad litem.	
20. District Judge serves notice of further hearing on persons mentioned in Step 14 and persons served with notice acknowledge receipt of it.	
21. Judge hears Application and makes or refuses adoption order.	
22. In any case: *when adoption order is made:* Applicant sends to or lodges with Proper Officer letter confirming that child has been continuously in actual custody of Applicant for at least 13 consecutive weeks immediately preceding date of Order, where one of Applicants is a parent or relative of child or child was placed by an adoption agency[19] **In other cases:** period is 12 months and child must be 12 months old[20].	
23. Proper officer sends copy of Adoption Order to Registrar-General and Applicant. *Time:* Within 7 days of drawing order. In the case of an interim order, order is sent only to the Applicant. District Judge may not supply a copy of order except at request of Registrar-General, Applicant or one of Applicants or on application of any other person under an order of Judge.	r 52 (8) r 52 (3) r 52 (10)
24. Proper Officer serves notice of making of an order for adoption or interim order or refusal to make an adoption order upon any Court[21] in Great Britain which appears to have made an order relating to parental responsibility and in respect of maintenance of child.	r 52 (7)
25. In any case: *If it is desired to apply for:* 1. *amendment of adoption order*[22]*; or* 2. *revocation of direction in adoption order to Registrar-General for making of entry in register*[23]*; or* 3. *revocation of adoption order on marriage of child's father and mother where child was adopted by his father alone*[24]*:* Person seeking order applies ex parte in first	

Steps to be Taken	Adoption Rules 1984[1]
instance in proceedings in which the adoption order was made.	r 49 (1)
26. Judge may require notice of application to be served on such person as he thinks fit.	r 49 (1)
27. *If Judge requires notice to be served:* party seeking Order: (1) issues summons in adoption proceedings; (2) files supporting affidavit exhibiting statement of facts.	
28. Party seeking order serves copy summons as directed by Judge.	r 49 (1)
29. Party seeking order lodges with District Judge: (1) office copy affidavit and statement of facts; (2) adoption order; (3) Certificate of entry in Adopted Children Register.	
30. Judge hears application and makes order.	
31. Proper Officer sends to Registrar-General notice specifying date of adoption order, names of adopter and adopted person as given in schedule to adoption order, and either amendments made by Court or the fact that the direction or adoption order has been revoked.	r 49 (2)

1 See the Adoption Rules 1984, SI 1984/265 (as amended by the Adoption (Amendment) Rules 1991, SI 1991/1880).
2 As to the authorised court see Adoption Act 1976 s 62 (as amended).
3 Ie in the High Court the district judge; in the county court the proper officer as defined by CCR Ord 1 r 3: Adoption Rules 1984 r 2 (1).
4 Family Proceedings Fees Order 1991, SI 1991/2114, Fee 3 (a).
5 See the Adoption Rules 1984 Sch 1 Form 6 note 3.
6 See ibid Sch 1 Form 6 note 5.
7 Under the Adoption Act 1976 s 24 (1), the court must not proceed to hear an application for adoption where a previous application made by the same person has been refused and the exceptions do not apply.
8 A reporting officer will be appointed from a panel established by the Guardians ad Litem and Reporting Officers (Panels) Regulations 1991, SI 1991/2051: see the Adoption Rules 1984 r 17 (3) (as amended by the Adoption (Amendment) Rules 1991, SI 1991/1880).
9 In the High Court the Official Solicitor will be the guardian ad litem (Adoption Rules r 18 (4)) unless the applicant desires some other person or the Official Solicitor does not consent in which case the applicant should seek a direction for the court to appoint a guardian ad litem from the panel who may not be an employee of the applicant or of any respondent: see ibid r 18 (5). The county court appoints such a member of the panel. The guardian ad litem may be the reporting officer who has been appointed under ibid r 17 (1): see ibid r 18 (3). For duties of guardians ad litem see: ibid r 18 (6).
10 The medical reports in relation to the parents and child where the child has not been placed by an adoption agency.
11 Adoption Act 1976 s 22 requiring the applicant for an adoption to notify the local authority within whose area he has his home of his intention to apply for an adoption order at least three months before an order can be made.
12 A statement of facts should set out the material facts upon which the applicant intends to rely when requesting the court to dispense with parent's or guardian's consent to freeing the child for adoption: Adoption Rules 1984 r 19 (1)–(3).

13 Grounds for dispensing with a parent's or guardian's consent are set out in the Adoption Act 1976 s 16 (2).
14 Where the applicant has been assigned a serial number for his identity to remain confidential the statement of facts must not disclose his identity: Adoption Rules 1984 r 19 (2).
15 The guardian ad litem may submit an interim report with a view to obtaining such directions and directions as to the attendance of the child.
16 This report is confidential Adoption Rules 1984 r 22 (5).
17 Persons served with notice under ibid r 21 (1) being all the parties, the reporting officer guardian ad litem and any person directed to be served with notice.
18 Adoption Act 1976 s 25 (1).
19 See ibid s 13 (1).
20 Ibid s 13 (2).
21 Ie any court which has made an order referred to under ibid s 12 (3).
22 Ie under ibid Sch 1 para 4.
23 Ie under ibid Sch 1 para 4.
24 Ie under ibid s 52 (1). The procedure would also presumably apply to an application under ibid s 52 (2) to revoke an adoption order on the ground that a person adopted by his father and mother before 29 October 1959 had been subsequently legitimated by the operation of the Legitimacy Act 1976 s 1.

Table 6: Application for return or removal of child to or from home of prospective adopter: High Court and county court[1]

Steps to be Taken	Adoption Rules 1984
1. *If application for adoption order is pending:* Applicant applies by summons in those proceedings.	r 47 (2) (a)
2. *If there is no application for adoption order:* Applicant applies by originating process. *Fee: £30[2].*	r 47 (2) (b)
3. *If there is no application for adoption order but application under this rule made by originating summons is pending:* Applicant applies by summons in those proceedings.	r 47 (2) (a)
In any case:	
4. Proper Officer, after giving any necessary directions, fixes date for hearing in Judge's chambers.	r 47 (5)
5. Any respondent to summons or originating process who wishes to claim relief files answer within 7 days of service of process upon him.	r 47 (4)
6. Proper Officer serves copy of summons or originating process (as the case may be) to parties concerned and copy of any answer and notice of the date of hearing.	r 47 (5)
Persons to be served:	
(a) *in a case where adoption proceedings are pending or proceedings for an order under Section 18 or 20 of the Adoption Act 1976:* all parties to the proceedings;	r 47 (5) (a)
(b) *in any other case:* on any person against whom an order is sought and local authority in receipt of notice under Section 22 of the Adoption Act 1976.	r 47 (5) (b)

Steps to be Taken	Adoption Rules 1984
7. Proper Officer ensures no breach of any confidential serial number case by any documents served at this time.	r 47 (6) (a), (b)
8. Prospective adopter, wishing to oppose application, files application for adoption order. *Time:* Within 14 days of hearing application.	r 47 (7)
9. Court may at any time give directions and in particular may give directions as to appointment of Guardian ad litem of child.	r 47 (8)
10. Court hears application in chambers and, in determining application, may treat hearing as hearing of process for adoption order and refuse adoption order accordingly.	r 47 (9)
11. Proper Officer serves notice on all parties of effect of determination of the Application.	r 47 (10)

1 Adoption Act 1976 ss 27–30.
2 Family Proceedings Fees Order 1991, SI 1991/2114, Fee 3(a).

Table 7: Wardship proceedings: Family Division

Steps to be Taken	Family Proceedings Rules 1991
1. Plaintiff applies to have minor made ward of court by originating summons[1] issued out of Principal Registry or district registry[2] If there is no appropriate Defendant, an ex parte application must be made to District Judge for leave to issue either an ex parte originating summons or an originating summons with minor as Defendant[3].	r 5.1 (1)
2. Plaintiff serves copy originating summons on Defendant.	
3. Defendant lodges in registry, notice stating Defendant's address and minor's whereabouts or that minor's whereabouts are unknown to him[4]. *Time:* On service of summons.	r 5.1 (8)
4. Defendant files acknowledgment of service at registry. *Time:* Within 14 days of service of originating summons upon him.	
5. Defendant serves copy of notice on Plaintiff. *Time:* On lodgment of notice in registry.	r 5.1 (8)
6. Minor becomes ward of court on issue of summons[5].	

Steps to be Taken	Family Proceedings Rules 1991
Either:	
7. Plaintiff applies for appointment for hearing. *Time:* Within 21 days after issue of summons.	r 5.3
8. Court gives directions for determination of application (*wardship continues pending such determination*), determines application and order is made making minor a ward of court or application is rejected and minor ceases to be ward of court.	
Or:	
9. Application for appointment for hearing is not made within the required time and minor ceases to be ward of court on expiration of that period[6].	r 5.3 (1)

1 The summons must state the whereabouts of the minor or that the plaintiff is unaware of his whereabouts: Family Proceedings Rules 1991, SI 1991/1247, r 5.1 (7). The minor's date of birth must also be stated in the summons and the plaintiff must on issuing the summons or before or at the first hearing lodge in the registry a certified copy of the entry in the Register of Births or in the Adopted Children Register relating to the minor or at the first hearing of the summons the plaintiff must apply for directions as to proof of the minor's birth: ibid r 5.1 (5). The originating summons must be indorsed with a notice stating "IMPORTANT NOTICE: It is a contempt of court which may be punishable by imprisonment to take any child named in this Summons out of England and Wales even to Scotland, Northern Ireland, the Republic of Ireland, the Channel Islands or the Isle of Man without the leave of this Court". The name of each party to the proceedings must be qualified by a brief description in the body of the summons of his interest in or relationship to the minor: ibid r 5.1 (6).
2 Particulars of any summons issued in a district registry are sent by the district judge to the Principal Registry for recording in the Register of Wards: ibid r 5.1 (4). No minor can be made a ward of court except by an order to that effect made by the court (Supreme Court Act 1981 s 41 (1)) and where application is made for such an order the minor becomes a ward of court on the making of the application but may cease to be a ward of court under Family Proceedings Rules 1991 r 5.3 (1) or if the court so orders: Supreme Court Act 1981 s 41 (2), (3).
3 Where leave is given to make the ward the defendant it is now the practice to ask for an undertaking by the plaintiff's solicitor to notify the ward when the wardship ceases. In cases where the ward has formed or is seeking to form an association which is considered undesirable with another person that other person should not be made a party to the originating summons. He or she should be made a defendant in a summons within the wardship proceedings for injunction or committal. Such a person should not be added to the title of the proceedings nor allowed to see any documents other than those relating to the summons but should be allowed time within which to obtain representation and any order for injunction should in the first instance extend over a few days only: Practice Direction 1983 2 All ER 672, (1983) 1 WLR 790.
4 Where any party other than the minor changes his address or becomes aware of any change in the minor's whereabouts after the issue or service of the summons he must notify the registry of such change and serve a copy of the notice on every other party: Family Proceedings Rules 1991 r 5.1 (9).
5 Ie under ibid r 5.1.
6 A wardship order may be made by a judge and accordingly a minor may continue to be a ward despite no appointment having been taken within 21 days of the issue of the summons. Such an order is, however, usually expressed to be temporary, a substantive order being made on the hearing of the summons: see the Supreme Court Practice 1991 (Cumulative Supplement) notes to Family Proceedings Rules 1991 r 5.3. The plaintiff must notify the registry stating whether he intends to proceed with the application made by the summons immediately after the expiration of that period: Family Proceedings Rules 1991 r 5.3 (3). The President has directed that in wardship proceedings in the Principal Registry except where special circumstances are

shown the district judge should in future order that unless the case is brought before the judge within three months from the date of the first appointment or an application is made to extend time the child will cease to be a ward of court at the expiry of that period: see the Supreme Court Practice 1991 para 90/3/13.

Form I

Parental Responsibility Agreement

Parental Responsibility Agreement

Section 4 (1) (b)   The Children Act 1989

▶ Please use black ink.
▶ The making of this agreement will seriously affect the legal position of both parents.
   You should both seek legal advice before completing this form.
▶ If there is more than one child, you should fill in a separate form for each child.

—————————————————— THE ▬▬ CHILDREN ▬▬ ACT ——————————————————

This is a parental responsibility agreement between

the child's mother	Name
and	Address
the child's father	Name
	Address

We agree that the father of the child named below should have parental responsibility for [him] [her] in addition to the mother.

Name	Boy / Girl	Date of birth	Date of 18th birthday

Ending of the agreement

Once a parental responsibility agreement has been made it can only end :

- by an order of the court made on application of any person who has parental responsibility for the child.
- by an order of the court made on the application of the child with leave of the court.
- when the child reaches the age of 18.

Signed (**mother**)		Date	
Signature of witness		Date	
Signed (**father**)		Date	
Signature of witness		Date	

This agreement will not take effect until this form has been filed with the Principal Registry of the Family Division. Once this form has been completed and signed please take or send it and two copies to :

> The Principal Registry of the Family Division
> Somerset House
> Strand
> London WC2R 1LP

—————————————————— THE ▬▬ CHILDREN ▬▬ ACT ——————————————————

Form 2

ORIGINATING SUMMONS by a parent for enforcement or registration of a decision of a foreign court on custody or rights of access in the United Kingdom[1]

(Royal Arms)

IN THE HIGH COURT OF JUSTICE   19... No. ...
  Family Division
  Principal Registry
  In the matter of J. D. a minor
  And in the Matter of [Part I *or* Part II] of the Child Abduction and
Custody Act 1985[2]
            Between   A. B.   ...   Plaintiff
                                     and
                                     C. D.   ...   Defendant

LET C. D. of (*address*) attend before Judge .... in chambers at
.... on the .... day of .... 19... at ... o'clock on the hearing
of an application by the Plaintiff A. B. of (*address*) that an order of the
[Mexican *or* Norwegian] court giving him custody of the said J. D. be
[enforced *or* registered] in accordance with the terms of [Part I *or* Part
II] of the Child Abduction and Custody Act 1985.
    1. The full name of the child in respect of whom this application is
brought is J. D. who was born on the .... day of .... 19...
    2. The child's parents are A. B. and C. D.
    3. The child is believed to be in England and Wales.
    4. The Plaintiff is the child's mother who in divorce proceedings in
[Mexico *or* Norway] was awarded custody of the child J. D. together
with an order that the child's father the defendant should not have
access to the child.
    5. On the .... day of .... 19... the child's father, the Defendant
C. D. in breach of the custody and access orders removed the child
from his school in [Mexico *or* Norway] and removed him out of the
jurisdiction of [Mexican *or* Norwegian] courts and brought him to
England and Wales.
    By this Summons the Plaintiff A. B. seeks custody and access orders
and the return to her of the said J. D. in accordance with the terms of
such orders.
    AND let the Defendant within 7 days after service of this summons
on him counting the day of service, return the accompanying
Acknowledgment of Service to the appropriate Court Office.

DATED the .... day of .... 19...
NOTE: This Summons may not be served later than [4 months *or if
leave is required to effect service out of the jurisdiction*, 6] calendar
months beginning with the above date unless renewed by order of the
Court.

1 Family Proceedings Rules 1991, SI 1991/1247, rr 6.2–6.4.
2 Child Abduction and Custody Act 1985 Parts I, II.

Form 3

AFFIDAVIT by plaintiff in support of an application for enforcement or registration of a decision of a foreign court on custody or right of access in the United Kingdom[1]

A. B.: Plaintiff: 1st: .... 19...

IN THE HIGH COURT OF JUSTICE
Family Division
[Principal *or* .... District Registry]
In the Matter of J. D. a minor
And in the Matter of [Part I *or* Part II] of the Child Abduction and Custody Act 1985[2]

Between	A. B.	...	Plaintiff
	and		
	C. D.	...	Defendant

I, A. B. of (*state residence or workplace, and occupation or, if none, description*) of [Mexico *or* Norway] make oath and say as follows:

1. I am the mother of the above-named minor J. D. and am the Plaintiff in these proceedings.

2. I was married to the Defendant on .... 19... in [Mexico *or* Norway] and there was one child of the marriage the said J. D.

3. The marriage was dissolved by order of the [Mexican *or* Norwegian] court dated .... 19... and a custody order in respect of J. D. was made in my favour together with an order preventing the said C. D. from having contact with the child J. D.

4. In breach of those orders the Defendant C. B. unlawfully removed the said J. D. from [Mexico *or* Norway] and brought him to live here at (*state address*) in England and Wales.

5. I therefore seek the [enforcement *or* registration] of the [Mexican *or* Norwegian] order and return of the child the said J. D. to me.

SWORN at (*address*) this .... day of .... 19... before me,

(*Signature*) } *Deponent's Signature*)

A [Commissioner for Oaths *or* Solicitor *or* other Proper officer]

1 Family Proceedings Rules 1991, SI 1991/1247, r 6.7.
2 Child Abduction and Custody Act 1985 Parts I, II.

Form 4

ORDER enforcing a foreign custody or access order in the United Kingdom and the return of a child wrongfully removed[1]

(Heading and formal parts as in Form 130)
UPON THE APPLICATION of the Plaintiff by Summons dated ....
19...
AND UPON HEARING [Counsel *or* Solicitors] for the Plaintiff and Defendant
IT IS ORDERED:
1. that the said C. D. the Defendant do forthwith return the child to the Plaintiff the said A. B. in compliance with the order of this court and that of the [Mexican *or* Norwegian] court dated the .... day of .... 19...

1 For the application and affidavit see Forms 2, 3 ante.

Form 5

SUMMONS by a parent for a declaration of unlawful removal of a child from the United Kingdom - expedited form[1]

(Heading and formal parts as in Form 130)
LET C. D. of (*address*) attend before Judge .... in chambers at .... on the .... day of .... 19... at ... o'clock on the hearing of an application by the Plaintiff A. B. of (*address*) that C. D. unlawfully removed the child J. D. from the United Kingdom in breach of a sole residence order granted to A. B. and in breach of [Part I *or* Part II] of the Child Abduction and Custody Act 1985
1. The full name of the child in respect of whom this application is brought is J. D. who was born on the .... day of .... 19...
2. The child's parents are A. B. and C. D.
3. The child is believed to be in [Mexico *or* Norway].
4. The Plaintiff is the child's mother who in divorce proceedings on the .... day of .... 19... was awarded a sole residence order in her favour together with a prohibited steps order preventing the child having contact with his father the said C. D.
5. On the .... day of .... 19... the child's father C. D. in breach of the said prohibited steps order collected the said J. D. from school and informed the headteacher J. S. that he was taking the child to [Mexico *or* Norway].
By this Summons the Plaintiff seeks a Declaration that the removal of the said child J. D. was lawful.

DATED the .... day of .... 19...
This Summons was taken out by G. H. & Co. of (*address*) Solicitors for the Plaintiff.
To the Defendant, and to E. F. & Co. of (*address*) his Solicitors.

1 Child Abduction and Custody Act 1985 s 8; Family Proceedings Rules 1991, SI 1991/1247, rr 6.2–6.4.

INDEX